T0214187

Communications in Computer and Information Science 1032

Commenced Publication in 2007
Founding and Former Series Editors:
Phoebe Chen, Alfredo Cuzzocrea, Xiaoyong Du, Orhun Kara, Ting Liu,
Krishna M. Sivalingam, Dominik Ślęzak, Takashi Washio, and Xiaokang Yang

More information about this series at http://www.springer.com/series/7899

Constantine Stephanidis (Ed.)

HCI International 2019 - Posters

21st International Conference, HCII 2019
Orlando, FL, USA, July 26–31, 2019
Proceedings, Part I

 Springer

Editor
Constantine Stephanidis
University of Crete
and Foundation for Research
and Technology – Hellas (FORTH)
Heraklion, Crete, Greece

ISSN 1865-0929   ISSN 1865-0937 (electronic)
Communications in Computer and Information Science
ISBN 978-3-030-23521-5   ISBN 978-3-030-23522-2 (eBook)
https://doi.org/10.1007/978-3-030-23522-2

This Springer imprint is published by the registered company Springer Nature Switzerland AG
The registered company address is: Gewerbestrasse 11, 6330 Cham, Switzerland

Foreword

The 21st International Conference on Human-Computer Interaction, HCI International 2019, was held in Orlando, FL, USA, during July 26–31, 2019. The event incorporated the 18 thematic areas and affiliated conferences listed on the following page.

A total of 5,029 individuals from academia, research institutes, industry, and governmental agencies from 73 countries submitted contributions, and 1,274 papers and 209 posters were included in the pre-conference proceedings. These contributions address the latest research and development efforts and highlight the human aspects of design and use of computing systems. The contributions thoroughly cover the entire field of human-computer interaction, addressing major advances in knowledge and effective use of computers in a variety of application areas. The volumes constituting the full set of the pre-conference proceedings are listed in the following pages.

This year the HCI International (HCII) conference introduced the new option of "late-breaking work." This applies both for papers and posters and the corresponding volume(s) of the proceedings will be published just after the conference. Full papers will be included in the *HCII 2019 Late-Breaking Work Papers Proceedings* volume of the proceedings to be published in the Springer LNCS series, while poster extended abstracts will be included as short papers in the HCII 2019 *Late-Breaking Work Poster Extended Abstracts* volume to be published in the Springer CCIS series.

I would like to thank the program board chairs and the members of the program boards of all thematic areas and affiliated conferences for their contribution to the highest scientific quality and the overall success of the HCI International 2019 conference.

This conference would not have been possible without the continuous and unwavering support and advice of the founder, Conference General Chair Emeritus and Conference Scientific Advisor Prof. Gavriel Salvendy. For his outstanding efforts, I would like to express my appreciation to the communications chair and editor of *HCI International News,* Dr. Abbas Moallem.

July 2019   Constantine Stephanidis

HCI International 2019 Thematic Areas and Affiliated Conferences

Thematic areas:

- HCI 2019: Human-Computer Interaction
- HIMI 2019: Human Interface and the Management of Information

Affiliated conferences:

- EPCE 2019: 16th International Conference on Engineering Psychology and Cognitive Ergonomics
- UAHCI 2019: 13th International Conference on Universal Access in Human-Computer Interaction
- VAMR 2019: 11th International Conference on Virtual, Augmented and Mixed Reality
- CCD 2019: 11th International Conference on Cross-Cultural Design
- SCSM 2019: 11th International Conference on Social Computing and Social Media
- AC 2019: 13th International Conference on Augmented Cognition
- DHM 2019: 10th International Conference on Digital Human Modeling and Applications in Health, Safety, Ergonomics and Risk Management
- DUXU 2019: 8th International Conference on Design, User Experience, and Usability
- DAPI 2019: 7th International Conference on Distributed, Ambient and Pervasive Interactions
- HCIBGO 2019: 6th International Conference on HCI in Business, Government and Organizations
- LCT 2019: 6th International Conference on Learning and Collaboration Technologies
- ITAP 2019: 5th International Conference on Human Aspects of IT for the Aged Population
- HCI-CPT 2019: First International Conference on HCI for Cybersecurity, Privacy and Trust
- HCI-Games 2019: First International Conference on HCI in Games
- MobiTAS 2019: First International Conference on HCI in Mobility, Transport, and Automotive Systems
- AIS 2019: First International Conference on Adaptive Instructional Systems

Pre-conference Proceedings Volumes Full List

34. CCIS 1033, HCI International 2019 - Posters (Part II), edited by Constantine Stephanidis
35. CCIS 1034, HCI International 2019 - Posters (Part III), edited by Constantine Stephanidis

http://2019.hci.international/proceedings

HCI International 2019 (HCII 2019)

The full list with the Program Board Chairs and the members of the Program Boards of all thematic areas and affiliated conferences is available online at:

http://www.hci.international/board-members-2019.php

HCI International 2020

The 22nd International Conference on Human-Computer Interaction, HCI International 2020, will be held jointly with the affiliated conferences in Copenhagen, Denmark, at the Bella Center Copenhagen, July 19–24, 2020. It will cover a broad spectrum of themes related to HCI, including theoretical issues, methods, tools, processes, and case studies in HCI design, as well as novel interaction techniques, interfaces, and applications. The proceedings will be published by Springer. More information will be available on the conference website: http://2020.hci.international/.

General Chair
Prof. Constantine Stephanidis
University of Crete and ICS-FORTH
Heraklion, Crete, Greece
E-mail: general_chair@hcii2020.org

http://2020.hci.international/

Contents – Part I

Multimodal Interaction

Security and Trust

Accessibility and Universal Access

Design and User Experience Case Studies

Contents – Part II

Interacting with Games

Human Robot Interaction

AI and Machine Learning in HCI

Physiological Measuring

Object, Motion and Activity Recognition

Virtual and Augmented Reality

Intelligent Interactive Environments

Contents – Part III

Learning Technologies

HCI in Transport and Autonomous Driving

HCI for Health and Well-Being

Interacting with Cultural Heritage

Design, Development and Evaluation Methods and Techniques

System Usability Scale Evaluation
of E-Participation in Malaysia

Nasrah Hassan Basri[1]([⊠]), Wan Adilah Wan Adnan[2],
and Hanif Baharin[3]

[1] Kolej Poly-Tech MARA, Ipoh, Malaysia
nasrah@gapps.kptm.edu.my
[2] Universiti Teknologi MARA, Shah Alam, Malaysia
adilah@tmsk.uitm.edu.my
[3] Universiti Kebangsaan Malaysia, Bangi, Malaysia
hbaharin@ukm.edu.my

Abstract. E-government holds tremendous potential for improving the
authoritative effectiveness of public institutions, empowering democratic governance, and building trust between citizens/private sector and governments.
One of the module in e-government that are expanding gain consideration is e-
participation. However, most e-government activities to date have neglected to
achieve their maximum capacity, since they are progressively tormented by
usability issues. Therefore, there have been expanding calls for assessing the
usability of e-government sites, as they are broadly viewed as the essential stage
for government communication with citizens. This empirical study, therefore
seeks to extant knowledge by assessing the usability of Malaysia e-government
site concentrating on the e-participation. This is especially vital as little is known
about the usability of e-participation and four ministries websites were selected
for such evaluation. A total of 10 participants volunteered in this study that
employed System Usability Scale method. Analysis of the SUS demonstrated
that the usability of the chosen site was marginal with all the average usability
score was below 70%.

Keywords: E-participation · System Usability Scale · Usability evaluation

1 Introduction

Governments nowadays are utilizing Information and Communication Technologies
(ICTs) to support its operations, engage citizens and provide services [16]. In fact,
e-government has been applied to support the many activities of government [1] and
one of the key factors that motivate the use of e-government solutions among different
entities is the strong aspiration to foster higher levels of citizen satisfaction and trust in
governments [3, 14]. One of the unique module in e-government that shows an
increasing consideration is e-participation [8, 15]. [18] stated that e-participation is a
fundamental component making a good e-democracy by helping people getting
involved in politics and policy-making.

© Springer Nature Switzerland AG 2019
C. Stephanidis (Ed.): HCII 2019, CCIS 1032, pp. 3–8, 2019.
https://doi.org/10.1007/978-3-030-23522-2_1

Despite the advancements of e-participation, there is still lacks of usability evaluation for this effort [7]. The idea of usability has been characterized and estimated diversely by various authors. For instance, [11] expressed that usability is certifiably not a solitary quality; rather, usability is characterized as far as five attributes: learnability, efficiency, memorability, errors and satisfaction. This definition shows that usability is characterized as far as a lot of traits or plan objectives of a system or product. Nonetheless, the International Standards (ISO 9241-11, 1998) give a more extensive meaning of usability, expressing that: "Usability is the extent to which a product can be used by specified users to achieve specified goals with effectiveness, efficiency and satisfaction in a specified context of use".

Usability of a website is a crucial determinant in attracting new visitors and has a direct influence on satisfaction [10]. [9] further stressed the importance of website usability by claiming that it is "a necessary condition for survival," since its absence is very likely to frustrate and confuse users leading them to abandon that website for another competing one [5, 12]. Users are unlikely to revisit a website that exhibits poor usability and hence, users' loyalty to a website is significantly influenced by website usability [6].

Measuring usability is often difficult, as usability of a product or service is highly subjective [10]. As such, there are quite a number of ways to measure usability and one of it is the System Usability Scale (SUS). An empirical systematic evaluation of SUS studies of over 10 years found the tool to be useful as a quick and easy method of measuring system usability [2].

This paper presents a first attempt to empirically research the people's subjective perceptions of the usability of e-participation in Malaysia by using the standardized System Usability Scale (SUS). SUS is a well-researched and widely used method for measuring users' perception of usability evaluation of websites, software, and other human-machine systems [13]. This simple scale was shown to be more reliable across numerous sample sizes compared to other usability scales [17] and according to [4], the SUS method has been cited in more than 1200 publications.

For this purpose, four ministries websites which are Ministry of Finance, Ministry of Health, Ministry of Human Resource and Ministry of Women, Family and Community Development had been selected to study the possible effect of service usability as a contributing factor in service adoption of e-participation.

2   Methods

2.1   Participants

Ten participants were recruited for this usability studies and they were selected on a voluntarily basis. All participants are over 21 years old and out of the total number, two were male and another eight were female. They were given a token of appreciation after the session ended.

2.2   Materials and Equipment

The session were running simultaneously in a computer laboratory at the college by using iMac computers with the same specifications (Intel Core i5; 8 gb; 1 TB; web browser: Google Chrome).

2.3   Usability Questionnaire

For this study, A System Usability Scale (SUS) questionnaire consisting of 10 items (5 Likert scale) was used to measure the usability. Participants provided their feedback by filled out System Usability Scale (SUS) forms and on the SUS form, ten statements about the related website were given to the participants. Participants could indicate their level of agreement based on the scores provided on the form (from 1 to 5; with 5 means strongly agree).

2.4   Procedures

For this study, usability tests were conducted simultaneously with a researcher conducting the project. All the participants would come into the laboratory type setting and give their consent on participating with this study.

Once they filled up the consent form, a short briefing on the purpose of the study and how the study will be conducted was given by the researcher. Next, participants were asked to browse the website and performed random tasks with the website especially on the e-participation module. Upon completion of the usability tests, the participants would complete the SUS. A flow of the experimental procedure is given in the diagram shown in Fig. 1 below.

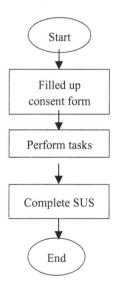

Fig. 1. Experimental procedure

3   Results

3.1   Descriptive Statistics

Table 1 provides the frequencies and mean System Usability Scale (SUS) scores for each different groups of participants.

Table 1. Frequencies and mean System Usability Scale (SUS) scores, $n = 10$

Factor	Category	Frequency	Percentage	Mean SUS score
Gender	Male	2	20%	60
	Female	8	80%	52.2
Age	21–30	2	20%	60
	31–40	6	60%	52.5
	41–50	1	10%	42.5
	Above 50	1	10%	60
Education	Bachelor	4	40%	65
	Master	6	60%	45.4
Internet frequency of use	Daily	3	30%	44.2
	More than 3 times per day	7	70%	57.9

3.2   Mean SUS Scores Rating

All the participants completed SUS forms after browsing each website. The average SUS score based on the method suggested in [4] for each website is presented in Fig. 2.

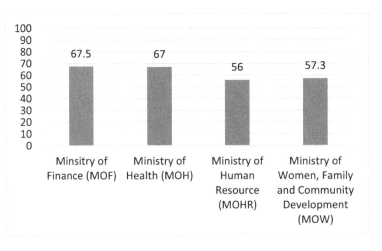

Fig. 2. Average SUS score for each website

3.3 Adding Adjective Rating Scale

[2] suggested adding adjective ratings scale to SUS scores in order to better comprehend the scores. Thus, this study also applied the mapping of average SUS scores to an adjective rating scale for each website as presented in Fig. 3.

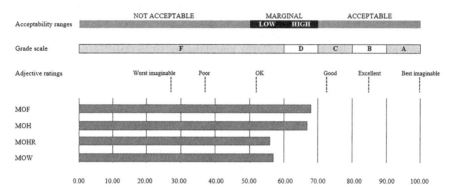

Fig. 3. Adjective rating scale added to SUS scores for each website

4 Conclusion

This study reports on the SUS assessment of e-participation in Malaysia. The results show that all participants were experienced users of the Internet and thus having no problem in participating in this study. The findings of this study highlight that the e-participation modules reside in e-government websites are in the 'marginal' range and yet some improvement need to be done in order to enhance their usability.

One limitation of this study is that the sample is biased towards 10 users who participated in this study. Furthermore, the paper is restricted to the usability evaluation dependent on the SUS measurement tool, which includes 10 item questionnaire to measure usability. Consequently, a more comprehensive usability evaluation of e-participation can be obtained by utilizing an in-depth survey tool that specifically investigates a variety of usability principles.

Acknowledgement. The authors are grateful to Universiti Teknologi MARA, Shah Alam for the financial support and to Kolej Poly-Tech MARA Ipoh for recruiting the participants and also for providing at no charge the laboratory facilities that were used in this study.

References

1. Anjoga, H., Nyeko, S., Kituyi, M.: A framework for usability of e-Government services in developing countries. J. Acc. Audit. Res. Pract. (2017). https://doi.org/10.5171/2017.313796
2. Bangor, A., Kortum, P.T., Miller, J.T.: An empirical evaluation of the system usability scale. Int. J. Hum.-Comput. Interact. **24**(6), 574–594 (2008). https://doi.org/10.1080/10447310802205776

3. Bannister, F., Dublin, T.C.: The trouble with transparency : a critical review of openness in e-Government, **3**(1) (2011). https://doi.org/10.2202/1944-2866.1076
4. Brooke, J.: SUS: A retrospective. J. Usability Stud. **8**(2), 29–40 (2013)
5. Cappel, J.J., Huang, Z.: A usability analysis of company web sites. J. Comput. Inf. Syst. **48**(1), 117–123 (2007)
6. Flavia, C., Guinalı, M., Casalo, L.: The role of perceived usability, reputation, satisfaction and consumer familiarity on the website loyalty formation process (2006). https://doi.org/10.1016/j.im.2005.01.002
7. Loukis, E., Demakis, A., Charalabidis, Y.: An evaluation framework for e-participation in parliaments. Int. J. Electron. Gov. (2010). https://doi.org/10.1504/IJEG.2010.032729
8. Macintosh, A., Whyte, A.: Evaluating how eParticipation changes local democracy (2006)
9. Mclellan, S., Muddimer, A., Peres, S.C.: The effect of experience on system usability scale ratings. J. Usability Stud. **7**(2), 56–67 (2014)
10. Mujinga, M., Eloff, M.M., Kroeze, J.H.: System usability scale evaluation of online banking services : a South African study. South Afr. J. Sci. **114**(3/4) (2018). https://doi.org/10.17159/sajs.2018/20170065
11. Nielsen, J.: Usability 101: Introduction to Usability (2003). https://www.nngroup.com/articles/usability-101-introduction-to-usability/. Accessed 12 Oct 2018
12. Nielsen, J., Loranger, H.: Prioritizing Web Usability. New Riders Press, Berkeley (2006)
13. Peres, S.C., Pham, T., Philips, R.: Validation of the system usability scale (SUS): SUS in the wild. In: Proceedings of the Human Factors and Ergonomics Society 57th Annual Meeting, pp. 192–196 (2013). https://doi.org/10.1177/1541931213571043
14. Porumbescu, G.A.: Linking public sector social media and e-government website use to trust in government. Gov. Inf. Q. (2016). https://doi.org/10.1016/j.giq.2016.04.006
15. Sæbø, Ø., Rose, J., Skiftenes, L.: The shape of eParticipation: characterizing an emerging research area. Gov. Inf. Q. **25**, 400–428 (2008). https://doi.org/10.1016/j.giq.2007.04.007
16. Sakowicz, M.: How to evaluate e-Government? Different methodologies and methods (2003)
17. Tullis, T.S., Stetson, J.N.: A comparison of questionnaires for assessing website usability (2004). ABSTRACT: Introduction
18. Vrabie, C.I., Tirziu, A.-M.: E-participation - a key factor in developing smart cities (2016)

Human-Food Interaction Framework: A New Design Tool Used to Understand Amateur Home Cooks' Needs

Sohyeong Kim[(✉)], Da Hyang Summer Jung, Anand Upender,
Sahej Claire, and Ion Esfandiari

Center for Design Research, Stanford University, Stanford, CA, USA
{sohkim,summerjung,anandx,
saclaire,ionesfan}@stanford.edu

Abstract. Our present research focuses on gaining a better understanding of the relationships between food and different human stakeholders in order to develop our Human-Food Interaction framework. This paper focuses on the key stakeholders of people new to the kitchen called "amateur cooks." We noticed there is a gap in research on this group regarding how they transition between taking stored food and choosing how and what to cook. We discovered from initial interviews that more amateur home cooks initially strictly follow recipes and therefore create food waste on the niche ingredients they buy for each recipe. More advanced cooks see recipes as composed of an essential base (like pasta or salad) and extras which are added on to that base (like nuts, sauces or cheese). As a result, we sought to develop a tool to help amateur cooks unleash their creativity and gain confidence while cooking. Our research led us to develop a prototype called *Flavor Explorer*, a new algorithm and corresponding interface that allows amateur cooks to find the best ingredient pairings depending on what they have stored in their kitchens. With this tool and our research, we thus hope to highlight the importance of the needs of this user group while proposing a novel tool that could actually help amateur cooks around the world.

Keywords: Food design · Ingredients · Confidence · Home cooks · Design thinking

1 Background

1.1 Human-Food Interaction (HFI)

Food is significant in every walk of human life from physical and mental health to social and cultural perspectives. There have been attempts to understand food-related behaviors based on Human-Computer Interaction (HCI), framed as Human-Food Interaction (HFI) [1, 2]. HFI is the study of the interface between food and people, whether at the level of food production, preparation, or consumption. To understand the interactions more systematically, we adopted a conceptual framework from existing literature on food systems. Food systems have been understood as a "set of activities ranging from production through to consumption" [3]. This framework operates with

© Springer Nature Switzerland AG 2019
C. Stephanidis (Ed.): HCII 2019, CCIS 1032, pp. 9–14, 2019.
https://doi.org/10.1007/978-3-030-23522-2_2

several different stakeholders, defined as those who have an intentional interest or designated role in the food system. Examples of stakeholders are farmers, cooks, and consumers (Table 1).

Table 1. Primary food-related activities in the food subsystems [2]

Subsystems	Examples of activities
Production	Farming, growing, harvesting
Storage	Packaging, labeling, freezing
Culinary processing	Preparing, cooking
Foodservice	Serving, catering, transporting, wholesale/retailing
Food data management	Communicating, collecting, storing and accessing data (e.g., nutrition, culinary know-how, and knowledge, etc.)
Consumption	Eating, digesting
Waste	Composting, recycling

1.2 Amateur Home Cooks

In this qualitative study, we decided to focus on one main transition period people face with food: their move to a first apartment or home that requires them to learn to cook for themselves and possibly others (non-commercially). This group's development is crucial as we know that adolescent's confidence in their cooking ability in this stage can even have long-term impacts on diet and consumption of fast food [4]. We define amateur cooks as individuals or couples in their twenties who do not have a background in cooking from their childhood. These people are a large entry group to the funnel of people who cook in America and by studying them, we hope to display opportunities for changes in how we perceive culinary confidence, grocery shopping, and food waste.

2 Research Process

We adopted the design thinking process as a research process, which is heavily grounded user-centric [5]. The process, which is a novel user-centric approach to problem solving and innovating, is broken down in the steps of empathizing, defining, ideating, prototyping, and testing. We started our research by conducting extensive interviews with our target user group to learn more about their needs (empathize). From these interviews, we then identify research questions we can focus on based on patterns observed, before diving into more interviews (define). Finally, as we seek to develop a solution which would solve our target user's need, we engage in brainstorming (ideate) and then develop and iteratively test that solution (prototype and test). By the end of that process, we have thus identified an important user need and a solution that successfully responds to that need. As this research is still in the pilot study, research method was only qualitative, though we plan to include a quantitative method in the future.

3   Research Questions

Of the different stages of the HFI framework, we decided to focus on the transition from storage to culinary processing in this paper (Fig. 1).

Fig. 1. Summary of interactions between consumers and their food. "X" indicates a gap in research and solutions.

Compared to others stages of HFI framework, such as logistics and food waste, there is less research on the transition between storing (fridge and pantry) and cooking food. We adopted the approach of observing user groups with extreme needs because this research style has been shown to fluidly lead to new insights on future high-technology products [6]. We explored various extreme groups and decided to focus on a precise segment of consumers: amateur home cooks, as described in the Background. We had a general understanding of how amateur cooks store and prepare ingredients, but we identified opportunities in the interactions between these two processes, such as deciding what to make or handling leftover ingredients after cooking. This gap led to one main research question: what barriers do amateur cooks face in transforming a set of raw ingredients into complete dishes given their diverse cultural, societal, and personal preference constraints [7]?

4   Results

4.1   Preliminary Findings

We interviewed five individuals and couples in the Bay Area, 20–30 years old, who had recently gone through a transition in which they began to cook more. Through deep interviews with this group, we identified a few key findings.

People who are new to cooking often express a deep fear of "messing up," saying things like "I would burn a pot of boiling water" or "I just know how to make toast." One mom said of her daughter, "My daughter is…afraid to cook something and it not coming out the same, also afraid that her new husband will judge her cooking, so she doesn't feel comfortable moving away from a recipe." Many interviewees spoke about this desire for consistency and fear of letting others down with a failed attempt. They would stick to a recipe in order to deflect blame in case of a poor meal. There seems to be no incentive to experiment or time set aside from busy weekday eating hours to learn about cooking. Therefore, people who do not grow up in a household of cooking end up passively learning while cooking day-to-day meals often with the stress of a full-time job.

Furthermore, there is a desire in these new cooks to differentiate what is essential and what is extra. Essential ingredients are objective ingredients at the core of a dish like a chicken breast or pasta and extra ingredients are subjective ingredients that could be substituted like thyme or sesame oil. Traditional recipes tend to be inflexible, not informing users which ingredients can be exchanged or even left out entirely with a similar result. These amateur cooks hold a shared belief that they must follow recipes exactly as written, buying specific, niche ingredients to do so. These ingredients are often specific to a single recipe, making it difficult to use the leftover ingredients without a deeper knowledge of them. This leads to increased food waste from unused ingredients and also perpetuates a feeling of intimidation. Recipes are designed for one meal, but ingredients are packaged for many.

In addition, we found that amateur cooks' discomfort with modifying recipes may be due to gaps in knowledge around simpler cooking techniques and dishes. For example, they would find it difficult to cook a chicken piccata if they had never mastered the simple act of grilling chicken. We began to define a recipe framework centered around this finding called "bases," in which standard dishes, such as a quiche, omelet, or grilled chicken, should be taught first so amateur cooks feel comfortable preparing a wide array of more sophisticated variants of these bases. We even saw with two more culinarily advanced interviewees that they had organically developed this mental framework in which they would cook a base dish routinely but then experiment with new additions as their pantry changed. In talking about omitting an extra ingredient, one said, "But then I just made it without it, and it was fine. It just wasn't as deep flavor and that was fine." This sense of play and improvisation is a key trait that is common around more culinary confident individuals even if they are early in their learning and experience.

Finally, along with this notion of "base" ingredients, we uncovered that certain ingredients may seem simple and foolproof to most amateur cooks. We heard that eggs are one of these "because you can like, even if you're a bad cook... always make something with it. You can always put it in... anything." Recipes with these staple ingredients could be used to build confidence in those new to cooking.

4.2   Guiding Questions

After analysis of the interviews, we formulated guiding "How Might We" (HMW) questions to base our research on as part of the design thinking process [8]. These included: HMW help new cooks reuse leftover raw ingredients in creative ways? HMW help new cooks learn "base" skills and dishes? and HMW encourage new cooks to modify and personalize these "base" recipes? The relationships between these varied questions guided us in understanding how beginner cooks can gain the efficiency and creativity that more experienced cooks have. The main question simplified down to "How can we help new home cooks make use of seemingly-disparate leftover ingredients in their storage?"

4.3   Prototype

Ideating and prototyping in cycles gave our team the opportunity to explore diverse solutions from new types of bento-box Tupperware to modular cookbooks. After receiving feedback from users, we concentrated our efforts on a single prototype addressing our key goals: instilling culinary confidence in amateur cooks, leveraging their leftover ingredients, and teaching them to master simple "base" recipes.

"The Flavor Explorer" is our vision of a tool that allows amateur cooks to explore relationships among the ingredients in their home as they plan a meal. A user can select anchor ingredients that they know they want in their meal, and the algorithm suggests appropriate pairings and how to bring them together into a dish (Fig. 2).

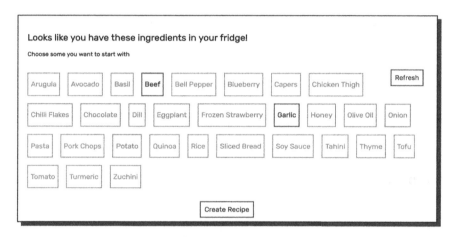

Fig. 2. Recommendation of pairings when garlic and beef are chosen as anchors. Blue ingredients are selected by the user and green are recommended. (Color figure online)

For example, if one chooses the leftover garlic and beef from their fridge as anchors, the algorithm may recommend they use basil, potato, and onion from their pantry to make dinner. On the other hand, if they choose blueberries, the system recommends that the blueberries could go well with chocolate, frozen strawberries, or honey. Their personalized "recipe" is then generated—relieving the cook of the stressful task of finding their own—formatted for easy comprehension and flexible enough that the cook can add their own twist (still being built). In taking a closer look at a modern recipe's structure, we considered adjustable parameters such as time, difficulty level, and novelty. Our aim goes beyond a simple recipe generator; we wish to give beginner cooks the confidence to personalize basic recipes through tools that inspire such improvisation. We hope the output of our research can be the stepping stone that builds amateur cooks' intuition for flavors and ingredients.

5 Conclusion and Limitations

Our current iteration of the Flavor Explorer is limited to a small set of 30 ingredients that have manually labeled similarities. In future tests, we would like to use a large open-source dataset of ingredient similarities to create a more robust system. The system assumes that there exists adequate technology to know what ingredients a user has. We believed this to be a fair assumption given the rise in smart fridges as well as more simple receipt apps. We also determined unanswered questions that require new prototypes and tests. Much of it would revolve around the subjective quality of confidence and how an interactive product (rather than a human or a teacher) could instill confidence. Furthermore, if we are going to replace modern, static recipes with more dynamic ones, it is important to understand which aspects of current recipes are constraining and which are supportive and adequately prescriptive.

Through the presented research, we intend to create a welcoming platform for amateur cooks to feel more confident in their creative choices. Our future research, however, focuses more broadly on defining the human-food interaction framework by understanding its stakeholders and their experiences with food. In addition, the human-food interaction framework will elucidate the interconnected relationships between such stakeholders and the many other stakeholders they deal with. We aim to enhance this framework and provide it as a design tool for food design researchers, food entrepreneurs, and food corporations to identify and augment future ventures. Through doing so, we hope to create a network of both knowledge and interpersonal relations that can be leveraged as not only a design tool but as a means to effect change.

References

1. Grimes, A., Harper, R.: Celebratory technology: new directions for food research in HCI. In: Proceedings of the SIGCHI Conference on Human Factors in Computing Systems, pp. 467–476. ACM, April 2008
2. Park, S.Y., Kim, S., Leifer, L.: "Human Chef" to "Computer Chef": culinary interactions framework for understanding HCI in the Food Industry. In: Kurosu, M. (ed.) HCI 2017. LNCS, vol. 10271, pp. 214–233. Springer, Cham (2017). https://doi.org/10.1007/978-3-319-58071-5_17
3. Ericksen, P.J.: Conceptualizing food systems for global environmental change research. Glob. Environ. Change 18(1), 234–245 (2008)
4. Utter, J., Larson, N., Laska, M.N., Winkler, M., Neumark-Sztainer, D.: Self-perceived cooking skills in emerging adulthood predict better dietary behaviors and intake 10 years later: a longitudinal study. J. Nutr. Educ. Behav. (2018). https://doi.org/10.1016/j.jneb.2018.01.021
5. Dym, C.L., Agogino, A.M., Eris, O., Frey, D.D., Leifer, L.J.: Engineering design thinking, teaching, and learning. J. Eng. Educ. 94(1), 103–120 (2005)
6. Von Hippel, E.: Democratizing Innovation. MIT Press, Cambridge (2005)
7. Asp, E.H.: Factors affecting food decisions made by individual consumers. Food Policy 24(2–3), 287–294 (1999)
8. Carroll, M., Goldman, S., Britos, L., Koh, J., Royalty, A., Hornstein, M.: Destination, imagination and the fires within: Design thinking in a middle school classroom. Int. J. Art Des. Educ. 29(1), 37–53 (2010)

Leveraging Personality to Design Expression for AI Based Embodied Agents

Gaeun Lee[1(✉)], Jung-Mi Park[1], Yoojin Won[1], Hankyung Kim[2], and Youn-kyung Lim[2]

[1] Samsung Research, Seoul, Republic of Korea
{gganni.lee,jungmipark,yoojin.won}@samsung.com
[2] KAIST, Daejeon, Republic of Korea
{hkkim31,younlim}@kaist.ac.kr

Abstract. Conversational agents empowered by artificial intelligence, for instance Siri, Alexa, and more, are widely adopted and used nowadays. Users tend to perceive certain characters or personalities to those agents, interact with them. These situations lead us to following research questions; Can we leverage personality as a medium to design agents? How can we use it for designing dialogues and other modalities in early-stage of design? We conduct a remote design-sessions with designers who experienced designing dialogues for CA with two different types of pre-defined personality. (N = 16, total 268 sentences) They are asked to write scripts with stage directions based 26 situation units according to five functions on healthcare agents.

We find major findings according to open-coding and theme-coding analysis. First, providing certain personality types leads dialogues and other modality-expressions differentiated. Second, utilizing stage directions with scripting enact designers to design not only dialogues but also other modality-expressions were effectively done even without high-fidelity prototypes such as physically-enabled devices. Several kinds of modality-expressions for instance facial expressions, voice tones, head gestures were successfully designed following two different types of personality.

All in all, it is effective leveraging personality in early-stage of design process for embodied conversational agents. Moreover, simply scripting with stage directions enables designers to explore and elaborate behaviors of CA without highly-developed prototypes. It is expected to be the next step designing systematic procedures for creating personality for CA and reflecting it to various behaviors.

Keywords: Embodied agent · Robot personality · Robot expression · Modality

1 Introduction

Conversational agents empowered by artificial intelligence, for instance Siri, Alexa, and more, are widely adopted and used nowadays [1, 2]. Users tend to consciously or unconsciously attribute agents, and the nature of these agents affects many aspects of the interaction. There is no general definition of a personality. However, personality is what makes it possible to predict how an individual will behave in a particular

© Springer Nature Switzerland AG 2019
C. Stephanidis (Ed.): HCII 2019, CCIS 1032, pp. 15–20, 2019.
https://doi.org/10.1007/978-3-030-23522-2_3

situation, and it is defined as relevant to all human actions in a related research [3]. In the previous research, there have been a lot of studies on the nature of virtual agent including conversational agent, but there is little research considering physical agent [4–7].

In order to communicate with humans, robots express their intentions in a variety of ways, such as voice, facial expression, and behavior [8] in this study, we propose a way to design and develop modality that can give character in the early stage of agent design and express personality factors well.

2   Research Purpose

As for the importance of agent personality design, we think of the following research questions.

– Can we leverage personality as a medium to design agents?
– How can we use it for designing dialogues and other modalities in early-stage of design?

This study was started to investigate how the personality is reflected in design when providing the given personality in AI based embodied agent design process. Moreover, we want to design various modalities including conversation.

3   Research Process

We conduct a remote design-sessions with designers who experienced designing dialogues for CA with two different types of pre-defined personality (N = 16, total 268 sentences). Prior to scripting, we provided an introduction to the agent (Fig. 1), the roles and preferences of the user (Table 1). Two different health care agents for the general public who experienced the use of the interactive agent had to write a dialogue script based on the scenario (Table 2). As a pre-study stage, the trait of the nature given to the agent was designed differently according to the three traits. We define that common traits is a general character element defined by the selection of the service domain, and distinctive traits is a personality element that can be given to give personality to the personality. Also, Neutral traits should be constantly considered to define which conversation topics or situations to avoid conveying personalities [9]. In this study, the scope of the service provided by the agent is limited to 26 Conversational situation based on five service scenarios (Table 2).

In addition, we proposed that the robot's dialogue and the corresponding characteristics of the robot that we design should be well presented. Thus, we validate the differences in the expression of agents of different personalities.

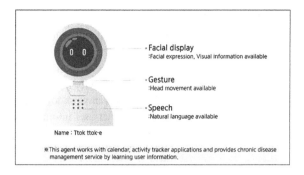

Fig. 1. List of given robot role and character

Table 1. List of given user role and character

User name	Jiwon
Using application	Google calendar, Apple health, Fitbit
Chronic disease	High blood pressure
Taking medicine	Taking blood pressure pill Frequently forget to take daily blood pressure pill
Preference of food ingredients	Food ingredient that user like: potatoes Food ingredient that user dislike: spinach

Table 2. List of given personality by traits

	Agent 1	Agent 2
Personality keyword	Strict Instructor	Golden Retriever
Common traits	Accurate, Trustworthy, Friendly	
Distinctive traits	Uptight, Flawless, Charismatic	Emotional, Youthful, Humorous
Neutral traits	Older Than User, No Obvious Hobbies or Preferences	Similar Age With User, Share Hobbies and Preferences

4 Findings

We found that it is effective to provide the given personality in the robot's dialogue interaction design. First, providing specific personality types differentiates conversations and other forms of expression. For example, when it comes to one scenario 'first greeting', different types of expressions such as facial expressions, voice tones, and head gestures are designed differently according to the two types of personality. (Table 4) Second, designers were able to effectively design expressions without high-fidelity prototypes types (N = 462) (Table 5). Based on the dialog data collected according to the 27 cases (Table 3) for the five service scenarios, we conducted a

Table 3. Table of service scenario & situation

Service scenario #	Service situation	Conversational situation
S1_First meeting	S1.1 First greeting	First greeting
		Introduced the agent himself
	S1.2 Initial setup	Ask if user activity tracker and calendar information can work together
		Indication that user information link is completed
		Based on the connected information
		Tell you to provide customized services
S2_Post-weather management	S2.1 Opening/Closing	Good morning greeting
	S2.2 Sleep management	Reports sleep tracking results
	S2.3 Provide daily information	Provide the date and day of the week
		Inform current weather
		Notify the user that the requested function cannot be executed
S3_Pre-meal health check	S3.1 Check blood pressure	Ask for blood pressure check
	S3.2 Medication	Notification of timing to take medicine
	S3.3 Diet planning	Suggested diet suggested breakfast meal with good spinach for high blood pressure
		Suggest a good potato salad for high blood pressure with another diet
		Notice that agent will not recommend spinach dishes in the future
S4_Chronic disease management	S4.1 Health management	Notification of the current number of steps
		Suggestion of 30-minute alert exercise
	S4.2 Medication	Ask if user has taken your blood pressure medication
		Recommendation of taking pills right now
S5_Pre-sleep management	S5.1 Health management	Notification of lack of daily exercise
		Recommendation of stretching before going to bed
	S5.2 Chat	Free chat with users
		Notice that agent did not understand the user response correctly
	S5.3 Sleep management	Ask if agent can turn off the lights after 30 min from now
		Tell user to turn off the lights after 30 min
	S5.4 Opening/Closing	Goodnight greeting before bedtime

frequency analysis on the use of expressive form related keywords. As a result, a variety of additional modality expressions have been created in agents that are warmer and more friendly (N = 235).

Table 4. Sample coding of scripting (User scenario 1: First greeting)

User scenario 1: First greeting				
A#_P#	Scripting of additional modality	Facial display	Gesture	Other
A1_P1	(Moving head up and down)	–	O (Head up and down)	–
A1_P2	(Head shaking slightly)	–	O (Head up and down)	–
A1_P3	(Nods)	–	O (Head up and down)	–
A1_P4	–	–	–	–
A1_P5	(Making a cuddle)	–	O (Head up and down)	–
A1_P6	(Nods the head up and down, puts a smile on the display)	O (Smile)	O (Head up and down)	–
A1_P7	(Nods his head up and down)	–	O (Head up and down)	–
A1_P8	(Shakes his head)	–	O (Head up and down)	–
A2_P9	(Blinking eyes with big smiles)	O (Smile)	–	–
A2_P10	(Screens flash and shake)	O	–	–
A2_P11	(Waving the head to the right and left to welcome)	–	O (Shake head from side to side)	–
A2_P12	–	–	–	–
A2_P13	(With a smile on his eyes and shaking his head from side to side)	O (Smile)	O (Shake head from side to side)	–
A2_P14	(To greet the user with a smiling face and shake his head)	O (Smile)	O (Head up and down)	–
A2_P15	(He looks around and big smiles	O (Smile)	O (Shake head from side to side)	–
A2_P16	(Nods his head in smile)	O (Smile)	O (Head up and down)	–

In addition, about 3 times 'related keyword' is indicated for the 'face expression' in the Display. Similarly, in the case of 'sound of voice' there was a reference only to the agent corresponding to type 2 (light/bright/warm/worry/etc.) It is also more common in type 2 to 'Call the user's name'. By writing a script, modality design other than dialogue was possible in early-stage design. By expressing various modalities together, we found that low-fidelity robot could design multi-modality embodied agent personality.

Table 5. Overall results of analysis

Additional modality	Facial display (displaying facial expression & visual information)	Gesture (head tilting)	Other	Total
Agent 1	138	44	9	191
Agent 2	149	62	24	235
Total	287	106	33	426

5 Discussion

In this study, we found that personality setup was effective in the early-design stage of the agent. In addition, simple scripting without a high-fidelity profile showed that not only dialogues but also other modality designs were possible. It is meaningful that we showed the possibility of designing other modality through 'Dialogue situation' proposed in this study. For a specific modality (e.g. motion, facial design, etc.), there will be more appropriate design methodologies using visual base tools. In the future, the next step is to conduct a study to further detail the personality setup and to refine the modality design methodology.

References

1. Cohen, M.H., Giangola, J.P., Balogh, J.: Voice User Interface Design, pp. 75–84. Addison-Wesley, Boston (2004)
2. Dryer, D.C.: Getting personal with computers: how to design personalities for agents. Appl. Artif. Intell. **13**(3), 273–295 (1999)
3. Mccrae, R.R., Costa Jr., P.T.: A five-factor theory of personality. In: Handbook of Personality: Theory and Research, vol. 2, pp. 139–153 (1999)
4. Ball, G., Breese, J.: Emotion and personality in a conversational agent. In: Embodied Conversational Agents, pp. 189–219 (2000)
5. Oliveira, E., Sarmento, L.: Emotional valence-based mechanisms and agent personality. In: Bittencourt, G., Ramalho, G.L. (eds.) SBIA 2002. LNCS (LNAI), vol. 2507, pp. 152–162. Springer, Heidelberg (2002). https://doi.org/10.1007/3-540-36127-8_15
6. Malatesta, L., et al.: Agent personality traits in virtual environments based on appraisal theory predictions. In: Artificial and Ambient Intelligence, Language, Speech and Gesture for Expressive Characters, AISB 2007 (2007)
7. Dezonno, A.J., et al.: Personality based matching of callers to agents in a communication system. U.S. Patent No. 7,184,540, 27 February 2007
8. Custódio, L., Ventura, R., Pinto-Ferreira, C.: Artificial emotions and emotion-based control systems. In: 7th IEEE International Conference on Emerging Technologies and Factory Automation, Proceedings ETFA 1999 (Cat. No. 99TH8467), vol. 2. IEEE (1999)
9. Kim, H., Koh, D.Y., Lee, G., Park, J., Lim, Y.: Designing personalities of conversational agents. In: Proceedings of CHI EA 2019 Late-Breaking-Work. ACM Press, Glasgow, 4–9 May 2019

A New Framework of Interactive System Theory in Jewelry Design

Jiaqi Li and Jian Shi[(⊠)]

Shanghai Jiao Tong University, Shanghai, China
jshi@sjtu.edu.cn

Abstract. The rapidly developed interaction design has been introduced into the jewelry field. The early interactive system theories were proposed to help human-computer interaction or product interaction design, having great significance as a design guideline, but not very suitable for interactive jewelry design. In this paper, we propose a new framework of interactive system theory, special for interactive jewelry design, consisting of six elements: User, Emotion, Product, Activity, Context, and Technology (UEP-ACT). We first demonstrate the necessity of 'UPACT' components. Through the method of statistics and user research, we then analyze the importance of 'Emotion'. We also illustrate the mutual relationship between these six components. To identify the availability and feasibility, we use an example and take an experimental design. The aim of this proposal is to make this theory widely used in jewelry interactive design so as to create a better user experience.

Keywords: Interactive system · Jewelry design · Theoretical framework

1 Introduction

Modern interactive jewelry is added accessorily interactive function, incorporating the technique of wearable smart devices, which enable wearers to have interactive or sensual experience. Jewelry interaction has led to a surge of many smart jewelry companies, and many companies such as Nike and Fitbit have begun to collaborate with jewelry designers to develop smart jewelry [1]. Meanwhile, researchers like Marti et al. [2] and Rantala et al. [3] have carried out related studies on interactive jewelry.

Jewelry interaction design should conform to the normal principles of interaction design, whereas systematic thinking is also needed. Benyon [4] initially proposed an interactive system theory(Hereafter we called IST) to help an interaction designer's work in the 20th century. Later, Li [5], and Gu [6] expanded IST. These ISTs are based on human-computer interaction, and more suitable for computer and industrial products. Applications can be seen in the studies conducted by Huang et al. [7] and Liu et al.[8]. However, there have been very few researches on using IST to jewelry design yet, and previous ISTs are not very suitable for jewelry interaction design.

Therefore, in this paper, we propose a new systemic framework called 'UEP-ACT' interactive system theory, special for jewelry interaction design. In this theory, we define six components: User, Emotion, Product, Activity, Context, and Technology. It can be used in pre-design analysis and as an important tool of iterative evaluation.

© Springer Nature Switzerland AG 2019
C. Stephanidis (Ed.): HCII 2019, CCIS 1032, pp. 21–31, 2019.
https://doi.org/10.1007/978-3-030-23522-2_4

The general interactive system refers to devices and systems that interaction designers work with and responds to people's actions [4]. In this paper, the term interactive system means a systemic thinking method that is commonly used in the design field and focuses on integral analysis, being shown by visual chart and theoretical demonstration.

This paper is organized as follows. Section 2 introduces some related theories. Section 3 defines our proposed theory framework in detail and describes an example. In Sect. 4, we apply this new theory for experimental design. Section 5 discusses the limits and concludes the paper.

2   Related Theory

2.1   PACT Interactive System Theory [4]

David Benyon put forward an Interactive System Theory consisting of four elements: People, Activity, Context, and Technology (PACT). In David's view, the interactive system should be human-centered so 'people' is placed at the center rather than technology. Technology enables People to perform various Activities in different Contexts. Taking a PACT analysis can provide designers useful guidance for designing and principles of evaluation.

2.2   PACT-P Interactive System Theory [5]

The PACT-P interactive system theory was proposed for product design. The 'Product' was added into PACT and placed at the center because the product is the object interacting with a user directly. In PACT-P, People are defined into three categories based on their use of the product: primary users, secondary users, and tertiary users. Activity includes the behavior and feedback from users' use of the product.

2.3   UACP Interactive System Theory [6]

The theory of UACP interactive system was presented for product design too, which comprising four elements: User, Activity, Context, and Product. It uses the term "User" to replace "People" in the center. The product is thought as a materialized and visual form of technology, containing the required technical elements for interaction, thus replacing "Technology" with "Product". User, Activity, Context, and Product interact with each other.

3   Proposed Theory Framework

3.1   UEP-ACT Interactive System Theory Framework

In this section, we propose a new theoretical framework of interactive system for jewelry interaction design, called UEP-ACT theory (User, Emotion, Product, Activity, Context, and Technology), as shown in Fig. 1(a). We add the 'Emotion' element on the basis of PACT theory and integrate into the 'Product' element. In this theory, User,

Emotion, and Product are at the central position, being the core of the whole system, and they interact with each other. Meanwhile, these three interact with the remaining components, their relationships are shown in Fig. 1(b).

Users have many differences in both physical and psychological characteristics.

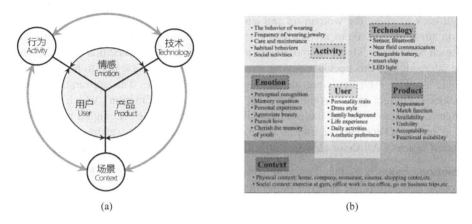

(a)   (b)

Fig. 1. UEP-ACT Interactive System Theory and the relationship of 'UEPACT'

Emotion can affect users directly. Interactive products usually involve lots of input-output information conversion and are inseparable from technology. Users use products via different technologies in diverse contexts. Contexts are divided into two types here: physical context and social context [4]. Physical contexts are solid places like home, office, bar, park and etc. The social context refers to a social situation or environment when the interaction occurs. These six components are key points in design. Jewelry interaction designers should have knowledge of them and their relationships.

User, Product, Activity, Context, and Technology. As described in previous theories above, User, Product, Activity, Context, and Technology are of great necessity and significance in interaction design. Here we use the storyboard approach to make a further demonstration.

(a)   (b)   (c)   (d)

Fig. 2. Storyboards

Storyboards. Figure 2 mainly depicts four storyboards. In part (a), the woman felt pleasant when she saw the prettier necklace, so her husband bought it for her. In part (b), the woman was in a good mood on the subway to work because she wore the newly purchased necklace. In part (c), the woman missed her husband when she touched the necklace, meanwhile, the necklace seemed to be understood and send a signal making her husband informed. After that, the husband sent a phone message right back to cheer the woman up and she felt happy again in part (d).

In these stories, there are various interactions such as visual interaction that the woman seeing a necklace, the movement interaction that she touched this necklace, and the interaction of this necklace giving a response and sending a signal to her husband, where these five elements are all playing an important role. The appearance of the necklace (Product) gives people (User) an intuitive feeling (Emotion), which to a large extent determines whether the product will be purchased. The sent signal needs technical support (Technology), and all these behaviors (Activity) occur in specific situations (Context). All these elements constitute the whole system of interaction.

Emotion. Emotion is the dominant component that affects users. "Emotion is the experience and attitude that the individual has got when his/her needs are met [9]." Concerning jewelry, the experience generates along with a series of actions like appreciating, wearing, storing and maintaining [10], where users have experience in different levels and give diversely corresponding emotional feedback.

Research. Since the emotion is more subjective than the other five components in IST, the assessment of emotion can only be achieved by self-report measures, direct observation or inquiring [11]. Therefore, to demonstrate the importance of 'Emotion', we use the approach of semantic differential scales, conducting surveys by questionnaires and focus groups. First, we collected and sorted out a number of jewelry pictures to make a two-dimensional (value and interactivity) diagram and selected six evenly-distributed necklaces as the sample, and Fig. 3 shows part of this diagram (The selected ones are circled with a red frame). Then, combined with the Geneva Emotion Wheel [12] and six prototypic emotions (joy, sadness, fear, disgust, anger, and surprise) [11], we listed about 100 adjectives and selected 10 pairs out of the most representative adjectives. These 10 adjective pairs describe both visual and subjective feelings, which were set in the form of seven-point differential scales to describe chosen jewels in a questionnaire. We invited 10 female participants aged predominantly 18–29 years into these focus group sessions, where half of them are college students and the remainder are office workers.

The steps of the focus group sessions are shown below:

1. Briefly introduce the concept of interactive jewelry and the topic: How do you like these jewels?
2. Fill in the questionnaires of adjective-pairs scales.
3. Discussion: What kind of jewelry do you prefer? What factors will you value if buy a smart jewel?
4. Discussion: Each participant describe her desired interactive jewelry.

Fig. 3. Part of the two-dimensional jewelry-picture diagram (Color figure online)

Results. Figure 4 shows the average score of six chosen jewels got from ten participants. Each participant gave her own score for each jewel in the order from the favorite to the least favorite (the corresponding score is 5–0). As can be seen, the NO. 4 jewel has the highest score of 4.09, indicating its most popular, compared to the NO. 5 jewel with the lowest score of 2.36.

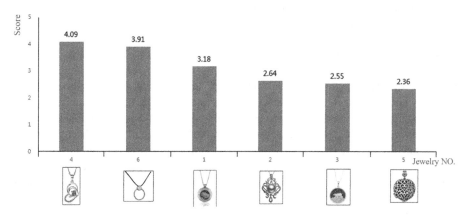

Fig. 4. The statistical data of scores on six jewels

We also sorted out the completed questionnaires, collected the scores of each adjective pair, and plotted them into radar charts. Figure 5 shows two of six jewels' radar charts, (a) is the NO.5 jewel and (b) is the NO. 4 jewel. In radar charts, seven colored polylines represent different given scores (1–7); each direction of the radar

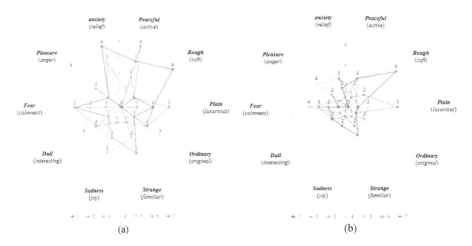

Fig. 5. Two radar charts with adjective pairs

represents an adjective pair; the bold words represent the outermost circle(where the score is 7), and the words in brackets indicate the innermost circle(where the score is 1).

According to the radar chart, we can clearly see the emotional state of the participants. It can be found that in Fig. 5(a), the distribution of the polyline is relatively scattered; equally 3–4 subjects gave the same score to each emotional adjective in the outer circle. This indicates that jewel NO. 5 bring people different feelings including the best and worst, that is why it becomes the lowest-rated favorite jewelry. While in Fig. 5(b), the distribution of polylines is relatively tight, where the scores are different but concentrated. Through the vocabulary ranges, it can be found that jewel NO. 4 gives participants more positive feelings and therefore becomes the most favorite jewelry with the highest score.

During the discussing session, the subjects expressed their different opinions. Similar to what was described by Rantala et al. [3], people are very concerned about the appearance of jewelry. They thought "Interactive jewelry must first look good before someone wants to wear it, and the function is secondary." Some participants thought it was appealing to add intelligent interaction if the aesthetics was not affected. Several participants hoped that jewelry can provide some functions like health supervision, message and weather reminder, making it more convenient than cell phones.

In short, people's emotional feelings can affect their cognition and preference for jewelry. Users expect that interactive jewelry should first possess the aesthetics of jewelry, and then be intelligent and interactive. Grasping the emotional needs of users can correctly guide the direction of jewelry design.

3.2 Example

We show an example of the We Bloom Smart Pendant in TOTWOO Company. To give a primary verification of UEP-ACT theory, we studied this case by group discussion and made a reverse analysis. Based on the collected information (Fig. 6), we analyzed these six elements 'UEPACT' respectively.

■Material: gold-plated brass & Swarovski crystals

■Function: Fitness Tracker, Daily Horoscope, Call &App Notification, Love Message, Break Reminder

■Description: Being Classic Baroque style, Shape like an inner bloom flower, the side hollow is embedded in colorful crystal and gold-plated silver, meaning that each woman has its own unique and magical charm

Fig. 6. We Bloom Smart Pendant

User. The user research was done first, a foundation for the follow-up research and design. The target users of this pendant are modern fashionable women. Their common characteristics are as follows: fashion, like freshness and beauty, often wear jewelry, concern quality and personality, and have an ordinary family life and social activities.

Emotion. Understand the expected emotions of target women from their perspective. The emotion can be summarized here: One is the yearning for beauty and expressing of self. Another is the desire and blessing of love.

Activity. The target women's behaviors were observed during the user research: work or study during the daytime; exercises, read books or watch movies online at night; on weekends, enjoy shopping, meet friends, travel with partners or take course training. Interactions occur in these activities.

Context. Users can wear We Bloom Smart Pendants in most places (physical context) of their daily lives, such as homes, companies, restaurants, cinemas, shopping malls, etc. As for social context, it can be seen including fitness exercise scene, work in the office, go on business trips and so on.

Product. Based on the analysis of User, Emotion, Activity, and Context, the due features of product and interaction design were determined. The shape is inspired by the flower blossom in nature, in line with the feminine characteristics and aesthetic preferences. The choice of Gold-plated brass and crystals gives the pendant a higher aesthetic beauty and value, which can get more affection by women.

Technology. The proper techniques to achieve this pendant's interactive function were chosen. Contemporary technologies, including that the smart chips combining with a mobile phone app, charging within the jewelry box, shining LED light and sensors, are fully utilized. Moreover, traditional crafts are innovatively inherited, like crystal inlay and cutting techniques.

4   Experimental Design

The process of applying UEP-ACT theory to interactive jewelry design is following. Here we design a jewelry piece for fashionable women as an experiment, and the subjects involved are the same 10 females.

4.1   UEP-ACT Analysis

Step 1: User and Emotion Research

User: Through the method of questionnaires, focus groups and interviews, conduct user research, collect available data, and build a user model at last (Table 1).
Emotion: Deeply track the subjects who accord with the user model. Communicate directly with them by interview to gain an in-depth understanding of their emotions.

Table 1. The user model

	Name: Miss. Zhou **Age:** 24 **Gender:** Female	
	Job: office clerk, medium income	
	Education: Master degree	**Residence:** Shanghai, China
	Family: live alone but falls in love, have an ordinary Chinese family with the elder and younger members	**Character:** fashionable, independent, optimistic, outgoing, enjoy beautiful things and love jewelry
		Hobby: music, yoga, keep pets, baking, travel
Normal activity: work in the daytime; practice yoga, read books, listen to music, or watch movies after work at night; make baking, go shopping, take pets for a walk, attend courses or go short-trips on weekends		
Dress style: bright color, high quality, in the look of elegance, simple but delicate, value details, like beautiful jewelry and accessories		

Step 2: Activity and Context Analysis

Activity: With the method of tracking observation and interview in Step1, analyze the user's behavioral routine and activities referring to the factors in Fig. 1(b). Then summarize the feature of their activities.
Context: Based on the above research, combined with the scenario method, the physical and social contexts of target users' wearing jewelry are identified: Physical contexts include home, office, and gym, etc. Social contexts consist of going shopping in malls, take walks in parks, etc.

Step 3: Product and Technology Analysis

Product: List user's expectations and concerns about interactive jewelry based on the collected information. Then determine the feasible and reasonable interactive functions and appearance characteristics.
Technology: Choose the appropriate techniques and processing technologies according to users' requirements.

Step 4: Summary and Arrangement

Summarize above steps, and illustrate the result in an integrated table as shown in Table 2.

Table 2. The result of UEP-ACT analysis

User model (Table.1)
Emotion   ● Pursue beauty and happiness   ● Convey love to the dearest   ● Express the sense of self   ● Hope to be praised
Activity   ● Wear jewelry almost every day (earrings, necklaces, bracelets)   ● Wear different styles of jewelry in work, parties, hang out   ● Regular Maintenance for jewelry (2~3 times/month)   ● Be very happy when wear jewelry, the behavior will be gentle and careful   ● Unconsciously touch the ring or pendant sometimes
Context   ● Rest at home or work in the office: consider the impacts of indoor physical and environmental conditions   ● Go shopping in malls, take walks in parks and other outdoor activities: consider the impacts of outdoor environments and the intensity of outdoor operations   ● Attend formal social events, parties, etc.: emphasize the design style of jewelry to match clothes
Product   **User expectation**   **Design requirements**   ● **Appearance:** beautiful, unique, fashion, delicate; ● **Appearance:** combine with women's traits, absorb natural style or natural materials;   ● **Function:** change color according to mood / occasion/weather, time/break reminder; ● **Function:** switch function easily, smooth interactive operation; charge batteries repetitively;
Technology   ● science technology: Smart chip, rechargeable battery, tactile sensor, LED light, etc.;   ● processing technique: inlay, cutting, surface treatment, etc.

4.2 Concept Design

According to Table 1, propose 2–3 conceptual designs through the method of brainstorm, and present the design ideas by sketches. For example, get insights into the jewelry piece's shape from natural grasses. Add an interaction for wearers like the Mimosa pudica to augment its joyful experience.

4.3 Evaluation and Assessment

Choose several typical users to participate in the evaluation of the conceptual design, discuss the pros and cons, determine the best design idea and confirm its implementation and improvements.

4.4 Prototype and Final Design

Prototype is the important process of a product from concept to real model. The component elements of function and appearance, like touch experience or technological modules, can also be evaluated by the prototype experiment [13]. Built the prototype by computer-aided design or physical model, and then go on with the user-participated evaluation to iteratively push the optimization and improvement.

5 Discussion and Conclusion

In this paper, we have proposed a new theoretical framework of UEP-ACT Interactive System to facilitate jewelry interaction design. We can apply this theoretical framework to make analysis in the early stage of design research, and push forward the whole design process with this systematic thinking. Our findings suggest that in interactive jewelry design, we should comprehensively analyze these six components 'UEPACT'. Most importantly, User, Emotion and Product are the core of this system; the human-centered and aesthetic principles should be attached great importance.

However, there are still several limits. First, the number of subjects and sample data is small and limited. Second, the proposed theory framework has not been fully applied to real design environment yet. Third, the experimental design in this paper only gives a set of relatively complete process. In the future, we should perform more case studies and evaluation experiment with concrete data to fully facilitate the application of this theory.

References

1. Nantia, K.: Why should jewelers care about the "digital". J. Jewellery Res. **1** (2018). http://www.journalofjewelleryresearch.org/
2. Marti, P., Iacono, I., Tittarelli, M.: Experiencing sound through interactive jewellery and fashion accessories. In: Bagnara, S., Tartaglia, R., Albolino, S., Alexander, T., Fujita, Y. (eds.) IEA 2018. AISC, vol. 824, pp. 1382–1391. Springer, Cham (2019). https://doi.org/10.1007/978-3-319-96071-5_140
3. Rantala, I., Colley, A., Häkkilä, J.: Smart jewelry: augmenting traditional wearable self-expression displays. In: 7th ACM International Symposium on Pervasive Displays. ACM Press (2018). https://doi.org/10.1145/3205873.3205891
4. Benyon, D., Turner, P., Turner, S.: Designing Interactive Systems: People, Activities, Contexts, Technologies, pp. 20–66. Mateu Cromo, Madrid (2005)
5. Li, S.: Experience and Challenge: Product Interaction Design, pp. 22–36. Literature, Jiangsu Fine Art Press, Nanjing (2008)
6. Li, S., Gu, Z.: Interaction Design, pp. 17–24. Literature, China Water Power Press, Beijing (2012)
7. Huang, Y., Gao, Y., Sheng, T., Zhu, L.: Appearance design of X-ray instrument based on interactive system theory. J. Mach. Des. **32**(10), 126–128 (2015). https://doi.org/10.13841/j.cnki.jxsj.2015.10.026
8. Liu, W.: A study of mobile games design based on the theory of interactive systems design. Academic paper, Shenyang Aerospace University (2013)
9. Zhu, X.: The Comprehensive Dictionary of Psychology, pp. 940–942. Beijing Normal University Publishing House, Beijing (1989)
10. Shao, Y.: Discussion on the application of sensory experience in emotional jewelry design. J. Art. Des. **2**(9), 140–141 (2012). https://doi.org/10.16824/j.cnki.issn10082832.2012.09.038
11. Vieira, L.-C., da Silva, F.S.C.: Assessment of fun in interactive systems: a survey. In: Cognitive Systems Research, vol. 41, pp. 130–143. Elsevier B.V., Amsterdam (2016). https://doi.org/10.1016/j.cogsys.2016.09.007

12. Geneva Emotion Wheel Version 3.0. (GEW; see Scherer, 2005; Scherer, Fontaine, Sacharin, & Soriano 2013). https://www.unige.ch/cisa/gew/
13. Qu, Y., Chong, D., Liu, W.: Bring interaction design methods and experimental technologies together into designing and developing interactive products. In: Joint Proceedings of the 11th Asia Pacific Conference on CHI and the 5th Indian Conference on HCI, pp. 102–107. ACM Press (2013). https://doi.org/10.1145/2525194.2525196

Contextual Evaluation of Digital Media Through Experience-Focused Participatory Bodystorming in a Full-Scale Spatial Prototype

Yihyun Lim[(⊠)] and Federico Casalegno

Design Lab, Massachusetts Institute of Technology,
Cambridge, MA 02139, USA
yihyun@mit.edu

Abstract. Distributed digital media and services are becoming more integrated to the spatial experience. This experience of the digital-hybrid needs a tangible method to asses its spatial legibility, digital interaction, and user experience. We propose a two-phased body-storming design and testing, to evaluate a novel concept of the Learning Branch for the financial industry, a flexible space that supports learning of digital financial services. The body storming exercises in both phases occurred within a full-scale, low-fidelity spatial prototype, where proposed interior environment was simulated with lightweight foam construction. The prototyped space was overlaid with digital experiences by introducing mobile apps and interactive media, from touch screens to visual projections. Final layer of service experience was added during the workshop sessions through enactment of service scenarios to test interactions between potential users and employees. The two-phase testing involved over 130 employees in the corporate bank, from various departments. Overall, the full-scale bodystorming provided an opportunity to have a 'living-lab' where new services could be evaluated through physical simulation, perform in-situ iteration and brainstorming of ideas, as well as uncover related issues and values related to HCI, such as privacy, in/exclusivity, complexity, acceptability, and implement-ability.

Keywords: Human-computer-building interaction · Design research · Prototyping · Bodystorming · User-centered design · Participatory design · Ubiquitous computing

1 Introduction

With the increased embodiment of digital and media interactions in physical space, our engagement with spatial experience is no longer one dimensional. Users may receive location specific contextual information through their personal devices, or develop their own understanding of the space through interaction with digital media. The increasing amount of intelligence of buildings through the integration of digital media and spatial design [12] calls for a new approach to the evaluation of user experience, its related issues, and the experiential values embedded in human-computer-building interaction.

As discussed by architect Rem Koolhaas at Venice Architecture Biennale 2014, it is in this context of an increased exchange between architecture and interaction design

© Springer Nature Switzerland AG 2019
C. Stephanidis (Ed.): HCII 2019, CCIS 1032, pp. 32–40, 2019.
https://doi.org/10.1007/978-3-030-23522-2_5

that we need to establish the "architecture of the digital hybrid" [1], and methods to evaluate the experience of this hybridity.

1.1 Objectives

This paper reviews a case study that uses bodystorming practices, full-scale spatial prototyping, and media prototyping as in-situ design methods to co-design and evaluate with stakeholders and potential users. We intended to evaluate the spatial and digital media design of the Learning Branch in order to assess the acceptability of these features, and to guide discussions on the implement-ability of this novel concept in real contexts.

The results can inform the design and testing of new service concepts, as well as a broader discussion on how to provide a platform to unveil issues and values related to new digital experiences in the financial and retail field. Such results (and proposed methods) can potentially be applied to industries that are testing out novel retail concepts of the digital-hybrid space, with open distributed space and its embedded digital experiences.

2 Related Work

2.1 Bodystorming as Design and Testing Process

When designing digital media-based services, interactions, and supporting spaces, representational models, visual materials, and digital prototypes are used to communicate and test the design. These representations are limited in communicating the multi-faceted experience of the digital hybrid space. The complexity of experiences requires a multi-communicational method of design and testing [3]. As Latour argues, "collective experiment" becomes essential, involving both scientific knowledge and everyday-life performances [6] through a participatory process that invites people to become central actors. This process of experience prototyping and participatory bodystorming provides an 'enactive' way to build empathy through social experience between users and the simulated space [9].

2.2 Value of Bodystorming

There are additional values to conduct bodystorming sessions to evaluate the interaction of users and building experiences, especially when technology acts as a mediator between these experiences. First, participants can easily relate to and understand the "non-observable aspect of design, such as user needs and interactional elements" by experiencing it in space [9]. Second, by 'being-there' in the physical space of the prototype, it is easier for participants to evaluate and generate new ideas when relevant constraints are observable [5]. Third, contextual cues from the physical prototype can bring up their personal memories and experiences, generating empathy with experiences that are being tested [7, 9]. The shared reference points between participants can facilitate more in-depth discussions, a crucial part in the co-design process of bodystorming [2].

3   Case Study: The Learning Branch

In the following we present a case study where we designed and prototyped both digital and spatial experiences to support the concept of a 'Learning Branch' for the financial sector. Two-phase workshops were performed, where we actively used bodystorming practices to evaluate proposed spatial and digital experiences. In presenting these cases, we will mainly discuss the methods, tools we used, and how we conducted the bodystorming exercises.

3.1   From Vision to Prototype

The Learning Branch was conceived within the Branch of the Future project, developed by MIT Design Lab in collaboration with a major bank in Brazil. The concept was part of a future vision composed of digital and spatial solutions aimed at increasing digital literacy of their existing and new customers, to transition them into digital banking.

3.2   Design

The concept of the Learning Branch mainly focused on creating a community hub for education in digital banking financial management. It is also a place for personalized experiences, through the use of smart technology and easily approachable universal bankers. To enable this, the proposal comprised three elements: (1) modular and flexible space design to accommodate activities of varied privacy and engagement levels, (2) digital media design for both remote personal uses and in-branch use (Branch App with multiple features such as virtual check-in/appointments, and other in-branch media elements such as interactive calculator and virtual conferencing), (3) service design for 'floating experts' to facilitate these experiences (Fig. 1).

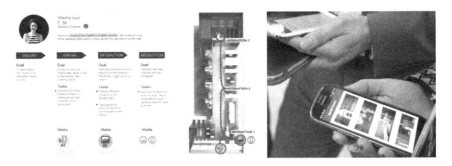

Fig. 1. User journey maps were developed based on digital educational needs. Learning Branch experiences can be enhanced with the use of its companion app.

4 Bodystorming Workshop

We conducted two phases of bodystorming workshops. The first phase focused on the spatial/physical experience of the proposed service concepts around the Learning Branch and its link to physical placement within the branch space. The second phase focused on the digital experience, during which we deployed media prototypes of digital services that utilized both personal mobile devices and on-site devices.

4.1 Spatial Experience – Bodystorming Workshop Phase 1

The first phase involved assembly of a full-scale mockup of the space using lightweight foam, which allowed easy construction and modification of the design. This mockup provided an opportunity to place various interaction and service design ideas in space, allowing users to form connections between digital and physical experience. The goal was to get feedback on the perceived usability and programming of the space (for which digital activities the space should be best used) in relationship to proposed digital media/digital banking experiences.

Participants. In total, 60 people across 6 sessions over several days participated in the first phase of the workshop. All participants were corporate bank employees from various departments and retail branches, selected on the basis of their roles and expertise.

Method. In each workshop session, participants were divided into two groups: customers and bankers. 'Programming' cards that described services in banking and digital learning were given out to each participant. Without first seeing the rendered image of the design that illustrated the function of the space, participants were asked to individually walk around the white foam prototype space and place relevant service concept cards where they thought they would best fit, based on the perspective of either the customer or the banker (Fig. 2). Participants also wrote in their ideas for new services and spatial features in empty cards. After all cards were placed, we regrouped to unveil renderings and interaction scenarios of the designed service and spatial features to the participants. With prior self-exploration in the prototype space and individual reflection on the service features, participants were able to actively engage in the discussion sessions. At the end of the workshops, the location and quantity of 'programming cards', along with comments and feedback, were recorded (Fig. 3).

Results. Overall, programming cards were widely distributed throughout the space, but the results show that cards were concentrated in specific zones. More so than the quantitative results, the key insights from this activity came from the follow-up discussions, where participants explained their reasoning behind card placement. These explanations unveiled each person's understanding of key issues related to the proposed learning and digital banking activities, such as complexity of digital interaction, required levels privacy, and exclusivity of the experience.

Privacy and Security. Discussions on privacy and security came up when digital/service experiences were related to disclosure of sensitive financial information. This was also closely tied to the perceived duration of digital interactions; digital banking features that

Fig. 2. Programming cards illustrating proposed digital banking services and digital learning experiences were given out to participants, and were asked to place them in the area that they found to be 'fitting' and 'appropriate' to run these functions.

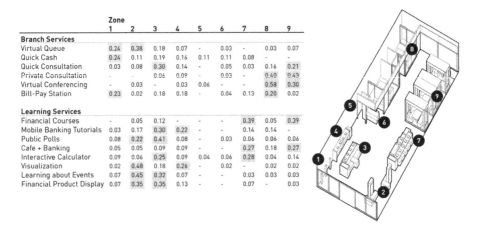

	Zone 1	2	3	4	5	6	7	8	9
Branch Services									
Virtual Queue	0.24	0.38	0.18	0.07	-	0.03	-	0.03	0.07
Quick Cash	0.24	0.11	0.19	0.16	0.11	0.11	0.08	-	-
Quick Consultation	0.03	0.08	0.30	0.14	-	0.05	0.03	0.16	0.21
Private Consultation	-		0.04	0.09	-	0.03	-	0.40	0.43
Virtual Conferencing	-	0.03	-	0.03	0.06	-	-	0.58	0.30
Bill-Pay Station	0.23	0.02	0.18	0.18	-	0.04	0.13	0.20	0.02
Learning Services									
Financial Courses	-	0.05	0.12	-	-	-	0.39	0.05	0.39
Mobile Banking Tutorials	0.03	0.17	0.30	0.22	-	-	0.14	0.14	-
Public Polls	0.08	0.22	0.41	0.08	-	0.03	0.06	0.06	0.06
Cafe + Banking	0.05	0.05	0.09	0.09	-	-	0.27	0.18	0.27
Interactive Calculator	0.09	0.06	0.25	0.09	0.04	0.06	0.28	0.04	0.14
Visualization	0.02	0.48	0.18	0.26	-	0.02	-	0.02	0.02
Learning about Events	0.07	0.45	0.32	0.07	-	-	0.03	0.03	0.03
Financial Product Display	0.07	0.35	0.35	0.13	-	-	0.07	-	0.03

Fig. 3. Placement of 'programming' cards in the full-scale white foam-prototype space. Yellow highlights indicate most concentrated zones for each service component. (Color figure online)

required a long time to perform were placed towards the back of the bank, and in areas with acoustic and visual protection from other users.

Complexity. Simple and seemingly quick services were placed by the entrance of the branch, whereas more complex and time-intensive services were placed in the rear/interior, which was perceived as more comfortable and private.

Exclusivity. Branch services such as private consultation, virtual conferencing, and financial courses and their related digital components (features within the app and digital media) were regarded as exclusive experiences. These cards were placed towards the rear/interior of the branch.

4.2   Media Experience – Bodystorming Workshop Phase 2

The guided Media Experience of the second phase of the workshop was designed around a specific goal: to simulate various media-technology experience points within the prototype space for user evaluation. Through demonstrations of media technology in digital learning and banking, participants in this second phase experienced the Learning Branch from the perspective of the 'visitor'. Experience points were designed based on selected user scenarios that targeted various levels of digital literacy and age groups, and their projected needs. We also introduced the "look and feel" layer to the white prototype space by introducing select color (materiality), music (sound), and coffee (aroma). These additional sensory features were added to create an ambience and mood of the learning branch, and to simulate a cafe-like environment for learning and to promote open conversations (Fig. 4).

Fig. 4. (left) Bodystorming spatial legibility in a full-scale prototype. (right) Testing the usability of digital features through simulation and role-playing.

Participants. A total of 67 participants joined this second phase of the workshop, representing 15 different departments around the corporate office, including 27 returning participants from the previous phase.

Method. In this second phase participants used their own devices to download the branch mobile app, a clickable interface prototype that was designed specifically for this workshop. The mobile app was designed as a mediator between the user and the space, to help users to navigate the open layout concept of the branch. To simulate the service experience with the media interaction, our team members played the role of the 'branch expert' to guide each 'visitors' around the branch space. Observations were made of participants using the branch app. Additionally, individual interviews and a digital survey were made, asking for comments on presented features.

Results. Media prototypes and role-playing of the services allowed participants to imagine and discuss actual applications in a real context. From acceptability of proposed media experience to brainstorming of additional features, participants were able to bring in their experiences to evaluate the usefulness and relevance of proposed ideas.

Acceptability. Participants discussed the overall concept of Learning Branch, especially how to make this concept acceptable to potential users. Participants drew from their own experiences to discuss the relevance of proposed concepts to their current business, and its acceptability to their current clientele.

Implement-ability. 73% of the participants said that this branch can be implemented now, if done gradually in order to acculturate the digitally illiterate to new technologies. Efforts should be made to include the older generation as well as those that are less familiar with digital devices. 23% of the participants said this could be implemented within 5 years.

Relationship Building. Participants talked about how the personalized guidance in learning digital banking using their own devices can bring clients emotionally closer to the brand and the branch itself. Participants mentioned that this type of space and its related digital interactions can assist in building the trust of account and non-account holders in digital channels as well as boost confidence of clients in performing digital banking. Also, the exclusive experience of the branch can make one feel 'special', which in return can increase loyalty to the bank.

Usefulness of the Bodystorming/Full-scale Prototype 95% of the participants said the full scale spatial prototype and digital mockups were useful. In terms of additional testing within the full-scale spatial mock-up, 81% of the participants said they would like to test real services and use the space to train employees. 18% mentioned they would test additional materials, colors, signage and other visual materials within the space.

5   Discussion

5.1   Benefits of 'Being-There': Immersive Evaluation

Full-scale prototyping and bodystorming workshops provided an immersive and empathy-driven way to evaluate the integration of digital media with the spatial experience [4]. 'Being-there' in a full-size mock up of a spatial environment opened up new ways to evaluate, experience, co-design, and quickly prototype features in-place [9]. In comparison to brainstorming, where participants gather around a table with visual materials, bodystorming forces participants to actively engage all senses to experience and generate ideas. Having a physical presence and the ability to move around in the prototype space, adds tangibility to digital mockups of technological experiences. Participants can better understand and imagine proposed innovative interaction features. In this high-context group communication model, the result is faster and better collaboration and communication with participants [10].

Bodystormed experiences are also better remembered, and the experiences are relatively easily recalled to be utilized in later design sessions [2]. Even after a few months of time between the first and second sessions, returning participants remembered the original spatial layout and pointed out the differences made in the second workshop. By 'being-there' in the spatial mock-up, participants were able to bring references from their own experiences and tie in their ongoing projects to come up with additional ideas, such as partnerships, and discuss from the perspective of an informed user.

5.2   A Collaborative 'Living Lab'

Another positive outcome of the full-scale prototype evaluation was how the space itself became a "collaborative room to accommodate Design Thinking and Agile work methods" [8]. With quick-to-build prototypes and immersive testing methods, the prototype space itself became a 'living-lab' for co-designing both digital and physical interactions. As in the two presented cases, we were able to bring together participants from different departments for discussion, consolidation, and iteration of ideas.

The 'living lab' is also economical, fast, and easy to create. It is a place to test low-fidelity prototypes, from spatial lightweight foam mock-ups for physical evaluation to quick simulations of digital media experiences. It is these foreseeable benefits of a full-scale prototyping and bodystorming methods that allows it to become a sustainable model for company's internal 'innovation lab' [11]. This space can be used by different departments to test new service features, spatial arrangements, digital media, and even interactive branding ideas. As suggested by one of the participants, the third phase to this workshop can be on 'how to make the proposals technically possible' through in-situ hackathons, where resulting prototypes can be easily deployed and tested within the prototype space.

5.3   Unveiling of Value-Driven Experiences for Discussion

The largest benefit of bodystorming practice in full-scale spatial and media prototypes was the opportunity it provided to unveil intangible, value-driven experiences of proposed digital media and service concepts. As mentioned previously, issues related to privacy, inclusivity, exclusivity, and acceptability were discussed, which wouldn't have been easily discussable if these experiences were presented with commonly used representation forms, such as 2D interfaces, 3D renderings, or even a VR space.

6   Conclusion

Bodystorming should be seen as a way of working with information in embodied ways, by 'being there'. These "contextually situated design sessions" [8] provide an immersive way to enhance the understanding and evaluation of human-building-computer interaction. Bodystorming sessions are also highly generative and partici-patory [10]; they allow participants to explore contexts to develop new ideas and uses, consolidate existing ideas, and allow everyone to become part of the design process. By putting the users into the simulated space of 'innovation', the empathy driven co-design process allows three key activities to happen: design by doing, learning by making, and innovation by understanding.

References

1. Alavi, H.S., Churchill, E., Kirk, D., Nembrini, J., Lalanne, D.: Deconstructing human-building interaction. Interactions **23**(6), 60–62 (2016)
2. Buchenau, M., Suri, J.F.: Experience prototyping. In: Proceedings of the 3rd Conference on Designing Interactive Systems: Processes, Practices, Methods, and Techniques, pp. 424–433. ACM, August 2000
3. Buxton, B.: Sketching User Experiences: Getting the Design Right and the Right Design. Morgan Kaufmann, Burlington (2010)
4. Giaccardi, E., Paredes, P., Díaz, P., Alvarado, D.: Embodied narratives: a performative co-design technique. In: Proceedings of the Designing Interactive Systems Conference, pp. 1–10. ACM (2012)
5. Klemmer, S.R., Verplank, B., Ju, W.: Teaching embodied interaction design practice. In: Proceedings of the 2005 Conference on Designing for User eXperience, p. 26. AIGA: American Institute of Graphic Arts, November 2005
6. Latour, B.: From "matters of facts" to "states of affairs": which protocol for the new collective experiments? (2001). http://www.bruno-latour.fr/node/372
7. Leonard, D., Rayport, J.F.: Spark innovation through empathic design. Harv. Bus. Rev. **72**, 102–113 (1997)
8. Löwgren, J., Reimer, B.: Collaborative Media: Production, Consumption, and Design Interventions. MIT Press, Cambridge (2013)
9. Oulasvirta, A., Kurvinen, E., Kankainen, T.: Understanding contexts by being there: case studies in bodystorming. Pers. Ubiquit. Comput. **7**(2), 125–134 (2003)
10. Schleicher, D., Jones, P., Kachur, O.: Bodystorming as embodied designing. Interactions **17**(6), 47–51 (2010)
11. Schrage, M.: Serious Play: How the World's Best Companies Simulate to Innovate. Harvard Business Press, Brighton (2013)
12. Wisneski, C., et al.: Ambient displays: turning architectural space into an interface between people and digital information. In: Streitz, Norbert A., Konomi, S., Burkhardt, H.-J. (eds.) CoBuild 1998. LNCS, vol. 1370, pp. 22–32. Springer, Heidelberg (1998). https://doi.org/10.1007/3-540-69706-3_4

Service Designers' Information Seeking: Consulting Peers Versus Documenting Designs

Yu-Tzu Lin[(⊠)] and Morten Hertzum

University of Copenhagen, Copenhagen, Denmark
{linyutzu, hertzum}@hum. ku. dk

Abstract. Service design is an information intensive activity. This study aims to investigate service designers' information behavior and understand the roles people and documents play as information sources for service designers. Ten designers were interviewed about their information seeking behavior in one service design project from its start to its completion. The interviewees were asked to describe and reflect upon their choice of information sources and their use of project documentation. Each interview lasted about 1.5 h. The interviews were transcribed in full and the transcripts were coded with respect to design activities, information sources used, and reflections on information behavior. People served five different roles as information sources and documents served four. Documents became increasingly important sources of information as projects progressed because still more information was recorded in writing. Consistent with previous research, people play an important role because of their easy accessibility and the good quality of the information they provide. In contrast, the forward-looking role of document creation restricts the backward-looking roles of the resulting documentation. We speculate that the consultancies suffer from poor integration across documents.

Keywords: Information seeking behavior · Information system design · Information sources

1 Introduction

Service design is an information intensive activity [3, 8]. Designers need information about the users' current practices, the technological possibilities and the envisioned future [6]. Numerous information systems and prototypes have been developed to support designers in managing this information. However, designers' information needs are complex and not well-understood [1, 2, 10]. This study investigates the information behavior of service designers. We are particularly interested in what information service designers need, how they go about finding it, what role design documentation plays in this process, and in service designers' reflections on the pros and cons of their information behavior. In this study, we identify the different roles that people and documents serve as information sources and investigate how the relative importance of people and documents evolves in the course of service design projects.

© Springer Nature Switzerland AG 2019
C. Stephanidis (Ed.): HCII 2019, CCIS 1032, pp. 41–48, 2019.
https://doi.org/10.1007/978-3-030-23522-2_6

2   Related Work

The *Wheel* model aggregates multiple models of the design process and consists of iterating through four activities: analysis, design, implementation, and evaluation [4]. Information seeking is central to these activities in that analysis involves gathering information about user needs, design involves matching information about user needs with information about technological possibilities, implementation involves acquiring the detailed technology information necessary to build designs, and evaluation involves collecting information about the extent to which the current version of the design meets user needs. To support the designers' information behavior, documentation is integral to the design process. While the *Wheel* model presents a general design process, other models describe a process specific to service design [11, 12]. For example, the *Multilevel Service Design* framework [12] distinguishes among three levels: service concept, service system, and service encounter.

In general, engineers and designers use people as information sources more often than documents [7]. Bruce et al. [2] find considerable differences in the information behavior of two design teams. For example, one of the teams had little communication with people in other design teams, whereas cross-team communication was common in the other team. With respect to documents, Hertzum [5] notes that designers tend to document their work to support their own sense-making process; they are less inclined to spend time expanding their writings into documents understandable to future readers. The resulting condensed forms of writing leave most of the context unsaid. To make documents understandable to a broader audience the condensed forms of writing must be elaborated. However, such elaboration often creates frustration among the current members of a design team, who can see the elaboration as redundant [1].

Designers also tend to satisfice in their balancing of source quality against source accessibility [14]. That is, once the quality of the information source is good enough for present purposes then their choice of source is determined by ease of access, not by a continued search for the best possible source. Designers often find that people provide information of good quality. For example, Poltrock et al. [13] found that asking people was considered to yield more benefits than simply obtaining the answer to a question. They cited a software designer for saying that '*you get what's important and their analysis of it*'. Conversely, documents leave it to the reader to interpret the meaning of the text and its applicability to present purposes [5]. An additional quality of people as information sources is that pertinent design knowledge, such as the design rationale, is often only held in the designers' mind and, thus, inaccessible from documents [9].

Hertzum [6] found that designers mostly obtained information from sources internal to their organization, with the exception that they mostly relied on external sources for information about the domain in which their design was to be used. In large organizations, it is sometimes recommended to look for information internally before turning to external sources because finding a good internal source provides valuable input about previous company-internal work on the issue, including the names of colleagues to consult [8]. In small and medium size organizations, external sources tend to be contacted more freely (e.g., [7]), probably because these organizations know that their size prevents them from having all the needed information internally.

3 Method

We interviewed ten service designers from five design consultancies, see Table 1. In an effort to avoid mono-cultural bias, the design consultancies are from different countries. The job titles of the interviewees span design lead, UX designer, and similar profiles. We opted for interviewees at different levels of seniority but required that they had completed at least one project in the design consultancy in which they were currently employed. The interviewees constitute a convenience sample in that they were selected from the first author's network and from the contacts of the people in this network. All ten interviewees gave their written informed consent to take part in the study.

Table 1. Profile of the interviewees

	Country	Gender	Seniority	Education	Project
A	China	M	6 years	Industrial design	Real estate
B	China	M	9+ years	Architecture	Entertainment
C	Italy	F	3–4 years	Interaction design	Insurance
D	Italy	M	10+ years	Communication design	Insurance
E	Spain	F	2–3 years	Media/interaction design	Consultancy
F	Spain	F	7–8 years	Service design and innovation	Design
G	Taiwan	F	1 year	Media/interaction design	Finance
H	Taiwan	F	4–5 years	Industrial design	Telecom
I	UAE	F	2–3 years	Industrial design	Airline
J	UAE	M	10+ years	Accessories design	Airline

The interviews were structured into three parts. First, the interviewees described their job and design experience. At the end of this description, the interviewees were requested to select a service design project they had recently been involved in. Second, they were asked to describe what they had done in that project from its start through to its completion: What information had they needed for completing their tasks? How had they gone about finding it? Had they documented information during the project? How had they reused previously documented information? Third, the interviewees were asked to reflect on their information and documentation practices in the project they had just described: Why had they behaved this way when they needed information? What were their opinions toward documentation and using documentation? The two designers from each consultancy were not required to talk about the same project, and they all chose to talk about different projects. Each interview lasted about 1.5 h.

The audio-recorded interviews were transcribed and coded in NVivo 11. We coded statements about three themes: the interviewees' activities, their information sources, and the reasons for their information seeking behavior. Activities were categorized into the four activities of the *Wheel* model [4] as well as into the three levels of the *Multilevel Service Design* framework [12]. Information sources were categorized into people or documents and into internal or external to the projects and consultancies.

4   Result

Team members and clients were the most frequently used sources. They were consulted more often than colleagues working on other projects in the company and more often than documents. Figure 1 shows the five roles that people played as information sources.

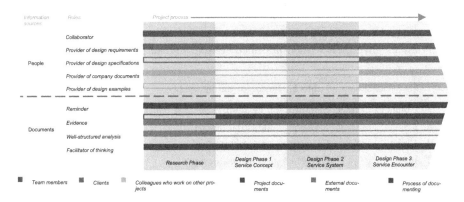

Fig. 1. The roles people and documents played in the service design projects

Team members were collaborators because all team members made design decisions together. For example, interviewee I said that she consulted her senior designers whenever she made design decisions. Sometimes designers worked by themselves, but there would always be a team discussion in each activity. Interviewee F stated that *"Everybody on the team needs to participate in everything"*. The designers sought information from clients when they needed design requirements (e.g., user data) and design specifications (e.g., legal regulations). For example, Interviewee C had acquired interface specifications during meetings with her client. She received a lot of information but later learned that it was incomplete. This made the situation stressful: *"So stressful, because the changes were so many. I added tons of information… I did my layout with logo and information. They were like 'no, no, we cannot do this'"*. The designers also sought information from colleagues who worked on other projects in the company. However, these colleagues were consulted infrequently compared to team members and clients. Designers sought information from colleagues on other projects to collect design examples and to learn about the existence of useful company documents. Interviewee J used colleagues as sources more often than the other interviewees. He often held workshops to collect input. The good peer-review culture in his company made the workshops an efficient way for him to collect useful information: *"You end up with ten, twenty examples of similar experiences, similar applications… Ultimately, it helps me as a designer to seek advice from other people without taking too much of their time."* In contrast, Interviewee B said that when he learned from colleagues on other projects, it was mainly by chance: *"You learn it coincidentally when people are chatting… In our company, we are not good at this [i.e., chatting]. We all want to know what projects are currently taking place in the company, but actually we don't know, unless we ask.*" He further stated that he would ask managers for information because they knew more about the projects. However, he had not done this in the project he shared in the interview. Corresponding with his statement that managers were the best sources of cross-project information, Interviewee D (an associate creative director) shared reusable documents from other projects with his team members.

Documents served four roles in the designers' information behavior, see Fig. 1. First, the process of creating documents facilitated the interviewees in thinking about their designs. In creating project documents, the designers were visiting, interpreting, and otherwise processing the information they had available. This way the information and its implications for the project became salient to them. Often the designers did not need to go back to the documents after they had written them because the information had become present to mind. Second, documents served as reminders of project activities in which the designers had taken part. For Interviewee E it was decisive to the usefulness of a document that it was about an activity in which she had been part. If she had been then the document could provide a useful summary and reminder; if she had not been part of the activity then she doubted that the document would be sufficiently detailed for her to learn much from reading it: "*If a person gives me a summary, I would not think reading it would be useful for me. However, if I experienced the process then – when I read the summary – it helps me to think of the things that happened… For me, what I need is a starting point to help me think about and recall the things that have happened.*" Third, documents served as well-structured analyses. For example, Interviewee B learned useful information from question-and-answer websites. Interviewee I also sought information that was structured by other people. She explained that depending on the quality of her design and the nature of her task, she would seek different types of information: "*It is easier if you pick things [i.e., examples] from the ones they have filtered… I think it depends on what you want to get from it. Whether your design is already good enough or you want to make a break-through. [In the latter case] you have to spend more time on competitor analysis.*" Fourth, documents served as evidence to show the rationale for designs. The rationale could, for example, be a client requirement or a design theory. Interviewee F said that the design materials and design theories she sought from external documents helped her explain to clients why the team made its design decisions. Interviewee A often used project-internal documents for similar purposes. For him, detailed documents were important: "*When we had some arguments with our client… we would go back to the strategy documents defined during concept design. We would tell them [the client] we did things on the basis of them [the strategies, defined together by the designer and his client].*"

The designers' use of information sources evolved over the course of the design process. Early in the design process, few project documents had yet been created and information was overwhelmingly obtained from people supplemented with external documents. Later in the design process, project documents played a larger role in the designers' information seeking. This evolution coincided with a somewhat restricted approach to iteration. Already during the analysis activity the designers began to experience a reduced need for additional information. Rather than consulting more people through additional interviews, they revisited the documentation of the interviews they had already conducted. Notably, they did not make changes in the revisited documentation. Interviewee F explained that she saw no need for changes: "*I have never seen it happen that we go back and change the research results because we discover something new... The things that you are discovering for this [i.e., for designing the screens], they are not gonna change what you have discovered in the research.*" Interviewee I mentioned that she maintained a document in which she kept track of whether her hypotheses were confirmed. Among the ten interviewees, this document was the only mention of a document that evolved over time. The other interviewees merely revisited documents from previous activities to obtain information from them. For example, Interviewee A returned to strategy documents to follow up on whether the design met client needs: "*During concept design and detail design, we needed to constantly go back to check research files... To verify whether our design fits client needs.*"

5 Discussion

5.1 People: Easily Accessible, High Quality, or Both

Team members are the most frequently used internal source and clients are the most frequently used external source. When the interviewed designers consult people who are internal to their organization but external to their project, it is primarily to get links to company documents and design examples. These findings echo those of previous studies [7, 8, 13]. During projects, the interviewed designers work closely with the other team members: sharing their own points of view, listening to those of others, and making decisions together. This way, the team members are easily accessible information sources and, at the same time, knowledgeable about the context in which information is sought, thereby increasing the likelihood that they can provide context-aware answers. In contrast, clients are the authoritative source of information about design requirements and design specifications but they are less accessible. Specifically, designers will normally be unfamiliar with the client's business domain and may therefore struggle to appreciate the details of the requirements and specifications. In addition, the commercial nature of the relationship between designers and clients makes communication more delicate. Interviewee C illustrates that the resulting information seeking may be stressful and lead to misunderstandings in spite of the client providing lots of information. The reduced accessibility of people who are not team members increases the interviewed designers' attention to documents as information sources. For example, Interviewee B seeks information on question-and-answer websites.

5.2 Documents: Important While They Are Being Created

The interviewed designers find that writing facilitates thinking. Thus, an important role of documents is to facilitate thinking during document creation. This role is forward-looking. It involves processing available information to make sense of it and to become able to act competently on it. The resulting document is secondary because its creation is a means to arrive at a coherent understanding of the available information. Once the designers have arrived at this understanding it will be salient to them and available in their mind. Although the document is secondary to the acquired understanding, the created document serves additional roles as documentation. In these additional roles, documents provide a means for designers to look back, for example at the rationale for a design decision. It must be expected that documents are restricted in their backward-looking roles because it is their forward-looking role that is designers' immediate motivation for creating documents. The forward-looking role is likely to produce condensed forms of writing by leaving out issues the designer already understands [1, 5]. Instead, the documents will focus selectively on the issues that are important to the designers for present purposes, often to the extent of being hard to understand for people who did not take part in the activities dealt with in the documents. For example, Interviewee E prefers reading documents that summarize activities in which she has taken part over reading documents that summarize design activities in which she has not taken part. The former reminds her of important issues and arguments, the latter will most likely not be of use to her because important information will be missing. Insisting that designers should elaborate their documents to make them more under-standable to future readers would add considerably to the designers' workload [1].

5.3   From People to Poorly Integrated Documents

The designers' information behavior changes as their projects progress from the first to subsequent iterations. As the projects progress the designers increasingly revisit the documentation of previous activities rather than, for example, re-interview users. In addition, they increasingly turn to the documents previously obtained from colleagues rather than consult these colleagues anew. That is, the designers convert people sources into easily accessible documents. This transition qualifies the designers' overarching preference for people as sources. The designers' source preferences evolve with their task progress because this progress increasingly provides the designers with project-internal documents that are tailored to the specifics of the project. Although the designers rely increasingly on documents, the documents appear to be poorly inte-grated. For example, Interviewee F mentions that discoveries made during subsequent iterations will not lead to changes in the documents from the first iteration. We speculate that the absence of such changes produces inconsistencies. One source of inconsistencies may be that the designers attend to the users' needs during the early analysis to get to grips with the design task but thereafter primarily attend to their client's needs. A primary focus on the client is unsurprising, given that the designers are consultants, but entails that the users' needs become supplementary information. Poor integration between user and client needs may limit the consultancies in the long run because it prevents them from incorporating a solid understanding of the user experience in their projects.

6   Conclusion

Three conclusions arise from this study. First, designers use people as information sources owing to their easy accessibility and the good quality of the answers they can provide. Second, the process of creating documents serves a forward-looking role for designers. This role likely yields condensed forms of writing that limit the documentary roles of the documents. Third, designers switch from primarily using people as sources during the initial project activities to making increased use of documents during subsequent project activities. However, the documents appear to be poorly integrated.

References

1. Brown, J.S., Duguid, P.: The social life of documents. First Monday 1 (1996). https://doi.org/10.5210/fm.v1i1.466
2. Bruce, H., Fidel, R., Pejtersen, A.M., Dumais, S., Grudin, J., Poltrock, S.: A comparison of the collaborative information retrieval behaviour of two design teams. New Rev. Inf. Behav. Res. 4, 139–153 (2003)
3. Gumienny, R., Dow, S.P., Meinel, C.: Supporting the synthesis of information in design teams. In: Proceedings of the 2014 Conference on Designing Interactive Systems, pp. 463–472. ACM, New York (2014)
4. Helms, J.W., Arthur, J.D., Hix, D., Hartson, H.R.: A field study of the wheel—a usability engineering process model. J. Syst. Softw. 79, 841–858 (2006)
5. Hertzum, M.: Six roles of documents in professionals' work. In: Bødker, S., Kyng, M., Schmidt, K. (eds.) ECSCW '99, pp. 41–61. Springer, Dordrecht (1999). https://doi.org/10.1007/0-306-47316-X_3
6. Hertzum, M.: People as carriers of experience and sources of commitment: information seeking in a software design project. New Rev. Inf. Behav. Res. 1, 135–149 (2000)
7. Hertzum, M.: Expertise seeking: a review. Inf. Process. Manag. 50, 775–795 (2014)
8. Hertzum, M., Pejtersen, A.M.: The information-seeking practices of engineers: searching for documents as well as for people. Inf. Process. Manag. 36, 761–778 (2000)
9. Ko, A.J., DeLine, R., Venolia, G.: Information needs in collocated software development teams. In: Proceedings of the 29th International Conference on Software Engineering, pp 344–353. IEEE Computer Society, Washington (2007)
10. Kwasitsu, L.: Information-seeking behavior of design, process, and manufacturing engineers. Libr. Inf. Sci. Res. 25, 459–476 (2003)
11. Pang, S.: Successful Service Design for Telecommunications: A Comprehensive Guide to Design and Implementation. Wiley, Hoboken (2009)
12. Patrício, L., Fisk, R.P., Cunha, J.F., Constantine, L.: Multilevel service design: from customer value constellation to service experience blueprinting. J. Serv. Res. 14, 180–200 (2011)
13. Poltrock, S., Grudin, J., Dumais, S., Fidel, R., Bruce, H., Pejtersen, A.M.: Information seeking and sharing in design teams. In: Proceedings of the 2003 International ACM SIGGROUP Conference on Supporting Group Work, pp 239–247. ACM, New York (2003)
14. Simon, H.A.: Rational choice and the structure of the environment. Psychol. Rev. 63, 129–138 (1956)

Research of Interaction Design Guided by Five Senses Theory

Jingjing Liu[✉] and QiJun Duan

School of Design Art and Media, Nanjing University of Science and Technology,
200, Xiaolingwei Street, Nanjing 210094, Jiangsu, China
allieliu@yeah.net

Abstract. This paper examines the value and application of five senses design theory in interaction design. Through the analysis of human sensory experience, we know that at present, designers have focused on the emotional aspects of product design, while problems such as lack of innovation and poor performance of product interaction still exist. Mainly manifested on the one hand, lack of sensory mobilization, many designs only focus on visual performance, while ignoring other sensory experience. On the other hand, some designers have noticed the importance of five senses in interaction design, but many of them are still in simple interaction stage, cannot trigger people's deep emotional memory.

Based on those problems, a method to score the designs by creating a Five Senses Map were proposed together with constructing five senses information chart system and methods for design improvement on emotional interaction for product design.

The experience of five senses is also one of the standards for assessing whether it is a good design. The results showed that the higher the score of Five Senses Map, the better the users' experience will be. Using the method of drawing Five Senses Map in interaction design can awaken users' emotional memory and simplify the process of interaction design, also provide users a more pleasant experience.

Keywords: Five senses · Interaction design · User experience · Emotional satisfaction

1 Introduction

Excellent designs touch people's hearts. For designers, emotional designs have attracted more and more attention, design directions has gradually transferred from individual product design to interactive products that focus on users' sensory experience.

With the development of product interaction design, consideration of users' emotional needs and integration product with the five senses experience of human has become an important issue faced by interactive product design [1]. At present, The main problems of interactive product design as following: (1) Lack of sensory mobilization. Many designs only focus on visual performance, while ignoring other sensory experience. (2) Some of the designers have noticed the importance of sensory

C. Stephanidis (Ed.): HCII 2019, CCIS 1032, pp. 49–55, 2019.
https://doi.org/10.1007/978-3-030-23522-2_7

experience in interaction design, but those are still in simple interaction stage, cannot touch users' deep emotional memory.

Based on problems mentioned above, a method of drawing a Five Senses Map was proposed to evaluate the five senses of product design by constructing five sensory information chart system. We proposed design improvement methods for emotional interaction of product design, and carries out the following research: The first step is to do user research. Second step is to extract the elements of human five senses experience. Last step is to study and practice the five senses design strategy, and form an interactive design strategy based on the five senses theory, and bring users a better interactive experience.

From the perspective of cognitive psychology. The information processing system of the human brain consists of receptor, effector, memory and processor. Receptors are human sensory organs whose functions include vision, hearing, smelling, touching and tasting. At this stage, people produce subjective feelings to products through the sensory system. The five senses design theory advocates optimizing the feedback perceived by the human brain at the cognitive level. Good product design can mobilize multiple sensory effectively, thus leaving deeper emotional memory and experience for users. Using five senses design theory will help interaction designers to find out users' requirements and improve the design quality.

2   Methodology

This research focused on potential users of interactive products. Through the analysis of five senses experience design, an interactive design model of modern products was formed and product design model that can ultimately support five-sense experience was established.

2.1   User Research of Interactive Products

From users' point of view, designers can discover users' emotional needs by understanding the product using process and emotional behaviors of users. Then the designers need to consider from the sensory point of view to stimulate new design inspiration and come up with designs that can convey emotions.

In interactive design, the experience of the five senses at the cognitive level is more of an "intuitive experience". Users make intuitive judgments on products through their own instinct on their feelings. When an interactive link arouses people's sense of deja vu and mobilizes their existing experience habits and memories, it will naturally give feedback to the product. In this way, users can use the product without re-learning. This process effectively reduces the learning cost of users and makes the interaction process of the whole product more smoothly.

2.2   Five Senses Map

Users' experience can be improved by integrating different sensory experience into the designs. Based on this fact, we have established a creative to score the five sense experience of a product by user-participatory research, and drew the results of the research into a Five Senses Map. As showed in Fig. 1, the vertical axis of the Five Senses Map increases gradually from the origin to the positive direction, and the score ranges from 0 to 5.

The horizontal axis from the origin to forward include vision, sound, smell, touch and taste. According to the score of the five senses obtained from the calculation, a chart is drawn. In this way, we can intuitively see the degree of sensory mobilization of a product. The score of each point in the five senses rating table represents the average value of the corresponding item score after calculation. Then the points are connected and colored. As showed in Fig. 2, the larger the coloring area, the stronger the initiative of the product/experience to mobilize human senses, the richer the emotional mobilization in the process of using the product or experience.

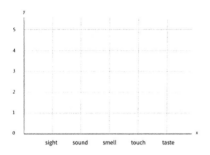 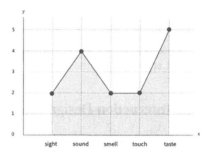

Fig. 1. Blank five senses map   **Fig. 2.** Five senses map

3   Sensory Elements Extraction

3.1   Extraction of Visual Color

Vision is the most basic and intuitive sensory of the five senses. It is often considered as the primary sensory. It also carries other sensory experience.

Color has been symbolized in the process of cognitive development as influenced by the cognitive habits and concepts in different regions. Color has diverse meanings, but also conveys different values and emotions. In order to fully express the visual signals of products, interactive product design should emphasize the emotional and symbolic significance of color.

3.2   Hearing in Interactive Design

The sound function of the product mainly includes prompting, warning and deepening memory [2]. It creates various atmospheres through sound to satisfy the psychological needs of customers. Warning sound can prompt users of wrong operations. Feedback sound refers to a kind of metaphorical sound effect, which can accurately reflect the interaction behavior of the user feedback to the interface system.

3.3   Touch and Feedback in Interactive Design

Touching is the earliest mature feeling of human beings. People will form their own touching experience and unique psychological feelings and habits for the temperature and texture of external objects [3]. Through touching, people can feel the shape, lines, subtle forms and textures of all objects. Touching experience of different things produces different psychological feelings.

3.4   Smelling and Tasting in Interactive Design

Smelling is a real-time physiological stimulation. Comparing with visual impacts, the impact of smelling is more profound. In interactive product design, the reminder function by emitting an odor is likely to be a new interactive reminder besides ringing, vibration and flickering in the future.

Comparing with vision and touching that played a leading role in sensory design, smelling and tasting have been overlooked in general product design. But the five senses of human beings are interlinked. They can be stimulated and guided by other senses, and at the same time they can bring the pleasure of taste.

4   New Interaction Design Method: From Effective to Pleasant

From the users' point of view, interactive design means to make products easier, more effective and more pleasant for people to use. The relationship between users and designers is bidirectional. As showed in Fig. 3, interaction designers are committed to exploring people's psychological and behavioral characteristics, finding out users' needs and optimizing the steps users take when using products.

At the same time, it can also enhance and expand interactive behavior through various effective interactions, and establish the organic relationship between products and users through behavior interaction, so that people transfer from using products effectively to pleasantly [4]. As shown in Fig. 4, users' requirements also have a shallow to deep level of requirements from "Available" to "Useful", then "Easy-to-Use" and finally "Want-to-Use".

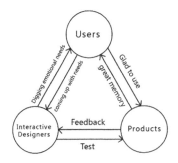   

Fig. 3. User relationships   **Fig. 4.** Hierarchy of user requirements

To sum up that, the key point of emotional design of interactive products is to impress, to make the products functional useful, to create an emotional bond with users, and to generate emotional deduction and thinking at the same time.

People start to feel objective things with the experience of the five senses [5]. Take the most common things in life as an example, as shown in Fig. 5, when drinking a coke acts on our sensory experience, we can hear the sound of "his" when opening the can through hearing, see its color through vision, distinguish its smell through smelling, taste its taste through tasting, and feel its temperature through touching. We integrate these sensory experience data and draw a Five Senses Map. We can clearly see the corresponding scores of the five senses.

The experience of the five senses is also one of the standards to evaluate product designs. The interactive experience of the alarm clock is a good example. The traditional alarm clock usually emits sound at regular intervals to wake up the users. The score presented by the Five Senses Map was summarized in Fig. 5. We can clearly see that the scores are not particularly ideal.

The Sensorwake alarm clock designed by Guillaume Rolland is somewhat like a retro TV. In addition to supporting light and sound to awaken users, it also releases its own fragrance to wake people up with various flavors to choose. Although, for alarm clocks, auditory stimulation is the most effective and direct, the experience of Sensorwake alarm clocks breaks the traditional alarm clock pattern, which relies solely on auditory stimulation. It started from the five senses experience.

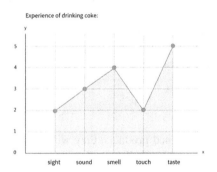

Fig. 5. Five senses map of drinking coke

It wake up users by visual awakening, auditory awakening and olfactory awakening. Many users' senses are stimulated and upgraded.

Overlapping the scores of two alarm clock products in a Five Senses Map by using this method, we can understand the advantages and disadvantages of different products more intuitively, and guide designers to upgrade the sensory experience with lower scores to design products with more experience enhanced (Figs. 6 and 7).

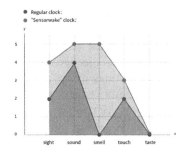

Fig. 6. "Sensorwake" alarm clock   **Fig. 7.** Five senses map of two clocks

The research results showed that enhancing only one of the five sensory experience would greatly improve the user's experience. The design method of enhancing the five sensory experience proposed for interactive design was based on the indispensable elements of in people's experience of life.

The interaction design strategy based on the five senses design theory can be formed by penetrating the five senses experience into the interaction design.

To listen to the voice in the eyes, the color in the ears, or to see the invisible shape can realize the complementarity and harmony of the design and enhance the competitiveness of the design works. The five senses design theory is part of the sources of inspiration for interactive design [6]. When products can satisfy users' sensory experience needs and emotional demands, the experience of interweaving sensory and memory will leave a deep impression on users.

5   Conclusion

When users use emotional designed products, they will produce a kind of familiar but also unfamiliar sensory experience, which stimulate people's interest in understanding, feeling the interactive experience of information and emotion beyond the product itself, and get feedbacks of the product naturally. It not only gives the product functionality, but also gives the product a unique personality.

This paper discusses the application of five senses design theory in interactive design. By extracting elements in vision, hearing, smelling, touching and tasting, the value of five senses design theory in interactive design was discussed by using user-participatory research and drawing Five Senses Map.

Nowadays, design should not be limited to the visual field, but a completed experience under the joint action of multiple sensory. The application of the Five Senses Map makes designers to find the balance of the five senses when conceiving, and provides new ideas for interactive design.

Based on the interactive product design, this paper analyses how to optimize product design from the perspective of experience. This paper not only provided measures and evaluation models for designers, but also clearly showed the spiritual value of interactive products and provided effective reference for the design and development of interactive products. Users and products interacts with each other that forms an interactive product design model based on five senses experience.

References

1. Huang, C.R.: Research on Emotional Design of Museum Creative Products in China (2018)
2. Wu, X.: Five Sensors Used in Product Design (2015)
3. Zhu, Z., Wang, K.Q.: From the Five Senses Design to the Emotional Design (2013)
4. Ch'ien, C.-S.: Synesthesia (2002)
5. Hara, K.: Designing Design (2006)
6. Kolko, J.: Thoughts on Interaction Design (2012)

Design Research of New Energy Imagery Transformation Based on Verb Semantics

Li-Jun Liu[1], Yi Li[1(✉)], and Yong Dai[2]

[1] School of Design, Hunan University, Changsha, Hunan, China
{sallyliu,2012171}@hnu.edu.cn
[2] School of Electrical and Information Engineering, Hunan University,
Changsha, Hunan, China
chd-dy@foxmail.com

Abstract. At present, due to large-scale development of non-renewable energy, its reserves are getting smaller and smaller and the use of fossil energy causes serious pollution. In order to cope with the dual pressure of energy and environmental protection, the products powered by new energy will become future directions. It is an urgent problem to be studied that how to apply new energy imagery to product design. The research is to perceive the new energy based on the study of verb semantics and transform its imagery into a perceptible design model. It is carried out in three parts: the extraction of "new energy" verb and the establishment of the word bank, the establishment of a gene bank and the extraction and transformation of new energy design elements. Perceived imagery from the perspective of the verb which analogies to the study of adjectives. Combined with card classification, correlation analysis, and other methods, a new energy word library and image library of verbs are formed and finally transformed into a perception and experience model reflecting new energy. The use of verb thinking can help designers create the immersive design to better convey the design in a variety of ways while enabling users to mobilize multiple senses to perceive new energy products, increase usability and experience, and arouse users' emotional resonance.

Keywords: New energy · Imagery cognition · Verb thinking · Experience model

1 Introduction

With the continuous development of the world economy, large industrial scale lead to large consumption of fossil fuels. We are facing a serious energy crisis. Only by vigorously developing new energy can the harmonious development between human and nature be maintained [9]. In the future, new energy products will become the mainstream, and how to apply new energy into product design

Supported by the National Natural Science Foundation of China (No. 61772186).

C. Stephanidis (Ed.): HCII 2019, CCIS 1032, pp. 56–63, 2019.
https://doi.org/10.1007/978-3-030-23522-2_8

has become an urgent problem to be studied. In product design, it is necessary to embody the image of new energy so that people can know its power source. In previous studies, the expression and description of product image are mainly based on adjectives [4,5,8]. This study perceives new energy from the perspective of verbs, which provides a new possibility for the study of product semantics.

2 Related Research

2.1 New Energy Perception Imagery

Perception imagery is the psychological emotion produced by the comprehensive sensory response. People receive information about product design elements through the perception system and then match the cognitive memory stored in the brain with the objects they see to complete the process of perceptual image perception [7]. Users can feel the design symbols of new energy products from multiple senses, which match the existing cognitive impression of new energy in the brain and eventually form the cognition of new energy products.

New energy is currently used more in the automotive sector. Due to the difference in power, new energy vehicles will have great changes in modeling design, and the corresponding design will convey different symbols. In order to let people perceive the difference between new energy products and traditional products through design, it is necessary to explore the difference between new energy and traditional fossil energy in users' perception image.

2.2 Extraction of Verb Semantics

Semantic expression and description are mainly based on adjectives, because they have the characteristics of cognitive economy and relative stability in the same language environment. Most studies use adjectives as the main form of semantic expression, and acquiring and expressing adjectives is an important basis for building a stable semantic space. This study uses verbs to describe new energy and tries to look at things from a new perspective, which is similar to the method of product semantic research.

Every word including noun, verb, and adjective has its own "meaning" and "image". When a word is mentioned, the memory of the word will be searched in the mind. Verbs are used to express actions or processes. They have a more dynamic picture sense than adjectives and nouns. They are easy to change with time and have the form of "body" [10]. In semantics, verbs have various forms, which can describe the dynamic characteristics and behavioral attributes of nouns and are closely related to people's image thinking. Looking at design from the perspective of verbs, we can better understand people's behaviors in the environment and meet users' changing needs in design. It is the uncertainty and flexibility of verbs that can bring designers and users different perceptual situations from adjectives.

Taking new energy vehicles as an example, cars are mobile "Spaces", which can be described by verbs to better reflect the characteristics of cars in all aspects. The car itself is a dynamic product. From the first sight of a car to the touch of a car, the relationship between a car and a person also changes dynamically. The whole process of using a car is in a changing interaction.

To sum up, this study perceived new energy from the perspective of verbs and tried to provide a new idea for the design of new energy products.

3   Research Process

The research is mainly divided into the following three parts: the establishment of new energy verb lexicon, the collection of new energy image resources and the final design transformation. Figure 1 shows the research flow. The semantic space is constituted by the semantic divergence of "new energy" subject words, the image space is constituted by a large number of relevant images, and the experiential situation space is finally designed by the designer. The whole process is complemented and stimulated by designers and users, and they participate in the completion together to get good user feedback.

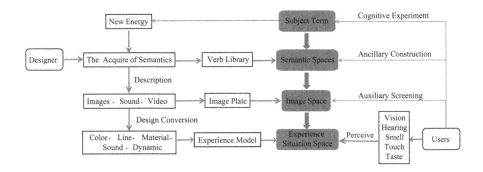

Fig. 1. The research process

3.1   Semantic Acquisition of New Energy Image and the Establishment of Verb Database

Establishment Process. There are generally two kinds of semantic (adjective) extraction methods: (1) taking the design object as the object, using morphological, color, texture and other elements as the carrier of semantic information, and using linguistic and statistical methods to establish the relationship between semantics and product features; (2) take people's cognition as the main body, use methods such as user survey and image scale analysis to study people's psychological perception of design objects and obtain the scale of cognitive adjectives [1]. In this study, two methods are used for reference and combined with natural language statistics to describe verbs of new energy. Users are also allowed to select verbs according to their psychological perception to construct semantic verb database to describe new energy. The method of multi-level and multi-layer filtering is adopted, and the following five steps (see Fig. 2) are adopted to construct.

Fig. 2. The formation of the verb library

Overlap the Lexicon. By using the method of literature survey and combining the data of the dictionary of verbs, the dictionary of modern verbs, the dictionary of Chinese verb usage, the dictionary of Chinese verbs, and the library of Chinese verbs resources, the words are overlapped through Python. The intersection of dictionaries is taken to get 1000 commonly used verbs.

Screen Out the Irrelevant Verb Categories. In this step, 500 verbs were obtained, and irrelevant items were deleted according to the verb category [3] of the Chinese verb resource library (Table 1 is the verb classification category). According to the subject word "new energy", two types of communicative verbs and relational verbs could be basically deleted, leaving the psychological verbs describing people's psychology and the action verbs describing things.

Table 1. The verb classification

Verbs			
Action verbs	Communicative verbs	Psychological verbs	Communicative verbs

Relevance Analysis. Eighty Chinese native speakers were selected to participate in the experiment, and their recognition of new energy-related words was obtained through a five-point scale. The "relatively reasonable" standard set by the experiment is that when the proportion of "strongly agree" and "relatively agree" of a word is more than 90%, the meaning of the word can be considered to be related to new energy by the public. Through cognitive experiments and statistical analysis, 200 verbs with high cognitive consistency were retained. The verb lexicon describing new energy sources is preliminarily obtained.

Synonym Screening. In order to ensure that the verbs in the word bank are familiar to the general public and the meaning of the words is clear, remove ambiguous meaning, multi-meaning, and unfamiliar words from the 200 words. Among them, 87 verbs were obtained by deleting words with duplicated meanings with the help of synonym word forest.

Expert Selection. In order to let designers better perceive new energy, 50 teachers and students majoring in design were selected to select the verb vocabulary with more visual sense, which made the verb bank more concise and accurate and prepared for the next step of immersive design. Finally, the verb lexicon (see Table 2) was obtained, with a total of 32 verbs.

Table 2. The verb classification

Regenerate	Evolve	Cycle	Refuse	Flow	Permeate	Breed	Breathe
Diffuse	Release	Filter	Balance	Extend	Intersect	Float	Cure
Absorb	Derive	Bloom	Rotate	Grow	Expand	Immerse	Germinate
Connect	Degrade	Spread	Alternate	Mutate	Coagulate	Surround	Purify

Analysis and Verification of Synonymy Thesaurus. In order to further understand the word library from the angle of the description of new energy, we adopt the method of card sorting. It's an index card or a similar function of the software written content, and then asked people to classify these cards according to preference and impression or rearrange the grouping method. The purpose is to understand people will put the content in any position. In the process of observing the card arrangement, the researcher can ask the respondents' feelings or opinions on the classification [6].

Thirty-two new energy verbs were arranged into cards and 30 Chinese native speakers were selected for the test. These verbs were classified according to the given category: five senses(audio-visual smelling touch) and new energy category. Because each verb has its own bias, it focuses on which of the five senses it senses and which of the new energy sources it describes better.

The experiment found that more than 90% of the 32 verbs were assigned to a new energy category and more than 90% of the 28 verbs were assigned to the same feeling. It further verifies that the thesaurus obtained through step by step filtering is basically in line with the general public recognition. By asking the subjects, we found that some verbs can be felt from a variety of senses, such as immerse, it can be perceived by the four sensory channels of sight, hearing, smell, and touch. The acquisition of these verbs provided a lot of inspiration for the designer's later work, which was more conducive to creating immersive design.

3.2 Image Board Establishment and Element Acquisition Based on Verb Library

Verb dictionary is helpful to describe the construction of a new energy, but because of the interpretation of the verb semantic uncertainty, people in understanding a word will have no understanding of exactly the same, it is necessary to add a set of analytical tools for verb. The interpretation of the word can't through more words to express, instead use it to describe objects reflect objectively and visual stimulation signal to convey. The generation of visual images depends on the analogy and expression of relevant visual images. Therefore, the acquisition of semantic-related visual images and the establishment of the image plate are of great help to complete the design conversion from semantics to image [2]. Therefore, we choose to build an image board based on the verb library to help understand and interpret verbs.

Image Board Establishment and Analysis. The image board mainly explains the verb through pictures, video, and audio of the object described by the passive words. The scope of describing the object includes: nature (animals and plants), architecture, people, objects, etc.It is hoped that the situational space of new energy can be constructed through the selection of objects of different categories and layers, so as to complete the transition from the semantic space of verbs to the multi-sensory perception situational space. Figure 3 is part of the image board.

Element Extraction. According to the image board to extract the color, line, material, sound, dynamic effect and other elements. In the end, different presentation methods are given for different energy sources, such as wind energy, which can be transformed from the three aspects of touch, hearing, and vision. Solar energy is mainly through smell and touch. In the sense of touch, the new energy gives people a cold feeling and blue can give the feeling of new energy more.

3.3 Construction of Perceptual Experience Model

Imagination and association are used to stimulate the visual situation in memory by verb description. Meanwhile, images in the resource database are combined, arranged or reconstructed to interpret the image information and integrate into the design language. It can be seen that the image transformation for new energy has been transformed into the transformation of the elements describing the verb database. Finally, these verbs and resource banks are transformed into multi-sensory experience models. Use various sensory stimuli, such as sight, hearing, touch, smell, etc., to create an immersive experience of new energy products. Figure 4 shows part of the multi-sensory experience model. Due to the limitation of expression forms, each model can only be presented in the form of images. Each model has dynamic effects, smells, and sounds, which can be felt from multiple sensory channels.

Fig. 3. Part of image board

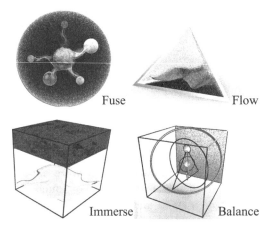

Fig. 4. Partial multisensory perception model

4   Conclusion

This paper mainly focuses on the cognition of new energy image, analyzes the image of new energy with the help of the tools of product semantic research, constructs the verb database describing new energy image, the image board based on the verb database, and the element transformation of the resource database, and transforms the semantics of new energy to multi-sensory perception. On this basis, a multi-sensory perception model of new energy is established to provide inspiration and ideas for the subsequent design of new energy products. This paper proves the feasibility of image transformation based on verb semantics and provides another possibility for future semantic research.

References

1. Ahmad, S., Chase, S.C.: Style representation in design grammars. Environ. Plann. B **39**(3), 486–500 (2012)
2. Eckert, C., Stacey, M.: Sources of inspiration: a language of design. Des. Stud. **21**(5), 523–538 (2000)
3. Ford, C.E.: English verb classes and alternations: a preliminary investigation. Beth Levin. Stud. Second Lang. Acquisition **17**(01), 105 (1995)
4. Hsiao, S.W., Chen, C.H.: A semantic and shape grammar based approach for product design. Des. Stud. **18**(3), 275–296 (1997)
5. Lindgren, H.C.: The measurement of meaning. Audio-Vis. Commun. Rev. **2**(7), 503–504 (1957)
6. Spencer, D.: Card Sorting: Designing Usable Categories. Rosenfeld Media, Brooklyn (2009)
7. Su, J.-N., Li, H.Q.: The perceive feature of material in industrial design. Mach. Des. Res. **21**(3), 12–14 (2005)
8. Tanoue, C., Ishizaka, K., Nagamachi, M.: Kansei engineering: a study on perception of vehicle interior image. Int. J. Ind. Ergon. **19**(2), 115–128 (1997)
9. Xu, B., Lin, B.: Assessing the development of China's new energy industry. Energy Econ. **70**, 116–131 (2018)
10. Zhang, G.X.: Study on the Function and Cognition of Modern Chinese Adjectives. The Commercial Press, Beijing (2006)

The Concept of Intelligent Interaction Design Based on the Perspective of the Production of Space

Feng Liu[1], Wei Yu[2(✉)], Hao Shan[2], and Sijia Jiang[2]

[1] School of Journalism and Communication, Shanghai University, Shanghai, People's Republic of China

[2] School of Art Design and Media, East China University of Science and Technology, Shanghai, People's Republic of China
Weiyu@ecust.edu.cn

Abstract. The application of AI technology has promoted the development of interaction design concept. The object of interaction design is gradually transferred from physical object to multi space based on the perspective of the production of space. This reflects the change of spatial logic in intelligent interaction design, which can be understood from three aspects: behavior, personalization and node. AI has changed the relationship between interaction design and social life, and the development of social relations and meaning is the connotation of the production of multi space, which provides feasibility for the research of intelligent interaction design from the perspective of the production of space. Taking the meaning of the production of space as the goal, this paper studies the trend of inclination from functional user interface design to behavioral user interface design, and gives some thoughts on the integration of "flow space" elements of design. The production of space is a complex concept, and the development of space form is its external performance, what is more important is the co-ordination of multiple elements in space. Only by establishing the relationship between intelligent interaction design and social change, urban development and user behavior can we solve the complex problems in the development of intelligent interaction design.

Keywords: Interaction design · The production of space · AI · Design concept

1 Introduction

With the application and popularization of digital technology in the field of design, the influence scale of interactive design concept is more and more extensive. The emergency of various new interactive design methods changes the interaction behavior between users, designers and products. In recent years, artificial intelligence technology has begun to enter social production and life, which also brings profound influence on interaction design and promotes the update and development of interaction design concept. Space is the environment of the designer's activity, at the same time the designer intervenes and shapes the space. The state and function of various elements in the space based on the application of intelligent technology produces new changes, and

© Springer Nature Switzerland AG 2019
C. Stephanidis (Ed.): HCII 2019, CCIS 1032, pp. 64–71, 2019.
https://doi.org/10.1007/978-3-030-23522-2_9

then drive the reconstruction of the spatial relationship of the interactive design. From the perspective of space production, this paper summarizes and analyzes the concept of intelligent interaction design through the comparison between interactive design methods before and after the application of intelligent technology.

2   Objects of Interaction Design: From Object to Space

This paper examines the concept of interactive design under the background of artificial intelligence development from the perspective of space. From 1960s to 1970s, the "spatial turn" appeared in the study of western philosophical and sociology. Space production, third space, mobile space and other theories triggered a cultural transformation. Space theory has gradually developed into one of the most cutting-edge criticism theory in the west. Lefebvre believes that "space is the product of a society, different social forms will have a different mode of production, and each mode of production has a corresponding, unique space to produce" [1]. Different social behavior, production methods will promote the production of the space with different natures and forms, including different social relations and behavioral significance; Interactive design emphasizes the interaction between people and devices and between people, with the expansion of the technical field and industry scope covered by interactive design, it makes more and more social subjects generate new relationships based on interactive behavior, which promotes the shaping and production of new spatial forms.

From the perspective of space production, the object of interactive design has shifted from matter to space. From the traditional sense, the object of interactive design is object. Unlike the ordinary design, as an object of interactive design, things need to carry the connection and interaction of different subjects' relations. With the "Creation" of interactive design, the object becomes the hinge and medium of interaction between different actors. In this process, the interaction design is not only to face the traditional and interactive objects, but also to consider all the factors that can relate to the object, which together constitute the spatial scene of interactive behavior generation and lasting, and this space becomes the object of "vitality" in interactive design. Park, a representative of the Chicago school, mentioned "There are some factors in space that lead to an orderly, typical combination" [2]. When talking about urban space. In the perspective of space production, things are still the object of interactive design. The difference is that the things here are no longer the physical things in the traditional design concept, nor is it simply an inanimate intermediary in the interaction.

The transfer of interactive design objects from matter to space is realized by the creative behavior of interactive design, and its focus shifts from the form of matter to the function of matter, and the function of matter is to connect various elements in space and make the interactive behavior produce meaning. Castells thinks that "Space is a material product that is associated with other elements of matter–elements that include humans themselves involved in specific social relationships that give form, function, and social meaning to space (and other interrelated elements)" [3]. The addition of different elements and the change of the correlation mode during the process of interactive design will change the function of the object, and then promote the production of new spatial form and meaning. With the change of current technical background, artificial intelligence technology has gradually become a strong factor which cannot be ignored in the transfer of interactive design object from matter to space, which has brought great impact to people's design concept and design method. Intelligent interaction design enhances the ability to schedule various elements in the target space, and gives the designer greater possibility of the realization of imagination. Facing the opportunities and challenges brought by artificial intelligence to the design industry, it is necessary for us to comb and master the spatial logic of intelligent interactive design to create conditions for the optimization of intelligent interactive design concept.

3   Spatial Logic of Intelligent Interaction Design

The transfer of objects is the external representation of the innovation of interactive design concept, which embodies the change of internal spatial logic, and the application of artificial intelligence technology further strengthens the spatial logic of interactive design. The designer starts with the spatial logic, which makes it easy to understand the meaning of interaction from a more macroscopic level, coordinate the effect of various spatial elements in interactive design more scientifically, and apply artificial intelligence technology to interactive design more effectively and creatively. The direct result of the development of intelligent interaction design is to get through the interaction between originally isolated elements in the space, strengthen the frequency of interaction between different subjects, and improve the spatial effect of intercommunication, so as to realize the production of spatial form and function. The goal of this kind of space production is based on the behavior of interactive design, and the behavior of different subjects will be directly affected by the factors of intelligent technology, so as to present the interactive characteristics of networking and node. Here, the spatial logic of intelligent interaction design is interpreted from three aspects of behavior, personalization and network node.

Intelligent interaction design focuses on the behavior of different users. The purpose, interaction mode and habit of users are all issues that designers need to focus on, which reflects the importance of behavior in space. Behavior is the starting point of the spatial logic of intelligent interactive design. The space production cannot be realized without behaviors. The purpose of improving the degree of intelligence is to serve the behavior. Grasping the behavior means grasping the core of space production. "From fixed space to mobile space, from a single space to a multi-dimensional space, from real space to virtual space, from natural space to intelligent space… Intelligent transformation from basic platform to application platform will further activate the normalization of media intelligent use" [4]. The design of interactive behavior can realize the correlation interaction of multiple relationships, make the interaction design have the function of intelligent media, and continuously improve the role of interactive design behavior in space production.

In the development of interactive design, designers always pay attention to the individual needs of users, but the realization of personalization is not easy. "Spatial polarization is the agglomeration of various things and elements in space, which reflects the uneven development of the region within a certain space range, the regional development differences in different polarization layers are getting bigger and bigger, and the development difference between the same types of space is becoming smaller" [5]. From the perspective of space, polarization phenomenon in the interaction design also has a universal existence. The designer's "personalized" efforts with the technology, space constraints often can only be achieved within a specific range, and has different degrees of distances away from the real personalization. However, with the development of intelligent technology, intelligent interaction design can make breakthroughs in the design and implementation of personalized behavior, such as in the face of the increasingly "silver" market, intelligent interaction design can "collect user needs and provide quantitative usability evaluation criteria for equipment and products of the elderly to improve user experience" [6]. It improves the matching degree of the digital carrier and its information expression and interaction with the elderly's life cognition experience through intelligent design, and changes "from 'simulated reality' to 'merged reality' to fit the lifestyle of the elderly" [7]. Thus it can be developed from spatial polarization to spatial personalization, which is an important content of intelligent interactive design's space logic.

Network node is a prominent feature of interactive design after it has developed to the intelligent stage. The characteristics of networking and node have already existed in the development process of interactive design, and it is also one of the characteristics of interaction design which is different from traditional design. But under the background of intelligent interaction design, the characteristics of network node have a new connotation. Before the application of artificial intelligence technology, the networking and node characteristics of interactive design focused on the comparison with traditional design, highlighted the realization of interactive behavior, but the degree of networking in interactive space still needs to be improved, and the spatial significance of nodes is relatively thin. Intelligent interaction design is different. Interactive behavior has the possibility of association with any object and makes a specific space a network node that is associated with other behaviors.

4 Spatial Meaning: Target Orientation of Interactive Design Under the Intelligent Background

The core problem of the concept of space production lies not in the development of space form, but in the change and production of spatial meaning, "space form is produced by human action. And according to certain production methods and development patterns, human actors have the ability to transform space and the significance of constantly challenging and changing the space structure" [8]. The development and application of artificial intelligence technology make the interactive design have more powerful ability to change the form of space, but also bring the problems that need to be considered and solved, which are not limited to the technical operation level of interactive design, but need to think from the level of the influence of intelligent interaction design on social life, customer use and humanistic value. If the macroscopical thinking of the design goal is missing, it will lead to the loss of interactive design in the era of artificial intelligence. Facing the opportunities and challenges brought by artificial intelligence to interactive design, society, industry and users are bound to think deeply from different angles, gradually reach a preliminary consensus on the development trend and concept of intelligent interaction design, and how to avoid negative effects and problems. The consensus here does not exclude the differences in personalized ideas between different designers, but rather emphasizes that the industry consensus is reached on the goal orientation of interaction design under the intelligent background.

Intelligent interaction design promotes the innovation of user's behavior mode and the development of space form. We need to take care of how to produce the spatial meaning and what kind of impact, and then give designers reasonable feedback, promote intelligent interaction design to play a positive role in social production and life. Taking the problem of social value bias brought about by intelligent development as an example, "The value bias of society under the background of intelligence refers to the social interaction between people. Because intelligent communication leads to results that are not conducive to social governance and good operation, such as the 'information cocoons' effect at the cognitive level, the value bias at the cognitive level can also lead to value bias at the behavioral level, such as 'group polarization' phenomenon" [9]. This kind of social value bias also exists in the field of intelligent interaction design, and it is also a problem that designers need to think about and avoid, otherwise the spatial significance of their interactive design cannot be effectively represented.

The interaction design enhances the correlation degree and interaction frequency of each subject behavior in space, and the application of intelligent technology further enhances this trend, which makes the interaction design play more and more large role in the process of urban development and social progress. And the interactive design begins to intervene in more cities and living space, makes more and more isolated subjects come into contact and endows more and more scenes with spatial significance. "With the development of the times, the competition of design has risen from the previous content, products, platform to the competition between the ecosystems. Mature ecosystem can achieve positive feedback and self-reinforcement, and realize common benign development. In the future, the development of intelligent technology can create an ecosystem with positive feedback to better serve users" [10]. In order to better serve users, interactive designers need to think about the goal orientation of interaction design in the new context from multiple perspectives. Intelligent interaction design has become an important part of the space ecosystem, whether to promote the production of meaning in the process of space production has become the standard to judge the value of interactive design, and is where its goals point.

5   Intelligent Interactive Design Concept Based on the Perspective of Space Production

By grasping the spatial logic and spatial meaning of intelligent interactive design, we can have a more comprehensive and profound understanding of the development trend of interactive design, the relationship with social life and the existing problems under the background of artificial intelligence, so as to make it easy to think about the innovative application of intelligent interaction design in different scenes from the macroscopic level of urban and social spatial interaction. Based on the above analysis, this paper summarizes and analyses the concept of intelligent interaction design from the perspective of space from the following two aspects.

First, it tilts from functional user interface design to behavioral user interface design. User behavior in space is the core element of intelligent interaction design, there is no spatial significance of production without user behavior. When it comes to the interface of interaction design, "it can be divided into functional user interface and behavioral user interface. The former uses the physical logic to organize interface to satisfy the function realization as the main purpose; the latter emphasizes the user experience, uses the behavior logic to organize the interface" [11]. Satisfying function is the initial goal of intelligent interaction design, and the organization and mobilization of user behavior through design activities is a higher level goal. However, the behavior of different subjects will be influenced by various factors in space, such as social psychology, personal emotion and scene environment. The advantages of intelligent interaction design are fully reflected here, intelligent technology can assist designers to scientifically and dynamically grasp the impact of the above factors on behavior, so that the design of behavioral user interface in line with the requirements of the production of spatial meaning. For example, in the design of intelligent in-vehicle infotainment system, it is necessary to realize that "the way of travel, driving behavior has become a part of modern life, so to understand the trip purpose of the target population, and its social, shopping, fitness, outings and other behaviors in the specific performance" [12]. This allows the interactive interface design to reflect the user's behavior needs, "make voice, screen touch, vibration and other ways become an effective extension of user behavior" [13]. The tilt of behavioral user interface design is the embodiment of attaching importance to the concept of spatial subject behavior, which not denies the importance of functional user interface design, but also embodies the application of spatial concept in intelligent interaction design.

Secondly, the interface is the display of interactive design concept. There are more and more unfixed and dynamic "flow" elements behind the interface of intelligent interaction design. The integration of these flow elements is the focus of intelligent interactive design concept. Castells has proposed the concept of "mobile space", "in addition to local space as a social material expression, society is increasingly built around the flow: capital, information, technology, the flow of organizational interaction and the flow of images, sounds and symbols, etc" [14]. This is a concept based on networked society, and its background is connected with the network node logic of intelligent interaction design, and in the future, valuable interaction design must be based on the effective organization of the multiple flow factors behind the interface. "Mobile space narrows the substantial interaction between reality and virtual world, which not only conquers and alters people's logical experience of local space, but also realizes the socialized production of spatial relations" [15]. The development of artificial intelligence will further strengthen the characteristics of mobile space. Drive interactive design to pay more attention to the socialized production of spatial relations, and improve interactivity to a new level.

In conclusion, the development of artificial intelligence has brought profound influence to interactive design, changed the interaction between interactive design and social life, and the development of social relations and meaning is the connotation of space production, which provides a feasible path to examine intelligent interaction design from the perspective of space. Space production is a complex concept. The development of spatial form is its external manifestation, more importantly, the integration of social multiple elements behind space, so as to get through the correlation between intelligent interaction design and social change, urban development, user behavior, etc., and solve the complex problems faced in the development process of intelligent interaction design. Intelligent interaction design that conforms to the spatial logic and is closely related to the meaning of space will gain wider recognition and greater vitality, on the contrary, if the intelligent interaction design violates the spatial logic, it is not easy to be recognized by the user, which will affect the normal function of the role of artificial intelligence technology in the interactive design, and even produce negative effects. Therefore, we should grasp the concept of intelligent interaction design with a spatial perspective from the perspective of multiple disciplines, which is not only the problem of interactive design itself, but is closely related to many disciplines such as sociology, communication, information science, Internet, psychology and so on. Taking the production of spatial meaning as the point, taking the grasp of spatial logic as the basis, promote the continuous improvement of intelligent interactive design concept, so that intelligent interactive design plays a greater role in social life.

References

1. Lefebvre, H.: The Production of Space, p. 154. Wiley-Blackwell, Hoboken (1991)
2. Spates, J., Macionis, J.: The Sociology of Cities, p. 109. St. Martin's Press, New York (1982)
3. Castells, M.: The Urban Question, p. 115. Edward Arnold Ltd., London (1977)
4. Gao, X.: On the five dimensions of the development of radio and television media in the era of intelligent communication. Telev. Res. 8, 21 (2018)
5. Carter, W.H., Schill, M.H., Wachter, S.M.: Polarisation, public housing and racial minorities in US cities. Urban Stud. 35(10), 1889–1911 (1998)
6. Moon, M.K., Kim, S.C.: Usability evaluation of movement support service robot for elderly. Adv. Ergon. Model. Usability Spec. Popul. 486(7), 517–526 (2017)
7. Zhang, P.: Research on the interaction design of intelligent products for the elder under the mechanism. J. Tuxue 4, 702 (2018)
8. Castells, M.: The City and the Grassroots: A Cross-Cultural Theory of Urban Social Movements, pp. 311–312. Edward Arnold Ltd., London (1983)
9. Chen, C.: Intelligent communication in the future: from "internet" to "people networking". Acad. Front. 12, 13 (2017)
10. Guo, Q.: Intelligent communication: the latest mode of communication of Internet media evolution in China. Media Rev. 1, 79 (2017)
11. Xin, X.: Interactive design: from physical logic to behavioral logic. Decoration 1, 61 (2015)
12. Wu, J.: Research on interactive design of vehicle infotainment system based on situational perception. Packag. Eng. 8, 191 (2018)
13. Koskinen, H., Laarni, J., Honkamaa, P.: Hands-on the process control: users preferences and associations on hand movements. In: CHI 2008 Extended Abstracts (2008)

14. Castells, M.: The Rise of the Network Society. Blackwell Publishing Ltd., Hoboken (2010)
15. Liu, T., Yang, Y.: Socialized media and the socialized production of space–contemporary interpretation of the "mobile space thought" of Custer. Literary Theory Criticism **2**, 75 (2014)

Optimize the Flow of Web Banners Design

Ren Long[✉], Chenyue Sun, Hongzhi Pan, Honglei Wang,
and Jiali Zhang

School of Mechanical Science and Engineering,
Huazhong University of Science and Technology,
Wuhan, People's Republic of China
547834629@qq.com

Abstract. With the development of information technology and business, the demand of advertising design grows rapidly and the life cycle of ad banners get shorter and shorter which requires more efficient and brief design flow. In order to optimize the flow of web banners design, the existing design flow of the studio was analyzed with the six sigma DMAIC method. The result of this study shows that the main problem of this studio's design flow is too much information can't be settled in time.

Keywords: DMAIC · Design flow · Design management

1 Introduction

DMAIC is a kind of process management method to improving, optimizing and stabilizing the work flow (Fig. 1). It is the core tool to drive six sigma projects in many fields.

Guo and Zhu [1] optimized the new student register system with the method of DMAIC, settling the problem of waiting in line. They found out the impact of the main factors through the questionnaire survey and positive Likert scales weighted evaluation method. Baral [3] assessed the impact of newly proposed DMAIC-KM integrated methodology in executing Six Sigma projects within an airbag manufacturing unit. Singh [4] reduced quality rejection by implementing DMAIC approach in a systematic manner on the shop floor of the manufacturing unit of northern India, which results in net savings of 17.66 lakhs per year. Nidhi applied DMAIC strategy to improve process of subsequent dissemination of cardiometabolic risk counselling, which led to significant improvement in assessment for central obesity in an ambulatory clinic practice. Rahman [9] demonstrated the empirical application of Six Sigma DMAIC methodology to reduce product defects within a garments manufacturing organization in Bangladesh which follows the DMAIC methodology to investigate defects, root causes and provide a solution to eliminate these defects. These studies have not applied DMAIC to design work. However, the occurrence of anonymous design led the part of design work to standardization, which provided the opportunity to optimize the design management with quality control.

There have been a great number of studies in design management. Mozota [2] introduced the four powers of design including differentiator, integrator, transformer

C. Stephanidis (Ed.): HCII 2019, CCIS 1032, pp. 72–77, 2019.
https://doi.org/10.1007/978-3-030-23522-2_10

Fig. 1. DMAIC model

and good business. Nurcan [7] presented a method, appropriate for group work analysis, and particularly well suited for the analysis and design of workflow applications. Bruce [5] identified the most effective methods of briefing, sourcing and evaluating design as part of the small business process.

This study attempted to introduce DMAIC method which is applied in quality control in design management in order to improve the efficient and quality of web banners design. The structure of the study follows DMAIC process (Define, Measure, Analyze, Improve and Control).

2 Define

The purpose of define is to clearly articulate the design objectives and the flowcharts of banner design. The information was captured within the investigation of designers and managers. The main point of the exiting design work was too much failing design, which led reworking and made it less efficient. We list all kinds of failing design, which includes wrong font style, inappropriate color scheme, wrong material, wrong size, wrong copy, untidiness, chromatic aberration, improper word spacing, wrong font size, inconsistent design style and the difference of font size.

3 Measure

This stage includes selecting the measurement factors to be improved and providing a structure to evaluate current performance as well as assessing, comparing and monitoring subsequent improvements and their capability. The authors measured existing process (Fig. 2) of design, defining what are flows and mistakes in banner design according to design objective from the first step. And then, seek failures of the practice of banner design and find the reasons of these failures as many as possible. Established the objective of banner design process modification.

4 Analyze

The aim of this step is to identify, validate and select root cause for elimination. Analysis the key factors in design output. The authors studied the failure cases in the existing process and clusters the reasons into four clusters including overload information, communication problems, personal abilities and disunity equipment (Fig. 3).

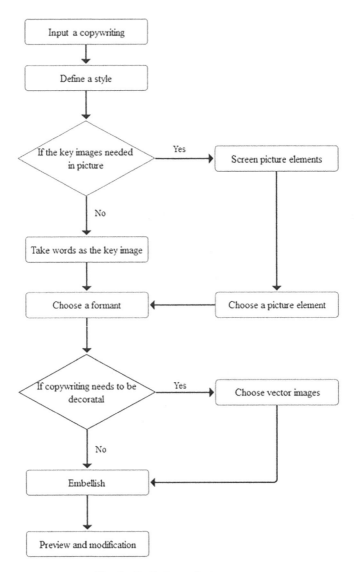

Fig. 2. Preliminary design process

The result of Pareto chart analysis showed the root reason was that designers had too much cognitive load when they faced a large number of design tasks, which caused banner design failures (Fig. 4). And then, the authors tried to explorer how overload information influenced design behavior with in-depth interview to the designers in SANGFOR project for data collection. The result of in-depth interview showed that designers couldn't tell what were important information, what were secondary information and what were irrelevant information, which would add to cognitive load. Besides, some designers would ignore the enterprise design objectives after referring too much design cases, leading the style confusion.

Too much information	The font used is not commercial
	Inappropriate color scheme
	Used the wrong material
	Inappropriate text effect (style)
Communication problems	Inconsistent with the target design style
	Wrong Size
	Wrong copy
Personal ability	Wrong font size
	Untidiness
	The font size difference is too large
	Improper word spacing
Disunity equipment	Chromatic aberration

Fig. 3. Cluster chart of failing factors

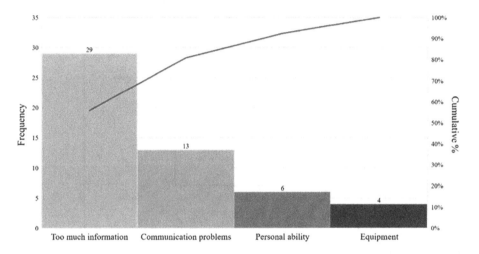

Fig. 4. Pareto chart

5   Improve

The purpose of this step is to identify, test and implement a solution to the problem; in part or in whole. This depends on the situation. The solution of information overload in web banners designing is pay more attention on modification. The design studio should consider more about modification and preview in the whole design flow (Fig. 5). The manager should realize the important of work checking and make the process of banners designing more deliberate. Designers will pay more time on element screening in order to decrease the frequent of failing design in each step.

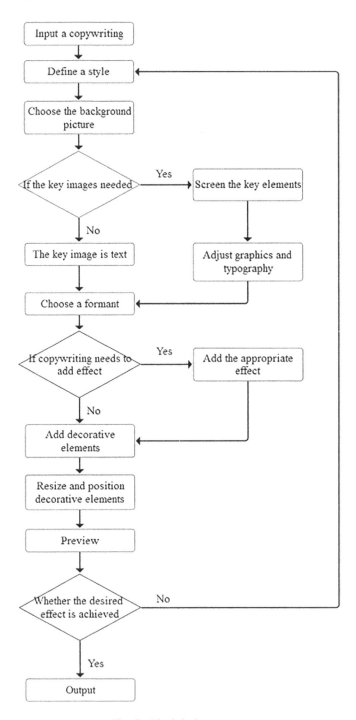

Fig. 5. Final design process

6 Control

The purpose of this step is to embed the changes and ensure sustainability, this is sometimes referred to as making the change 'stick'. The final system was developed by case-study according to the final design flow. Made it sure that designers will follow the design flow. Finally, the optimized design process should be tested if it improves the efficiency of banner design in practice. If it is not, the experiment of DMAIC should be repeated until the efficiency of banner design has great improvement.

7 Conclusion and Future Research Directions

The research studies the feasibility of optimizing the design flow with DMAIC model in the practice of web banner design. The final design flow can be used as an effective design management method in routine banner design. But it needs a further study to test and verify whether it has the extensive applicability. If the design flow failed to the situation of other design work, it needs more different design practice cases to sum up the common structure of most of the graphic design practice.

References

1. Guo, H.-N., Zhu, J.-M.: The research and application of DMAIC model in new student register system. In: Qi, E., Shen, J., Dou, R. (eds.) Proceedings of 20th International Conference on Industrial Engineering and Engineering Management, pp. 547–552. Springer, Heidelberg (2013). https://doi.org/10.1007/978-3-642-40072-8_54
2. Mozota, B.B.: The four powers of design: a value model in design management. Des. Manag. Rev. **17**(2), 44–53 (2010)
3. Baral, L.M., Kifor, C.V., Bondrea, I.: Assessing the impact of DMAIC-knowledge management methodology on six sigma projects: an evaluation through participant's perception. In: Buchmann, R., Kifor, C.V., Yu, J. (eds.) KSEM 2014. LNCS (LNAI), vol. 8793, pp. 349–356. Springer, Cham (2014). https://doi.org/10.1007/978-3-319-12096-6_31
4. Singh, J., Singh, H.: Performance enhancement of manufacturing unit using six sigma DMAIC approach: a case study. In: Khangura, S.S., Singh, P., Singh, H., Brar, G.S. (eds.) Proceedings of the International Conference on Research and Innovations in Mechanical Engineering. LNME, pp. 563–571. Springer, New Delhi (2014). https://doi.org/10.1007/978-81-322-1859-3_52
5. Bruce, M., Cooper, R., Vazquez, D.: Effective design management for small businesses. Des. Stud. **20**(3), 297–315 (1999)
6. Simpson, P.A.: Team Based Design Flow (2015)
7. Nurcan, S.: Analysis and design of co-operative work processes: a framework. Inf. Softw. Technol. **40**(3), 143–156 (1998)
8. Gupta, N., Lteif, A., Creo, A., Iqbal, A.M.: Improved utilization of waist-to-height ratio in cardiometabolic risk counselling in children: application of DMAIC strategy. J. Eval. Clin. Pract. **25**(2), 300–305 (2018)
9. Rahman, A., Shaju, S.U.C., Sarkar, S.K.: Application of six sigma using define measure analyze improve control (DMAIC) methodology in garment sector. Independent J. Manag. Prod. **9**(3), 810–826 (2018)

Optimization of Project Management Processes Using the A* Project Management System (AStarPM)
A Prototypical Implementation and Evaluation

Alexander Marbach[✉], Christian Roschke, Rico Thomanek,
Claudia Hösel, and Marc Ritter

University of Applied Sciences Mittweida, 09648 Mittweida, Germany
marbach@hs-mittweida.de

Abstract. The management of complex application development such as video game development warrants a separate consideration. Recurring creative tasks or process chains must be handled simultaneously to tasks of the domains of programming, implementation and testing of all project-relevant results. These drastically divergent domains create a field of tension between inter-task dependencies and resulting temporary team- or competence-related bottlenecks. Current project management approaches such as Scrum, Kanban lack the focussed linearity und structurization of recurring process chains while on the other hand rigid project management systems impede the developer's empowerment and through incorrect montitoring or prioritization hinder the solution efficiency within the project. This paper discusses a new approach that combines several project management methodologies to address the issues identified. Based on an analysis, a concept is developed and tested prototypically in the form of a project management system. The so called "AStar Project Management" incorporates specific areas from established agile project management methods combined with classic waterfall structures.

Keywords: Project management system · Project management · Education

1 Introduction

The practise of project management is regarded as a mandatory process in any company's struggle for survival. Over the last decades project management has evolved from philosophy to a system-inherent process supported by a multitude of approaches, softwaretools and possible applications. These aforementioned approaches range from a strictly linear processing of task chains through several authority levels to highly dynamic, almost hierarchyless systems for rapid adaptation to frequently varying requirements. The methodologies including waterfall, iterative, rapid, object oriented or agile approaches all have their respective

C. Stephanidis (Ed.): HCII 2019, CCIS 1032, pp. 78–85, 2019.
https://doi.org/10.1007/978-3-030-23522-2_11

fields of application when it comes to project-specific demands. In the case of software development the strong assumption is that the larger the project size the more likely it is to change its requirements in the course of development [5] thus favoring agile methods to react to those changes. While an increasing number of companies across all areas claim to use agile development processes it is most prominent in software development [2]. Software development for digital entertainment products such as games however comes with a variety of other demands that warrant a consideration of all available project management methodologies. The rapid change in ideas, styles, mechanics and needed software especially in the preproduction phase advocates the use of agile methods whereas in the production stage risk assessment and management increase in significance to prevent feature creep, problems in requirements engineering and to facilitate a consistent output of art and multimedia assets and foster continuous gameplay exploration and playtesting cycle [1,6].

Petrillo et al. [8] states that a considerable number of negative project issues could be attributed to management problems. In order to address these specific problems, several adaptions to project management in game development have been made. Although GameScrum or Game Unified Process for example combine ideas from other development methods like Rational Unified Process (RUP) or eXtremProgramming (XP) [3] they emphasize on the software development part, especially omitting or neglecting the integration of longer, interdependent tasks chains of artists. Those need to be handled differently than short iterative cycles in software development. Petrillo [7] states that game development teams instinctively adapted agile methods although they deemed them unsuitable beforehand but also clarifies that a gap between artists and developers may result in inefficient communication because of the vastly different quality features. Game fun or playtesting, like concept art or modelling lack the efficiency of programcode when it comes to determination if a certain goal is achieved.

This paper presents a specialized method of project management to overcome the issues mentioned above. The intentionist to create a more flexible environment that takes into account the interdependencies and time constraints of diverse fields of work. To ensure a common ground for how to operate under the new project management method a software tool has been developed as integral part to visualize the project's progress according to tasks, milestones and developers personal effort. The project management method and the accompanying softwaretool have then been used in an academic setting to develop a game with 48 students simultaneously over the course of one semester. The participants of the project were asked to provide information on project satisfaction, overview, progress and project management method at different times via questionnaire. These were finally evaluated together with qualitative interviews and personal assessment forms.

2   Methods

The decisions on the project management method presented here are based on the analysis of the preceding modules "Game Development" at the University of Applied Sciences Mittweida of the last 5 years, postmortems of German game developers, qualitative interviews with professional game developers and project managers as well as the analysis of existing established and proven project management methods. The resulting method has been subject to a number iterations of change and improvement. Key factors can only be spotlighted. In order to establish general guidelines for the new project management, meta-requirements for the method, participants and software support were first set. Requirements to the project management method are "the maximum overview of the complete project at any given time from any project participant", "the fastest possible overview of the amount of work to be carried out", "the definition and separation of technical and qualitative constraints and shift to multiple levels of control", "the initial visibility of task volumes" and "the team size or number-independent scalability of the method". whereas the requirements for personnel development are "promote independence", "promote an environment for learning", "force co-determination and self-motivation", "bridge the gap between creative and informatics development in your team", "transform time and competency pressures into a more engaged, participant facing environment", "involvement of all participants in the complete project plan" and "consistent and constantly visible planning".

The method of this paper was developed from these guidelines, the recommendations and best practices of Petrillo et al. [7] and the analysis of Kanode and Haddad [6]. In the following the most important components are explained.

Before the start of the project, all project-relevant areas are defined as working competences. In the concrete practical implementation in the student module "Game Development" these were Conception, ArtDesign, Modelling, Rigging, Animation, Texturing, Programming, Implementation, Sound, Testing, Event and Video. Depending on the desired result, these individual areas can show dependencies and parallelizability in the project. Dependency chains are represented by linear linking of areas in the A*Tool.

2.1   Project Classification

In order to meet the requirements relating to the overviewability of work tasks and effort, general graphic visualization options were evaluated in addition to list-based representations such as taskboards (for example Kanban boards) or text-based variants (such as sprint or product backlogs in Scrum), which serve to structure facts. In addition to its specific details, a single task should be equally embedded in the overall system of all tasks. Above all, however, in order to make the concatenation of creative tasks - inherent to creative workflows - directly visible, the decision was made to use a visual representation in mindmap form as seen in Fig. 1. Tasks thus are the smallest unit. They therefore require a concrete and clear formulation of the work to be done. A task is to be formulated as atomic and generally valid as possible. Great importance should be attached to clarity and comprehensibility. The possible intellectual or artistic effort of a task is assessed and converted into an abstract taskpoints value (referred to as TP). Before the start of the project, an evaluation of the complexity of a

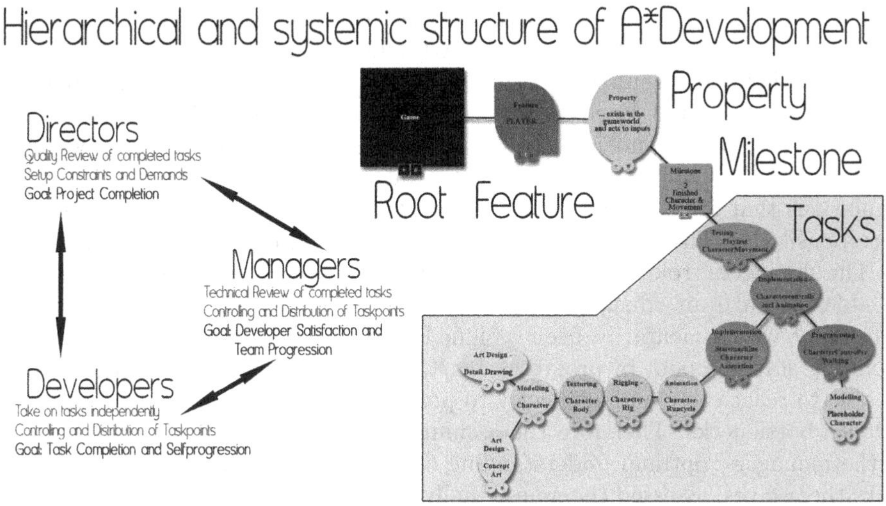

Fig. 1. Representation of structural and systemic main components in AStarPM

task is agreed for each area. What is the time interval to be observed in which tasks are to be processed (e.g. one day, four hours, one week)? If the effort is classified as "justified" - i.e. normal - and the task can be completed within one cycle, this task receives a value of 13 taskpoints. Based on the "Planning Poker" strategy of the agile development of Grenning (2002) [4] the efforts can be integrated accordingly from 1 (fast or trivial) to 100 (inestimable effort - must be planned/evaluated anew) in the gradations 1, 2, 3, 5, 8, 13, 20, 40, 100.

2.2 The Project Team

The project team is divided into three areas of responsibility. *Directors* divide the competence areas of the project among themselves and are responsible for the qualitative evaluation of the completed tasks therein. In addition, they are responsible for the allocation of area-specific constraints regarding the completion of tasks and the prioritisation of tasks. *Managers* are responsible for controlling the tasks. Together with the task planner, they estimate the effort required for the respective task and define this as the taskpoint value. They also check the speed and technical quality of the completed tasks. In the event of deficits or on special request, they are required to offer workshops or support measures. *Developers* take on the tasks of the project and receive the corresponding task points if the task meets the technical (tec review via manager) and qualitative (qua review via director) requirements.

The director posts will be assigned through democratic election within the project team - an adaptation to a fixed allocation of the posts is possible, but on the basis of the guidelines "Motivation, co-determination and dedicated work" the decision in the present case was taken against an external determination of the posts. In the case presented here, the division had initially used Creative, Implementation, Programming, Art and Managing Director. The later evaluation, however, resulted in a shift and renaming of the positions, which are explained in the Sect. 3. Each director has qualitative responsibility for his or her area of responsibility and is accordingly responsible for drawing up guidelines for achieving this quality. The constraints contain both technical and qualitative regulations that are essential for the completion of a task in the director's area of responsibility. These constraints are attached to each task of this area.

The managers' role in A*D is twofold. On the one hand, managers should be able to make an educated statement about which tasks of which level of difficulty have momentarily been assigned to which developer and their corresponding status (open, in progress, Tec/Qua Review, done). Managers should be able to react early and efficiently to possible TP discrepancies, task or competence bottlenecks. Therefore the assumption was obvious that it would lead to the managers' optimal understanding of the project if they planned out the tasks themselves, assessed them and finally assigned them to the developer. The development of all tasks should enable the managers to get a deep insight into the project and through that an exact picture of each developer and his qualification over the course of the project. The manager can create workshop tasks, assign several developers to a single task (e.g. for pair programming) or seek a personal meeting to get an exact picture.

Developers should strive to educate themselves further throughout the project. Self-motivation and self-responsibility are focussed. Since self determination was fixed as a guideline, it was decided to assign developers *to no particular department* for the study. It is therefore up to each developer to choose any task as long as he is aiming to achieve the required number of taskpoints per cycle. The contribution of own ideas for necessary tasks or workshops is encouraged and to be coordinated with the supervising manager or director. To avoid clustering every Developer may have only one task at runtime.

2.3   Prototypic Implementation

The A*D webtool as seen in Fig. 2 was developed to enable a smooth and efficient use of the method. The tool strives to not only simplify the management process through focusing, visibility and freedom, but also to integrate it naturally into the actual project operation and thus making it a valuable an understandable part of every developer's work.

The A*D tool offers several views, the most important of which is the *graph view*. Through the representation in mindmap form several requirements are met. The direct visibility of the task volume is implemented as follows. Each atomic task is visible in the context of the project and visually linked in the hierarchical structure. The amount of TP estimated for tasks changes the size of the task representation. So the bigger a node, the more complex it is to do. In addition, the colored representation of the individual nodes shows their status in the project as seen in Fig. 3.

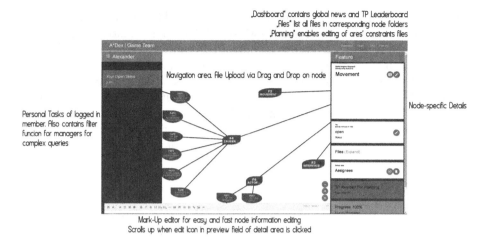

Fig. 2. Annotated graph view of AStarPM

Nodes can be deleted, restructured or their details changed at any time in the Graph view. A change history enables the user to trace individual changes in the graph. By separating complex tasks into atomic components - single points of interest - the information can be retrieved task-specifically at the respective node but can also always be viewed in the context of the neighbouring tasks. All details can be viewed and edited in the status window of the respective node. Files can be uploaded and assigned to a node by drag and drop. All files can also be accessed via the menu item *Files*. The *Dashboard* shows the current status of the TP of all project participants as well as general news.

2.4 Evaluation

The project management method and the A*D tool were used in the "Game Development" module of the fifth semester "Media Informatics and Interactive Entertainment". A total of 48 students took part in the module and corresponding study. The aim of the module was to complete a video game playable on PC within the three-and-a-half month deadline of the semester. All 48 participants worked on this one project. Thus structuring and planning of the project group was as necessary as the initial idea, concept art, blockout, playtesting, etc. In addition to the choice of directors and managers, the initial creative phase and the creation of tasks at the beginning were the most critical. The students were

Fig. 3. Depiction of all task stati of a "Concept"-Node in AStarPM

questioned in advance about their competences and whether they would like to take on a managerial or directorial position. After approximately 9 of the 14 weeks, each student was interviewed individually about their personal performance and their assessment of the A*D method. Near the end of the project, a retrospective survey was conducted to find out the student's opinion on the method and the tool. At the end of the project the qualitative performance of the students was evaluated and feedback was obtained via a questionnaire. Qualitative interviews with developers, managers and directors concluded the project. Of the 48 students, 29 took part in the online questionnaire.

3   Results and Discussion

As Fig. 4 shows, 80% of the respondents were enthusiastic about the project management method. Nevertheless, there is a particular need for improvement in the tool and method. The greatest need for improvement is in the functionality of the tool. Half of all respondents have expressed their support for this. The exact requirements were identified in a qualitative interview. Only 14% of the participants either saw no sense in the current method or were so dissatisfied with certain aspects of the method that there was a general rejection of the system. Here, too, the most important points of criticism were worked out in interviews.

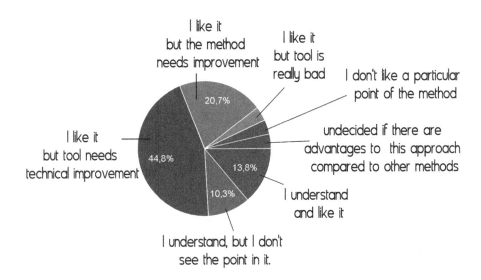

Fig. 4. In your opinion, which description best fits A*D at the moment?

The improvements demanded for the software were (1) filemanagement system which enables upload of task-specific files directly into the task, (2) a manager-specific tab that enables complex queries over tasks, developers and their respective states and (3) an option to merge task chains into list-chains to reduce cluttering of the mindmap with identical task-chains. The most frequently mentioned points of criticism are noted with the frequency of their occurrence. If there have already been changes to the method or the tool in the meantime, these are entered under "issue addressed".

4 Conclusion

In this paper, a new project management methodology was introduced to help overcome known difficulties in the software development process. By the implementation of a combining method and a software-side representation a research environment could be created. In the teaching module "Game Development" the method was applied and the test persons were interviewed. The analysis shows clear potentials of the method also in comparison to other agile or conventional methods. The most important findings are the transfer of the planning performance to developers and managers, the introduction of categories for developers and the clear improvement of the clarity and usability of the software tool. Furthermore, the results presented here can be used for further investigations due to the already started improvement and adaptation of the tool and the method.

References

1. Alshamrani, A., Bahattab, A.: A comparison between three SDLC models waterfall model, spiral model, and incremental/iterative model. Int. J. Comput. Sci. Issues (IJCSI) **12**(1), 106 (2015)
2. COLLAB.NET: 12th Annual State of Agile Report (2018). https://bit.ly/2EAEx9d
3. Godoy, A., Barbosa, E.F.: Game-scrum: an approach to agile game development. In: Proceedings of SBGames, pp. 292–295 (2010)
4. Grenning, J.: Planning poker or how to avoid analysis paralysis while release planning. Hawthorn Woods: Renaissance Softw. Consult. **3**, 22–23 (2002)
5. Jorgensen, M.: Relationships between project size, agile practices, and successful software development: results and analysis. IEEE Softw. **36**(2), 39–43 (2019)
6. Kanode, C.M., Haddad, H.M.: Software engineering challenges in game development. In: 2009 Sixth International Conference on Information Technology: New Generations, pp. 260–265. IEEE (2009)
7. Petrillo, F., Pimenta, M.: Is agility out there?: Agile practices in game development. In: Proceedings of the 28th ACM International Conference on Design of Communication, pp. 9–15. ACM (2010)
8. Petrillo, F., Pimenta, M., Trindade, F., Dietrich, C.: Houston, we have a problem...: a survey of actual problems in computer games development. In: Proceedings of the 2008 ACM Symposium on Applied Computing, pp. 707–711. ACM (2008)

An Automatic Modeling Method of Kansei Evaluation from Product Data Using a CNN Model Expressing the Relationship Between Impressions and Physical Features

Hidemichi Suzuki$^{(\boxtimes)}$, Atsuhiro Yamada, Kensuke Tobitani,
Sho Hashimoto, and Noriko Nagata

Kwansei Gakuin University, 2-1 Gakuen, Sanda, Hyogo, Japan
{hide4831,nagata}@kwansei.ac.jp

Abstract. In the field of Kansei engineering, the approach is often taken of Kansei evaluation modeling expressing the relationships between physical features and impression of an object. However, in the conventional modeling method, personnel and time costs are very high because multiple experiments and analyses are needed to high precision modeling. In contrast, study using machine learning has been conducted as a method of modeling the relationship between physical features and impressions of products. However, no studies have been reported that considering how the nature of an impression that there is evaluation vary from person to person. In this study, we work on automatically Kansei evaluation modeling using images and review-text data of products existing on the web. A convolutional neural network (CNN) is used for modeling, and variation in the impressions of each product are taken into consideration when learning. In the proposed method, we performed the following: (1) Extraction of the main impressions of target domain and calculation of values that express the strength of each impression from review-text data through text mining based on the previous study [1], (2) creation of a product image data set that uses the distribution of products' impression scores as a training label and (3) construction of the CNN model using the created data set. We applied proposed method to wristwatches as the target domain and verified the estimation accuracy of constructed CNN model. As a result, a high positive correlation was confirmed between estimated impression score and impression scores that were calculated from review-text data. In addition, since present results exceeded the estimation accuracy of CNN model hasn't learned distribution of impression scores, learning variations in the evaluation of peoples' impressions were shown to be effective for improving estimation accuracy.

Keywords: Kansei engineering · Text mining · CNN · Appraisal dictionary

1 Introduction

In the field of product design, it is important to reflect user's needs in products. Particularly in recent years, affective needs such as usability and comfort have attracted attention in addition to conventional manufacturing needs such as function, price and

C. Stephanidis (Ed.): HCII 2019, CCIS 1032, pp. 86–94, 2019.
https://doi.org/10.1007/978-3-030-23522-2_12

reliability [2]. Kansei engineering approach is accepted to be the most reliable and effective method to handle affective needs and is applied to various domains [3]. One specific approach is modeling Kansei evaluation that expresses the relationship between physical features and impressions of a product. With this approach, it is possible to accurately and efficiently reflect user's affective needs on product design.

However, in the conventional method of Kansei evaluation modeling based on a subjective evaluation experiment [4], a subjective evaluation experiment with semantic differential (SD) method and multiple experiments and analyses during the preparation stage are necessary. Therefore, there is a problem in that personnel and time costs are very high.

On the other hand, studies using machine learning have been conducted as a method to model the relationship between physical features and impressions of products has been conducted [5]. However, no studies have been reported that consider how the nature of an impression and its evaluation vary from person to person.

In this study, we work on automatically Kansei evaluation modeling using images and review-text data from many products existing on the Web. In proposed method, based on a previous study [1], the main impression of the target domain (impression topic) is first extracted from whole review-text data via text mining, and then the value that expresses the strength of the impression (impression score) is calculated from some review-text data for each product. Next, product image data set is created with the calculated distribution of the impression scores as training label. Finally, a CNN model that solves estimation of impression scores of product images as classification problem is constructed using created data set. This model solves the estimation of impression scores of product images as classification problem. Figure 1 shows the flow of automatically modeling Kansei evaluation using text mining and a CNN model.

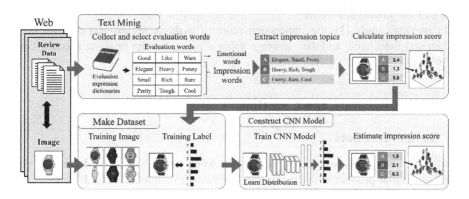

Fig. 1. Flow of the proposed method

2   Method of Extracting Impression Topics and Calculating Impression Scores Through Text Mining

First, evaluation words are collected and classified. At the stage of collecting, affective expressions (e.g. evaluation word candidates such as adjectives) contained in review-text data are collected by consult some evaluation expression dictionaries and part-of-speech information. This candidate evaluation word group compares high-order evaluation words (emotional words) related to a person's emotions and low-order evaluation words (impression words) describing product impressions [6]. However, since the emotional words (such as "want" or "joyful") do not express the features of a product, it is difficult to reflect them directly on the product even if the emotion can be estimated. Therefore, the candidate evaluation word group is classified into emotional words and impression words, and only impression words are used. Classification of evaluation words is performed by consult Japanese evaluation appraisal dictionary [7] in which attributes of internal evaluation and external evaluation are assigned to evaluation expressions. Internal evaluation is expression that indicates evaluator's emotions with respect to evaluation target, or action that represents emotion, an external evaluation is expression that indicates the characteristics of evaluation target. Based on these definition, internal evaluation words are classified as emotional words, and external evaluation words are classified as impression word.

Next, impression topics are extracted. Impression words obtained at previous section are input to HDP-LDA [8], which is a language model that probabilistically finds topics of words in sentences using sentences as input, and extracts impression topics.

Finally, using the frequency of impression words in each review-text data and the importance of each impression word in each impression topic, the impression topic score for the product is calculated. At that time, term-score [9] is used as the importance of each impression word.

In previous study [1], the impression score of multiple review-text data for each product was calculated, and their average value was used as the final impression score of the product.

3   Method for Data Set Creation

3.1   Review-Text Data

First, image and review-text data of products existing on the web are collected. At that time, we set that product with 10 or more review-text data are collected.

3.2   Election of an Impression Topic

Next, impression topics are extracted from review-text data through text mining. At that time, impression topic could include function of product or haptic impression. Such impression topics is considered difficult to estimate from images. Therefore, visual impression topic which is expected to be effective to estimate from images is collected.

3.3   Selection of Product Image

Among the product images collected, there are images of objects and backgrounds other than the product, and those of the target product that cannot be seen. When estimating impression scores from product images, these images are excluded from the data set because they are thought to lead to a reduction in estimation accuracy.

3.4   Creation of Training Label

First, select review-text data. Due to the nature of calculating impression scores method in previous studies [1], the scores calculated from review-text data with fewer impression words tend to be lower than actual scores. Therefore, top 10 review-text data with many impression words are used to calculate impression score of each product.

Next, clustering of impression scores is performed. Since the impression scores calculated from review-text data is continuous value, it is difficult to create a training label of classification problem. Therefore, using k-means method, all impression scores in one impression topic are classified into seven clusters, and class labels from 1 to 7 are assigned in descending order from the impression scores to the product. The reason why clustering number is 7 is to unify with following subjective evaluation experiment.

Finally, probabilities of each classes in which the product will be classified are calculated from 10 class labels of each product and obtained probability distribution is used as training label. This label makes it possible to learn distribution of impression scores and model Kansei evaluation that considers distribution of person's evaluation.

4   Impression Estimation Method of Product Images that Uses the CNN Model

4.1   Architecture of the CNN Model

The network architecture of CNN model used in this method is based on CNN-M [10]. In addition, Table 1 shows parameters that are readjusted from CNN-M for our model.

By learning data set described in this chapter, we constructed CNN model that estimates impression of product image.

Table 1. List of readjusted hyper parameters.

	Number of units in the output layer	Initial value of the learning rate	Normalization method	Initial value of the weight
CNN-M	1,000	10^{-2}	Local response normalization	Gaussian initialization
Proposed method	7	10^{-3}	Batch normalization [11]	He initialization [12]

4.2   Creation of Impression Estimates Using the Constructed CNN Model

The output of the constructed CNN model is a probability distribution of 7 classes. In this method, calculate the correlation coefficient with the impression scores that were calculated from the review-text data through text mining to verify the accuracy of CNN model's impression estimation. We used Eq. 1 to calculate the expected value for each product image from the probability distribution of the output result and used the expected values as the impression scores that the CNN model estimated. In Eq. 1, c_i indicates each evaluation value of 7 classes ($c_1 = 1$, $c_2 = 2, \ldots, c_7 = 7$).

$$E|x| = \sum_{i=1}^{n} c_i p_i \quad n = 7 \tag{1}$$

5   Creation of Data Set for Wristwatches

5.1   Collected Product Data

The data to be used were collected from Rakuten Market, an online mall that Rakuten, Inc., operate. The total number of wristwatch items was 2,811, and the number of targeted reviews was 252,228. As a result of morphological analysis and classification, 3,880 impression words were collected from the review-text data.

5.2   Selection of Impression Topics and Product Images

The number of extracted impression topics was 9. Table 2 shows each topic. Of these topics, Topic 1 (sophisticated, pretty, small) and Topic 5 (heavy, high grade, nicely textured) were considered related to visual impression.

Then, 1,936 images were selected from 2,811 product images of wristwatch, and training labels were created for data set. Figure 2 shows part of this data set.

Table 2. Extracted impression topics.

Topic number	Impression topics
1	**sophisticated, pretty, precious, tiny**
2	hard to see, dressed, affordable, easy
3	accurate, thin, useful, unnecessary, easy
4	hard, smart, casual, thin
5	**heavy, high grade, durable, Nicely textured**
6	cool, light, hard to see, childish
7	childish, affordable, breakable, enough
8	childish, undisturbing, forgettable, affordable, loose
9	luxurious, fulfilling, overjoyed, unfriendly

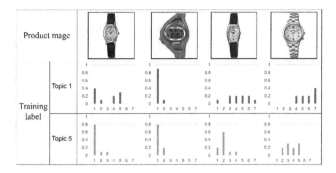

Fig. 2. A part of data set of wristwatches

5.3   Validation of the Impression Scores

To verify the accuracy of impression scores that were calculated based on text mining method [1], a subjective evaluation experiment which answered strength of impression topic feel to product image of data set at 7 stages was conducted. Then, average of 20 people's evaluation value was taken as person's impression score for the product image.

Result

The correlation coefficient between the impression scores calculated from the review-text data and the evaluation scores obtained from the experiment is shown in Table 3. The impression scores calculated for each impression topic is shown on the horizontal axis, and the plots for each impression topic are shown in Fig. 3.

Table 3. Correlation coefficient between average of calculated scores and evaluation scores.

Impression topic	Correlation coefficient
1	0.63
5	0.45

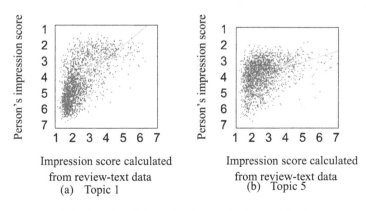

Fig. 3. Plot of the estimation results (text mining)

Discussion

From Table 2, correlation coefficient is 0.63 in topic 1, and strong positive correlation with person's evaluation scores is seen. In topic 5, correlation coefficient is 0.45 and moderate positive correlation with person's evaluation scores is confirmed.

The cause of result that high correlation was not found in topic 5 is considered to be "heavy". It involves not only visual but also tactile impressions, and the reviewer considers both impressions for evaluation. In contrast, it is difficult to estimate tactile impression from image in subjective evaluation experiment. It is thought that such a difference of the situation of evaluation influences correlation with person's evaluation.

6   Impression Estimation of Project Images Using CNN Model

In this study, we construct CNN model that estimates the scores of impression topic 1 (sophisticated, pretty, small), which has higher correlation with the person's evaluate scores. For accuracy verification, K-fold cross validation with K = 11 was performed.

In addition, to investigate the effect of using distribution of impression scores for training label on estimation accuracy, we created training label which does not consider distribution of impression scores. In procedure, first, an average value of impression scores calculated from review-text data is obtained for each product. Next, with k-means method, average scores are classified into 7 classes, and class labels from 1 to 7 are assigned as in Sect. 3. Finally, create an array whose element of class label number is 1 and the other is 0 (if the class label is 3, the array is [0, 0, 1, 0, 0, 0, 0]). Using this array as training label, we constructed CNN model with procedure described in Sect. 4 and compared with proposed method.

6.1   Result

The correlation coefficient between the estimation results obtained by the proposed method and the impression score calculated from the results obtained by the comparative method is shown in Table 4. In the proposed method and comparison method, the expected value calculated using Eq. 1 was used as the estimation result Fig. 4 shows a plot of the estimation results of each method.

Table 4. Difference of the training labels and the correlation coefficient

	Training label	Correlation coefficient
Proposed method	Impression distribution	0.67
Comparison method	Average of impression score	0.51

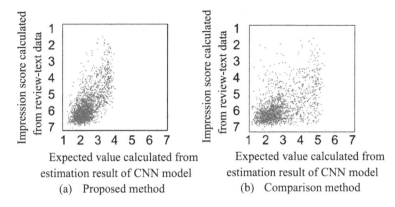

Fig. 4. Plot of estimated result (CNN)

6.2 Discussion

From Table 3, we confirmed positive correlation with correlation coefficient of 0.67 between expected value with proposed method and impression score calculated from review-text data, and effectiveness of proposed method was confirmed. In addition, since this result exceeds correlation coefficient 0.54 calculated with CNN model which hasn't learned distribution of impression scores, it was shown that learning distribution of impression evaluation is effective for improving estimation accuracy.

7 Conclusion

We created image data set considering impression distribution of images by collecting product images and review-text data on the web and using text mining. In addition, we proposed a method to automatically modeling Kansei evaluation that estimates impression from image by constructing CNN model using created data set.

In addition, effectiveness of proposed method was verified with wristwatch as target product. As a result, we confirmed high positive correlation between impression scores of training data and estimated impression scores, and confirmed effectiveness of method. Furthermore, this result exceeds estimation result of CNN model hasn't learned distribution of impression, and it was shown that learning distribution of person's impression evaluation is effective for improving estimation accuracy.

References

1. Hashimoto, S., Yamada, A., Nagata, N.: A quantification method of composite impression of products by externalized evaluation words of the appraisal dictionary with review text data. Int. J. Affect. Eng. **18**(2), 59–65 (2019)
2. Toyoda, N., et al.: Objective evaluation about texture for cosmetic ingredients by direct shear testing of powder bed. J. Soc. Pow. Technol. **52**, 694–700 (2015). https://doi.org/10.4164/sptj.52.694

3. Chen, C.H., Khoo, L.P., Chen, K., Pang, J.H., Huang, Y.: Consumer-oriented product form creation via Kansei engineering. In: Proceedings of the International Symposium for Emotion and Sensibility e Emotion Research in Practice, pp. 184–191 (2008)
4. Tobitani, K., Matsumoto, T., Tani, Y., Fujii, H., Nagata, N.: Modeling of the relation between impression and physical characteristics on representation of skin surface quality. J. Inst. Image Inf. Telev. Eng. **71**, 259–268 (2017)
5. Lu, X., Lin, Z., Jin, H., Yang, J., Wand, J.Z.: Rapid: rating pictorial aesthetics using deep learning. In: Proceedings of the 22nd ACM International Conference on Multimedia, pp. 457–466. ACM (2014)
6. Sano, M.: "Nihongo apureizaru hyooka hyoogen jisho -taido hyooka hen-" no koochiku ~ hyooka no tayousei wo toraeru tameno gengoshigen no kaihatsu ~. In: Proceedings of the Annual Meeting of the Association for Natural Language Processing, vol. 17, p. ROMBUN NO.E1-2 (2011)
7. Sano, M.: Japanese Dictionary of Appraisal -attitude-. Gengo Shigen Kyokai (2010)
8. Teh, Y.W., Jordan, M.I., Beal, M.J., Blei, D.M.: Sharing clusters among related groups: hierarchical Dirichlet processes. In: Advances in Neural Information Processing Systems, pp. 1385–1392 (2005)
9. Blei, D.M., Laffety, J.D.: Topic models. In: Text Mining: Classification, Clustering, and Applications, vol. 10, p. 34 (2009)
10. Chatfield, K., Simonyan, K., Vedaldi, A., Zisserman, A.: Return of the devil in the details: delving deep into convolutional nets. CoRR, abs/1405.3531 (2014)
11. Ioffe, S., Szegedy, C.: Batch normalization: accelerating deep network training by reducing internal covariate shift. CoRR, abs/1502.03167 (2015)
12. He, K., Zhang, X., Ren, S., Sun, J.: Delving deep into rectifiers: surpassing human-level performance on ImageNet classification. The IEEE International Conference on Computer Vision, pp. 1026–1034 (2015)

An Idea Support Method and a Tool for New Product Development

Yuichi Tsujiwaki[1(✉)] and Takako Nakatani[2(✉)]

[1] National Institute of Informatics, 2-1-2 Hitotsubashi, Chiyoda-ku
Tokyo 101-8430, Japan
yuichi.tsujiwaki@gmail.com
[2] The Open University of Japan, 2-11 Wakaba, Mihama-ku
Chiba 261-8586, Japan
tinakatani@ouj.ac.jp

Abstract. In order to develop a new product, we have to create more valuable user experiences in the product. The value of the product is able to satisfy the goals of stake holders of the product. Creating the value depends greatly on developers' inspirations and ideas. However, it is hard for humans to have good inspirations and ideas constantly. Therefore, in order to produce such ideas constantly, we need an engineering method. When we support developers to create new ideas systematically and continuously, we have to solve some problems. In order to solve these problems, we developed a method that was integrated into our empirical knowledge with KAOS, persona analysis, scenario analysis, etc. As a result, it becomes possible to analyze the user experiences based on their roles and, to add functions that improve the user experiences. In order to validate the effectiveness of the method, we applied the method to an actual product development. We also developed a tool for the method. We close this paper with the results of its validation and our future work.

Keywords: Requirement engineering · Goal oriented analysis · Idea creation

1 Introduction

In order to develop a new product, we have to create more valuable user experiences in the product. The value of the product is explored by developers so that it satisfies the goals of stakeholders of the product. Therefore, the value depends greatly on developers' inspirations and ideas. However, it is hard for humans to have good inspirations and ideas continuously. In order to produce such ideas continuously, we developed an engineering method named ICM (Idea Creation Method).

The method, ICM, was developed firstly, by developers as an idea support sheet based on their empirical knowledge. However, there were some problems. The purpose of our study is to clarify these problems and, develop a new method to solve them. Basically, the ideas must satisfy the goals of the customers of a product. Therefore, the method should be based on a goal-oriented method.

KAOS is a goal-oriented requirements analysis method proposed by Axel van Lamsweerde [1]. Its notation allows analysts to consider-and-refinement, or, refinement

© Springer Nature Switzerland AG 2019
C. Stephanidis (Ed.): HCII 2019, CCIS 1032, pp. 95–102, 2019.
https://doi.org/10.1007/978-3-030-23522-2_13

at the same time. Though KAOS works effectively to analyze the means to satisfy the customers' ends, we have to analyze each goal with regard to its owners, in other words, stakeholders who are involved in a new product. We need to extend KAOS with a process to explore the value of a new product for the stakeholders.

Tsumaki and Tamai provided a requirement engineering (RE) technology map with typical requirements engineering techniques and also provided representations of their characteristics [2]. Figure 1 shows their RE technology Map. The figure has two dimensions. The x axis represents the analysis processes based on their process; static or dynamic, and the y axis represents how the analysis domain is open. There are other methods that were not mentioned in their paper. When we analyze or explore the value of a new product, our analysis domain is relatively "open" and, the process of the analysis is "dynamic", since we apply our intuitions and/or inspirations to the first stage of our idea creation process. Therefore, our method must be placed in the third and fourth quadrants. This means that KAOS is placed in the third quadrant, and, we have to extend KAOS with a method placed in the fourth quadrant.

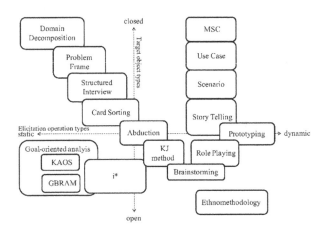

Fig. 1. RE technology Map [2]

There are several methods that are placed in the fourth quadrant. For example, Rich Picture and CATWOE analysis are tools in the fourth quadrant. They were proposed by Peter Checkland, et al. in their "Soft Systems Methodology (SSM)" to express a current problematic situation [3]. Rich Picture consists of illustrations and speech bubbles. By using Rich Picture, we can clarify various stakeholders and discover their issues in the real world. Figure 2 shows an example of a Rich Picture. If we apply a persona analysis [5, 6] that can also be placed in the fourth quadrant, we will be able to analyze problematic situations more concretely.

After we understand a problematic situation, we will be able to derive new requirements to solve the situation by applying KAOS. However, when we utilize these methods to create new values for a new product, we need some guides through the use of a computer supported tool. We have developed the tool, which we call ICM.

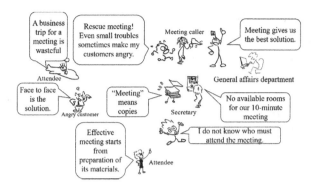

Fig. 2. Example of Rich Picture

The structure of this paper is as follows. In Sect. 2, we introduce an approach of our method to solve problems to create values continuously and give an overview of the tool. Section 3 presents the key factors of the method. In Sect. 4, we describe an experiment that we have applied to the method in order to develop a new product. We conclude this paper with our future work in the last section.

2 Approach to Solve Problems

2.1 Overview of a Method

According to the definition of Antón, maintenance goals are those goals that are satisfied while their target condition remains true and achievement goals are what stakeholders believe the purpose of a system to be [4]. She also defined achievement goals that are objectives of some enterprise or system. Discovering achievement goals is necessary to add new functions to existing products. Once we have discovered the achievement goals, it is possible to derive requirements by a goal-oriented requirements analysis method.

In order to create values of procedures continuously, ICM should support developers by solving the following problems of:

- There are only two layers of a purpose and functions.
- It doesn't have a structure to specify stakeholders.
- There is no systematic process for creating new ideas.

In order to solve the first problem, we apply KAOS, which provides multilayers with means-ends to ICM. In order to solve the second problem, we add a mechanism to define stakeholders with their role, as they are involved in the existing and/or future products. Furthermore, in order to solve the third problem, we add tips to help developers create new ideas by discovering achievement goals with regard to the known goals.

2.2   A Tool to Support ICM

We developed a tool to support our method called ICM. The tool enables developers to have good ideas. It provides the following functions:

- Support basic KAOS notation.
- Manipulate nodes as means-ends and arcs as relationships between nodes.
- Define stakeholders.
- Present tips to help developers create new ideas.

3   Key Factors of ICM

3.1   Notation

Basically, a tool of ICM followed the notation of KAOS. The means and ends are represented by square nodes in the goal graph. Therefore, nodes are goals, which includes operations and requirements. Contribution relationships between goals are represented by arcs. Goals are refined from an upper goal to lower goals. This means that a super goal is refined to subgoals. We extend a goal from that of KAOS with a role that owns the goal. The name of the goal is represented in the upper part of a goal node, and the role of the owner is also represented in the lower part of the goal node.

3.2   Analysis Process

ICM should have multiple layers between purposes and functions, because it is necessary to analyze unknown super goals and/or subgoals. Furthermore, it should also provide a structure to expand the scope of the analysis. We consider the following four approaches to analyze the achievement goals of stakeholders after creating the goal model of the existing functions of a product.

1. Vertical approach
   (a) Top-down refinement: the analysis starts from a known maintenance goal to derive unknown subgoals.
   (b) Bottom-up goal analysis: the analysis starts from a known goal to derive an unknown super goal.
2. Horizontal approach
   (a) Expansion with roles: the analysis starts by defining new roles and expanding the scope of the analysis *with* the roles. After that, new goals for each role are found and defined
   (b) Expansion with domains: the analysis starts by exploring other domains in order to explore new ideas that can be applied to the target domain

In the rest of this section, we specify the details of these analysis processes.

Top-Down Refinement
What is the super goal of known maintenance goals? If we answer this question repeatedly, we will be able to get a top goal as a new achievement goal. Such a top goal

has been an unknown goal and, may not have been fully achieved previously. If we define new achievement goals in this way, we will be able to analyze other subgoals of the newly defined achievement goals; then, we can elicit new requirements from the goal graph. Figure 3 shows the example of this approach.

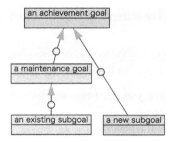

Fig. 3. The example of Top-down refinement

Bottom-Up Goal Analysis

What are super goals of the existing goals? In general, a product may have been used for multiple purposes. For example, surfactants are used in soaps, but are also used to spray magnetic material onto films. Figure 4 shows the example of this approach.

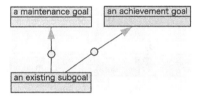

Fig. 4. The example of Bottom-up goal analysis

Expansion with Roles

Figure 5 shows the example of this approach. When we expand the goal scope with roles, we pose two questions. Are there any roles that are involved in the known goals? What are the goals that they want to achieve with the known goals? The dotted arrows in Fig. 5 represent dependency relationships between the known goal and new goals that are derived through answering these two questions. If we consider multiple roles, we may be able to find new achievement goals for each role. For example, the role of the maintenance goal of a car navigation system is a driver. The maintenance goal is "knowing the routes to a destination." When we take into account the role of a passenger, we may be able to find a new achievement goal, for example, "knowing a time required to reach the destination."

We added a mechanism to define stakeholders with their roles. In this approach, we can apply persona analysis in order to understand the situation of the real world with regard to a role and a product.

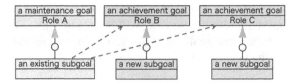

Fig. 5. The example of Expansion with roles

Expansion with Domains

When we expand the scope of the goal analysis, we pose the following questions.

(a) What a product/service have you used recently?
(b) Why do you use the product/service?
(c) What is the goal of the product/service?
(d) If a new product/service achieves the goal, what specific goals is the product/service able to achieve?
(e) What kinds of features are able to realize the goal? Who benefits by the features?

Figure 6 shows this approach. We may be able to apply various types or kinds of products or features to a new product. In other words, there may be able to be new achievement goals of a new product. In this figure, a generalization relationship between a general goal and a concrete goal is shown by a red triangle.

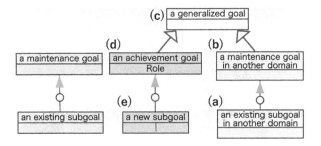

Fig. 6. The example of Expansion with domains

3.3 Tool Details

The tool of ICM is a Web-based application. It follows the notation described in Sect. 3.1. In order to promote the "Expansion with roles" approach, ICM provides a function to enumerate roles (see Fig. 7). In order to promote "Expansion with domains", the tool provides a button that brings out four hints. "What is similar?", "What have you used recently?", "What is the same color?" and "What is the old way?".

Fig. 7. A function to enumerate roles

4 Experiment

We verified how ICM can support engineers to create new ideas of an actual new product development. Figure 8 shows the result of their goal analysis.

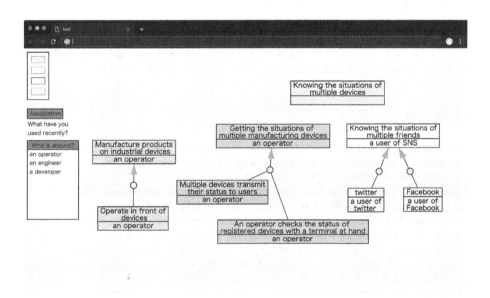

Fig. 8. The result of the goal analysis

In a manufacturing plant, one operator operates many industrial devices. In this situation, engineers tried to create new values for the operators and vender engineers. Firstly, the tool's associative function gave a hint: "What have you used recently?" This hint brought the engineers SNSs such as twitter or Facebook to mind. SNSs are the tools that support one-to-many relationships between people. Then, what kind of maintenance goals do these SNSs meet? As a result of the above question, the maintenance goal of "knowing the situations of multiple friends" could be derived. Finally, it was easy for the engineers to get the goal of "knowing the situations of multiple devices." The engineers applied the goal to the domain of manufacturing plants through the analysis process of "Expansion with domains." They got the achievement goal of "getting the situations of multiple manufacturing devices." After they found a means to meet the achievement goal, they were able to discover the following two new functions:

- Multiple devices transmit their status to users.
- An operator checks the status of registered devices with a terminal at hand.

According to the result, we could come to the conclusion that the proposed method, ICM, can support the process of creating new ideas for a new product.

5   Conclusion

In this paper, we presented an engineering method named ICM (Idea Creation Method) that supports the process of creating new ideas for new product development. The process is proceeded by simple questions to lead ideas.

In our future work, we will apply ICM and its tool for use within a practical domain in order to verify how much it can actually support new ideas and/or values continuously. In addition, we will improve the presentation of hints and tips. Especially, we will design questions and the timing to present the appropriate questions.

References

1. van Lamsweerde, A.: Goal-oriented requirements engineering: a guided tour, In: the 5th IEEE International Symposium on Requirements Engineering on Proceedings, pp. 249–263. IEEE Computer Society, Toronto (2001)
2. Tsumaki, T., Tamai, T.: A framework for matching requirements elicitation techniques to project characteristics. Softw. Process Improv. Pract. 11(5), 505–519 (2006)
3. Checkland, P., Scholes, J.: Soft Systems Methodology in Action. Wiley, Chichester (1990)
4. Antón, A.I.: Goal based requirements analysis. In: Second International Conference on Requirements Engineering on Proceedings, pp. 136–144. IEEE, Colorado (1996)
5. Cooper, A.: The Inmates are Running the Asylum: Why High Tech Products Drive Us Crazy and How to Restore the Sanity. Sams, Indianapolis (1999)
6. Rosenberg, D., Stephens, M., Collins-Cope, M.: Persona analysis. In: Agile Development with ICONIX Process, pp. 189–201. A-Press, Berkeley (2005)

Application of Fuzzy Analytic Hierarchy Process to Discuss the User's Favor of Electric Bicycle Modeling

Tianxiong Wang$^{(\boxtimes)}$, Meiyu Zhou$^{(\boxtimes)}$, and Zhengyu Wang$^{(\boxtimes)}$

School of Art Design and Media, East China University of Science
and Technology, No. 130, Meilong Road, Xuhui District,
Shanghai 200237, China
`1192913346@qq.com`, `753501966@qq.com`,
`zhoutc_2003@163.com`

Abstract. As a means of transportation, electric bicycle have characteristics of low pollution, low noise, energy saving and so on. In recent years, in addition to the increasing environmental awareness and the rising oil prices, the country has begun to pay attention to the problem of environmental pollution caused by transportation, so it is important to develop and promote electric bicycle design actively. At the same time, electric bicycles enable users to improve travel efficiency, and they are also fast and convenient to use. Therefore, the production get the favor of consumers, and the research enterprises of electric bicycles will also increase. However, in the design process of electric bicycles, most designers rely on the rich experience level of the research to explore the design schemes and criteria of electric bicycles, and lack the rational exploration of the electric bicycle design factors from the understanding of users. This study will combine the analytic hierarchy process and fuzzy theory to propose a fuzzy hierarchical analysis method, in order to study the user's preference for electric bicycles more accurately, and thus explore user's specific emotional demand factors of electric bicycle. Accordingly, the evaluation value is defined according to the fuzzy semantics and the questionnaire data is established into a paired matrix. The research method and results put forward the product development strategy of electric bicycle, which provides a solution to design electric bicycles that meet the needs of users.

Keywords: Fuzzy Analytic Hierarchy Process (FAHP) · User's need · Electric bicycle · Emotional needs · Product design

1 Introduction

Environmental protection is a major problem related to our life. In recent years, the rapid development of economy has not only improved people's living quality but also resulted in the greenhouse effect, serious haze and other environmental pollution problems. It is reported by US media that 5,000 people in EU countries die from air pollution caused by excessive exhaust emissions from diesel vehicles every year. In China, the direct loss caused by automobile exhaust pollution is as high as 68 billion Yuan every year.

© Springer Nature Switzerland AG 2019
C. Stephanidis (Ed.): HCII 2019, CCIS 1032, pp. 103–115, 2019.
https://doi.org/10.1007/978-3-030-23522-2_14

Therefore, it is necessary to promote new energy vehicles to reduce the harm of environmental pollution. Under various subsidy policies, China's new energy transportation industry is booming. More and more electric drive vehicles appear in the lives of urban residents. Users also prefer to choose electric bicycles as their travel tools and the electric bicycles can be seen everywhere in life. However, product indicators of many electric bicycles have exceeded the current standards, resulting in a large number of casualties. Therefore, Ministry of Industry and Information Technology organized the revision of the compulsory national standard of *Technical Specification for Safety of Electric Bicycles* and made it to be officially released. The emergence of the new national standard has paid unprecedented attention to safety, guaranteed the safety of consumers and promoted the upgrading of product quality.

At present, China is the world's largest producer and seller of electric bicycles, with a total number of about 200 million vehicles and an annual output of more than 30 million. The newly revised national standard is called Technical Specification for Safety of Electric Bicycles, which regulates that the maximum speed of the vehicle should be adjusted from 20 km per hour to 25 km per hour, the weight of the vehicle (including batteries) should be adjusted from 40 kg to 55 kg, and the power of the motor should be adjusted from 240 W to 400 W. Safety contents such as fire retardant, water spraying, charger protection are added and key performance such as shape and size are strictly limited. At the same time, electric bicycles are required to have the design of speeding up alarm. Compared with the previous standards, the new standard of electric bicycle has promoted the weight, speed, motor power and safety factor, which not only brings new development opportunities for products, but also provides safer and more secure services for products. It is necessary for the R&D Department to design products according to the new national standard so as to meet the industrial standards and provide better services for users (Table 1).

Table 1. Comparison of parameters of electric bicycle in new and old standard

New standard of electric bicycle		
Standard	New standard	Old standard
Maximum speed	25 km/h	20 km/h
Total weight	55 kg	40 kg
Mileage	/	25 kg
Continuous power output	400 W	240 W
Battery voltage	48 V	48 V
Pedal	Remained	Remained

In the international market, the electric bicycle market in Germany's is growing at an unprecedented rate. According to the latest data of Zweirad Industrie Verband in 2017, electric bicycle is not only a popular means of transportation, but also a popular sport and leisure activity in Germany. In 2017, 720,000 electric bicycles were sold in Germany in total, with a 19% increase in total sales. In the United States, sales of electric bicycles have an explosive growth in recent years, with an increase of more than 400% and a sales volume of 263,000. In Taiwan, the electric bicycle market is also developing rapidly. Giant and Merida electric bicycles sells best in Taiwan. In the first three quarters of this year, the two giants performed quite well in exports, among which the growth rate of Merida was as high as 77%. It can be seen that many countries in the world are vigorously developing electric bicycles, among which the sales and retention of electric bicycles in Europe, America and China are very prominent.

In view of the changes in the standards of the electric bicycle industry, we should redesign the models and deeply understand the psychological preferences of consumers. Like other industrial products, more and more consumers not only need the electric bicycle to meet the basic functional needs, but also need more products to meet their emotional needs. It has been a new issue how to design an electric bicycle that meets the users' psychological preferences. The market of electric bicycle industry is also developing rapidly and some new and fashionable products have been introduced by major brands. For example, the appearance of SUNRA L1MINI electric bicycle is fashionable and full of sense of science and technology. As a new vehicle confirming to national standard, this product is popular with consumers, as shown in Fig. 1 [1] below. Therefore, it is necessary to explore an effective method to design the model of electric bicycle based on customer's needs, so as to develop the electric bicycle with innovative characteristics.

Fig. 1. SUNRA L1MINI electric bicycle

2   Literature Review

2.1   The Analytic Hierarchy Process

Analytic Hierarchy Process (AHP) [2] is a quantitative and qualitative multi-objective analytic hierarchy process, which is a decision-making tools widely used in various fields. It was first proposed by professor of operational research of the University of Pittsburgh in the 1970s. Analytic hierarchy process (AHP) divide the decision-making problems into different hierarchical levels according to general objectives, evaluation criteria and specific schemes. Then, the final weight of each scheme to the total objective is obtained by solving the eigenvectors of the judgment matrix, and the optimal scheme is determined. Furthermore, AHP provides a proven and effective way to deal with complex decisions and speed up the decision-making process. Secondly, AHP provides a useful mechanism to check the consistency of evaluation measures, enabling decision makers to incorporate subjectivity, experience and knowledge into the decision-making process in an intuitive and natural way. AHP can calculate the weights of each criterion and the final weighted average scores of each alternative, which enables us to understand the elements of decision-making in depth, so that analysts can better understand the final decision [3].

However, there are some shortcomings when the AHP method is applied to decision-making process of industrial design. The reasons are as follows: 1. AHP method cannot cover the uncertainties of human perception to things. Generally speaking, AHP is used to represent the relative importance extent through a scale of 1 to 9, that is to say, the inaccurate value recognized by decision-makers subjectively is treated as an exact value, which makes the research results inaccurate. 2. The ranking of AHP method is quite unclear. 3. The subjective judgment, choice and preference of decision-makers have a great influence on the evaluation results obtained by AHP method, that is, the judgment is wrong, and the results of decision-making are also incorrect. It can be seen that the AHP method cannot fully cover the subjectivity, ambiguity and uncertainty of human cognition of things. When the problem is complex and the information is incomplete, it is impossible to point out a definite value to express the importance judgment of the comparison between two. Only language description will make the experimental results different from the actual problem.

2.2   Fuzzy Theory

Overview of Fuzzy Theory. Proposed by Professor Zadeh in 1965 [4], fuzzy set is mainly used to solve problems that cannot be distinguished by binary logic in real environment, for example, the data with ambiguity and fuzziness as high, short, fat and thin. Therefore, Professor Zadeh uses the concept of fuzzy sets to represent concepts that cannot be clearly defined in reality. When we use words to define a set, the boundaries whether an object belongs to the set are usually blurred. The definition of fuzzy theory is: Let U be the whole object under discussion, called Universe of Discourse, and each object in the universe is called an element, represented by u. A fuzzy subset A on U means that for any $x \in U$, a real number $u(x) \in [0, 1]$ is determined, which is called the degree to which X belongs to A.

$$u_A(x) : U \rightarrow [0, 1]$$

When the value range of A equals $\{0, 1\}$, $u(x)$ A becomes a characteristic function of a common subset, that is, A is a common subset. Height of fuzzy sets refers to the maximum Degree of Membership. A fuzzy set with at least one element subordinated to one degree is called a normalization fuzzy set. When the characteristic value of an element belonging to a set, are no longer either 0 or 1, instead, the degree that it belongs to the set is generally expressed by a number, usually between 0 and 1.

Triangular Fuzzy Numbers are the most common types of fuzzy numbers, and the formulas are as follows [5] (Fig. 2):

$$\mu_A(X) \begin{cases} 0, & x < a \\ \frac{x-a}{b-a} & a \le x \le b \\ \frac{c-x}{c-b} & b \le x \le c \\ 0, & x > c \end{cases}$$

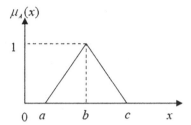

Fig. 2. Triangular fuzzy numbers

Fuzzy Algorithm. In this paper, the fuzzy algorithm used in this study is defined. According to the property and expansion principle of fuzzy numbers, suppose that there are triangular fuzzy numbers $\tilde{A}_1$ and $\tilde{A}_2$, $\tilde{A}_1 = (l_1, m_1, u_1), \tilde{A}_2 = (l_2, m_2, u_2)$ and then its algorithm is as follows [6]:

1. Addition

$$\tilde{A}_1 \oplus \tilde{A}_2 = (l_1 + l_2, m_1 + m_2, u_1 + u_2)$$

2. Subtraction

$$\tilde{A}_1 \ominus \tilde{A}_2 = (l_1 - l_2, m_1 - m_2, u_1 - u_2)$$

3. Multiplication

$$\tilde{A}_1 \otimes \tilde{A}_2 = (l_1 \times l_2, m_1 \times m_2, u_1 \times u_2)$$

4. Division

$$\tilde{A}_1 \oslash \tilde{A}_2 = (l_1/l_2, m_1/m_2, u_1/u_2)$$

Defuzzification is the conversion of fuzzy data into clear and representative data so as to make the comparison and sorting of the final stage. There is no definite method for defuzzification, which depends on the characteristics of the problem.

Fuzzy Analytic Hierarchy Process. Fuzzy Analytic Hierarchy Process (FAHP) [7] is a combination of Fuzzy Theory and AHP. The membership function of the fuzzy theory is used to replace the explicit value of the traditional AHP, so that experts can grasp the problem on a more humanized scale and give the comparative value of two factors in the evaluation framework, so as to improve the accuracy of the analysis results. In recent years, the Fuzzy Analytic Hierarchy Process has been widely used by some scholars. For example, in order to develop an experience-based framework for new product release strategy, Chiu and Chen et al. [8] proposed to evaluate by Fuzzy Analytic Hierarchy Process (FAHP). Taking the design scheme of the second-class seat of high-speed train as an example, Wei et al. [9] established the comprehensive evaluation model and evaluation process of seat comfort with the help of Fuzzy Analytic Hierarchy Process. Buckley [10] combined the fuzzy sets theory with the Fuzzy Analytic Hierarchy Process, and uses trapezoidal fuzzy number to transform expert opinions to form the fuzzy positive-reciprocal matrix in algorithm, and then obtains the fuzzy through the geometric mean. Weights are calculated by hierarchical cascade, and the fuzzy weights of alternatives are calculated. Because the real environment is a vague environment and human thinking is uncertain, the hierarchical analysis process is extended to the vague environment to make up for the lack of the hierarchical analysis process which cannot solve the problem of fuzziness.

In conclusion, scholars at home and abroad have pointed out that when using AHP to evaluate weights in complex environments, we must introduce the concept of ambiguity, because the subjective identification or the asymmetric semantic scales affect the decision-making results. On this basis, this study analyzes the design scheme of electric bicycle by Fuzzy Analytic Hierarchy Process and collects the opinions of experts and designers, screens out the evaluation criteria, then design the questionnaire with the method of pairwise comparison, establishes a pairwise matrix table, then calculates the fuzzy weight values, and finally ranks the data obtained from the evaluation criteria according to the criteria.

3   Method

3.1   Fuzzy Analytic Hierarchy Process

In the process of design and development of electric bicycle products, it is difficult to quantitatively study the user preference because there are many functions and rich modeling characteristics of electric bicycle. Therefore, the Fuzzy Analytic Hierarchy Process (FAHP) is introduced to measure the relative importance of the core function attributes of electric bicycle products, and to obtain the user preference value finally. After industry experts and designers mark and questionnaire feedbacks are collected from experts, user research is effectively and objectively completed through data statistics and calculation, thus avoiding the subjectivity and randomness of relevant decision makers in the design process, and more accurately capturing users' emotions and key needs to guide the design decision-making methods of electric bicycles.

Generally speaking, fuzzy AHP includes the following steps. Firstly, the evaluation criteria of products are screened after conducting a user research, and collecting opinions from experts and experienced product designers. After classifying and sorting out the corresponding hierarchical indicators, pair-wise comparisons are made. Secondly, judgment opinions of different experts are collected to establish a fuzzy pairwise comparison matrix [10, 11], shown as follows:

$$\tilde{B} = \begin{bmatrix} \tilde{b}_{11} & \tilde{b}_{12} & \cdots & \tilde{b}_{1m} \\ \tilde{b}_{21} & \tilde{b}_{22} & \cdots & \tilde{b}_{2m} \\ \vdots & \vdots & \vdots & \vdots \\ \tilde{b}_{m1} & \tilde{b}_{m2} & \cdots & \tilde{b}_{mm} \end{bmatrix} = \begin{bmatrix} 1 & \tilde{b}_{12} & \cdots & \tilde{b}_{1m} \\ \tilde{b}_{21} & 1 & \cdots & \tilde{b}_{2m} \\ \vdots & \vdots & 1 & \vdots \\ \tilde{b}_{m1} & \tilde{b}_{m2} & \cdots & 1 \end{bmatrix} \quad j = 1, 2 \cdots m \quad (1)$$

$\tilde{b}_{ij}$ represents the fuzzy preference between the two criteria, the formula is as follows:

$$\tilde{b}_{ij} = \left(L_{ij}, M_{ij}, U_{ij} \right), \tilde{b}_{ij} = \tilde{b}_{ij}^{-1} = \left(\frac{1}{U_{ij}}, \frac{1}{M_{ij}}, \frac{1}{L_{ij}} \right)$$
$$L_{ij} = \min_k \left(\tilde{b}_{ijk} \right), \quad M_{ij} = median \left(\tilde{b}_{ijk} \right), \quad U_{ij} = \max_k \left(\tilde{b}_{ijk} \right) \quad (2)$$

Compute and judge the relative weights of each criterion of the matrix $\tilde{w}_i$:

$$\tilde{w}_i = \left(\prod_{j=1}^{m} \tilde{b}_{ij} \right)^{1/m} \quad (i = 1, 2, \cdots, m) \quad (3)$$

Then the standardized weight values are further calculated $\tilde{W}_i$. The formulas are as follows:

$$\tilde{W}_i = \frac{\tilde{w}_i}{\sum\limits_{i=1}^{m} \tilde{w}_i} \quad (4)$$

The consistency index of the weights obtained by the judgment matrix is obtained and expressed by CI. Only when the consistency ratio CI is less than 0.10 and the maximum error must be less than 0.2, does the judgment matrix have consistency. The relevant formulas are as follows:

$$CI = \frac{\lambda_{max} - n}{n - 1} \quad (5)$$

In the process of calculation, the random consistency coefficient value RI corresponding to the order of matrix n is queried according to the table. The consistency ratio CR is calculated, CR = CI/RI. When the CR value is less than 0.1, the consistency of the judgment matrix can be determined to be acceptable. On the contrary, the judgment matrix needs to be readjusted until the condition is satisfied. The value of RI is shown in Table 2.

$$CR = \frac{CI}{RI} \quad (6)$$

Table 2. RI Random consistency index table

n	1	2	3	4	5	6	7	8	9	10	11	12
RI	0	0	0.58	0.90	1.12	1.24	1.32	1.41	1.45	1.49	1.51	1.48

Then, a simple centroid method is used to convert the fuzzy weight of each initial standard into a single value. The calculation method is as follows:

$$D(\tilde{W}_i) = \frac{|(W_U - W_L) + (W_M - W_L)|}{3} + W_L \tag{7}$$

Then the weight obtained by each scheme is normalized and the final weight is obtained. The formula is as follows:

$$W_i = \frac{D(w_i)}{\sum D(w_i)_L} \tag{8}$$

3.2   Research Methods

Taking the electric bicycle as the evaluation object, user interview method is used. The evaluation of fuzzy semantics is divided into 1 to 9 levels. Considering the efficiency of the survey in the scoring process, participants are only required to mark the corresponding degree numbers of the criteria on the questionnaire, which is easy to operate and is accepted by users. Table 3 is the levels of semantics [12].

Table 3. Level of numerical judgment

Judging scale semantic value	Triangular Fuzzy Endpoint	Index explanation
$\tilde{1}$	(1,1,1)	As important as
$\tilde{3}$	(2,3,4)	Slightly important
$\tilde{5}$	(4,5,6)	important
$\tilde{7}$	(6,7,8)	Quite important
$\tilde{9}$	(8,9,9)	Very important
$\tilde{2}, \tilde{4}, \tilde{6}, \tilde{8}$	Compromise use	Determining the importance level Based on Neighboring Indicators

In the interview, the participants were asked to compare the factors and indicators of the product. Choosing 1 means equal importance and mark the function he prefers. Choosing one of 2, 3 and 4 is slightly important, choosing one of 4, 5 and 6 is more important, choosing one of 7, 8 and 9 is very important, 23456789 is the level of importance, and the larger the number is, the more important it is.

4 Discuss the Case Study

As a kind of intelligent product that is popular with users, electric bicycles have been improved in the aspect of body weight, power and speed compared with the previous national standard and according to the new national standard and the change of the industry standard of electric bicycle. Therefore, it is necessary to redesign and develop the car models to meet the new standards. In the process of design and development of electric bicycle, it is the most important to deeply discuss the product shape design. Shape design has not only become a bridge between products and users, but also a key carrier to convey product information. In the era of sensibility-driven consumption, users pay more attention to product shape in the process of choosing and purchasing products. Therefore, it is necessary to study the psychological reflection of users on product shape and explore the consumer preferences, so as to design electric bicycle products that meet users' needs.

4.1 Extraction of Product Semantic Space

In order to obtain the standardized language for the cognitive description of product modeling image style, it is necessary to extract the psychological perception of abstract cognition of modeling entity features from user's language, so as to construct the semantic lexicon of modeling style description. Firstly, 18 sample electric bicycles with different brands are selected through online and magazine searches, and then the semantic evaluation of product style by users is investigated. The research team is composed of 15 experts or experienced product designers, including 8 males and 7 females. The questionnaire is shown in Table 4 below.

Table 4. Questionnaire on cognitive semantic evaluation of product image style

Research Questionnaire on Electric Bicycles							
Product	Sample 1	Sample 2	Sample 3	...	Sample 16	Sample 17	Sample 18
Electric Bicycle				...			
Style evaluation							

4.2 Simplifying Semantic Space

Afterwards, the image semantic words of user evaluation are further extracted, and all users' cognitive semantic adjectives are integrated into one. Then similar semantic integration and classification are carried out by KJ simplification method. That is to say, similar adjectives are classified as a corresponding adjective category. Through this method, 270 adjectives are merged into 12 categories of adjectives. Taking small and smart as an example, the specific merging method is shown in Table 5 below.

Table 5. Merging cognitive semantic vocabulary by simplification method (small and smart)

Product name	Semantic evaluation of original users	Semantic evaluation merged through KJ method
Electric bicycle	Small 18, Flexible and light 6, light 4, light and quick5, Smart and light6, Light and handy 8, Small and smart 2, Small and light, leisure and sports2, Jump and flexible	Small and smart (56)

4.3 A Modeling Evaluation Hierarchy Framework for Architectural Products

Through the above-mentioned research on product image semantics of electric bicycle, 12 categories of semantics vocabulary are formed after merging the same semantics vocabulary by KJ method. These 12 categories of semantics vocabulary are product style. Further, we should focus on the user's preference for these 12 types of shape style. However, the 12 categories of semantics vocabulary are too broad, and some semantic vocabulary are not frequently used by users, therefore, it is unnecessary to research on them. Thus, the semantic words mentioned more than 10 times are chosen in this paper for further study of user's preference for product image style, and seven adjectives are selected to discuss, namely 7 categories of Concise (A1), Small and Smart (A2), Cool and Technology (A3), Novelty and Personality (A4), Roundness and Fullness (A5), Dignified and Stable (A6). Elegance and Gentleness (A7). Finally, the evaluation index hierarchical analysis model of electric bicycle is obtained, as shown in Table 6:

Table 6. Hierarchical analysis model of electric bicycle evaluation index

Product	Product modeling style semantic space
Electric bicycle	Concise (A_1)
	Small and Smart (A_2)
	Cool and Technology (A_3)
	Novelty and Personality (A_4)
	Roundness and Fullness (A_5)
	Dignified and Stable (A_6)
	Elegance and Gentleness (A_7)

4.4 Investigate Process

Taking the electric bicycle as the evaluation object, eight experts were selected to conduct a questionnaire survey by means of user interviews, including 4 males and 4 females, that is to say, evaluating the importance of the indicators at the same level. The evaluation level is from 1 to 9. Considering the efficiency of the survey in the scoring process, participants are only required to mark the corresponding degree numbers of the criteria on the questionnaire, which is easy to operate and is accepted by users. The questionnaire is shown in Table 7 below.

Table 7. Questionnaire of product image style evaluation

	9	8	7	...	3	2	1	2	3	...	7	8	9	
Concise														Small and Smart
Concise														Cool and Technology
Concise														Novelty and Personality
⋮														⋮
Dignified and Stable														Elegance and Gentleness

4.5   Discussion of Semantic Weight

According to the (1–7) step of the formula, the data collected from the questionnaire survey are calculated. Finally, the weight values of the image semantic style of the electric bicycle products are calculated, and the consistency between CI and CR is tested. Finally, the weight values are normalized and simplified by means of defuzzification. Take the research and calculation results of an expert as an example, as shown in Table 8.

Table 8. An expert data calculation case

Evaluation factor	$\tilde{w}_l$	$\tilde{w}_m$	$\tilde{w}_u$	$D(\tilde{w}_i)$	W_i
Concise (A_1)	0.237	0.319	0.374	0.310	0.310
Small and Smart (A_2)	0.171	0.208	0.228	0.202	0.202
Cool and Technology (A_3)	0.120	0.124	0.131	0.125	0.125
Novelty and Personality (A)	0.074	0.072	0.068	0.071	0.071
Roundness and Fullness (A_5)	0.066	0.056	0.049	0.057	0.057
Dignified and Stable (A_6)	0.054	0.038	0.030	0.041	0.041
Elegance and Gentleness (A_7)	0.278	0.183	0.120	0.194	0.194
CI	CI = 0.03	CI = 0.04	CI = 0.08	CI < 0.1	
CR	CR = 0.02	CR = 0.03	CR = 0.06	CR < 0.1	

The final normalized weight values of eight research experts are averaged, and the weight values of stylistic image semantics of electric bicycle products are obtained, thus the weight preferences of users for products are calculated. The final statistical table is shown in the following Table 9:

From Table 9, we can see that Concise ranks first. It can be seen that the concise style is popular with consumers in the design process of electric bicycles. Because the Concise style chases after the combination of simple geometry and smooth and lively

Table 9. Weight statistical table of modeling style of electric bicycles

Evaluation factor	A_1	A_2	A_3	A_4	A_5	A_6	A_7
Expert 1	0.310	0.202	0.125	0.071	0.057	0.041	0.194
Expert 2	0.258	0.057	0.107	0.107	0.086	0.125	0.262
Expert 3	0.239	0.042	0.109	0.109	0.081	0.133	0.287
Expert 4	0.300	0.057	0.106	0.106	0.085	0.124	0.222
Expert 5	0.235	0.044	0.107	0.110	0.083	0.131	0.290
Expert 6	0.267	0.057	0.106	0.106	0.082	0.124	0.260
Expert 7	0.223	0.044	0.108	0.111	0.090	0.132	0.292
Expert 8	0.310	0.056	0.105	0.105	0.081	0.123	0.220
W_i	0.27	0.07	0.11	0.10	0.08	0.12	0.25
Sort	1	7	4	5	6	3	2

line instead of the exquisite and complicated decorations. When consumers find that the product has the characteristics of concise style, they will have the feeling of clarity and cleanliness psychologically, and they will be attracted by the appearance of electric bicycles. On this basis, the shape design of electric bicycle is summarized as an abstract geometric shape, and the permutation and combination are made by full use of points, lines and surfaces. The shape change in some places could be increased, so as to design a simple shape, which makes the electric bicycle more attractive.

From the perspective of Elegance and Gentleness, they rank second for the moment. Elegance and Gentleness refer to the smoothness of product shape. An arc in the form of bicycle product and a local large rounded corner shape will make the product present the Elegance and Gentleness style as a whole. When choosing electric bicycles, if consumers find that the electric bicycles have the shape characteristics of elegance and gentleness, they will have a feeling of delicacy and elegance, which will make them feel the bicycles are delicate and moving.

According to Table 9, it can be seen that Dignified and Stable rank third. From the prospective of the electric bicycle product design, the Dignified and Stable style originates from people's certain psychological dependence on products. As a transportation tool popular with users, the electric bicycle's safety factor is the most important, and it is also the key factor in the process of product design. Therefore, in the process of shape design of electric bicycle products, it is necessary to show the stable product shape so that users can rest assured to drive and ride.

5   Conclusion

In this study, Fuzzy Analytic Hierarchy Process is used to analyze the stylistic characteristics of electric bicycle. The evaluation criteria is selected with the help of user research of electric bicycle, collecting the opinions from experts and experienced product designers. The FAHP questionnaire is designed through the pairwise comparison of two criteria. Then the evaluation value is defined according to the fuzzy semantics. The questionnaire data are built into a pair-wise matrix table, and then the weight values based on the user's product modeling style are calculated and ranked, so as to reason out the emotional demand characteristics of consumers for electric bicycles. The research method and results provide a solution to designing electric bicycle products that meet users' needs.

References

1. http://www.qqddc.com/html/news/201812/news_50233.html
2. Saaty, T.L.: The Analytic Hierarchy Process. McGraw-Hill, New York (1980)
3. Chen, M.-F., Tzeng, G.-H., Ding, C.G.: Combining fuzzy AHP with MDS in identifying the preference similarity of alternatives. Appl. Soft Comput. **8**(1), 110–117 (2008)
4. Zadeh, L.A.: Fuzzy sets. Inf. Control **8**(3), 338–353 (1965)
5. Khoo, L.P., Ho, N.C.: Framework of a fuzzy quality function deployment system. Int. J. Prod. Res. **3**(24), 299–311 (1996)
6. Kwong, C.K., Bai, H.: Determining the importance weights for the customer requirements in QFD using a fuzzy AHP with an extent analysis approach. IIE Trans. **35**(7), 619–626 (2003)
7. van Laarhoven, P.J.M., Pedrycz, W.: A fuzzy extension of Saaty's priority theory. Fuzzy Sets Systems **11**(3), 199–227 (1983)
8. Han, S.H., Yun, M.H., Kwahk, J.: An evaluation model of new product launch strategy. Technovation **26**(11), 1244–1252 (2006)
9. Wei, F., Dong, S., Xu, B., Zhi, J., Guo, X., Lu, J.: Comfort evaluation and application of high-speed train passenger seats based on FAHP. J. Mach. Des. **34**(4), 119–123 (2017)
10. Buckley, J.J.: Fuzzy hierarchical analysis. Fuzzy Syst. **17**(3), 233–247 (1985)
11. Wang, C.-H., Wang, J.: Combining fuzzy AHP and fuzzy Kano to optimize product varieties for smart cameras: a zero-one integer programming perspective. Appl. Soft Comput. **22**, 410–416 (2014)
12. Chyu, C.-C., Fang, Y.-C.: A hybrid fuzzy analytic network process approach to the new product development selection problem. Math. Probl. Eng. **2014**, 1–13 (2014)

Research on the Application of Eye Movement Human-Computer Interaction in Jewelry Design

Chao Yu[✉] and Jian Shi

Jewelry Fashion Industry Research Center,
Shanghai Jiaotong University, Shanghai, China
jlthxyc@sjtu.edu.cn

Abstract. Eye movement human-computer interaction has become a new tool for user research, but it is rarely used in jewelry design. Based on eye movement experiments on jewelry materials, sketches and material quality, this paper acquires, identifies, interprets and processes consumers' internal needs and emotional signals, then evaluates the quality of related images of jewelry design. Finally, this paper discusses the feasibility and effectiveness of applying eye movement experiments to jewelry design and attempts to construct a jewelry design method based on eye movement experiments to guide the design.

Keywords: Eye movement experiment · User research · Quality evaluation · Design method

1 Introduction

Eye movement experiment, as a new human-computer interaction method, provides great convenience for the acquisition of human emotional signals. In the field of jewelry design, the application of eye movement is still infrequent. Through the understanding of the eye movement experiment, I believe that applying it to the jewelry design process is reasonable and valuable. It is an effective means to study the user experience and can guide the creation of the design.

2 The Relationship Between Eye Movement Human-Computer Interaction and Jewelry Design

2.1 The Rationality of Eye Movement Experiment Applied to Jewelry Design

About 80% to 90% of humans' access to external information depends on vision, and various physiological values of eye movements are also strongly related to human psychological changes. The present study revealed that eye movement data can indicate human behavior-directed intentions, intention classification, and inferences from such information [1].

At present, we are in a consumer-oriented consumer society. User-centric design becomes the trend and standard of design, which means designers need to understand

C. Stephanidis (Ed.): HCII 2019, CCIS 1032, pp. 116–122, 2019.
https://doi.org/10.1007/978-3-030-23522-2_15

the potential needs and preferences of users. The eye movement can tell the experimenter what the subjects are actually looking.

Therefore, it is feasible to use eye movement experiments for jewelry design. Facilitate knowledge discovery through information synthesis, which is the integration of data based on their meaning rather than the original data type [2]. We also need scientific analysis and explanation.

2.2   Application of Eye Movement Experiment in Jewelry Design

According to the various stages of jewelry design, the material quality evaluation experiment, sketch screening experiment and material selection experiment were designed to explore the feasibility of using eye movement experiments for jewelry design.

There were some errors in the data obtained from the eye movement experiment, the subjects were recorded a large amount of fixation time because they were confused when they saw the strange pattern for the first time. Therefore, questionnaires and in-depth interviews can eliminate error data and dig out more information.

3   Eye Movement Experiment and Experimental Analysis

3.1   Experimental Preparation

Prepare before the experiment: select representative experimental material, Fig. 1 shows the Chinese bronze pattern, the sketch of the flower theme ring, the modeling of the nine-tailed fox and bi fang. Design an objective questionnaire. Prepare the experimental site and time. Recruited five males and five females with a total of 10 subjects, aged between 20 and 30 years old, who are university students, all subjects have naked eyesight or corrected visual acuity of 1.0 or above. The experimental equipment is Tobii Glasses 2. Then experiment.

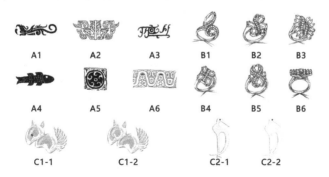

Fig. 1. Eye movement experimental materials

3.2   Material Quality Evaluation Experiment

After research and user interviews, the quality evaluation elements of the materials are divided into formal beauty, uniqueness, culture, and pleasure. According to the analytic hierarchy process, the weight of the quality evaluation elements is determined. First, the score table is obtained by scoring the subjects, and then the final weight result is obtained by calculation (see Table 1).

Table 1. Evaluation element weight table

	Formal beauty	Uniqueness	Culture	Pleasure	W%
Formal beauty	0.578	0.644	0.500	0.500	55.50%
Uniqueness	0.192	0.214	0.300	0.300	25.10%
Culture	0.115	0.071	0.100	0.100	9.70%
Pleasure	0.115	0.071	0.100	0.100	9.70%

We can see that the weight of the formal beauty is 55.5%, the uniqueness is 25.1%, the cultural is 9.7%, and the pleasure is 9.7%. Then, a test was performed to obtain:

$$CI = (4.047 - 4)/3 = 0.016 \tag{1}$$

$$RI = 0.9 \tag{2}$$

$$CR = 0.016/0.9 = 0.018 \tag{3}$$

$CR < 0.1$, so it meets the criteria for consistency testing. The result is simplified, and the formal beauty weight is 55%, the uniqueness weight is 25%, the cultural weight is 10%, and the pleasure weight is 10%. As a five-point system, the test materials are scored by subjects. Then the four scores are weighted and summed to obtain the subjective quality evaluation score of each picture, which is finally converted into a percentage system. The materials of the six bronze patterns were scored as questionnaires, and the results were as shown in Table 2.

Table 2. Bronze pattern score table

	A1	A2	A3	A4	A5	A6
Formal beauty	4.5	3.9	3.1	2.8	3.5	2.6
Uniqueness	4.2	4.3	3.8	2.6	3.9	2.3
Culture	3.1	3.5	3.2	3.1	3.2	2.8
Pleasure	3.4	3.3	3.2	2.8	3.1	2.5
Score	83.5	78	65.9	55.6	70.6	50.7

10 subjects were tested using the Tobii Glasses 2 eye tracker. The above material pictures are displayed to the subjects for observation for the 20 s, and all data is recorded. The data of 10 subjects are integrated, and a heat map is obtained based on the absolute gaze time length of the fixation point (see Fig. 2). The heat map can show the line of sight distribution of the subjects on the materials. It is obvious that A1, A2, and A5 patterns have the highest degree of fixation.

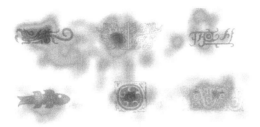

Fig. 2. Group A heat map

Get the AOI Average Fixation Duration (AAFD) and AOI Fixation Count (AFC) for Group A, and calculate the proportion of each of A1–A6, final summary into a table (see Table 3). You can see that the data results and the heat map have a strong correlation, that the AAFD and AFC of the three patterns A1, A2 and A5 with the highest degree of gaze are also the most prominent, and the comprehensive index of A1 is the highest.

Table 3. AAFD & AFC for Group A

Group A	A1	A2	A3	A4	A5	A6	SUM
AAFD (s)	6.30	4.21	2.07	1.48	3.57	2.62	20.25
W%	31.1%	20.8%	10.2%	7.3%	17.7%	12.9%	100.0%
AFC (times)	131	71	43	32	55	52	384
W%	34.1%	18.5%	11.2%	8.3%	14.3%	13.6%	100.0%

Taking the proportion of AAFD and AFC of A1–A6 as scores, the scores, and the subjective quality evaluation scores are together as a line chart (see Fig. 3). It can be seen that the trends of the three curves are basically the same. Therefore, it is preliminarily believed that high-quality materials receive more attention and are more favored by the tested groups.

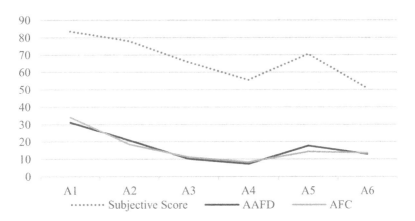

Fig. 3. Line chart of scores

3.3   Sketch Screening Experiment & Material Selection Experiment

Using the experimental method of Group A, ten subjects were subjected to a flower-themed ring sketch (Group B) test and a nine-tailed fox (C1 group) and Bifang (C2 group) modeling test. Among them, the choice of the main stone in the C1 group is different, C1-1 is set with ruby and C1-2 is set with colorless diamond; the choice of C2 group main material is different, C2-1 selects 18 K gold, C2-2 selects 925 silver.

Get the heat maps (see Figs. 4 and 5). It can be seen that B1 has the highest degree of attention, while B2, B3, B4, and B5 have the same degree of attention, and B6 has the lowest degree of attention. C1-1 was more highly gaze in the C1 group, and the upper half of the C2-2 in the C2 group was more highly looking, but the overall degree of gaze was basically the same.

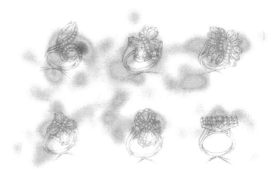

Fig. 4. Group B heat map

Fig. 5. Group C heat map

Obtain AAFD and AFC from Group B and Group C, and calculate the proportion of each(see Table 4). It can be seen that the data of AAFD and AFC of B1-B6 is consistent with the visual focus area of the heat map. The AAFD and AFC of C1-1 are higher, while C2-1 and C2-2 are basically the same. According to the preliminary conclusions of Group A, the quality of B1 is the highest in the opinion of the subjects, B2, B3, B4, and B5 are the second, and B6 is the most common. The quality of C1-1 is higher, while the quality of C2-1 and C2-2 is basically the same.

Table 4. AAFD & AFC for Group B and C

Group B	B1	B2	B3	B4	B5	B6	SUM
AAFD (s)	4.65	3.52	3.33	3.37	3.16	1.94	19.97
W%	23.3%	17.6%	16.7%	16.9%	15.8%	9.7%	100.0%
AFC (times)	124	72	82	72	60	34	444
W%	27.9%	16.2%	18.5%	16.2%	13.5%	7.7%	100.0%
Group C1	C1-1	C1-2	SUM	Group C2	C2-1	C2-2	SUM
AAFD (s)	13.67	6.37	20.04	AVFD	10.62	9.43	20.05
W%	68.2%	31.8%	100.0%	W%	52.9%	47.1%	100.0%
AFC (times)	227	151	378	AFC	183	187	370
W%	60.1%	39.9%	100.0%	W%	49.4%	50.6%	100.0%

3.4   Experimental Summary

The experiment achieved the expected effect, and we can conclude: in the case of excluding incorrect data, the materials with a higher degree of attention are of higher quality.

However, there is a strong correlation between the test results and the subjects. The same group of materials will have different preferences among subjects of different ages, genders, and cultural backgrounds. In future studies, the scope can be expanded to analyze the preferences of different user groups through eye movement experiments. At the same time, the more subjects are recruited, the higher the effectiveness of the experimental results and the more stable the results will be.

3.5   Jewelry Design Flow Chart Based on Eye Movement Experiment

We try to construct the jewelry design flow chart based on eye movement human-computer interaction (see Fig. 6), which is divided into Preparation Phase: first of all, the design project is studied to determine the test object, at the same time, choose the age, gender, cultural background, sample size and other factors of the testee; Implementation Phase: first, perform eye movement test, then use questionnaires and interviews to reduce erroneous data, and finally extract data after experiment; Analysis Phase: analyze the data, and obtain the quality evaluation of the measured object to predict the user's preference and guide the design.

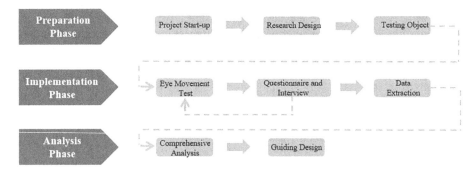

Fig. 6. Flow chart of jewelry design based on eye movement human-computer interaction

4   Summary

For jewelry design, everything is designed to meet user needs and thus achieve higher profits, and eye movement experiments provide a new and effective way to understand the real needs of users. According to the eye movement experiment, the more the gaze is, the longer the gaze is, the more information is obtained, the better the memory effect, and the more likely the purchase is [3]. This experiment proves that the method of using eye movement in the field of jewelry can well study the user's preference tendencies and guide the design.

References

1. Park, H., Lee, S., Lee, M., et al.: Using eye movement data to infer human behavioral intentions. Comput. Hum. Behav. **63**(C), 796–804 (2016)
2. Thomas, J., Cook, K.: Illuminating the Path: The Research and Development Agenda for Visual Analytics. IEEE Press (2005)
3. Li, C., Yang, Z., Wang, X.: Eye movement research on web ads with different presentation modes. Psychol. Sci. **2007**(03), 584–587+591 (2007). ISSN 1671-6981

Multimodal Interaction

Glass-Beads Display: Evaluation for Aerial Graphics Rendered by Retro-Reflective Particles

Shinnosuke Ando[1(✉)], Kazuki Otao[1,2], and Yoichi Ochiai[1,2]

[1] University of Tsukuba, Ibaraki 3058577, Japan
ando@digitalnature.slis.tsukuba.ac.jp
[2] Pixie Dust Technologies, Inc., Tokyo 1010041, Japan

Abstract. We present a novel method for rendering aerial images using retro-reflective particles. Retro-reflective particles are composed of glass beads that are half-coated with mirror films. They reflect light in different directions without any significant reduction in brightness because the falling particles can rotate in all directions. We evaluate the proposed method through a comparison with conventional aerial screens, such as fog and gas.

Keywords: Aerial imaging system · Projector-screen · Retro-reflective particles

1   Introduction

There is a huge demand for aerial screens in the entertainment industry, because they extend the expression of imaging in the air. In addition, this allows images to be displayed in places where physical screens cannot be installed.

The fog display, which projects images onto fog screens formed by artificially generated mist, is the most common aerial screen [5]. In the last decade, the study of fog displays has shifted towards human-computer interaction research, and novel applications are constantly being proposed [4,6,7]. Fog screens are primarily used for entertainment and production; however, they contain several problems: (1) narrow field of view and image blurring due to Mie scattering, (2) Instability of the display screen due to turbulent flows, and (3) excessively bright projector light. Narrow viewing angles, of magnitude of 20° or less, are also to be noted. In addition, direct light from the projector is often hazardous for children, and limits the design space between the projector and the screen.

We propose a novel aerial imaging system using the retro-reflective particle screen. Retro-reflective particles are composed of glass beads that are half-coated with mirrors [2,8]. They are commonly used in road signs to provide highlights in the dark [3]. Here, the retro-reflective particles are arranged on the road signs to reflect the incident light.

© Springer Nature Switzerland AG 2019
C. Stephanidis (Ed.): HCII 2019, CCIS 1032, pp. 125–133, 2019.
https://doi.org/10.1007/978-3-030-23522-2_16

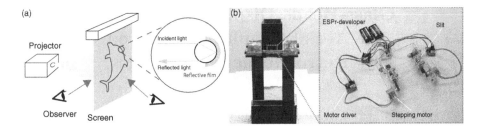

Fig. 1. The retroreflective particles fall from the control device. By projecting images from the projector on the screen, observers can clearly see the aerial images from all directions. (a) System overview. (b) Prototype and control device.

We present an alternative application that uses glass beads as the aerial screen for augmented reality (AR). The proposed method possesses some advantages:

– Glass-beads display has a wide viewing angle because the incident light enters the retro-reflective particles rotated in all directions.
– By placing the projector towards the observer, one can see the aerial images without receiving direct light from the projector. Moreover, the screen has high luminance as the incident light is reflected by the mirror without scattering.

All aerial imaging systems have both positive and negative attributes; hence, we aim to contribute towards the study of aerial imaging systems by presenting a novel method for visualizing images in the air. In this paper, we quantitatively evaluate the characteristics of the proposed method. In addition, we conduct a comparative evaluation with existing aerial screens, such as fog and gushed displays. This paper is based on our previous study [1].

2   Glass-Beads Display

In this section, we describe the implementation of our system. Our system consists of retro-reflective particles, a control device, and a projector. In the proposed method, we form a screen comprising of the retro-reflective particles prepared by dropping these particles in air and projecting images using a projector.

2.1   Retro-Reflective Particles

The retro-reflective particles are made from glass beads that are mirror-coated on one side via aluminium evaporation, as shown in Fig. 1(a). The coated inner surface functions as a mirror and the outer surface functions as a diffuser. In case the surface of the particle is not coated (i.e., clear), then the light entering on the bead will be refraction and transmission. On the other hand, when

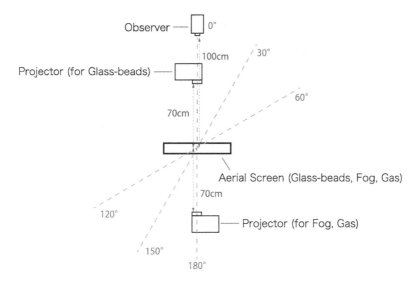

Fig. 2. Configuration of experimental setup. The observer represents people, cameras, and luminance meters. The same configuration was used in all the experiments. Note that the position of the projector varies but the distance from the screen remains the same.

the entire surface of the bead is coated, the incident light diffuses because it is simply a spherical diffuser. However, because half-coated reflective particles have both transmission surfaces and retro-reflection inner surfaces, a see-through (transparent) screen with high luminance display is obtained.

Commercially, retro-reflective particle sales are rare; hence, they must be purchased directly from the vendor. We use UB-24MSJ (Unitika Ltd.) as the retroreflective particle. The particle itself is 1 to 45 μm in diameter and 4.2 g/cm³. This particle size allows aerial images to be high resolution, and the particle weight is enough to fall vertically by gravity to form an aerial screen.

2.2   Control Device

We constructed an aerial screen by dropping retro-reflective particles using a control device as shown in Fig. 1(b). Retro-reflective particles pass through the slit and subsequently fall due to gravity. We can control the width of the slit using this system. The control device consists of an ESPr-Developer, a motor driver, and a stepping motor. In this paper, we set the width of the screen to 50 mm. The size of the device was 170 mm × 150 mm × 80 mm, and the weight of the device was 537 g. The control device opens and closes a slit between 1 mm. The slit of the screen nozzle was 50 mm × 1 mm. Wireless operation of the control device was enabled with the ESPr-Developer.

3   Experimental Evaluation

3.1   Experimental Setup

Figure 2 shows the setup for the experimental evaluation. We installed the projector and the aerial screen at a distance of 70 cm. The short focus projector TH682ST (BENQ)[1] is used for all sections of the experiment and user study. The display method was DLP, the resolution was Full HD (1920 × 1080), and the brightness was 3000 lm. The observer (e.g., human, camera, and luminance meter) is present/placed at a specific angle 100 cm away from the screen. We used three types of display for the aerial screen: glass-bead, fog, and gushed. Note that the position of the observer, the position of the projector, and the respective properties all remain the same. However, for the glass-bead display, a projector is placed between the observer and the screen. For the fog and gas displays, a screen is installed between the observer and the projector.

Fog Display. A fog display was constructed to conduct comparative experiments. The hardware consists of an ultrasonic transducer, blower fan, blower PVC pipe, and 3D printed nozzle. The atomization capacity of the ultrasonic oscillator was 500 ml/h and the slit of the nozzle was 50 mm × 8 mm.

Gushed Display. We also prepared a gushed display for comparative experiments. To build the gushed display, we referred to the study by Suzuki *et al.* [6]. A cooling spray employed for cooling the human body in sports was adopted as a gas.

3.2   Display Result

We captured photographs from each aerial screen (fog, gas, and glass-bead) at angles from 0 to 50°, as shown in Fig. 3. All ISO were 6400, the F value was 8, and the shutter speed was 1/60. For all aerial screens, clear images were obtained from the front. However, as the angle increased the Mie scattering caused blurring on both the fog and gas screens.

Then, we captured the glass-bead screen from angles of 0 to 180°, as shown in Fig. 4. The proposed method obtained clear results irrespective of the viewing angle.

3.3   Luminance and Viewing Angle

We measured the luminance with respect to the viewing angle for each display. The procedure for measuring the luminance is as follows.

---

[1] https://www.benq.com/en/projector/home-entertainment/th682st.html (last accessed February, 12th, 2019).

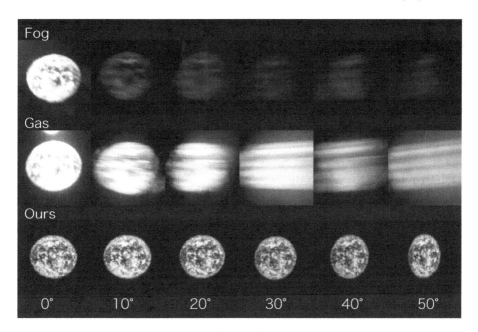

Fig. 3. Comparison of images obtained from different angles on fog, gas, and glass bead screens.

1. Construct an aerial screen of fog, gas, or glass beads.
2. Place the luminance meter at a distance of 70 cm at an angle of N degrees.
3. Project a white image from the projector.
4. Considering the turbulence of the screen, five measurement values are recorded and averaged.
5. Change the angle N with increments of $10°$ in a range from $0°$ to $80°$.

We employed LS-160 (KONICA MINOLTA, INC.)[2] as a luminance meter. All experiments were conducted in a dark room.

Result. The luminance values in the case of center (i.e., $0°$) was 89.93 cd/m^2 for fog, 506.82 cd/m^2 for gas, and 119.86 cd/m^2 for ours. From the results, the gas screen possesses the highest brightness value. Glass beads possessed higher brightness values compared to the fog screens.

Figure 5 shows the decrease in luminance versus angle. The horizontal axis represents the angle and the vertical axis represents the normalized luminance. The luminance in fog and gas screens sharply decrease at $20°$. The luminance becomes 10% or less when the fog is $20°$ and the gas is $40°$. In addition, it was difficult to measure the luminance over $80°$. Contrarily, though the luminance

---

[2] https://sensing.konicaminolta.us/products/ls-160-luminance-meter/ (last accessed February, 12th, 2019).

of the glass bead screen decreased by 50% at 10°, a detectable luminance value
was obtained even at 80°.

4 User Feedback

We conducted a user study with 15 participants (13 males and 2 females, with
a mean age of 21 and a standard deviation (SD) of 3.43) for evaluating the
performance of each aerial screen.

4.1 Procedure

Three screens of fog, gas, and glass beads were arranged side by side, each with
the configurations as follows Sect. 3. To prevent the participants from identifying
the material of the screen, each screen was called display 1 (fog), display 2 (gas),
and display 3 (glass beads) during the experiment. We projected three images of
earth, text, and a colored checker pattern on each screen. Participants observed
the images from the front of each display. Each image (earth, text, and checker
pattern) was displayed for approximately 5 s. Subsequently, the participants were
asked to rate each screen on a scale of 1 to 5, where 1 = poor, 2 = unsure, 3 = fair,
4 = good, and 5 = excellent. The screen features being rated were as follows:

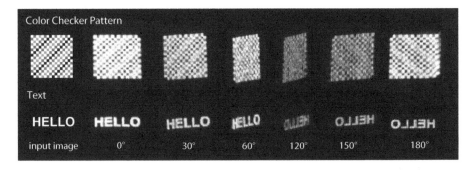

Fig. 4. Photograph of the projected image of colored checker pattern and text at each
angle. Input image is shown in the leftmost column.

- Luminance: bright or dark.
- Contrast: high or low.
- Sharpness: sharp or blurred.
- Visibility: easy to see or hard.
- Prefer: like or hate.

After observing displays 1 to 3, the participants could re-observe another
display and were able to update their ratings. After observing from the front,
the experiment was conducted for observations from an oblique angle of 30°
using the same procedure.

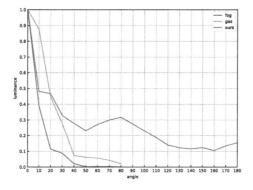

Fig. 5. Decrease of the luminance value with respect to the angle. The maximum value is 1 and the ratio is as shown. Glass beads possess a wide viewing angle, whereas fog and gas possess a large brightness value (depending on the viewing angle).

4.2   Results

The results of the questionnaire are shown in Fig. 6. Our method recorded a higher average value than fog and gas screens despite the viewing angle (front or obliquely) for all the rated features.

When observed from the front, it was equivalent in luminance/contrast, but its sharpness/visibility was higher than both fog and gas. When observed from an angle, the contrast/sharpness/visibility of glass-beads screen was higher than both fog and gas. Moreover, its luminance did not change substantially, as compared to the other screens. Participants preferred our method in both the cases. Further, unlike fog and gas, our approach is robust against viewing angle.

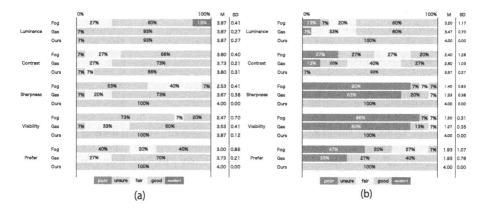

Fig. 6. Results from user feedbacks. (a) Observed from the center. (b) Observed from an angle of 30°.

5   Discussion and Future Work

5.1   Risk

We emphasize that the particles itself does not pollute the atmosphere and are safe to touch. However, because the size of the particles is exceedingly small, a risk similar to that associated with volcanic ash exists. Accordingly, it is necessary to prevent them from entering the body and inhalation through the mouth and nose must be avoided. Wearing a dust prevention mask could be a solution, but wearing such masks creates negative user experiences for the observers.

5.2   Sustainability

It is impossible to reuse the retro-reflective particles in event of the inability to collect them back. The projectable time of the aerial image depends on the number of beads. For instance, we dropped 1 kg of beads from the 50 mm × 1 mm slit and were able to project the image on the aerial screen for 60 s. Because the projection time per particle number is not very long, it is necessary to be able to reuse the glass beads for longer projection times. Retro-reflective particles in itself can be reused multiple times as they do not wear. For reusing these particles, methods such as sucking up the particles with the help of a vacuum cleaner or lifting them (such as on a belt conveyor) can be used.

6   Conclusion

In this study, we presented a novel method to visualize aerial images using retro-reflective particles and evaluated its display quality, luminance, and viewing angle. The results from the quantitative evaluation and the user feedback indicated that our proposed screen has a wider viewing angle, better sharpness, and higher contrast compared to the conventional screens such as fog and gas. Our system enables the exploration of new application areas for the aerial imaging system and the expression of AR.

References

1. Ando, S., Otao, K., Takazawa, K., Tanemura, Y., Ochiai, Y.: Aerial image on retro-reflective particles. In: SIGGRAPH Asia 2017 Posters, SA 2017, pp. 7:1–7:2. ACM, New York (2017). https://doi.org/10.1145/3145690.3145730. http://doi.acm.org/10.1145/3145690.3145730
2. Bingham, W.K.: Retroreflective sheet with enhanced brightness, US Patent 4,763,985, 16 August 1988
3. Bischoff, A., Bullock, D.: Sign retroreflectivity study. Joint Transportation Research Program, p. 190 (2002)
4. Lee, C., DiVerdi, S., Hollerer, T.: Depth-fused 3D imagery on an immaterial display. IEEE Trans. Vis. Comput. Graph. **15**(1), 20–33 (2009)

5. Rakkolainen, I., et al.: The interactive FogScreen. In: ACM SIGGRAPH 2005 Emerging Technologies, SIGGRAPH 2005. ACM, New York (2005). https://doi.org/10.1145/1187297.1187306. http://doi.acm.org/10.1145/1187297.1187306

6. Suzuki, I., et al.: Design method for gushed light field: aerosol-based aerial and instant display. In: Proceedings of the 8th Augmented Human International Conference, AH 2017, pp. 1:1–1:10. ACM, New York (2017). https://doi.org/10.1145/3041164.3041170. http://doi.acm.org/10.1145/3041164.3041170

7. Tokuda, Y., Norasikin, M.A., Subramanian, S., Martinez Plasencia, D.: MistForm: adaptive shape changing fog screens. In: Proceedings of the 2017 CHI Conference on Human Factors in Computing Systems, CHI 2017, pp. 4383–4395. ACM, New York (2017). https://doi.org/10.1145/3025453.3025608. http://doi.acm.org/10.1145/3025453.3025608

8. Yukawa, S., Iwamoto, Y.: Retroreflective sheet. US Patent 7,906,193, 15 March 2011

Generation of Atmosphere with Haptic Impressions by Using Surrounding Visual Stimuli

Midori Ban[1(✉)], Hideyuki Takahashi[1], Naoko Omi[2], Ryuta Ueda[2],
Sanae Kagawa[2], Hisashi Ishihara[1], Yutaka Nakamura[1],
Yuichiro Yoshikawa[1], and Hiroshi Ishiguro[1]

[1] Osaka University, Toyonaka, Japan
ban@irl.sys.es.osaka-u.ac.jp
[2] Daikin Industries, Ltd., Osaka, Japan

Abstract. This study aimed to develop an environment control system for generating an atmosphere with haptic impressions. Although the atmosphere cannot be touched in reality, it may occasionally induce haptic impressions. In this experiment, we prepared an experimental room whose walls were projected with animated stimuli, and thereafter, the relationship between the patterns of visual stimuli projected on the walls and the haptic sense of the room's atmosphere was investigated. First, participants were recruited, and after obtaining written informed consent, they were instructed to create visual stimuli corresponding to several themes and project them on the wall. Second, after collecting adequate data on the visual stimuli created by participants, we extracted the common stochastic features quantities of these visual stimuli, among the participants, for each tactile sensation and created a generative model for wall-projected visual stimuli by using machine learning methods. Furthermore, when projecting the generated visual stimulus, we examined the type of impression experienced by the participants in the laboratory. Preliminarily, we show that the proposed model autonomously generated visual stimuli which subsequently, to a certain extent, evoked various haptic senses of the atmosphere, and its use was shown to change the participant's impression.

Keywords: Haptic impression · Atmosphere of the room ·
Automatic generation · Onomatopoeia

1 Introduction

The subjective characteristics of the atmosphere, beyond its physical features, are commonly described using colloquial phrases such as "feeling the tension in the atmosphere" or "she brightens up the atmosphere". Although direct physical contact with the atmosphere is impossible, it occasionally induces qualitative haptic impressions. For example, many people feel the haptic sense on a resort island to be softer than that in a business district, despite no significant differences among the quantified physical parameters in the two atmospheres. Similarly, air is intangible, however, the perceived tactile impressions for air may be subjectively described as "soft" or

© Springer Nature Switzerland AG 2019
C. Stephanidis (Ed.): HCII 2019, CCIS 1032, pp. 134–141, 2019.
https://doi.org/10.1007/978-3-030-23522-2_17

"clammy". Therefore, we envisaged the possibility of creating and manipulating such an "atmosphere with tactile impression". This study aimed to develop an environmental control system to create an atmosphere with tactile impression.

Furthermore, we deliberated on the choice of method to be used for creating an atmosphere with a tactile impression of air, and subsequently, focused on visual stimuli for its implementation. Visual information is the dominant among the human senses [1], and moreover, it has been reported that visual information affects human cognition and emotions [2]. Additionally, the definite possibility for changing the "tactile and sense of existence" of the object, and evoking various impressions in the audience by projecting visual information such as light and shadow using projection mapping, has been pointed out [3]. Therefore, we implemented the use of projection mapping in this study to create an atmosphere with a tactile impression of air.

Specifically, the experimental participants created their own stimulus using the builder application of projection mapping. Furthermore, we implemented this system to develop a machine learning-based generative model by extracting feature quantities pertaining to the haptic sense generated in response to the created stimuli, universally shared among the users. By this strategy, we believe that it is possible to create a more sustainable social implementation system because the accuracy of this system increases with users.

In this study, additionally, we evaluated the generated visual stimuli. In many conventional studies, the evaluations have been made using rating scale-based methods, or the semantic differential method, a representative method using adjectives to quantify impression (e.g., [4, 5]). However, with the conventional methods, there is a possibility that the tactile impression generated by the visual stimulus cannot be measured. For example, although adjectives used in the semantic differential method are suitable for expressing a single texture, the expression of fine and comprehensive tactile sensations is difficult [6]. Therefore, for evaluating abstract concepts such as "tactile impressions," dealt with in this research, we realized the need for new indicators of evaluation alongside the conventional methods. Therefore, in this study, in addition to the semantic differential method, the evaluation was performed using onomatopoeia, which has been shown to be strongly associated with tactile sensation [6, 7]. Using this strategy, it possible to measure the tactile impression of air not captured by conventional method.

As aforementioned, in this research, we examined two objectives. First, presenting a specific theme to the participants using the builder application of projection mapping such that the user creates their own stimuli, and subsequently, extracting feature quantities of the universally shared haptic sense generated in response to the created stimuli, by machine learning. Therefore, we devised a system for developing generative models. Second, to measure the tactile sensation of air that could not be captured by the conventional semantic differential method.

Experiment 1

2   Method

2.1   Participants

In experiment 1, 50 Japanese participants (30 male, mean [M] = 22.82 years old (Standard deviation [SD] = 6.16), range = 18–42 years old) were recruited, with no history of neurological or psychiatric illness. All the participants provided written informed consent prior to the start of the study, and the study was granted ethical approval by the university to which the authors are affiliated.

2.2   Procedure

Participants were asked to create images based on 3 themes using the projection mapping builder which would, eventually, change the atmosphere of the room. The builder was presented on a 23 computer screen, with the following instruction, "Please use this builder to create visual images based on the following 3 themes [air feelings]: a feeling of well-being, a feeling of being wrapped, and a feeling of tension" (Fig. 1).

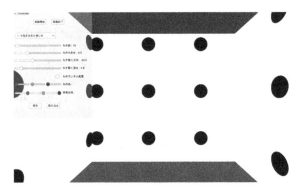

Fig. 1. Projection mapping builder used in the experiment (Example of a screen with a projected circle)

As instructed, the participants created their respective images on the computer screen on the three air feelings- "a feeling of well-being", "a feeling of being wrapped", and "a feeling of tension". The projection mapping builder was created using Unity. The participants were provided with 12 elements on the screen such as: randomness of the circles projected on the wall, number of circles, size of circles, direction of movement of circles (X), direction of circle movement (Y), speed of movement of circle, circle color (R), circle color (G), circle color (B), wall color (R), wall color (G), and the color of the wall (B) was set to be manipulated freely. The experiment concluded when the participants created images on all the three air feelings.

3 Result

3.1 Extraction of Feature Quantities of Three Air Feelings

Subsequently, in order to extract the feature quantities of the three senses of air from the image data, we performed principal component analysis for the 12 elements.

We defined y as a 12-dimensional element and projected it onto a low-dimensional feature vector.

$$\begin{array}{c} projection\ f \\ f : y \rightarrow x = (W_{PCA})y \end{array} \tag{1}$$

As a result, four components with an eigenvalue of 1.0 or more were extracted (Table 1). The contribution of the components were found to be the following: first component, 21.06% (eigenvalue = 2.53); second component, 15.17% (eigenvalue = 1.82); third component, 12.68% (eigenvalue = 1.52), and fourth component, 9.40% (eigenvalue = 1.13). The cumulative contribution was 58.31%.

Table 1. Four components in principal component analysis (description of those with an eigen value of 1.0 or more)

Element	Component			
	1	2	3	4
Number of circles	−0.690	−0.103	−0.295	0.137
Size of circles	0.661	−0.158	0.166	−0.240
Wall color (G)	0.621	−0.572	−0.178	0.172
Speed of movement of circle	−0.419	−0.074	0.408	0.112
Circle color (G)	0.543	0.586	−0.179	0.075
Randomness of the circles	0.196	0.565	−0.171	0.350
Wall color (R)	0.390	−0.540	0.243	0.312
Wall color (B)	0.416	−0.385	−0.586	−0.060
Circle color (R)	0.404	0.411	0.558	−0.002
Circle color (B)	0.282	0.417	−0.497	−0.174
Direction of circle movement (X)	0.202	−0.033	0.313	−0.686
Direction of circle movement (Y)	0.333	0.069	0.298	0.528

Furthermore, we used K-means clustering algorithm for the space feature quantity extracted by principal component analysis. As a result, four clusters were obtained. The content rate was calculated to evaluate the participants' extent of inclusion with the selected feeling among "a feeling of well-being", "a feeling of being wrapped", and "a feeling of tension". A high (56.0% or higher) air feeling label was assigned a cluster. As a result, the air feeling "a feeling of tension" was assigned to cluster 1, "a feeling of well-being" to cluster 3, and "a feeling of being wrapped" to cluster 4. Therefore, no labels were provided by us, and we could evaluate the three air feelings by extracting the respective feature quantity.

3.2 Automatic Generation of Parameters for Each Cluster

Here, we describe the process of automatically generating parameters from each cluster. First, we generated 12 parameters for each of the 4 clusters based on the mean and SD, and the parameters were generated by random numbers. Next, the parameters of each of the 12 elements generated were normalized, and the inner product of eigenvectors was taken to project onto the clustered feature space. However, since there was no guarantee that the parameters generated belonged to a specific cluster in the space where clustering process was performed, they were judged on the basis of their inclusivity in the space feature quantity. The criterion for its judgment was the product of its eigenvector falling to within ±1SD in the space feature quantity. If the projected parameters belonged to a specific cluster in four-dimensional space (the four components derived from principal component analysis), they were considered to be included in the cluster, and adopted. If not, they were rejected, and the parameters were regenerated with the same procedure.

In experiment 2, we performed an evaluation using a new index for identifying the nature of impression the participants felt when projecting the parameters of each cluster generated by the above method.

Experiment 2

4   Method

4.1   Participants

In experiment 2, 14 Japanese participants (8 male, M = 21.21 years old; SD = 2.04; Range = 18–25 years old), with no history of neurological or psychiatric illness, were recruited. All participants provided written informed consent prior to the start of the study, and ethical approval was granted by the university to which the authors are affiliated. The recruited participants were exclusive from that of experiment 1.

4.2   Procedure

From the observation room, the experimenter instructed the participants to answer questions regarding the atmosphere of the room where projection mapping was performed. The participants were asked to observe the room and wait for sound cues. On hearing the cue, the participants were instructed to answer questions using the tablet provided to them. After that the participants then moved to the laboratory. The laboratory is shown in Fig. 2.

In experiment 2, visual stimuli in the form of projection mapping of eight automatically generated clusters (two parameters generated from four clusters were presented sequentially, two by two) were randomly presented to each participant. The participants were instructed to sit in the center of the laboratory for 30 s and observe

Fig. 2. Projection mapping laboratory where experiment 2 was performed

the visual stimulus of projection mapping. After 30 s, the cue was sounded and the participants answered questions using a tablet.

4.3   Question Items

SD Method Question: The experimenter instructed them to select the appropriate number for the impression presented in the room. The following seven adjective pairs were used for questioning: "discomfort-comfort", "uninteresting-beautiful", "tired-fine", "quiet-noisy", "tensed-relaxed", "muddy-clear", and "poor air-good air". Each item was ranked in a 7-point scale.

Onomatopoeia Question: The experimenter instructed the participants to taught as follows "Please select one of the following two words (Onomatopoeias) which that is more appropriately described to the impression of this room". The following ten onomatopoeia pairs were used for question items.
"PasaPasa-PuruPuru", "SubeSube-CasaCasa", "TsuruTsuru-ShakaShaka", "MosaMosa-PokoPoko", "ZaraZara-FukaFuka", "SuruSuru-ShoriShori", "HowaHowa-FuniFuni", "ChickChick-GasaGasa", "MocoMoco-TubuTubu", and "FuwaFuwa-SaraSara" [6, 7]. Each item was ranked in a 2-point scale. These indicators were for measuring the tactile sensation to air.

5   Result

First, principal component analysis was performed on the semantic differential method question items. Two components having an eigenvalue of 1.0 or more were extracted. The contribution of the first component was 54.32% (eigenvalue = 3.80) and that of the second component was 20.54% (eigenvalue = 1.44). The cumulative contribution was 74.86%. The analysis of variance of one factor, with the corresponding four clusters as independent variables, was carried out. As a result, the main effect of only one component was observed (F (3, 81) = 10.61, p = .0001, η^2 = .28). Multiple comparisons identified the air feeling of "a feeling of wrapped" to be significantly higher than "a

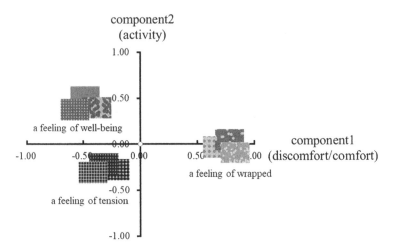

Fig. 3. The average value of three clusters on the principal component score

feeling of tension" and "a feeling of well-being". It was observed that the participants felt differently for each of the three clusters (Fig. 3).

Next, we describe the results for the new indicator, the onomatopoeic pair. Following a principal component analysis of the onomatopoeic pairs, three components with an eigenvalue of 1.0 or more were extracted. The contribution of the first component was 32.44% (eigenvalue = 3.24); the second component, 14.79% (eigenvalue = 1.48), and that of the third component was 10.48% (eigenvalue = 1.05). The cumulative contribution rate was 57.71%.

Next, after calculating the correlation between the components of the onomatopoeia pairs and semantic differential method, a moderately significant positive correlation was found between the first components ($r = .50$, $p = .0001$). In other words, we hereby, show that measuring "discomfort-comfort" using an onomatopoeia pair was possible. On the other hand, no significant association was found between the components of the semantic differential method and the second and third component. That is, using the new index, it was possible to extract an axis related to the tactile sensation that otherwise, could not be captured by conventional semantic differential method.

6   Discussion

The present study had two objectives. First, to present a specific air feeling to the participants, who, by using the builder application of projection mapping, created their own stimuli. Machine learning algorithm was used to create a generative model and extract data pertaining to feature quantities of the haptic sense, generated as a result of the visual stimuli, and is universally shared among users. Using the data collected in experiment 1, the characteristics of the three air feelings, i.e. "a feeling of well-being", "a feeling of being wrapped", and "a feeling of being tense" were extracted. Furthermore, the system can be automated. In other words, by using the system proposed in this study, it was possible to identify the sense shared by the group and present it to the participants. Additionally, we observed that the participants felt different impressions when different air feeling automatically presented.

The second purpose of this research was to measure the tactile sensation of air that could not be captured by the conventional semantic differential method. By using onomatopoeic pairs, we identified the second and third axes that could not be captured by the semantic differential method. These axes included the onomatopoeia pair related to the skin sensitivity. In other words, it was suggested that the participants felt a tactile impression of the presented visual stimuli. From the two experimental results of the study, though preliminary, it may be suggested that we succeeded in developing an environmental control system to create an atmosphere with tactile impression.

However, our research only shown the relationship between the impression and the touch of the air by using a questionnaire. In future, we propose subjecting the participants to tactile sensations and conducting experiments to create an atmosphere with those tactile sensations. Furthermore, we aim to create the atmosphere with tactile impression by automatically generating the data of the relation between air and tactile sense using the present system.

References

1. Kato, H.: Origin and future of the theory that humans have obtained, 80% of information input from vision. Natl. Univ. Corp. Tsukuba Univ. Technol. Techno Rep. **25**(1), 95–100 (2017)
2. Seno, T., Kawabe, T., Ito, H., Sunaga, S.: Vection modulates emotional valence of autobiographical episodic memories. Cognition **126**(1), 115–120 (2013). https://doi.org/10.1016/j.cognition.2012.08.009
3. Furugori, Y., Campana, R.J.M., Kobayashi, T., Hirabayashi, M.: Systematization of the representation techniques of contents for projection mapping. Inf. Process. Soc. Jpn **2014**, 391–396 (2014)
4. Osgood, C.E., Suci, G.J., Tannenbaum, P.H.: The Measurement of Meaning. University Illinois Press, Oxford, England (1957)
5. Russell, J.A.: Core affect and the psychological construction of emotion. Psychol. Rev. **110**, 145–172 (2003). https://doi.org/10.1037/0033-295X.110.1.145
6. Kwona, J., Yoshino, J., Kosahara, M., Nakauchi, S., Sakamoto, M.: Relation between naturalness and luxuriousness through onomatopoeia expressing texture. Jpn. J. Psychon. Sci. **36**(1), 40–49. http://doi.org/10.14947/psychono.36.7
7. Sakamoto, M., Yoshino, J., Doizaki, R., Haginoya, M.: Metal-like texture design evaluation using sound symbolic words. Int. J. Des. Creat. Innov. **4**, 181–194 (2015). https://doi.org/10.1080/21650349.2015.1061449

OPDisp - Open Architecture
for Extensible Public Displays

Miguel Almeida Carvalho[1]([✉]), Ana Tomé[2,3], and João Nuno Silva[1,2]

[1] INESC-ID, Lisbon, Portugal
miguel.d.carvalho@tecnico.ulisboa.pt, joao.n.silva@inesc-id.pt
[2] Instituto Superior Técnico, Universidade de Lisboa, Lisbon, Portugal
anatome@tecnico.ulisboa.pt
[3] CERIS - Civil Engineering Research and Innovation for Sustainability,
Lisbon, Portugal

Abstract. Currently public displays have many functionalities, but still present several challenges with respect to content producing and user interaction. Most are non-interactive, only used for static information dissemination, while others rely on tactile displays adding interactivity, but limiting to single-user interactions. Displays that resort to mobile devices to promote engagement and enhance user experience usually require the installation of specific applications.

This work proposes an open architecture for the production and deployment of interactive presentations: content on the mobile device complements the information presented on the display. We developed a prototype and conducted a real world experiment to evaluate the usability of the system, achieving good preliminary results.

Keywords: Mobile computing · Public displays · User interaction · Open display networks

1 Introduction

Public displays have become part of our lives allowing to present information, advertisements or services in users surroundings, but still present several challenges in order to become ubiquitous. Most of these challenges are related to user interaction and the production and design of contents [1,2]. The majority of displays in public spaces are non-interactive, usually used to provide static information, e.g., bus and train stations schedules, or advertisements. Others rely on tactile displays adding interactivity, but usually limiting to single-user interactions. There are some approaches that explore multi-user interaction but people do not feel very comfortable with this, specially due to privacy concerns. Displays that are complemented by mobile devices allow a richer user experience [3–6] but usually require the installation of specific applications [5] which can be cumbersome and time-consuming to allow interaction with users [7].

© Springer Nature Switzerland AG 2019
C. Stephanidis (Ed.): HCII 2019, CCIS 1032, pp. 142–148, 2019.
https://doi.org/10.1007/978-3-030-23522-2_18

Therefore, this work proposes an open architecture for the production of interactive presentations for public displays and mobile devices. The public display presents information like a regular presentation, and the complementary contents are accessed by user's personal devices. The proposed architecture is based on open standards such as HTML, JavaScript and HTTP. One of the main advantages is that it does not require the installation of any mobile application, since contents are accessed by any browser on the mobile device. Another advantage is that OPDisp allows the use of multiple media types (images, videos) and HTML/JavaScript to implement complex interactions.

2   Related Work

Multiple studies explore the interaction between people and public displays, and present several advantages of using smartphones [3–6]. Others investigate the phenomenon of display blindness, concluding that people are mostly attracted by content related to them. Our work focus on providing a tool for the easy production of these contents and their extension to mobile devices.

SlideTalk [8] presents a similar experiment using smartphone-based approaches to promote interactivity with slideshow content for public displays. The proposed prototype is based on the automatic generation of presentations from different University source contents, thus not acting as a generic tool. Another similar test was conducted by Pattanakimhun et al. [9] to evaluate the use of a mobile application as a way to enhance users' engagement with the contents. They focused on the interaction phase, and did not take into account issues like device pairing or the content design mechanism. Also mobile based application models can be a downside to peoples interest in interaction.

Other related systems propose the use of public displays to share contents between users. PresiShare [10] is a web-based platform for presenting and sharing multimedia contents on a public display. They propose the use of QR codes to facilitate interaction with public displays, similar to our solution. Though our architecture goes further by providing an open tool for content production. SnapAndGrab [11] propose a system that allows users to access and share multimedia contents via situated public displays and Bluetooth enabled camera phones. Their solution also does not require any client software to be installed on the user's device, but the interaction is limited by the adopted content package creation. A user can create a package uploading a contact card and selecting a representative image to be displayed on the big screen. When someone takes a picture of that image they automatically receive all the media associated with that package. Besides this limitation the system is patented.

Other works [12,13] focus on a specific application domain, for example public notice areas (PNA). Their research also support that people are interested in using smartphones to interact with public displays, specially because it provides privacy and brings information closer to the users. Our system provides an architecture that can facilitate the design and dissemination of contents for this kind of applications.

3   OPDisp

In this section we present a set of requirements that systems similar to ours should follow, and detail the architecture and implementation of the prototype.

3.1   Requirements

The proposed system should provide a tool that allows the simple and effective design of contents for public displays, and additional information to be displayed in mobile devices. It should be open in order that anyone can produce contents, even without having any programming skills, and interoperable to allow the use by any kind of display and mobile device. It also should support a wide variety of contents, such as multimedia or html code. These requirements can be summarized as followed:

- Simplicity
- Openness
- Genericness
- Interoperability

3.2   Architecture

Figure 1 illustrates the system architecture. The content manager is someone responsible for designing the display content and the mobile information. All data is encapsulated in a single web page: a part is rendered on the display, and the other on user's mobile devices. Mobile information is synchronized with the display content. The infrastructure is simple: a server with public address, a browser connected to the display and regular mobile devices, connected by a public or private Wi-Fi network.

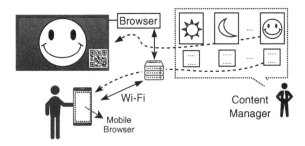

Fig. 1. OPDisp system architecture

Content Production. As mentioned, each presentation consists in a set of web pages divided in two parts: display and mobile content. This is achieved using regular HTML with different *<div>* classes, that define both parts. The display content is similar to a regular presentation, with the template presented in Fig. 2: title of presentation at the top, one or two images at the center and the caption below. The sidebar can be used to create sections that help people visualize content types or categories, and also to provide the QR Code to be scanned by nearby users.

All other complementary contents are to be presented on the user's mobile devices, including multiple media types such as images and videos.

At the end of each page should be a link that indicates the next page of the presentation.

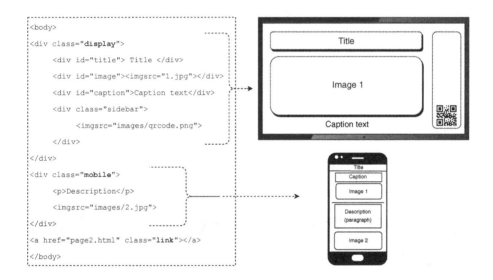

Fig. 2. Template of the presentation - code (left) and preview (right)

Interaction. System interaction is very simple. The public display only requires a web browser to access the server and display the main presentation.

A QR-Code [8] allows users to automatically access the presentation with their mobile device. This QR-Code encodes the URL of the presentation.

The pages are displayed in a loop, and the time of the transitions can be programmed. Every time the main display is updated a notification appears on the smartphone to inform the user. This way one can choose to continue accessing information of interest and not be forced to jump to the next slide. The use of JavaScript allows the implementation of complex interactions with the display contents: we tested the zooming and panning of images. A delimited area on the mobile UI allows the manipulation of images on the big screen. It is also possible - and easy - to implement other types of interaction, like manually controlling the transitions of the main presentation.

3.3 Implementation

The system prototype was developed in JAVA and consists of three main components. The first is an HTML parser that reads the produced HTML files of the various pages and splits the information for the display and mobile device.

The second component is a web server that assures the communication with the public display. This web server cycles over the various HTML pages allowing the refresh of the display information. It supports multiple displays, as long as each of them has access to a web browser.

The third component is a server that sends information to the mobile devices. This server uses WebSockets to communicates with a JavaScript interface on the browser. This server is synchronized with the web server so that it sends the correct mobile information.

4 Evaluation

In order to evaluate the system we have deployed a prototype at a museum in Instituto Superior Técnico - Lisbon University as a complementary display to the "Desenho técnico no Técnico" exhibit[1]. This scenario is presented by Fig. 3, where the mobile phone is showing the complementary contents of the main public display. The displayed contents were produced by different groups

Fig. 3. Prototype of the system at Lisbon University

---

[1] http://desenhotecnico.museudec.tecnico.ulisboa.pt.

of students. These groups were asked to define the content (for the display and mobile) and answer a questionnaire based on the After-Scenario Questionnaire (ASQ) [14] and the System Usability Scale (SUS) [15].

The answers showed that the participants were very satisfied with the production method, with a percentage of above 90% of the slides corresponding to the expected (without the need of changes). Some just stated that could have benefited from the use of a graphic HTML editor, or a Word Editor to better visualize the input data structure.

5   Conclusion

The emergence of public displays have imposed new challenges, specially regarding user interaction and content presentation, requiring the creation of new tools and practices. Our contribution is two fold: first we provide a generic tool for the easy design of interactive presentations for public displays; second we allow the extension of complementary contents to mobile devices, enhancing the user experience.

The developed prototype satisfies the requirements proposed in Sect. 3.1, and the results achieved on a preliminary analysis support the system usability.

Acknowledgements. This work was supported by national funds through Fundação para a Ciência e a Tecnologia (FCT) with reference UID/CEC/50021/2019 and UID/ECI/04625/2013.

References

1. Taivan, C., Jose, R., Silva, B.: Web-based applications for open display networks: developers' perspective. Comput. Syst. Sci. Eng. **30**, 79–88 (2015)
2. Langheinrich, M., Schmidt, A., Davies, N., José, R.: Open display networks: a communications medium for the 21st century. Computer **45**(05), 58–64 (2012)
3. Shirazi, A.S., Winkler, C., Schmidt, A.: Flashlight interaction: a study on mobile phone interaction techniques with large displays. In: Proceedings of the 11th International Conference on Human-Computer Interaction with Mobile Devices and Services, MobileHCI 2009, pp. 93:1–93:2. ACM, New York (2009)
4. Panhey, P., Döring, T., Schneegass, S., Wenig, D., Alt, F.: What people really remember: understanding cognitive effects when interacting with large displays. In: Proceedings of the 2015 International Conference on Interactive Tabletops & Surfaces, ITS 2015, pp. 103–106. ACM, New York (2015)
5. Scheible, J., Ojala, T.: MobiLenin combining a multi-track music video, personal mobile phones and a public display into multi-user interactive entertainment. In: Proceedings of the 13th Annual ACM International Conference on Multimedia, MULTIMEDIA 2005, pp. 199–208. ACM, New York (2005)
6. Alt, F., Shirazi, A.S., Kubitza, T., Schmidt, A.: Interaction techniques for creating and exchanging content with public displays. In: Proceedings of the SIGCHI Conference on Human Factors in Computing Systems, CHI 2013, pp. 1709–1718. ACM, New York (2013)

7. Vepsäläinen, J., et al.: Personal device as a controller for interactive surfaces: usability and utility of different connection methods. In: Proceedings of the 2015 International Conference on Interactive Tabletops & Surfaces, ITS 2015, pp. 201–204. ACM, New York (2015)

8. Patterson, J., Clinch, S.: SlideTalk: encouraging user engagement with slideshow displays. In: Proceedings of the 7th ACM International Symposium on Pervasive Displays, PerDis 2018, pp. 4:1–4:7. ACM, New York (2018)

9. Pattanakimhun, P., Chinthammit, W., Chotikakamthorn, N.: Enhanced engagement with public displays through mobile phone interaction. In: SIGGRAPH Asia 2017 Mobile Graphics & Interactive Applications, SA 2017, pp. 27:1–27:5. ACM, New York (2017)

10. Geel, M., Huguenin, D., Norrie, M.C.: PresiShare: opportunistic sharing and presentation of content using public displays and QR codes. In: Proceedings of the 2nd ACM International Symposium on Pervasive Displays, PerDis 2013, pp. 103–108. ACM, New York (2013)

11. Maunder, A.J., Marsden, G., Harper, R.: SnapAndGrab: accessing and sharing contextual multi-media content using Bluetooth enabled camera phones and large situated displays, pp. 2319–2324, January 2008

12. Alt, F., et al.: Digifieds: insights into deploying digital public notice areas in the wild. In: Proceedings of the 10th International Conference on Mobile and Ubiquitous Multimedia, pp. 165–174. ACM (2011)

13. Alt, F., et al.: Designing shared public display networks – implications from today's paper-based notice areas. In: Lyons, K., Hightower, J., Huang, E.M. (eds.) Pervasive 2011. LNCS, vol. 6696, pp. 258–275. Springer, Heidelberg (2011). https://doi.org/10.1007/978-3-642-21726-5_17

14. Lewis, J.R.: Psychometric evaluation of an after-scenario questionnaire for computer usability studies: the ASQ. SIGCHI Bull. **23**(1), 78–81 (1991)

15. Brooke, J.: SUS: a quick and dirty usability scale. Usability Eval. Ind. **189**, 4–7 (1995)

Horizontal Wide-Range Gaze Detection System by Combination of Pupil Ellipticity and Pupil-Corneal Reflection Methods

Yoshinobu Ebisawa[✉], Kiyotaka Fukumoto, and Yuichi Nakazawa

Graduate School of Integrated Science and Technology,
Shizuoka University, Hamamatsu, Japan
ebisawa.yoshinobu@shizuoka.ac.jp

Abstract. We have developed gaze detection systems based on the pupil-corneal reflection method for driver monitoring, digital signage, and so on. However, when a user looks at angularly remote positions ($>\pm30°$ – $\pm40°$) on a monitor screen from the optical systems for the gaze detection, the gaze detection becomes impossible because the corneal reflection does not appear. In the present paper, to expand the measurable horizontal range of the gaze, we proposed a method combing the pupil-corneal reflection method and the pupil ellipticity method. These two types of the gaze detection methods functioned on the same platform. In this combined method, a line of sight was always calculated using the ellipticity of the pupil ellipse and the inclination of the minor axis of the pupil ellipse. When the angle of the line of sight exceeded 30°, the gaze detection was determined using the pupil ellipticity method. When it was 30° or less, the pupil-corneal reflection method was used. When the pupil ellipticity method is used, it is unclear which direction a subject looks on the minor axis of the ellipse, e.g., right or left. To solve this problem, we proposed a method utilizing the difference in the pupil ellipticity between the right and left camera images. In the experiment, subjects were asked to look at 27 visual targets evenly arranged on horizontally arranged three monitors' screens. The experimental result showed that the measurable range of the gaze detection was expanded into approximately $\pm45°$ horizontally by the combination of the two types of the gaze detection methods. In the total range, the average angular gaze error for all subjects was $2.02 \pm 1.38°$.

Keywords: Gaze detection · Pupil detection · Pupil ellipticity · Corneal reflection

1 Introduction

We have developed gaze detection systems based on the pupil-corneal reflection method. Gaze points on a monitor screen are calculated from a 3-D pupil coordinate and the relative positional relationship between the pupil center and the corneal reflection (glint) in camera images captured by stereo-calibrated two optical systems each consisting of a camera and a two concentric near-infrared LED rings light source [1]. This system allows users' large head movements and achieves high accuracy of the

© Springer Nature Switzerland AG 2019
C. Stephanidis (Ed.): HCII 2019, CCIS 1032, pp. 149–157, 2019.
https://doi.org/10.1007/978-3-030-23522-2_19

gaze detection. However, when the user looks at angularly remote positions on the monitor screen from the optical system about 30 to 40° or more, the accurate gaze detection using the pupil-corneal reflection method becomes impossible because the corneal reflection does not appear. In driver monitoring systems, for example, a wider measurable angular range of the gaze detection is needed.

In the present paper, to expand the measurable horizontal angular range of the gaze detection, we propose a combination method for calculating the direction of a line of sight by using the of the pupil's ellipticity (pupil ellipticity method) and the pupil-corneal reflection method. The two types of methods simply function in the same platform.

In the similar study using both the two types of methods, stereo-calibrated cameras were installed at remote positions under a PC monitor, and gaze detection on an angularly remote PC screen was performed [2].

2   Method

2.1   Gaze Detection Based on Pupil-Corneal Reflection Method [1]

The inner (850 nm) and outer (940 nm) LED rings of the light source generated bright and dark pupil images, respectively. The pupils were detected from the difference image created by subtracting the bright and dark pupil images. However, when the user moves the head, the pupil position changes between the bright and dark pupil images because of the time difference of image acquisition for the both pupil images. Therefore, the image difference processing was performed after shifting the small areas (small windows) including each pupil in the dark pupil image so that the corneal reflection in this dark pupil image may coincide with that in the bright pupil image. Ellipse-fitting the pupil contour determined the ellipse center as the pupil center in the camera image.

The 3-D pupil position (P) of both eyes were calculated by stereo-matching of the pupil center. Figure 1 shows our gaze detection theory for a combination of one eye and one camera [3]. Point Q means the gaze point on the PC screen. The line of sight is defined as the line connecting P and Q. The virtual gaze plane H is perpendicular to the line connecting P and the camera (light source), O. It rotates depending on the pupil positions. Point T indicates the intersection point of the line of sight and plane H. Here, the X' axis corresponds to the intersection line of plane H and the horizontal plane ($X - Z$) in the world coordinate system. The angle between the line of sight and the line OP is denoted as θ in the 3-D space (Fig. 1(a)). The angle between line OT and the X' axis on plane H is denoted as ϕ. An angular vector between lines OP and PQ is defined as $\boldsymbol{\theta} = (\theta, \phi)$. The vector from the corneal reflection center to the pupil center, $\boldsymbol{r}$, is obtained from the camera image (Fig. 1(b)). The vector is replaced by its actual size vector $\boldsymbol{r}$ in the 3-D space using the pinhole model. It is defined as $\boldsymbol{r} = (|\boldsymbol{r}|, \phi')$,

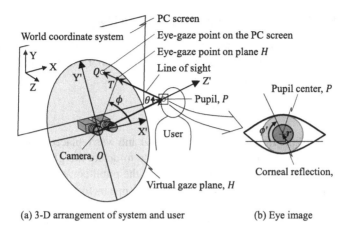

(a) 3-D arrangement of system and user   (b) Eye image

Fig. 1. Gaze detection theory.

where ϕ' is an inclination of r in the 3-D space. Here, assuming that $\theta = k|r|$ and $\phi = \phi'$, the following formula is established:

$$\theta = kr, \tag{1}$$

where k is a constant. However, the innate difference exists between the optical and visual axes of the eyeball. In order to correct the difference, r was replaced by the following formula:

$$r = r' - r_0, \tag{2}$$

where r and r' are vectors corresponding to the visual and optical axes of the eyeball, respectively, and r_0 is a vector corresponding to the difference between both axes. r' is measured by the gaze detection system. Equation (3) is obtained from Eqs. (1) and (2).

$$\theta = kr' - kr_0 \tag{3}$$

However, in general, when θ is increased, the linear relationship between θ and r' may not maintained. Therefore, if assuming a nonlinear relationship and changing k as a function of r', the second term in Eq. (3) comes to change depending on k [3]. This means that the invariable and inherent difference between the optical and visual axes of the eyeball changes. Therefore, the following equation was used instead of Eq. (3).

$$\theta = kr' - \theta_0 \tag{4}$$

θ_0 was an angular vector indicating the difference between the optical and visual axes of the eyeball. To obtain the values of k and θ_0 as the user calibration, the user must have fixated on one calibration target whose coordinates were known, which was presented at the center of the PC screen (one-point calibration).

2.2   Gaze Detection Based on Pupil Ellipticity Method

In this method, an angle θ'_{el} corresponding to the amplitude of $\theta' (= kr')$ in Eq. (4) was calculated by using Eq. (5) from the ellipticity, el, (the minor axis divided by the major axis) of the ellipse fitted to the pupil contour.

$$\theta'_{el} = \cos^{-1}(el) \tag{5}$$

An inclination ϕ_{el} of the minor axis was calculated and was replaced as ϕ' in the pupil-cornea reflection method. Therefore, we were able to detect the gaze points using the pupil ellipticity method with the same platform as the pupil-corneal reflection method. However, θ'_{el} has an error because the pupil contour appears to be misaligned due to the refraction of light by the cornea. Therefore, in the present paper, in order to correct the error, the value of el in Eq. (5) was replaced by empirically determined formula: $0.3(el)^2 + 0.7(el)$. This formula was used for all subjects in gaze detection.

The angle of the line of sight, θ'_{el}, was always monitored by the pupil ellipticity method. When θ'_{el} was 30° or less, the gaze direction was determined by the pupil-corneal reflection method. When it exceeded 30°, it was determined by the pupil ellipticity method.

2.3   Judgement of Right or Left Gaze Direction in Pupil Ellipticity Method

In our system, the two optical systems were spaced apart and aligned horizontally as shown Figs. 2 and 3. When the user looks at bilaterally symmetrical positions with respect to the optical systems for example, it cannot judge between right and left because the ellipticity shows the same value. To solve this problem, we propose the

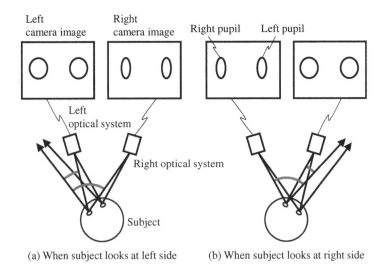

(a) When subject looks at left side   (b) When subject looks at right side

Fig. 2. Relationship between gaze direction to optical systems and pupil ellipticity.

following method. As shown in Fig. 2, when the subject looks at the left side from the optical systems (cameras), the angles between the left optical system and the lines of sight of both eyes are smaller than those of the right optical system. Therefore, the pupil ellipticities in the left camera image become larger than those of the right camera image (Fig. 2(a)). In contrast, when the subject looks at the right side, it shows the opposite tendency (Fig. 2(b)). The pupil ellipticities in both camera images were compared, and the right and left of the gaze direction were judged.

3 Experiment

Three male university subjects participated in the experiment. Three monitors (one 19 in. and two 24 in.) were arranged in the same plane and horizontally as shown in Fig. 3 to present many visual targets in a horizontally wide range. The vertical width of the screens of these monitors were the same. The two optical systems were set up to be attached under the central 19-in. monitor. The subject was asked to be seated at approximately 75 cm from the central monitor. The user calibration was performed by looking at one calibration target presented at the center of the central monitor. The subject was asked to look at 27 (9 in horizontal × 3 in vertical) visual targets evenly arranged on the three monitor screens every approximately one second. During the experiment, the subject was asked to put the chin on a rotational chin-rest stand and to rotate the head so that the subject easily looked at each target. The horizontal angle between the right and left end targets was approximately ±45°.

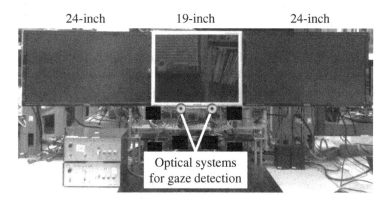

Fig. 3. Positional relationship between optical systems and monitors presenting visual targets.

Figure 4 shows the typical camera images. You can see the elliptical pupils, the sclera reflections (SR), and the corneal reflections (CR).

Left camera image   Right camera image

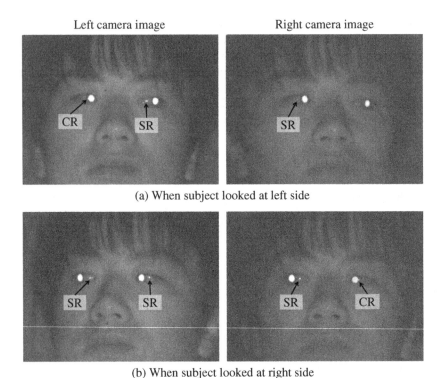

(a) When subject looked at left side

(b) When subject looked at right side

Fig. 4. Typical camera images when subject looked at right or left side. The brightness and contrast of these images have been modified. CR: corneal reflection; SR: scleral reflection.

Figure 5 shows the gaze point distributions of the average of both eyes in subject C for the following four analysis conditions; (a) the pupil-corneal reflection method, (b) the pupil ellipticity method with the judgement of the right and left gaze direction, (c) the combination of the two gaze detection methods without the judgement of right and left, and (d) the combination of the two methods with the right and left judgement, respectively. The dot color is changed for each target. In the pupil-corneal reflection method only (no monitoring by the pupil ellipticity method; Fig. 5(a)), the dots are seen even in the right and left areas, but most were false detections. In addition, many false detections can be seen in the central area. They were caused by the sclera's reflection image being falsely detected as the corneal reflection. In the pupil ellipticity method with the judgement of the right and left gaze direction (Fig. 5(b)), it can be seen that the accuracy was low in the entire areas. Especially, in the central area, the distribution was shifted to the top.

In the combination of the two methods (Figs. 5(c) and (d)), the pupil-corneal reflection method and the pupil ellipticity method were selected with $\theta'_{el} = 30°$ as the border as mentioned before. In the combination method without the judgement right

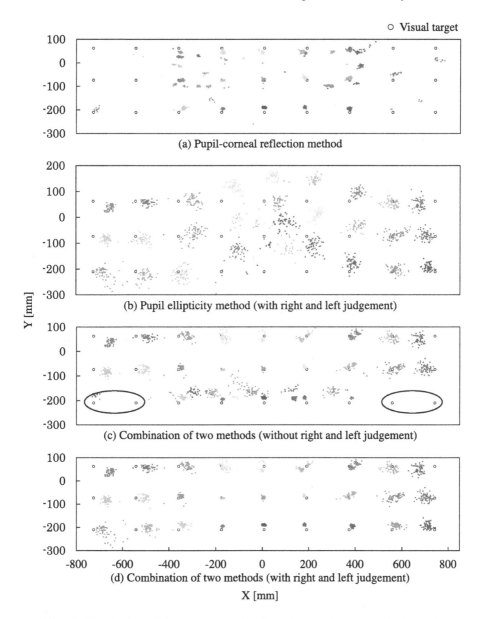

Fig. 5. Distributions of detected gaze points for 27 targets (average of both eyes).

and left (Fig. 5(c)), we assumed that ϕ_{el} was in the range of 0 to 180° since the screens were on the upper of the optical systems. The gaze points for the visual targets in the right and left bottoms, enclosed by the ellipses in this figure panel, were not detected correctly. On the other hand, these errors were almost perfectly corrected by adding the judgment of the right and left (Fig. 5(d)).

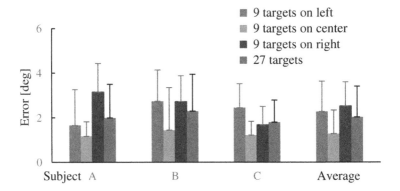

Fig. 6. Gaze detection errors for visual targets on center, right, and left monitor screens.

Figure 6 shows the average gaze detection errors of the nine targets on the center area by the pupil-corneal reflection method and the nine targets on the right or left area by the pupil ellipticity method, respectively. The average error of the three subjects when looking at the right and left areas was 2.40° while that of the center area was 1.27°. The average error and standard deviation for all of 27 visual targets were 1.99 ± 1.50° in subject A, 2.29 ± 1.65° in subject B, 1.79 ± 0.99° in subject C, and 2.02 ± 1.38° in the average of all subjects, respectively.

4   Conclusion

Although the pupil-corneal reflection method is an accurate gaze detection method, the measurable angular range is narrow because the corneal reflection does not appear when the gaze angle is more than ±30 to ±40°. In the present paper, we proposed the combination method of the pupil ellipticity and pupil-corneal reflection methods to enlarge the measurable horizontal gaze direction. The pupil ellipticity method functioned on the same platform as the pupil-corneal reflection method. The two types of methods were switched with the border of 30-deg gaze angle and used to determine the gaze direction, by monitoring the gaze angle obtained by the pupil ellipticity method. In the pupil ellipticity method, we proposed the method to judge the right and left direction of the gaze. We have not yet considered the refraction of the cornea. But the empirically determined formula corrected the gaze accuracy to some extent. The experimental result showed that the horizontal measurable gaze angle was enlarged to ±45°. The average gaze detection error and standard deviation was 2.02 ± 1.38° in the three subjects. The accuracy by the pupil-corneal reflection method was 2.40° (when the subjects looked at the central area) while that of the pupil ellipticity method was 1.27° (when the subjects looked at the right and left areas). The proposed combination method would be suitable for applications where the high accuracy is desired when looking at the front while the low accuracy is allowed when looking at the right or left.

References

1. Fukumoto, K., Tsuzuki, T., Ebisawa, Y.: Improvement of accuracy in remote gaze detection for user wearing eyeglasses using relative position between centers of pupil and corneal sphere. In: Kurosu, M. (ed.) HCI 2015. LNCS, vol. 9170, pp. 13–23. Springer, Cham (2015). https://doi.org/10.1007/978-3-319-20916-6_2
2. Lai, C.C., Shih, S.W., Hung, Y.P.: Hybrid method for 3-D gaze tracking using glint and contour features. IEEE Trans. Circ. Syst. Video Technol. **25**(1), 24–37 (2015)
3. Ebisawa, Y., Fukumoto, K.: Head-free, remote gaze detection system based on pupil-corneal reflection method with using two video cameras – one-point and nonlinear calibrations. In: Kurosu, M. (ed.) HCI 2013. LNCS, vol. 8007, pp. 205–214. Springer, Heidelberg (2013). https://doi.org/10.1007/978-3-642-39330-3_22

Peripheral Distortion on Views in a Fish Tank Could Be Corrected Using a Trapezoidal Glass and Microlens Array

Yukio Ishihara[1(✉)] and Makio Ishihara[2]

[1] Shimane University, 1060 Nishikawatsu-cho, Matsue-shi, Shimane 690-8504, Japan
iyukio@ipc.shimane-u.ac.jp
[2] Fukuoka Institute of Technology, 3-30-1 Wajiro-higashi, Higashi-ku,
Fukuoka 811-0295, Japan
m-ishihara@fit.ac.jp
http://www.fit.ac.jp/~m-ishihara/Lab/

Abstract. In this study, we discuss a way of correcting the distortion of views that look into fish tanks. It is widely known that those views are all seen distorted due to light distortion. That is, light rays traveling inside the tank towards an observer are refracted on the boundaries between different media: water, glass and air. Therefore, those rays come away from the observer, which are however necessary for constructing the observer's view without distortion. To capture the rays, a trapezoidal glass and microlens array are placed at specific positions and an image formed behind the array is taken by a camera. Finally, the observer's view is constructed from the single image without distortion.

Keywords: Distortion correction · Trapezoidal glass · Microlens · Aquarium · Light distortion

1 Introduction

In aquariums, there are various kinds of fish tanks used to display sea creatures. Those tanks are mainly made of flat glass walls and hold tremendous amount of water inside. Although the tanks give many views of things such as fish, plants and rocks, people already know that those views appear distorted due to light distortion. You may feel dizziness and faintness when getting closer to the tank because your view is more badly affected. To deal with it, we previously presented a way to construct distortion-free views from a set of photos of the tank [1]. Those photos are taken at specific positions in advance and are obviously all distorted. Then, they are merged as a single distortion-free view from those photos using image based rendering technique [2]. In that way, multiple photos are required for a distortion-free view. In the next approach, a microlens array was introduced to reduce the number of the photos down to one [3]. However the array needs to be made of germanium in order to raise the refractive index

© Springer Nature Switzerland AG 2019
C. Stephanidis (Ed.): HCII 2019, CCIS 1032, pp. 158–164, 2019.
https://doi.org/10.1007/978-3-030-23522-2_20

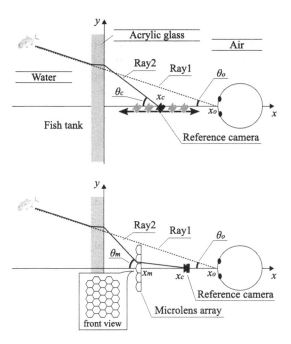

Fig. 1. Our previous approaches to correct the distortion of an observer's view. Multiple photos are required in the first approach (upper) while a single photo is sufficient by placing a microlens array in front of the reference camera in the next approach (lower).

up to 4.0, which is two or three times as high as those of common lens materials. In addition, the high refractive index can be achieved only in infrared light. To make this practical, in this study, a trapezoidal glass is introduced in front of the microlens array.

There have been various studies dealing with light distortion. Treibitz et al. study a way of measuring underwater objects with accuracy [4]. Photos taken by an underwater camera are affected by light distortion in the same way as mentioned above. It leads to inaccuracy of measurement on the photos. To deal with this problem, correspondence from each pixel on the photos to a light ray, called ray-map, is created during the calibration process. The map enables accurate measurement of objects on the photos even though the objects are seen distorted. In contrast, Sedlazeck et al. study a way of creating photo-realistic underwater images by modeling light refraction, light scattering and light attenuation [5]. So far, no studies are found attempting to construct observer's views without distortion. 3D structure estimation of underwater objects studied in [6] could construct those views using the extracted geometric information, but it seems inappropriate to create underwater atmosphere by including drifting dust, ascending air bubbles, tiny creatures and the like. Therefore, in this study, we exploit the image based rendering technique and construct observer's views without distortion.

The rest of this manuscript is organized as follows. In Sect. 2, our new approach is explained comparing with the previous approaches. In Sect. 3, a fish tank, microlens array and trapezoidal glass are simulated on a PC and distortion-free views are constructed. Finally, we give concluding remarks in Sect. 4.

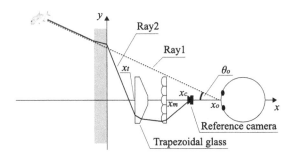

Fig. 2. Our new approach. A trapezoidal glass is placed and relays much angled light rays towards the microlens array.

2   Constructing Distortion-Free Views

Figure 1 shows the sectional top view of a fish tank and illustrates how to construct distortion-free views. In the upper figure, an observer stands in front of a fish tank and looks at a fish. The solid line Ray2 represents a light ray travelling in the tank directly towards the observer. Then it is refracted twice on the boundaries between the water and acrylic glass, and between the acrylic glass and air. Thus even though the observer is looking at the fish, he/she does not see it in that direction represented by the dotted line Ray1. To let him/her see the fish, the light ray Ray2 needs to be captured and displayed to the observer as Ray1.

To be more specific, let x_o be a constant value and the observer's position. Let θ_o be the angular direction of the fish. x_c and θ_c are the position and orientation of a reference camera that captures Ray2. These two variables x_c and θ_c vary as a function of θ_o [1]. In order to capture Ray2, the camera is placed at a series of positions x_c and pointed in θ_c. Then, it takes multiple photos and the color of Ray2 is obtained, which is going to be the same as of Ray1. Finally pixels on the perspective image from the observer, which corresponds to Ray1, are painted with the obtained color. After that, the complete perspective image, or the distortion-free view, is displayed to the observer. As a result, the observer sees the fish in the right direction.

In the next approach shown in Fig. 1 (lower), a single photo is sufficient for distortion-free views. A microlens array is introduced in front of the reference camera. It consists of many tiny lenses arranged in a hexagonal pattern. Each tiny lens forms a perspective image from the lens's position, which appears right behind the microlens array. Then, the reference camera takes that image. In the

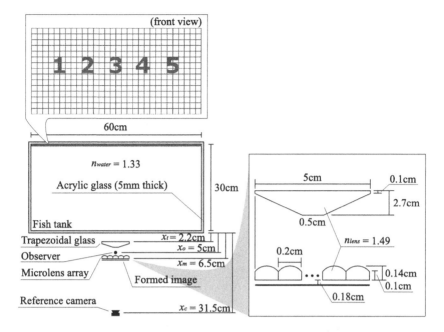

Fig. 3. An experimental setup (sectional top view).

similar way to the previous approach, pixels on the perspective image from the observer are painted from the corresponding pixels on the taken image.

Although it succeeded in reducing the number of photos, there still remains a limit to how much angled light rays the microlens array could receive and relay to the reference camera. When the observer looks in 45° of θ_o, for example, θ_m increases up to 70°. Such angled light rays cannot be received by the microlens array when it is made of common materials such as glass and acrylic glass. In this study, a trapezoidal glass is placed and bends that light rays as shown in Fig. 2 so that the microlens array could receive them.

In the next section, we confirm that the observer's view is constructed without distortion.

3   Simulation

Figure 3 shows an experimental setup for simulation. The fish tank is 60×30 cm in size and 30 cm in depth. The glass of the tank is 5 mm thick. As an object in the tank, a number image is placed on the back surface of the tank, where letters one to five are printed. A reference camera, trapezoidal glass and microlens array comprised of about 900 tiny lenses are placed as shown in the figure. This setup was simulated on a PC and the view from an imaginary observer being at 5 cm from the tank was constructed.

First of all, Fig. 4(a) shows how badly the observer's view is affected by light distortion when any our approaches are not taken. Figure 4(b) shows the view

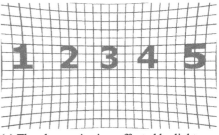

(a) The observer's view affected by light distortion.

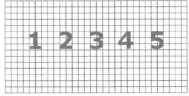

(b) The ideal observer's view that constructed views should appear close to.

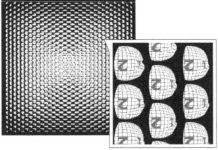

(c) The image formed behind the microlens array.

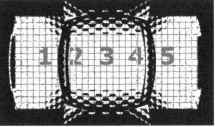

(d) The observer's view constructed by our new approach.

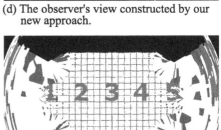

(e) The observer's view constructed by our previous approach.

Fig. 4. Simulation results.

that could be seen if no tank and no water, but only the number image existed. This is also the one that the observer's view should be constructed as close to as possible.

To construct the observer's view without distortion, the reference camera took an image formed behind the microlens array, which is shown in Fig. 4(c). The image includes about 900 circular segments and each of them represents a perspective view from the corresponding tiny lens. Figure 4(d) shows the observer's view that has been constructed from (c) in the way mentioned in Sect. 2. In comparison, Fig. 4(e) shows the observer's view constructed based on our previous approach in Fig. 1 (lower). The central part is successfully constructed, but the peripheral is not. This is because much angled light rays, which are represented by Ray2 and are as high as $70°$ in θ_m, cannot be relayed towards the reference camera. In our new approach, the peripheral part is successfully constructed as shown in Fig. 4(d). However some parts sill remain a problem and are left blank between '1' and '2', and between '4' and '5'. This is mainly due to the edge of the upper base of the trapezoidal glass that causes a sudden change to the direction of the light rays and breaks the smoothness of the constructed view. In the future work, we will improve our approach for complete construction of distortion-free views.

4 Conclusions

In this study, we discussed a way of correcting the distortion of views that look into fish tanks. To correct it, a trapezoidal glass and microlens array are placed at specific positions and an image formed behind the microlens array is taken by a camera. Finally, the observer's view is constructed from the single image. We performed a simulation on a PC and confirmed that the observer's view was successfully constructed without distortion, but except for some parts off-center. This is due to the edge of the trapezoidal glass. Thus, further improvements to our approach are necessary for complete distortion-free views.

References

1. Ishihara, Y., Ishihara, M.: Correcting distortion of views into aquarium and its accuracy. IEICE Trans. Inf. Syst. **E97.D**(9), 2552–2553 (2014)
2. Gortler, S.J., Grzeszczuk, R., Szeliski, R., Cohen, M.F.: The lumigraph. In: Proceedings of SIGGRAPH 1996, pp. 43–54 (1996)
3. Ishihara, Y., Ishihara, M.: Correcting distortion of views into fish tanks based on a microlens array. In: Proceedings of 33rd International Technical Conference on Circuits/Systems, Computers and Communications, pp. 785–788 (2018)
4. Treibitz, T., Schechner, Y., Kunz, C., Singh, H.: Flat refractive geometry. IEEE Trans. Pattern Anal. Mach. Intell. **34**(1), 51–65 (2012)

5. Sedlazeck, A., Koch, R.: Simulating deep sea underwater images using physical models for light attenuation, scattering, and refraction. In: Proceedings of Vision, Modeling, and Visualization Workshop 2011, pp. 49–56 (2011)
6. Kang, L., Wu, L., Yang, Y.-H.: Two-view underwater structure and motion for cameras under flat refractive interfaces. In: Fitzgibbon, A., Lazebnik, S., Perona, P., Sato, Y., Schmid, C. (eds.) ECCV 2012. LNCS, vol. 7575, pp. 303–316. Springer, Heidelberg (2012). https://doi.org/10.1007/978-3-642-33765-9_22

A Novel Semantically Congruent Audiovisual Interface for Assisting Brain-Machine Interface (BMI) Performance Enhancement

Sungyong Kim[1(✉)] and Jeounghoon Kim[1,2]

[1] Graduate School of Culture Technology, KAIST, Daejeon 34141, South Korea
simonksy@kaist.ac.kr
[2] School of Humanities and Social Sciences, KAIST, Daejeon 34141
South Korea

Abstract. Brain-Machine Interfaces utilize distinct brain patterns as control commands. However, many BMIs suffer from low performance issue even with the state-of-the-art classification algorithms in hand. Herein, we propose a novel BMI interface using semantically congruent audiovisual stimuli involving contextual motions to assist BMI performance enhancement. We designed two motion classes of "up" and "down" using two paradigms: visual only and congruent audiovisual pair. We first compared the level of spectral discernibility between the two given commands within each paradigm using frontal, temporal, and occipital channels. We then applied these paradigms onto a EEG-controlled drone system. Although the power spectral density did not show any statistically significant differences, the subjects' drone controlling performance increased by 16% with the audiovisual interface compared to the visual only interface. Thus, this semantically congruent audiovisual BMI interface using contextual motion stimuli may be used as a supportive tool for enhancing BMI performance.

Keywords: Brain-Machine Interface (BMI) · Electroencephalogram (EEG) · Multisensory integration · Audiovisual congruence

1 Introduction

For several years, non-invasive BMI systems have utilized ensemble of electroencephalograms (EEGs) to determine the intent of the user and translate them into commands, providing an additional channel for communication and control. Due to its non-muscular nature, BMI was primarily conceived as an option for restoring functions to those with neuromuscular disabilities [1, 2]. Recently, with the advent of low-cost, wireless consumer EEG headsets (NeuroSky, Emotiv, OpenBCI etc.) and increased computing power of mobile devices, BMIs became a useful supplementary channel of communication in special circumstances for those without disabilities [3].

Generally, BMI design process requires testing combinations of different cognitive tasks and machine learning algorithms to achieve satisfactory performance [4–6]. However, numerous cognitive and psychological factors such as concentration, frustration, and distraction constantly add undesired noise to EEG signals, making it more difficult to detect discernible changes [7]. This fundamental problem of ambiguous

© Springer Nature Switzerland AG 2019
C. Stephanidis (Ed.): HCII 2019, CCIS 1032, pp. 165–171, 2019.
https://doi.org/10.1007/978-3-030-23522-2_21

nature of EEG response requires longer subject training time with more trial sessions and delays the overall BMI design process regardless of chosen cognitive task and classifying algorithm.

Encoding and interpreting cognitively significant events from environmental cues by combining each sensory modality are one of the primary functions of brain's information processing. Several studies ranging from single cell studies to fMRI studies report that heteromodal brain areas interact effectively to process spatially, temporally, and semantically congruent audiovisual stimuli in order to enhance the salience of contextually meaningful events [8–11]. Previous EEG studies also reported audiovisual integration effects in early sensory processing time window in alpha band activity of several cortical sites providing evidences of the effectiveness of multisensory integration [12–15].

In this paper, we propose a novel audiovisual interface using semantically congruent audiovisual stimuli involving contextual motions "up" and "down" to assist BMI performance enhancement. By comparing the spectral discernibility and measuring BMI task performance between visual only and audiovisual paradigms, we show a robust performance enhancement effect of the audiovisual congruence.

2   Materials and Methods

2.1   Experiment 1

Subjects. A total of 16 undergraduate students with normal or corrected-to-normal hearing participated in experiment 1 in exchange for course credit. The subjects were naïve as to the specific purpose of this study. Every aspect of this experiment was carried out in accordance to the regulations of the KAIST Institutional Review Board (IRB).

Apparatus and Stimuli. An Emotiv EPOC+ headset and Emotiv Pro software were used to collect the EEG data from 6 electrodes based on the international 10–20 system (F3, T7, O1, O2, T8, F4) with the sampling rate of 256 Hz. The recordings were carried out in an acoustically and electromagnetically shielded room to minimize the effects of various noise sources.

The visual stimuli were sinusoidal gratings generated using PsychoPy [16]. The size of gratings was approximately 9.65° in the viewing distance of 50 cm with the spatial frequency of 0.83 cycles/deg. The gratings moved upward or downward according to the command. The auditory stimuli were Shepard tones matching the directions of the sinusoidal gratings (ascending or descending tones).

Experimental Procedures. The subjects participated in two sessions: visual task, and audiovisual task. In the visual task, subjects were told to fixate the gaze on the superimposed red cross on the sinusoidal motion and actively concentrate on the upward or downward motions as guided on the monitor. At the beginning of each trial, a text message of "Up" or "Down" appeared for 5 s to let participants be prepared for the task. Next, a red fixation cross appeared on the center of the screen for 1 s as a baseline period, followed by 8 s of "Up" or "Down" trial period with the sinusoidal motion. Each command trial was repeated 30 times, comprising total of 60 epochs for the session. The audiovisual task started with a simple congruency matching task to ensure that subjects learn the audiovisual semantic association. Here, the subjects were presented with a random pair of visual and auditory stimuli in either congruent or incongruent manner as shown in Table 1. The subjects pressed "O" or "X" key on the keyboard according to the congruency ("O" for congruent, "X" for incongruent). The session lasted until the subjects reached 20 consecutive correct answers to ensure the audiovisual association is attained. Next, the subjects actively concentrated on the upward and downward motion 30 times respectively while attending to the congruent audiovisual stimuli pair.

Table 1. The audiovisual matching rules.

Visual	Auditory	Correct answer
Up	Up	O
Up	Down	X
Down	Up	X
Down	Down	O

Data Processing. The acquired raw EEG signals were processed using EEGLAB [17]. Individual continuous recordings were band-pass filtered with the cutoff frequencies of 0.1 Hz and 30 Hz. We then ran ICA in order to decompose the multichannel EEG data into distinct components. Artifactual components were removed using the SASICA plugin [18]. Additional artifact removal was done by eye inspection of each epochs. The epochs of 8 s were extracted for each stimulus condition from the stimulus onset (visual up, visual down, audiovisual up, audiovisual down). After rejecting one subject's data due to severe channel artifacts, a total of 60 datasets (15 Ss × 4 conditions) were collected for multiple subject study.

In the study, the channel spectra for frontal (F3, F4), temporal (T7, T8), and occipital (O1, O2) regions were averaged and compared by each channel using two study designs: 'visual up vs visual down' and 'audiovisual up vs audiovisual down'. The power spectrum density (PSD) was plotted for delta (1–3 Hz), theta (4–7 Hz), alpha (8–12 Hz), and beta (13–25 Hz) bands. The gamma band was excluded as the EEG headset used here did not have any separate channel recording neck muscle activity which can interfere with the gamma band activities. A non-parametric permutation statistics with FDR correction method was used. The alpha significance level was set to 0.05.

2.2   Experiment 2

Subjects. A total of 11 undergraduate students participated in experiment 2 in exchange for course credit. All subjects had normal vision and hearing and were naive to the purpose of the study. Every experimental procedure was performed under KAIST IRB.

Apparatus and Stimuli. The Emotiv EPOC+ headset and a compatible drone were used to send the acquired EEG signals to the drone. The subjects were seated in a shielded room to block ambient noises and power line noise. The same visual and audiovisual interfaces using sinusoidal motion and Shepard tones were used.

Experimental Procedures. The procedures were identical to the experiment 1 except that each 30 trials of either "up" or "down" command were now used to control the drone pilot task. In the visual drone task, the subjects actively concentrated on sinusoidal motions of "up" and "down" 30 times respectively which were directly sent to the drone movement. The audiovisual trial began with the simple audiovisual matching task of sinusoidal motions and Shepard tones followed by congruent audiovisual up & down trials ensuring the subjects learn the semantic audiovisual congruence beforehand.

Performance Measure. The drone control performance of each command P_{Com} was calculated by averaging each participant's drone control accuracy measure which is the number of correct movements divided by the number of total attempts. Equation (1) below shows how the performance of a given command P_{Com} was measured, where n is the number of subjects, NT is the number of trials, N_i is the number of correct hits of the i th subject. in this study there were 4 commands, 'visual up (VU)', 'visual down (VD)', 'audiovisual up (AVU)', and 'audiovisual down (AVD)'.

$$P_{Com} = \frac{1}{n} \cdot \sum_{i=1}^{n} \frac{N_i}{N_T} \tag{1}$$

3   Experimental Results

The average power spectral density of visual and audiovisual tasks on selected channels (F3, F4, T7, T8, O1, O2) are shown in Fig. 1. In the visual task, the alpha band PSD of 'down' command was higher than 'up' command in right frontal, temporal regions and bilateral occipital region. Similarly in the audiovisual task, the alpha band PSD values were higher in bilateral frontal, temporal and occipital regions. However, overall analysis of spectral difference between 'visual up' vs 'visual down' and 'audiovisual up' vs 'audiovisual down' did not show any statistical significance using permutation statistics with FDR multiple comparison correction method. We believe this may be due to the relatively long epoch window (8 s) which could have averaged out any local spectral changes.

Although there were no discriminative features found in the spectral analysis, the paired sample t-test revealed that the subjects could yield statistically significant higher performance rates of drone control in audiovisual paradigm than in visual paradigm. In the case of 'up' command, there was a significant increase in the drone control performance for audiovisual up (M = 0.56, SD = 0.14) than visual up (M = 0.39, SD = 0.16); t(10) = 3.25, p = 0.009. Similar paired sample t-test on 'down' command showed a significant increase in the drone control performance for audiovisual down (M = 0.77, SD = 0.14), than visual down (M = 0.62, SD = 0.20); t(10) = 2.66, p = 0.024. Figure 2 shows the average performance scores of 'up' and 'down'

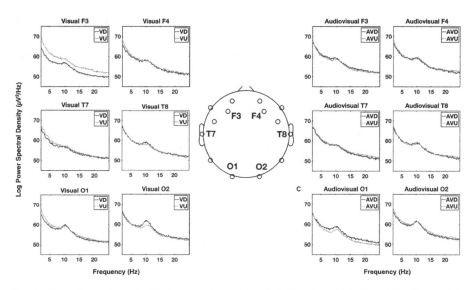

Fig. 1. Experiment 1 results. Each graph shows delta (1–3 Hz), theta (4–7 Hz), alpha (8 – 12 Hz), and beta (13 – 25 Hz) spectral responses of upward and downward motion commands. In visual task, the alpha band PSD of 'down' command was higher than 'up' command in F4, T8, O1, and O2. In audiovisual task, the alpha band PSD of 'down' was higher in bilateral frontal, temporal, and occipital regions.

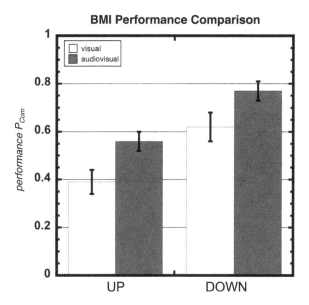

Fig. 2. BMI drone-piloting performance results using visual and audiovisual paradigms. Audiovisual commands enhanced the P_{Com} of "Up" by 17% and "Down" by 15%. The error bars denote standard errors.

commands comparing the visual and audiovisual trials with standard errors. The average performance of 'visual up' was 0.39 ± 0.05 whereas 'audiovisual up' rated 0.56 ± 0.04 which was about 17% performance increase. Similarly, 'audiovisual down' scored 0.77 ± 0.04 which was about 15% higher than 'visual down' of 0.62 ± 0.06. In summary, the subjects could control the drone more easily using the contextual motions in the audiovisual interface than the visual only interface with the average performance increase of 16%. This result indicates that factors other than spectral differences in the audiovisual congruence of contextual motion stimuli could have affected the subjects BMI performance which we will discuss in the discussion section below.

4 Discussion

In this study, we proposed a novel audiovisual interface using semantically congruent motion stimuli to help subjects maintain selected command by increasing the likelihood of contextual cues. The results showed that subjects could yield higher BMI performance in audiovisual interface with the performance increase of up to 17%.

Audiovisual integration is known to be a fast and synergistic process that significantly modulates the brain's interpretation of environmental cues [19]. Previous studies reported several perceptual modulation effects of visual cues on auditory stimuli and vice versa. The McGurk effect showed that our interpretation of auditory stimuli can drastically change just by seeing different lip motions [20]. Shimojo and Shams reported that sound can alter several aspects of vision such as intensity, duration or presence of visual motion [21]. In similar vein, Chen, Yeh, and Spence reported that audiovisual semantic congruence can help distinguish an ambiguous stimuli [22]. These studies indicate that different sensory modalities do not operate independently of each other, but rather work in tandem to significantly affect the primary experience of multisensory environmental cues leading to distinct unequivocal interpretations of given sensory input.

In this study, we attempted to adopt the previous findings above and investigate the effects of those principles on users' BMI performance enhancement. Although the spectral analysis done in this study could not confirm any particular increase of spectral differences in audiovisual congruence, the evident performance increase in actual BMI task imply that developing BMI interfaces based on cognitive tasks with semantic audiovisual congruence could provide a certain level of assistance to users, enhancing the overall performance.

References

1. Lebedev, M.A., Nicolelis, M.A.: Brain-machine interfaces: past, present and future. Trends Neurosci. **29**(9), 536–546 (2006)
2. Wolpaw, J., Birbaumer, N., McFarland, D.J., Pfurtscheller, G., Vaughan, T.M.: Brain-computer interfaces for communication and controls. Clin. Neurophysiol. **113**, 767–791 (2002)

3. Debener, S., et al.: How about taking a low-cost, small, and wireless EEG for a walk? Psychophysiology **49**(11), 1617–1621 (2012)
4. Lotte, F., et al.: A review of classification algorithms for EEG-based brain-computer interfaces. J. Neural Eng. **4**(2), R1–R13 (2007)
5. Johannesen, J.K., et al.: Machine learning identification of EEG features predicting working memory performance in schizophrenia and healthy adults. Neuropsychiatr. Electrophysiol. **2**, 3 (2016)
6. Samuel, O.W., et al.: Motor imagery classification of upper limb movements based on spectral domain features of EEG patterns. In: 2017 39th Annual International Conference of the IEEE Engineering in Medicine and Biology Society (EMBC). IEEE (2017)
7. Curran, E.: Learning to control brain activity: a review of the production and control of EEG components for driving brain–computer interface (BCI) systems. Brain Cogn. **51**(3), 326–336 (2003)
8. Czigler, I., Balázs, L.: Event-related potentials and audiovisual stimuli: multimodal interactions. NeuroReport **12**(2), 223–226 (2001)
9. Hein, G., et al.: Object familiarity and semantic congruency modulate responses in cortical audiovisual integration areas. J. Neurosci. **27**(30), 7881–7887 (2007)
10. Calvert, G.A.: Crossmodal processing in the human brain: insights from functional neuroimaging studies. Cereb. Cortex **11**(12), 1110–1123 (2001)
11. Meredith, M.A., Stein, B.E.: Interactions among converging sensory inputs in the superior colliculus. Science **221**(4608), 389–391 (1983)
12. Doehrmann, O., Naumer, M.J.: Semantics and the multisensory brain: how meaning modulates processes of audio-visual integration. Brain Res. **1242**, 136–150 (2008)
13. Molholm, S., et al.: Multisensory auditory–visual interactions during early sensory processing in humans: a high-density electrical mapping study. Cogn. Brain. Res. **14**(1), 115–128 (2002)
14. Talsma, D., Doty, T.J., Woldorff, M.G.: Selective attention and audiovisual integration: is attending to both modalities a prerequisite for early integration? Cereb. Cortex **17**(3), 679–690 (2006)
15. van Driel, J., et al.: Interregional alpha-band synchrony supports temporal cross-modal integration. Neuroimage **101**, 404–415 (2014)
16. Peirce, J.W.: PsychoPy—psychophysics software in Python. J. Neurosci. Methods **162**(1), 8–13 (2007)
17. Delorme, A., Makeig, S.: EEGLAB: an open source toolbox for analysis of single-trial EEG dynamics including independent component analysis. J. Neurosci. Methods **134**(1), 9–21 (2004)
18. Chaumon, M., Bishop, D.V., Busch, N.A.: A practical guide to the selection of independent components of the electroencephalogram for artifact correction. J. Neurosci. Methods **250**, 47–63 (2015)
19. Stein, B.E., Stanford, T.R.: Multisensory integration: current issues from the perspective of the single neuron. Nat. Rev. Neurosci. **9**(4), 255–266 (2008)
20. McGurk, H., MacDonald, J.: Hearing lips and seeing voices. Nature **264**(5588), 746–748 (1976)
21. Shimojo, S., Shams, L.: Sensory modalities are not separate modalities: plasticity and interactions. Curr. Opin. Neurobiol. **11**(4), 505–509 (2001)
22. Chen, Y.C., Yeh, S.L., Spence, C.: Crossmodal constraints on human perceptual awareness: auditory semantic modulation of binocular rivalry. Front. Psychol. **2**, 212 (2011)

Tactile Presentation Scheme Based on Physiological Characteristics of the Fingertip

Yoichi Yamazaki$^{(\boxtimes)}$ ⓘ, Masataka Imura, and Noriko Nagata ⓘ

Kwansei Gakuin University, 2-1, Gakuen, Sanda, Hyogo 6691337, Japan
y-yamazaki@kwansei.ac.jp

Abstract. In the case of the product purchase decision making in e-commerce, the tactile sensation a user can obtain from products is restricted. Our goal is to construct a framework for tactile measurement and presentation to remove such restrictions. To realize high-accuracy tactile presentation, we analyze the mechanical characteristics of the fingertip. We measured and analyzed the interactional force of the contact face when stroking the surface of fabrics. We found a filter-bank like structure of vibration information processing on the fingertip. In addition, we propose a tactile presentation scheme based on this physiological characteristic. To evaluate the validity of the proposed scheme, we produced a tactile presentation device for fabrics and evaluated the reproducibility of tactile sensation. The results demonstrate that it is possible to represent basic material texture characteristics, such as roughness and softness. This study provides key technological knowledge for constructing a framework for tactile measurement and presentation. Furthermore, this study promotes the use of sensory information relative to tactile sensation in e-commerce, such as the visual and auditory senses.

Keywords: Tactile presentation · Biomechanical analysis · Fingertip

1 Introduction

Recently, diversification of user needs has occurred with the globalization of the market environment accompanied by the spread of e-commerce [1]. In consideration of product purchase decision making in e-commerce, the sensory information a user can obtain from products is restricted. Despite the fact that tactile sensation is important information relative to the value of a product, there is no existing framework for measurement and presentation.

Tactile presentation using vibration is effective when mounting on a small communication device, such as a smartphone [2]. In particular, a DC motor reproduces vibrations in a wide frequency band as flat [3]. The vibrations sensed by mechanoreceptors that have different frequency characteristics [4]. However, presenting vibration using a DC motor makes it impossible to independently control vibration, which corresponds to the frequency characteristics of the mechano-receptor. Moreover, it is unclear how to realize tactile presentation using a DC motor.

© Springer Nature Switzerland AG 2019
C. Stephanidis (Ed.): HCII 2019, CCIS 1032, pp. 172–179, 2019.
https://doi.org/10.1007/978-3-030-23522-2_22

In this study, we demonstrate the vibration features of an interactional force occurring while stroking a surface texture with a fingertip. We propose a physiological characteristics-based construction scheme for tactile presentation that is realized using multiple vibrators. Based on the proposed construction scheme, we realize the tactile presentation of fabrics, which is desirable in the e-commerce field. We also evaluate the validity of the tactile presentation.

2 Mechanical Information Processing of Fingertip

We developed a specialized device [5] to measure contact force that occurs on the contact surface between the fingertip and surface texture during a stroking movement (Fig. 1). This device simultaneously measures frictional (horizontal) force and press (vertical) force while stroking an object's surface. To clear the vibration characteristics of the fingertip, we measured and analyzed interactional force when stroking the surface of fabrics.

2.1 Participants

Twenty healthy college and graduate students (15 males and five females; 22.2 ± 0.97 years)

2.2 Materials

Thirteen fabrics (Fig. 2) were included in a texture sample set provided by Takei Scientific Instruments Co. Ltd.

2.3 Frequency Analysis

First, we performed frequency analysis of the measured data using Welch's method to obtain the frequency characteristics of each fabric (Fig. 3). Note that differences in spectrum contribute to the formation of tactile sensation for each fabric.

To represent the difference as features, principal component analysis was applied to the entire spectrum set. We found that the vibration of the contact force can be expressed as a multichannel filter bank-like structure in time-frequency space (Fig. 4).

The power of the frequency corresponding to each of the six bases was obtained as the feature value. The differences between the samples of these features were visualized using multi-dimensional scaling (Fig. 5). We confirmed that the features provide sufficient information to represent differences in tactile sensations.

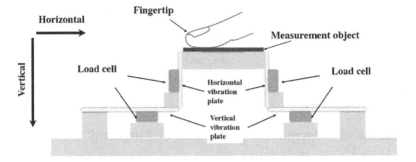

Fig. 1. Schematic of measurement device

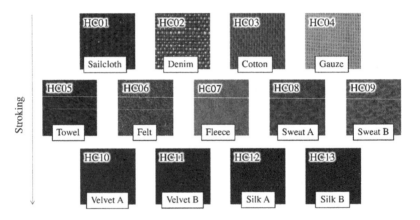

Fig. 2. Fabric samples

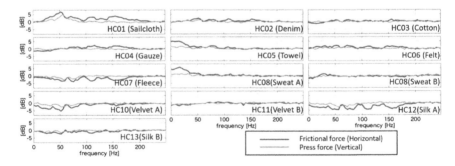

Fig. 3. Frequency characteristics of interactional force vibration

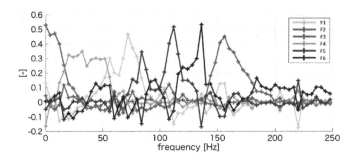

Fig. 4. Plot of the basis set of PCA (six components) of the frictional force of fingertip when stroking fabrics

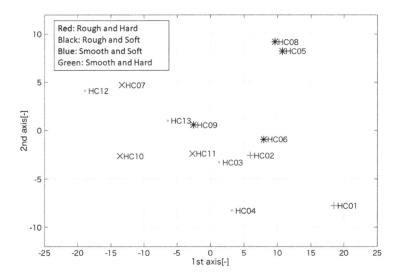

Fig. 5. Distribution of fabric samples in six-dimensional feature space

3 Tactile Presentation Scheme Based on Vibration Characteristics of Fingertip

3.1 Basic Concept

The result shown in Fig. 4 suggests that vibration during stroking can be represented using a number of vibrators that correspond to the passing frequencies of the bandpass filters that comprise the filter bank.

This makes it possible to control tactile presentation performance relative to the number of vibrators because the contact force is the primary information comprising tactile sensation, and the reproduction accuracy of the vibration corresponds to tactile presentation performance.

In this study, we developed a tactile presentation device based on the vibration characteristics of the fingertip (Fig. 6).

3.2   Implementation

To control each element of the features independently using a DC motor, the control parameters (motor type, voltage, and duty ratio) of the pulse wave modulation were searched comprehensively. As a result, we were able to present each element of the features with two intensity levels, except for a part (Table 1). The control parameters were determined from the difference of features with H12 for four samples (H01, H02, H05, and H12) with different features, as shown in Fig. 5 (Table 2). Thus, the standard material used the silk-like fabric, which provides the same tactile sensation as H12.

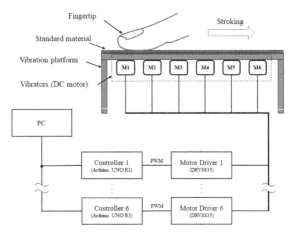

Fig. 6. Schematic of tactile presentation device based on proposed presentation scheme

Table 1. Enhancement intensity of the element of features using DC motor.

Motor ID	Vibration Intensity	Degree of Enhancement					
		F1 (56–80Hz)	F2 (0–16Hz)	F3 (144–180Hz)	F4 (20–52Hz)	F5 (84–116Hz)	F6 (120–140Hz)
M1	High	34.7	−5.1	2.6	4.0	−4.6	−9.4
	Low	12.0	−0.7	−5.7	3.2	−14.5	−4.3
M2	High	−10.2	30.9	1.6	−5.4	8.4	38.1
	Low	−5.2	20.2	−2.1	−0.2	17.4	37.8
M3	High	4.8	0.6	25.7	−3.0	−2.9	12.0
	Low	3.0	−0.7	13.4	−1.4	1.7	0.4
M4	High	−0.4	0.3	−2.4	9.2	−2.3	5.3
	Low	–	–	–	–	–	–
M5	High	−5.5	−1.3	12.6	1.7	41.4	11.1
	Low	−1.8	4.3	8.1	6.2	28.1	8.1
M6	High	2.7	0.9	−4.1	−2.3	9.4	21.9
	Low	−6.6	1.6	2.3	−1.9	4.0	9.7

Table 2. Control state of each experimental sample.

Stimuli	Control state					
	M2 (0–16 Hz)	M4 (20–52 Hz)	M1 (56–80 Hz)	M5 (84–116 Hz)	M6 (120–140 Hz)	M3 (144–180 Hz)
HC01 (Sailcloth)	Off	High	High	High	High	High
HC03 (Cotton)	Off	High	Low	Low	Low	Low
HC05 (Towel)	High	High	Low	Low	Off	Low
HC12 (Silk A)	Off	Off	Off	Off	Off	Off

4 Evaluation of Proposed Scheme

To evaluate the capability of the proposed tactile presentation scheme, we performed a subjective evaluation of each of the presented tactile sensations and the tactile sensation obtained from real fabrics. We also evaluated the similarity between these tactile sensations.

4.1 Participants

Four healthy college and graduate students (two males and two females; 23 ± 1.4 years) participated in this evaluation.

4.2 Materials

Four fabrics were evaluated (Table 2).

4.3 Experiment 1: Subjective Evaluation

Procedure
The participants sensed the tactile perception from the tactile presentation device and performed a 5-point Likert scale evaluation of 12 tactile impression words for each sample. Then, the participants stroked the real fabric surface and evaluated the tactile impression words.

Results
To evaluate the effect of vibration presentation, we demonstrated the differences in the evaluation values relative to the reference samples, e.g., H12 and the standard material (Fig. 7). The vertical axis is the amount of change from the evaluation value relative to the reference sample (e.g., H12 and standard material). The results indicate that the produced tactile presentation can reproduce the differences in tactile sensations for different samples.

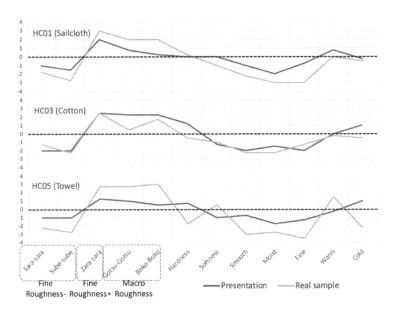

Fig. 7. Reproducibility of tactile sensation relative to the 12 tactile impression words

4.4   Experiment 2: Similarity Evaluation

Procedure

First, the participants sensed the tactile perception from the tactile presentation device. Then, the participants selected a sample similar to the presented perception from four fabric samples.

Results

We confirmed that the presentation device could present the tactile perception of HC02 (cotton) with good accuracy (Table 3). Note that HC01 (sailcloth) was evaluated as HC02 (cotton) with less roughness than HC01 (sailcloth). Although the unevenness of the surface of HC01 (sailcloth) is large, the standard material has a flat surface. We believe that this result was caused by the strong perception of this difference in the surface condition.

Although the surfaces of HC01 (sailcloth) and HC05 (towel) have the same degree of unevenness, the concordance rate was relatively high. HC05 (towel) is a soft material, and the surface structure deforms when stroked, which suggests that deformation can be expressed by vibration.

Note that M2 could not selectively control the feature amount of F2 and may have contributed to the reduction in concordance rate. This was due to the motor structure. In addition, the motor type and control method must be considered to realize tactile presentation with higher accuracy.

Table 3. Evaluation of similarity between presented tactile and actual tactile sensations.

		Selection				rate of concordance
		HC01	HC02	HC05	HC12	
Presentation	HC01	0	3	1	0	0%
	HC02	0	3	1	0	75%
	HC05	2	0	2	0	50%
	HC12	0	0	0	4	100%

5   Conclusions

We have demonstrated the filter-bank-like structure of vibration information processing on the fingertip. In addition, we have proposed a physiological characteristics-based construction method for tactile presentation. To evaluate the availability of the proposed method, we produced a tactile representation device for fabrics. Evaluation results indicate that it is possible to represent basic material texture, e.g., roughness and softness. As a result, we confirmed the validity of the proposed method.

Acknowledgement. This research is the Center of Innovation Program from Japan Science and Technology Agency, JST. This work was supported by a Grant-in-Aid of Research from the Telecommunications Advancement Foundation.

References

1. BIS: International Banking and Financial Market Developments. BIS Quarterly Review (2018)
2. Yatani, K., Truong, K.N.: SemFeel: a user interface with semantic tactile feedback for mobile touch-screen devices. In: Proceedings of ACM Symposium on User Interface Software and Technology (UIST 2009), pp. 111–120 (2009)
3. Yem, V., Okazaki, R., Kajimoto, H.: Vibration presentation using a DC motor. Trans. Virtual Reality Soci. Jpn. **21**(4), 555–564 (2016)
4. Genscheider, G.A., Balanowski, S.J., Hardick, K.R.: The frequency selectivity of information-processing channels in the tactile sensory system. Somatosens. Mot. Res. **13**, 191–201 (2001)
5. Asai, T., Yamazaki, Y., Tani, Y., Tobitani, K., Yamamoto, H., Nagata, N.: Sensibility evaluation of an exfoliating lotion with supreme tactile impression during wiping. In: IFSCC 2018 CONGRESS, P-S5-373 (2018)

Security and Trust

The Relationship Between Usability and Biometric Authentication in Mobile Phones

Carly Grace Allen$^{(\boxtimes)}$ and Sashidharan Komandur

Norwegian University of Science and Technology, 2815 Gjøvik, Norway
carlygraceallen@gmail.com, sash.kom@gmail.com

Abstract. It is estimated that over 1 billion people are active mobile phone users in 2018. When using a mobile phone, there are a variety of ways to authenticate and "secure" the device, and biometric authentication is becoming an increasingly common way to do this, however, biometric authentication is not always as usable as it could be. Both usability and security are important, yet many people believe that there is a trade-off between the two. The focus of this paper was to better understand usability, computer security, and within computer security more specifically biometric authentication, and how all three can work together to create systems that are both usable and secure. A survey and interviews were conducted based on previous research to understand perceptions from the general population, usability experts, and security/biometrics experts. The results do indicate that there is indeed a perceived trade-off between usability and computer security.

Keywords: Usability · Biometrics · Authentication · Security · Mobile phone · User experience · Computer security

1 Introduction

Both usability and computer security are important, yet many people believe that there is a trade-off between the two [1, 12, 15]. A device that isn't usable won't be used, and if a device isn't secure, then it will be rendered useless [1]. This can often be seen with regards to mobile phones. With mobile phones being accessed and used by so many people, sometimes over 100 times a day [2], it is vital for these devices to have authentication methods that are both secure and usable. Biometric authentication is a growing option; however, it is not as widely adopted as many had thought it would be. Many people still rely on passwords, pins, patterns, or no authentication method because these are the methods they are used to. The problem that comes with these methods is that often, they are not very secure. Patterns leave smudges on screens, pins and passwords are often only a couple of digits or letters, and no authentication is an easy option. Biometric authentication could solve these problems. In theory, biometrics are both secure and usable, however in practice this is not always the case. Thus, it is important to understand how we can increase the usability and security of biometric authentication together so that there is a stronger option for securing mobile phones.

C. Stephanidis (Ed.): HCII 2019, CCIS 1032, pp. 183–189, 2019.
https://doi.org/10.1007/978-3-030-23522-2_23

2 Background

2.1 A Trade-Off Between Usability and Security?

When computers were first built, they were predominantly used by experts, so security was a concern, not usability. Now with computers ranging in sizes, functions, and being used by millions of people, usability as well as security are important concerns. If it is not usable, it won't be used, and if it's not secure, then it will become useless [1]. There has been debate as to whether there is a trade-off between security and usability. Some research has stated that there is a trade-off showing that usability reduces security [10], that usability and security have different goals [14], or that this trade-off poses serious problems for system designers [15]. However, a majority of research today seems to go the other way; it predominantly depends on how security and usability are integrated into systems. The "'received wisdom' on the inherent conflict between usability and security goes against common sense" [1].

Discussions surrounding a trade-off between usability and security are often shallow [11]. There isn't discussion on the level of security that will be obtained and how usability will "hurt it" [11]. But usability can improve security. When usability and security are both incorporated into the design process, they can have the same goals [12]. And with an increased focus on users, there has been more research on the usability of security systems. Users make errors, so systems need to be designed to be either insensitive to those errors, to use metaphors and such to allow users to use security software more intuitively or provide users with the knowledge needed to make informed decisions [1]. When a system can interpret user desires correctly, then usability and security are working in harmony [12].

One problem that seems to arise is with the word "trade-off" itself. The way that security and usability are viewed must be changed and not thought of as a trade-off. When they are not integrated into the design process and are only seen as features, then there will of course be a trade-off. However, when viewed as qualities instead of features and are integrated into the design and development process, the perceived "trade-off" between usability and security can be reduced [12].

2.2 Biometric Security

Biometric authentication is about authenticating a person for who they are, not by what they remember or what they have with them [13]. It can be a more long-term and cost-efficient authentication method, and in theory it should be both secure and usable [17]. This is not always the case though. Each biometric trait has their own pros and cons, and some issues that can come up with biometrics are noise, distinctiveness, and non-universality [13, 17]. These issues can cause problems in the enrollment and authentication modes [13].

A few errors that can arise in the enrollment and authentication modes are failure to enroll (due to noise, distinctiveness, or not being able to use a specific biometric trait), false acceptance rate (accepting a non-match as a match), and false rejection rate (not accepting the enrolled trait) [19]. These errors can greatly influence the usability of a mobile phone, and a balance is needed between the usability and security [16]. It is crucial when it comes to user safety; however, user interfaces for authentication often encourage either secure or insecure behavior depending on its security requirements [16].

2.3   Usability and Biometric Authentication in Mobile Phone Devices

Usability issues arise from a variety of sources. One large usability issue with regards to biometric authentication can come from the detection error trade-off curve. Unlike passwords, pins, and patterns that are either 100% correct or not, biometrics are based on how close of a match it is to the collected template from the enrollment mode [19]. The threshold that has been established will decide if the biometric is to be accepted or not. The accuracy and thresholds in biometric authentication do not always relate to the ease of use or convenience that users are used to and are looking for [19].

Some people believe that biometrics are not the default authentication mode due to usability and user experience [18]. Many users have not experienced a noticeable difference when using biometrics than using the authentication methods they have already been using [18]. A very common problem with usability in biometric authentication systems is that those who create a system or design often think that it is intuitive and that users will easily understand; that is rarely the case. There is almost nothing that is inherently usable, and biometrics is no exception [19]. That is why biometric authentication systems should be designed with usability and security in mind throughout the whole design and development process [10, 11, 16].

3   Methodology

An explanatory research design was followed by using a survey in phase 1 followed by interviews in phase 2. As most research on biometric authentication and usability in mobile phones has focused on the general population, the goal here was to gather data on perceptions of biometric authentication and usability not just from the general population, but also from those who work in or with usability, computer security, and within that biometrics in particular. To accomplish this, survey and interview methods were used. The first phase consisted of the survey which had three user groups: the general population, usability experts, and computer security/biometrics experts. The second phase consisted of interviews with usability experts and computer security/biometrics experts for more in-depth data collection based on the survey and its results. A majority of the survey questions were based on research previously conducted.

Questions such as gender [4, 6, 7], age [4–7, 9], education level [6], knowledge about biometrics and usability [4, 6, 7], usability perceptions of biometrics [4], ease of use as well as security of biometrics [4, 5], operating system [8, 9], security tools (or authentication methods) used [8, 9], convenience [5, 7, 8], frequency of authentication [8], experience with failure to authenticate [8], and why participants use biometric authentication or not [7, 9] were used in the survey.

The survey design ensures potential bias is minimal. Before conducting phase 1 and 2, pilot tests were conducted on both the survey and the interview questions. To recruit participants for the survey and interviews, multiple channels were used. They can also be characterized convenience sampling. The survey was posted on multiple usability, design, computer security, and biometrics forums, Facebook groups, and LinkedIn groups. Also, 250 emails were sent to usability, design, computer security, and biometrics companies across 10+ countries to find more diverse participants.

4   Results

4.1   Survey Results

24% of participants work in biometrics, security, or related fields. 31% of participants work in usability, UX, UI, or related fields. The remaining 45% of participants worked in neither of those areas. 96% of participants in this study use some form of authentication for unlocking their device, 75% of whom have had issues with unlocking their phones. Those who work in usability, security, or related fields tended to say that biometrics were the most secure and easy to use authentication method (86% and 83% respectively) however, only 67% of those who worked in neither of those areas chose biometrics as the most secure or easy to use authentication method. Those working in security or related fields believed in a link (96%) and trade-off (65%) between usability and security at a much higher level than the other two participant groups (80% and 50% for usability participants respectively and 63% and 47% of general participants respectively). The percentage of participants who were uncertain if there was a link or a trade-off between security and usability increased from security participants (0% were uncertain of there being a link and 13% for a trade-off), to usability participants (3% were uncertain of there being a link and 17% for a trade-off), to general participants (28% were uncertain of there being a link and 37% for a trade-off). However, across the board, a majority of participants (63%) believe that mobile phones can be secure and usable, but they are not always like that today. When asked about their understanding of biometrics, the average understanding was a 3 on a scale of 1–6. 53% of general participants said that they had little to no understanding of biometrics, 60% of usability participants said that they had a novice to intermediate understanding of biometrics, and 57% of biometrics participants said that they have an advanced or expert understanding. When asked about their understanding of usability, the average understanding was a 4 on a scale of 1–6. 44% of general participants said that they had a novice to intermediate understanding of usability, 48% of security participants said that they had an advanced or expert understanding of usability, and 70% of usability participants said that they had an advanced or expert understanding of usability. 83% of security participants said that they have worked with usability experts whereas only 33% of usability experts said that they have worked with security experts.

There was a high correlation between participants who use a particular well-known brand of mobile phones and use of biometrics (94%) and having the belief that biometrics are the most secure and easy to use authentication method. A majority of participants whose age was between 35–44 years old use biometrics (90%) and had perceptions of biometrics being the most secure (85%) and easy to use (91%) authentication method. 100% of participants over the age of 45 said that biometrics are the most secure and easy to use authentication method. Overall, as the understanding of biometrics and usability increased, so did the belief of a link between the two increase.

4.2 Interview Results

One common theme that emerged from the interviews was about users of mobile phones. Several participants discussed how everything "goes back to the user" and how there is much that "depends on the person". These users discussed how users "shouldn't be locked into letting go of something or using something specifically", and that users will disable or circumvent security measures. Many people use the same passwords or pins "as their default method because they are used to it". Security measures now often depend on "what people are willing to do" or "what effort people are willing to make".

Another common theme that emerged was about the weaknesses of security in mobile phones. Multiple participants discussed margins of error, type I and type II errors, and how information is sent mainly around biometric authentication. When discussing the weaknesses of biometric authentication specifically, one participant said, "theoretically it can work and [security] can increase, but in practice it hasn't been that way", and another said that "when it comes down to it, it can be done, but at a cost". Another participant discussed how "you can use a backup method as heightened security, but... the methods used as a backup aren't secure methods".

In five of the six interviews when it came to the question about there being a trade-off or not between usability and security, it was mentioned that there needs to be a balance between usability and security; and even though there is a trade-off, it is not necessarily a bad thing or a problem. Another specific point that was discussed with four of the six participants was 2-factor authentication. Some of these participants mentioned how some data is stored due to two-factor authentication or that it is often recommended for heightened security, though it may be "overboard" or "not always practical for the end user".

There were a few phrases that participants said that were important to them. "Usability is the reason why biometrics are used". "Authentication needs to just work". "UX should not interrupt security". "Bigger phones" reduce the number of usable methods for authentication, although it was not clear what they meant by "bigger phones". "There needs to be an explanation to the user". "Independent testing is so important". "There needs to be a way to protect the device even when there is no physical access to it". "There is always the question about what is the best option today".

5 Discussion

In general, the survey results showed corroboration with what [3, 8], and [5] stated in that overall there is a belief outside of the security profession that security is important.

Similar to what [3], 76% of participants said that biometrics were the most secure authentication option followed by pins and passwords (22%).

As the other studies mentioned showed as well, fingerprint authentication was the most preferred and used biometric.

Something that was noticed during data analysis was about perceptions and understanding of usability. There were more people than expected outside of the field of usability who said that they have an advanced or expert understanding of usability, and this could be due to the simple definition of usability provided in the survey.

Throughout the interviews there were some common factors that came up. Participants discussed how usability is a large reason as to why biometric authentication is used, and as of now there is a lot of variation between biometric authentication methods and their levels of usability. Humans are an important factor that are often overlooked or thought of as a problem when it comes to authentication. Several participants also mentioned how if security is not usable, then users will circumvent it. Usability should not get in the way of security and vice versa. It was also discussed how there is a trade-off between usability and security, however that it may not necessarily be a problem to have that trade-off. Perhaps by saying it is not a problem the users imply that a healthy balance can be reached through good design between a desirable level of usability and computer security.

6   Conclusion

All groups of users see a link between usability and computer security (specifically with biometric authentication). All groups of users see a trade-off between them and simultaneously believe that an optimum level of both is possible through good mobile phone design.

6.1   Future Work

As of now we do not know exactly how the trade-off between usability and computer security manifests itself. We need to establish that they are related through objective data. As of now we have concluded the link based on subjective self-reported data from three categories of users. The interviews bring up several good hypotheses for future usability and computer security studies but each of them needs to be investigated in greater detail so that there are findings that can be in the form of clear design guidelines.

References

1. Cranor, L., Garfinkel, S.: Guest editors' introduction: secure or usable? IEEE Secur. Priv. **2**(5), 16–18 (2004)
2. Griffin, A.: iPhones are unlocked 80 times per day, Apple says as part of security briefing, The Independent UK (2016)
3. Zirjawi, N., Kurtanovic, Z., Maalej, W.: A survey about user requirements for biometric authentication on smartphones. In: 2015 IEEE 2nd Workshop on Evolving Security and Privacy Requirements Engineering (ESPRE), pp. 1–6 (2015)

4. Riley, C.W., Buckner, K., Johnson, G., Benyon, D.: Culture & biometrics: regional differences in the perception of biometric authentication technologies. AI Soc., 295–306 (2008)

5. Lovisotto, G., Malik, R., Sluganovic, I., Roeschlin, M., Trueman, P., Martinovic, I.: Mobile biometrics in financial services: a five factor framework. University of Oxford (2017)

6. El-Abed, M., Giot, R., Hemery, B., Rosenberger, C.: A study of users' acceptance and satisfaction of biometric systems. In: 44th Annual 2010 IEEE International Carnahan Conference on Security Technology, pp. 170–178 (2010)

7. Bhagavatula, C., Ur, B., Lacovino, K., Mon Kywe, S., Cranor, L., Savvides, M.: Biometric authentication on iphone and android: usability, perceptions, and influences on adoption. In: Workshop on Usable Security at USEC 2015 (2015)

8. Al Abdulwahid, A., Clarke, N., Stengel, I., Furnell, S., Reich, C.: Security, privacy and usability – a survey of users' perceptions and attitudes. In: Fischer-Hübner, S., Lambrinoudakis, C., Lopez, J. (eds.) TrustBus 2015. LNCS, vol. 9264, pp. 153–168. Springer, Cham (2015). https://doi.org/10.1007/978-3-319-22906-5_12

9. Ahmed, I.U.: Smartphone authentication, user experience, expectation and satisfaction. Master's thesis (2017)

10. Alshamari, M.: A review of gaps between usability and security/privacy. Int. J. Commun. Netw. Syst. Sci. **9**, 413–429 (2016)

11. Sasse, M.A., Smith, M., Herley, C., Lipford, H., Vaniea, K.: Debunking security-usability tradeoff myths. IEEE Secur. Priv. **14**, 33–39 (2016)

12. Yee, K.P.: Guidelines and strategies for secure interaction design. In: Usability and Security: Designing Secure Systems That People Can Use (2005)

13. Böhm, I., Testor, F.: Biometric systems. Department of Telecooperation University of Linz (2004)

14. Sahar, F.: Tradeoffs between usability and security. Int. J. Eng. Technol. (2013)

15. Ben-Asher, N., Meyer, J., Möller, S., Englert, R.: An experimental system for studying the tradeoff between usability and security. In: 2009 International Conference on Availability, Reliability and Security (2009)

16. Nwokedi, U.O., Amunga, B., Rad, B.B.: Usability and security in user interface design: a systematic literature review (2016)

17. Pocovnicu, A.: Biometric security for cell phones. Informatica Economica (2009)

18. Brostoff, G.: Adoption problems? How UX could boost biometrics. Biometric Technol. Today **2017**, 9–11 (2017)

19. Coventry, L.: Usable biometrics. In: Security and Usability: Designing Secure Systems that People Can Use (2005)

Trust in Software: Attributes of Computer Code and the Human Factors that Influence Utilization Metrics

August Capiola[1]([✉]), Alex D. Nelson[1], Charles Walter[2],
Tyler J. Ryan[3], Sarah A. Jessup[1], Gene M. Alarcon[1],
Rose F. Gamble[2], and Marc D. Pfahler[3]

[1] Air Force Research Laboratory, Wright-Patterson AFB, Dayton, USA
`august.capiola.1@us.af.mil`
[2] University of Tulsa, Tulsa, USA
[3] General Dynamics Information Technology, Dayton, USA

Abstract. The proliferation of technology has led to increased reliance on software. In software development, efficiencies can be gained by developers who reuse previously written code rather than starting from scratch. Although this practice has advantages, it can lead to security vulnerabilities. As such, it is important to understand the antecedents to software reuse. The present study explored how personality affects the decision to reuse software. Fourteen participants were recruited to evaluate 18 code artifacts. Results indicated that those participants higher in agreeableness were more likely to reuse the computer code than those lower in agreeableness. However, we found no evidence that the trustworthiness–reuse relationship was strengthened for those higher in agreeableness. In addition, there was no relationship between openness and reuse, nor did the interaction between openness and trustworthiness predict reuse. Post hoc exploratory analyses revealed agreeableness, but not openness, weakened the relationship between perceptions of code trustworthiness and time spent reviewing code.

Keywords: Trust · Computer code · Software reuse · Personality

1 Introduction

Software driven systems are ever-present in modern society. This abundance of computer software, or code, has led to the necessary practice of software reuse, which has associated vulnerabilities. The decision to reuse code indicates that the programmer trusts the code, as they are willing to be vulnerable to the consequences of reuse [1]. Moreover, the programmer's trust is influenced by their state-specific perceptions of the code as well as other individual difference variables [1, 2].

Certain individuals may be more prone to trust (i.e., reuse) code than others, highlighting the importance of investigating individual differences affecting software reuse. To replicate and extend past research [2], we explored how global programmer personality affects software reuse.

This is a U.S. government work and not under copyright protection in the U.S.;
foreign copyright protection may apply 2019
C. Stephanidis (Ed.): HCII 2019, CCIS 1032, pp. 190–196, 2019.
https://doi.org/10.1007/978-3-030-23522-2_24

1.1   Code Reuse

The reuse of existing computer code is a critical efficiency in software driven industries. These efficiencies include sustaining existing platforms, avoiding redundancies in manpower, and streamlining drivers of schedule and cost. Additionally, implementing extant code may reduce the probability of errors and vulnerabilities, as the code has been vetted by several programmers. On the other hand, the reuse of existing code without proper vetting introduces a level of risk as unseen errors and/or vulnerabilities could be incorporated into an overarching software system. Clearly, the implications of code reuse are far-reaching.

Trust is the willingness to accept vulnerabilities from others with the expectation of positive outcomes [3]. Research on trust in sociotechnical systems has flourished in recent years, as the trust process plays a major role in acceptance and use of technology [4]. In code reuse contexts, it is easy to see how accepting potential vulnerabilities (e.g., error or exploitation in the code) can lead to positive outcomes (e.g., efficiencies in developing new software). Lee and See [4] have discussed the ideas of trust calibration and performance which may pertain to trust in code reuse. Through the lens of their model, over-trusting extant code could introduce errors into the system or create cybersecurity vulnerabilities. On the other hand, under-trusting code creates inefficiencies in software development, as resources may be wasted creating new code. Thus, software reuse decisions may depend on how trustworthy programmers perceive the code, as well as their individual differences [2].

Recently, researchers adapted the heuristic-systematic processing model [5] of persuasion to the trust in code literature [6]. In the HSM of code reuse, Alarcon and Ryan [6] discuss the two different processes programmers may use to evaluate code. Heuristic processing describes a "strategy that ignores part of the information, with the goal of making decisions quickly and frugally" [7]. Heuristics are mental short cuts such as biases or norms which are stored in memory, and thus require less mental effort to process [5]. Systematic processing is an analytical assessment of relevant information used to form a decision. Systematic processing involves more cognitive resources, but often results in more accurate evaluations [5, 6]. Under this model, individual differences may influence how and when heuristic versus systematic processing is used. In other words, certain personality types may be more apt to perform certain types of processing.

The implications of code reuse are far-reaching, and the antecedents to such reuse, such as personality, are beginning to be investigated (e.g., [2]). Certain types of people may be more prone to trust code than others. Research has demonstrated that personality relates to the entire trust process [8]. In software-development contexts in particular, Ryan and colleagues [2] demonstrated that the relationship between perceptions of code trustworthiness and reuse was moderated by suspicion propensity, or the general likelihood to perceive mal-intent, be uncertain, and engage in cognitive activity when evaluating information [9].

In an effort to replicate and extend past findings from [2], we hypothesized that increased perceptions of code trustworthiness would be related to more decisions to reuse code. Moreover, we hypothesized that personality would moderate the trustworthiness–trust relationship. We chose to focus on global personality traits (i.e., agreeableness, openness) rather than facet personality traits (see [2]). Recent research has shown that global versus facet traits may be differently predictive in the trust process [10]. Relatedly, programmers who are more agreeable should be more likely to trust the code, as trust is a facet of agreeableness [11]. In comparison, we had no *a priori* hypotheses regarding the effects of openness on the trustworthiness–trust relationship, leaving all hypotheses related to openness entirely exploratory. We hypothesized that the relationship between perceptions of code trustworthiness and reuse decisions would be influenced by agreeableness and openness, such that greater trustworthiness leads to more reuse, and this positive relationship will be stronger for those higher in agreeableness, and potentially stronger or weaker for those high in openness.

2   Method

Participants. Fourteen participants (13 males; average age = 23) were recruited from the engineering department of a Midwest university. Participants were required to have at least three years of coding experience and a working knowledge of the Java language to participate. The sample had an average of 6 years programming experience. The study employed a 3 (readability) × 3 (organization) × 2 (source) full factorial design. Participants evaluated code that varied in readability, organization, and source within-subjects as in past research (see [12]). Factor levels for readability and organization included "high", "medium", and "low", while factor levels for source included "reputable" and "unknown". Conditions were counter-balanced to control for potential carry-over effects. More detail on stimuli can be found in the Stimuli section below. For extensive detail on stimuli development, see [12].

2.1   Measures

Each participant completed the Mini IPIP [13], a five factor model scale that assesses global personality constructs: neuroticism, extraversion, conscientiousness, agreeableness, and openness to experience. It consists of twenty items that use a 5-point Likert scale ranging from "strongly disagree" to "strongly agree". In the present study, we focused only on agreeableness and openness to experience.

For each code artifact, we assessed perceived trustworthiness, trust intentions, and time to complete. Perceived trustworthiness was assessed for each artifact with the item, "How trustworthy is the code?" using a 7-point Likert scale (1 = completely untrustworthy, 7 = completely trustworthy). Trust intentions in each code artifact were measured with a mutually exclusive option to either "use" or "don't use".

2.2   Stimuli

The study was conducted using an online application platform running the CodeTrust testbed [14], seen in Fig. 1. Stimuli comprised 18 Java code artifacts taken from a variety of sources that compile successfully, producing the intended output. Artifacts in the testbed were sanitized of existing comments or reference to authorship as to avoid confounding variables that could influence trustworthiness. Each artifact was presented to the participants in image form on its own page with a formatting style consistent with the widely used Eclipse Java development environment. A description of what the class is intended to do along with the source manipulation were given at the top of the page. The code class appears below this header with the trustworthiness rating scale and "Use" and "Don't Use" options at the bottom of the page.

Fig. 1. Code trust testbed example (Source: [14])

Each artifact was augmented with a unique combination of readability and organization degradations and source value as discussed in prior research (see [14]). A class with high readability or organization contained syntax with best practices and common coding standards (see [14]). A class with medium readability or organization contained three to seven degradations within the artifact, and a class with low reliability or organization contained eight or more degradations. Each artifact was designed to be complex enough to require attentive review to understand, but simple enough to be understood in less than ten minutes. For greater detail on stimuli, see [14].

2.3 Procedure

After consenting to participate and completing baseline questionnaires, participants were trained on how to perform the experimental task in the Code Trust testbed [14] and completed a short practice session. Then, each participant performed the experimental task, where they were prompted to evaluate 18 Java artifacts and rate their perceived trustworthiness of each artifact and then make a decision to either "Use" or "Don't Use" the code. Upon completion, participants were debriefed, received remuneration for their participation, and were dismissed.

3 Analysis and Results

A generalized estimating equation approach was used to model the relationships between the manipulated factors, personality, and reuse intentions. A model building approach was taken, adding independent variables in successive models and comparing fit using Wald χ^2 and quasi-information criterion [15] fit indices. An initial model was fit with the readability, organization, and source factors, QIC(6) = 335.81. Model 2 included perceived trustworthiness, and was significantly better fitting than model 1, Wald $\chi^2(1) = 15.24$, $p < .001$, QIC(7) = 187.23. The main effects of agreeableness and openness were added for model 3, which had marginally better fit than model 2, Wald $\chi^2(2) = 5.93$, $p = .052$, QIC(9) = 186.97. In order to test the moderating effects of personality on the trustworthiness-trust relationship, model 4 included the interactions between the personality variables and trustworthiness to predict reuse intentions. Model 4 did not fit the data significantly better than model 2, Wald $\chi^2(2) = 0.09$, $p = .954$, QIC(11) = 195.66. The test of model effects found readability, Wald $\chi^2(2) = 12.71$, $p = .002$, organization, Wald $\chi^2(2) = 9.05$, $p = .011$, trustworthiness, Wald $\chi^2(1) = 15.24$, $p < .001$, and agreeableness, Wald $\chi^2(1) = 5.92$, $p = .015$, provided significant contributions to the model. However, source, Wald $\chi^2(1) = 1.79$, $p = .181$, openness, Wald $\chi^2(1) = 0.09$, $p = .764$, the interaction between trustworthiness and openness, Wald $\chi^2(1) = 0.08$, $p = .771$, and the interaction between trustworthiness and agreeableness, Wald $\chi^2(1) = 0.02$, $p = .881$, were all non-significant. The parameter effects for model 3 were all non-significant.

Previous research suggests increased systematic processing, indicated by increased time for reviewing code, leads to increased levels of trust and therefore reuse, given functionally trustworthy code [6, 12]. We further investigate the influence of personality on code review time to better understand the process of code comprehension and decision making. An exploratory model was run with the three factors (trustworthiness, openness, and agreeableness), the interaction between trustworthiness and openness, and the interaction between trustworthiness and agreeableness, predicting code review time. Test of model effects suggest that readability, Wald $\chi^2(2) = 10.10$, $p = .006$, organization, Wald $\chi^2(2) = 10.30$, $p = .006$, source, Wald $\chi^2(1) = 11.07$, $p < .001$, and the interaction between trustworthiness and agreeableness, Wald $\chi^2(1) = 4.25$, $p = .039$, were all significant predictors of review time. Trustworthiness, openness,

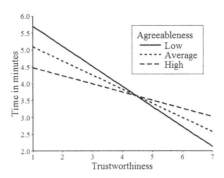

Fig. 2. Trustworthiness predicting review time, moderated by Agreeableness

agreeableness, and the interaction between openness and trustworthiness were all non-significant. The moderating relationship between trustworthiness and agreeableness predicting time is represented in Fig. 2.

4 Discussion

In the present study, we investigated how personality moderates the trustworthiness – trust relationship in software reuse contexts. Results indicated that higher perceptions of trustworthiness predicted greater reuse, replicating past research on the trust process in software reuse contexts [2]. Specifically, regardless of the code manipulations, programmer trustworthiness perceptions influence their subsequent decisions to reuse code. Agreeableness also predicted subsequent reuse decisions over code manipulations. The direct impact of an individual's general tendency to trust has been shown in past literature [10]. In addition, those higher in agreeableness were more likely to reuse the computer code than those lower in agreeableness. This finding shows evidence that global traits do have a main effect on trust, extending recent findings [10] to the code reuse context. As trust is a facet of agreeableness [11], those with higher agreeableness may be more likely to trust in general and thus more likely to reuse code. However, we found no evidence that the trustworthiness–reuse relationship was strengthened for those higher in agreeableness. Still, trust and agreeableness share some conceptual overlap [10, 11]. That said, it is not surprising that those who are higher in agreeableness were more likely to reuse the code.

There was no relationship between openness and reuse, nor did the interaction between openness and trustworthiness predict reuse. Though non-significant, these latter findings contribute to not only the general interpersonal trust literature but also the literature on trust in code [1, 2, 6, 12, 14]. It may be that some personality traits are more relevant as moderators of the trust process than others. Future research may wish to investigate traits outside the FFM and their moderating role of the trustworthiness – trust relationship [see 2].

In our exploratory analyses, agreeableness moderated the relationship between trustworthiness perceptions and time spent on code. In general, higher trustworthiness perceptions led to less time spent on the task. However, this relationship was weaker for those who were high in agreeableness. One interpretation of these findings is that those who are highly agreeable may be less influenced by state-specific perceptions of trust and are more so guided by their dispositions. Those higher in agreeableness take less time to assess the trust relevant characteristics of a referent before making trust-based decisions. As trust is a personality facet of agreeableness [11], those with higher agreeableness may be more likely to trust in general and thus relied less on perceptions of trustworthiness, thus taking less time on code. Our research is another step towards understanding the moderating role of personality on the trust process.

References

1. Alarcon, G.M., Militello, L.G., Ryan, P., Jessup, S.A., Calhoun, C.S., Lyons, J.B.: A descriptive model of computer code trustworthiness. J. Cogn. Eng. Decis. Making **11**, 107–121 (2017). https://doi.org/10.1177/1555343416657236
2. Ryan, T.J., Walter, C., Alarcon, G.M., Gamble, R.F., Jessup, S.A., Capiola, A.: The influence of personality on code reuse. In: Proceedings of the 52nd Hawaii International Conference on System Sciences, 8–11 January 2019. University of Hawaii, Manoa (2019)
3. Mayer, R.C., Davis, H.C., Schoorman, F.D.: An integrative model of organizational trust. J. Acad. Manag. Rev. **20**, 709–734 (1995). https://doi.org/10.5465/amr.1995.9508080335
4. Lee, J.D., See, K.A.: Trust in automation: designing for appropriate reliance. Hum. Factors: J. Hum. Fact. Ergon. Soc. **46**, 50–80 (2004). https://doi.org/10.1518/hfes.46.1.50_30392
5. Chaiken, S.: Heuristic versus systematic information processing and the use of source versus message cues in persuasion. J. Pers. Soc. Psychol. **39**, 752–766 (1980). https://doi.org/10.1037/0022-3514.39.5.752
6. Alarcon, G.M., Ryan, T.J.: Trustworthiness perceptions of computer code: a heuristic-systematic processing model. In: Proceedings of the 51st Hawaii International Conference on System Sciences, pp. 5384–5393 (2018). https://doi.org/10.24251/hicss.2018.671
7. Gigerenzer, G., Gaissmaier, W.: Heuristic decision making. Ann. Rev. Psychol. **62**, 451–482 (2011). https://doi.org/10.1146/annurev-psych-120709-145346
8. Colquitt, J.A., Scott, B.A., LePine, J.A.: Trust, trustworthiness, and trust propensity: a meta-analytic test of their unique relationships with risk taking and job performance. J. Appl. Psychol. **92**, 909–927 (2007). https://doi.org/10.1037/0021-9010.92.4.909
9. Calhoun, C., Bobko, P., Schuelke, M., Jessup, S., Ryan, T., Walter, C., et al.: Suspicion, trust, and automation. Technical report, SRA International Inc. (2017)
10. Alarcon, G.M., Lyons, J.B., Christensen, J.C., Bowers, M.A., Klosterman, S.L., Capiola, A.: The role of propensity to trust and the five-factor model across the trust process. J. Res. Pers. **75**, 69–82 (2018). https://doi.org/10.1016/j.jrp.2018.05.006
11. Costa Jr., P.T., McCrae, R.R., Dye, D.A.: Facet scales for agreeableness and conscientiousness: a revision of the NEO Personality Inventory. J. Personality Individ. Differ. **12**, 887–898 (1991). https://doi.org/10.1016/0191-8869(91)90177-D
12. Alarcon, G.M., et al.: Application of the heuristic-systematic model to computer code trustworthiness: the influence of reputation and transparency. Cogent Psychol. **4**, 1–22 (2017). https://doi.org/10.1080/23311908.2017.1389640
13. Donnellan, M.B., Oswald, F.L., Baird, B.M., Lucas, R.E.: The mini-IPIP scales: tiny-yet-effective measures of the Big Five Factors of personality. J. Psychol. Assess. **18**, 192–203 (2006). https://doi.org/10.1037/1040-3590.18.2.192
14. Walter, C., Gamble, R.F., Alarcon, G.M., Jessup, S.A, Calhoun, C.S.: Developing a mechanism to study code trustworthiness. In: Proceedings of the 50th Hawaii International Conference on System Sciences, pp. 5817–5826 (2017)
15. Pan, W.: Akaike's information criterion in generalized estimating equations. J. Biometrics **57**, 120–125 (2001). https://doi.org/10.1111/j.0006-341X.2001.00120.x

Layered Information Structure
for Hierarchical Security Management
of Critical Infrastructure Using Network
Security Appliances

Seungoh Choi[✉], Yesol Kim, Jeong-Han Yun, Byung-Gil Min,
and HyoungChun Kim

The Affiliated Institute of ETRI, Daejeon, Republic of Korea
{sochoi,yesol89k,dolgam,bgmin,khche}@nsr.re.kr

Abstract. Critical infrastructure can be found in many locations in
a wide range of areas such as energy and water transportation. Security surveillance can be implemented by installing and operating network security equipment at each site. However, to defend such a large
number of sites against cyber threats, systematic security surveillance of
the critical infrastructure must be implemented. A hierarchical setup for
managing this wide-ranging critical infrastructure already exists. In this
paper, we propose a layered information structure for the event logs of
network security devices that are based on that hierarchy. We partition
the information into three layers according to the user's roles. In the
future, we will apply this proposed information structure to the design
of a hierarchical security monitoring system for critical infrastructure.

Keywords: Layered information · Network security ·
Hierarchical monitoring

1 Introduction

With the steady increase in the number and severity of security threats, there is a
need for a systematic means of monitoring the security of a wide range of critical
infrastructures [3]. The generated event logs are vast and varied in format given
that they are produced by a diverse network of security appliances. In addition,
the information on which the personnel responsible for security management
must focus depends on their role in each level of the hierarchical monitoring, as
shown in Fig. 1. Therefore, it is essential to organize the field information of the
event logs according to the roles of security management and their position in
the hierarchy.

To satisfy these demands, we analyzed each field of the event logs using network security appliances for security management in the critical infrastructure.
Based on the results of this analysis, we propose a layered information structure having areas that are separated according to the hierarchy of the security
monitoring and the degree of data processing.

© Springer Nature Switzerland AG 2019
C. Stephanidis (Ed.): HCII 2019, CCIS 1032, pp. 197–204, 2019.
https://doi.org/10.1007/978-3-030-23522-2_25

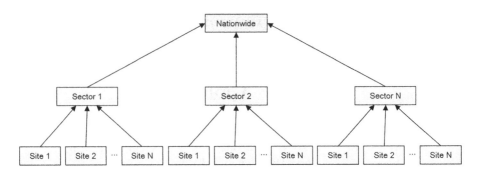

Fig. 1. Security management in hierarchy manner

We assigned information types according to the operational environment and user requirements for hierarchical security management. The basis area was allocated such that the degree of data processing increases with the monitoring hierarchy. Additional information, which is higher or lower than the basis area, is allocated on the extended information. To set the role of the hierarchical security management, we considered the information flow required for sharing information between different layers, policy propagation, and feedback. Furthermore, we provided an information flow when additional information was required within the same hierarchy of the security management. We believe that this basic structure could be used to visualize target information according to the users' requirements for individual sites or layers.

This paper is composed as follows. In Sect. 2, we analyze the information generated by network security appliances and introduce requirements for hierarchical security management. Section 3 introduces a layered information structure that fulfills these requirements, while Sect. 4 describes an actual application. Finally, we conclude this paper in Sect. 5.

2 Motivation

Network security appliances provide essential information for real-time security monitoring or post-analysis such as IP addresses and port numbers in various domains. We analyzed security-related information for the appliances used for hierarchical security management. Although there may be differences in the method of representation and the depth of meaning depending on the appliances, the information has been confirmed to include that listed in Table 1.

Most of this information could be expressed using three levels of data processing. For example, in the case of IP-related information, the data has no IP address information, which is a value itself (i.e., original data). In addition, the information can be expressed explicitly in the form of a host name, a server, and a device name, or a category that could be a country, an operating organization, or a network zone as a higher level.

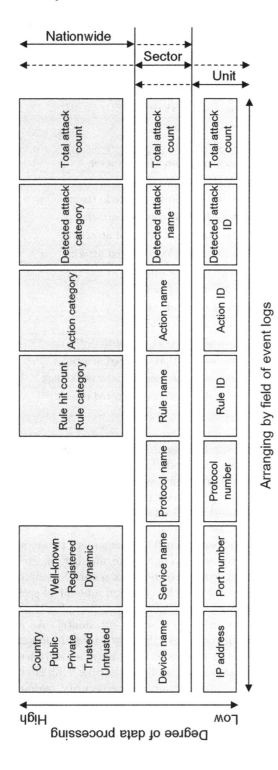

Fig. 2. Some of the fields selected from an event log by application of the proposed information structure

Table 1. Typical information on network security appliances

Category	Information of event log
IP	IP address of device that detected attack
	IP address of attacker
	IP address of victim
Port	Port of attacker
	Port of victim
Protocol	Transport protocol of attacker
Identifier	Rule ID that detected attack
	Action ID against detected attack
	Attack ID that detected attack
Statistics	Total number of detected attacks
Name	Device name that detected attack
	Device name of attacker
	Device name of victim
	Service name of attacker
	Service name of victim
	Name of transport protocol
	Name of rule that detected attack
	Name of action against detected attack
	Name of attack that detected attack

We arranged fields with similar meanings as shown in Fig. 2, according to their semantics. Moreover, we arranged the security information vertically by varying the location of the data processing and security management. As a result, we were able to structure the layered security information with the two criteria, such that the information could be utilized for hierarchical security management and monitoring in critical infrastructures.

However, the information-based security management incurs some problems because the critical infrastructure covers a large number of sites over a wide area, with each site operating a range of network security equipment for either security or operational reasons. First, the type and amount of security information that can be obtained at each site constituting the infrastructure increases exponentially when it is forwarded to a sector or country. As a result, users who perform security monitoring exceed their own information and processing limits such that, eventually, the user experience may be degraded. Second, the information to be monitored depends mainly on the operating environment (e.g., whether it is in the infrastructure domain or the security management layer). Last, it is necessary to consider the results of self-analysis or higher-level analysis of the information acquired by the role of the user as a security manager. To deal with these problems, in the following section, we introduce a layered information structure that is suitable for hierarchical security management.

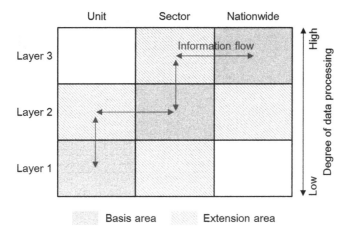

Fig. 3. Layered information structure for hierarchical security management

3 Layered Information Structure for Hierarchical Security Management

We are proposing a layered information structure observing the fields of an event log generated by a network security appliance. As shown in Fig. 3, the proposed information structure is divided into nine areas according to the degree of data processing and the security monitoring layer.

The security monitoring layer accommodates hierarchical monitoring and consists of three stages: unit, sector, and nationwide. The degree of data processing consists of three steps according to the information level. The degree of data processing precision is the same as the corresponding value in the information provided by the raw data, although the information is identified at a higher level.

Each area that is split according to our criteria is allocated to the basis and extension areas, with the unallocated area being assumed to be irrelevant. We designate three kinds of areas, as shown in the figure, because the information, limit of cognition, and security information on which the personnel in charge of security management must focus may differ depending on the step. Of course, the gathering and monitoring of all the information for all the security monitoring areas of a site will help us to pinpoint the exact situation, but it is very difficult for the user to understand the situation in real-time while being flooded with information. Furthermore, the location where the security management is applied may differ depending on the information to be monitored.

Proximity of the site to the infrastructure operation will enhance the raw data acquisition and analysis. Based on this, with an increase in the degree of data processing, the security management layer is allocated to a basis area such that it can be increased by one level. The basis area indicates that information which should always be monitored. For example, the basis area can act as a dashboard

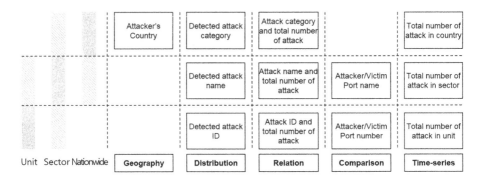

Fig. 4. Information organization in hierarchical security monitoring

that provides a real-time view directly to the user. The extension area is specified as being adjacent to the basis area. The extension area holds that information to which the user should refer if a specific situation occurs, such as an attack or an alarm. The result of a brief analysis is visualized through a separate view on the dashboard. We designated the unallocated area as being irrelevant due to the limitations of information cognition. In reality, it is impossible to monitor the entire area of information in either a unit or the whole country.

We also considered the flow of information used and produced with respect to the role of the security manager, such as information monitoring, analysis, and reporting. Information flow can be bidirectional between the basis and extension areas. Therefore, each step is scalable and flexible to the limited information.

4   Application of Proposed Information Structure

4.1   Organizing Information

We applied the proposed structure to the identification of information that can be verified by each hierarchy of security management according to the visualization method [1]. In general, there are many ways of actual implementations for the visualization. But here we presented an example of applying the five typical visualization types: geography, distribution, relation, comparison, and time-series, as shown in Fig. 4.

In the case of geographic information, the country corresponding to the attacker is suitable and can be assigned to the highest security management layer. Of course, such visualization methods can be applied to all layers according to the various infrastructure domains, such as traffic and energy supply networks. In the case of distribution, it is suitable for application to the attack-related information detected in the security situation. Information closer to the category can be allocated to a higher layer. This applies similarly to relations, comparisons, and time-series. Once the information has been organized, the dashboard for security management can be configured by combining the information corresponding to each step.

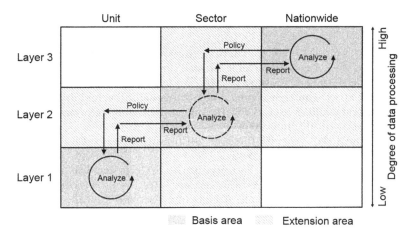

Fig. 5. Information flow for hierarchical security management

4.2   Assigning Information Flow

Anomaly detection in a network can be divided into three steps: monitoring, analysis, and response [2]. These actions are performed by the personnel at each stage according to the security monitoring. The US Department of Homeland Security introduced its National Cyber Incident Response Plan (NCIRP), a cyber operational plan for national, sector, and individual organizations, having a common doctrine and a strategic framework [4].

We applied this to the information structure and the proposed information structure for each action performed according to the security monitoring layer, as shown in Fig. 5. Each layer analyzes the network anomaly activity for the information in its basis area. If an anomaly is detected, the information that has been analyzed can be reported, or information that requires further analysis can be communicated to an upper level using the extension area. Once the analysis is complete, information in the basis and extension areas can be used to identify the root cause, and policy enforcement, including information to control the security threat, can be implemented.

5   Conclusion

In this paper, we have proposed a hierarchical information structure aimed at an infrastructure security management system. To this end, we first analyzed the information contained in the actual event log for security management in an infrastructure configured using network security appliances. Based on the results, we constructed a layered information structure which is suitable for hierarchical security management, as well as monitoring, using the security appliances. The proposed structure could be implemented as a primary information structure for identifying important monitoring target information according to the user requirements at individual sites or layers, accompanied by the design of a dashboard.

References

1. Friendly, M., Denis, D.: Milestones in the history of thematic cartography, statistical graphics, and data visualization: an illustrated chronology of innovations. Statistical Consulting Service, York University (2009)
2. Goodall, J.R.: User requirements and design of a visualization for intrusion detection analysis. In: Proceedings from the Sixth Annual IEEE SMC Information Assurance Workshop, pp. 394–401, June 2005
3. NCCIC: ICS-CERT Year in Review (2016). https://ics-cert.us-cert.gov/Year-Review-2016. Accessed 28 Mar 2019
4. U.S. Department of Homeland Security: National Cyber Incident Response Plan (NCIRP) (2016). https://www.us-cert.gov/sites/default/files/ncirp/National_Cyber_Incident_Response_Plan.pdf. Accessed 28 Mar 2019

Usability and Security: A Case Study of Emergency Communication System Authentication

Akintunde Jeremiah Oluwafemi[✉] and Jinjuan Heidi Feng[✉]

Towson University, Towson, USA
{aoluwafemi, jfeng}@towson.edu

Abstract. Usability and Security are two important concepts in any design. A system must be easy to use and at the same time secure, to prevent unauthorized users from gaining access to the system and the data stored in the system. The goal of this study is to review the efficacy of the user authentication methods implemented in systems used in emergency communication centers. Due to the nature of the tasks and the environment of emergency responding teams, their system needs to be available and easily accessible because time is an important factor for success. At the same time, the systems need to be highly secure due to the sensitive nature of the data being collected and communicated during the process. Surveys and interviews are used for this study to understand the user authentication methods currently adopted in public emergency communication systems, and the impact of the authentication method on the usability and security of the systems. The information collected through this study will inform developers and practitioners to design and choose more effective authentication mechanisms for emergency communication systems.

Keywords: Usability · Security · System · Authentication · Emergency

1 Introduction

Emergency responders, also referred to as first responders, are people with specialized training that arrive first on the scene of an emergency situation such as an accident, fire outbreak, natural disaster, or terrorist attack to provide assistance and curtail the situation. Emergency responders include police officers, firefighters, paramedics, emergency medical technicians, rescuers, and other people trained to handle emergency situations. They make use of different electronic equipment to perform their duties such as the computer-aided dispatch, 9-1-1 Phone System, mobile data computers, fire station alerting system, etc. Emergency responders are expected to arrive at the scene of an emergency as fast as possible. A delay of a few minutes may result in loss of lives or properties. Therefore, it is critical for the responders to receive notices and access necessary information as fast as possible.

Usability is defined in ISO 9241-11 (ISO 9241-11 2018) as the extent to which a system can be utilized by specified users in a particular context of use, to achieve specified goals effectively, efficiently, and with satisfaction. The usability of the

© Springer Nature Switzerland AG 2019
C. Stephanidis (Ed.): HCII 2019, CCIS 1032, pp. 205–210, 2019.
https://doi.org/10.1007/978-3-030-23522-2_26

emergency communication system focuses on the accessibility and ease of use of the system. The primary goal of an emergency responder is to access a system as fast as possible to acquire the necessary information needed to perform his duties. In the meanwhile, it is also extremely important that the systems remain as secured as possible in order to prevent unauthorized access, which can lead to destruction, alteration, and unauthorized disclosure of sensitive information.

Security measures are crucial for emergency communication systems, especially with the increased level of attacks on public emergency communication systems. It was reported in June 2016 that the hackers attacked emergency communication center in Howard, Tennessee using a weak password of a previous employee. The hackers shut down the center's computer-aided dispatch system, and it took the emergency communication center three days to recover the system. A similar incident occurred in March 2018 when hackers breached a computer-aided dispatch system in Maryland. Investigators revealed that the intrusion was an attempted ransomware attack, although they did not provide details of the investigations to the public.

User authentication is an important security measure for access control. There are three different authentication approaches based on the nature of the information used for authentication; knowledge-based authentication, biometric authentication, and possession-based authentication. The choice of a specific authentication method depends on the nature of the tasks, the sensitivity of the information collected and used by the system, the users of the system, and the context of use of the system. To date, there is limited research on the user authentication practice in emergency communication systems. The goal of this project is to provide preliminary understanding regarding the use of authentication mechanisms in the context of emergency response as well as the challenges that the emergency responders encounter when interacting with those mechanisms.

2   Related Work

During an emergency situation, different personnel usually work together to save lives and community resources. One of the main challenges in an emergency situation is access control to the facilities and the systems (Portman et al. 2008). Emergency communication systems are expected to be easily accessible, but the user authentication mechanisms implemented in the system could be a potential barrier for prompt access to information. In the past, some systems were designed to be as easy to use as much as possible with insufficient attention to security. With rapidly increasing security breaches and threats, designers nowadays have to ensure that the system is both usable and secure. Yee (2004) argued that system implementers usually consider security and usability as an add-on to a finished product without placing the two important concepts into perspective at the early stage of designs. He proposed that the trade-off between usability and security might be alleviated if the two concepts are incorporated into the design in the early stage of system development.

In 2007, Braze et al. developed Security Usability Symmetry (SUS) model. This model provides guidance on usability constraints and the potential impacts of these constraints on security. A large body of researches has been conducted to investigate user authentication approaches. Researchers have reviewed the different authentication methods to determine the pros and cons of each method. Knowledge-based authentication depends on what the user must know to verify his identity to the information system, which is implemented through challenge and response (Katsini et al. 2016). The Knowledge-based authentication method is the most popular authentication method, with various forms such as numeric password (also referred to as personal identification number (PIN)), alphanumeric password, or graphical password. Despite the popularity of the knowledge-based authentication approach, there are both usability and security challenges associated with this approach. Users usually find it difficult to remember a complex password, especially in an emergency situation (Komanduri et al. 2011). Katsini et al. (2016) argued that the problem of memorability affects the security of knowledge-based authentication method because many users write down their passwords or choose weak passwords that are easy to remember but also easy to break.

Biometric authentication is based on what the user is, using either physiological or behavioral traits of the users such as fingerprint, iris, retina, face, signature, and DNA technologies (Fang et al. 2009). It was suggested that biometric authentication is more usable than knowledge-based authentication because it does not require users to memorize any information. It is also more secure because of the uniqueness of the biometrics to an individual. However, once a biometric feature is compromised, it remains permanently compromised because biometric features cannot be changed like alphanumeric passwords (Cohen et al. 2011). Biometric authentication has a higher cost of implementation when compared with knowledge-based authentication. It was also reported that culture may have a direct impact on user acceptance of biometrics (Riley et al. 2009).

Possession-based authentication authenticates a user through a device known as a token, such as smart card, common access card, hardware token, software token, etc. (Schneier 2004). When this authentication method is used with other authentication methods, it provides stronger authentication. Possession-based authentication usually requires users to carry the token around, which could be easily lost or stolen. The introduction of software-based token lessens this burden (Acharya et al. 2013).

Although there are significant work in the HCI field that focuses on supporting emergency responders through various solutions such as mobile systems or sensors (Buttussi et al. 2010), limited research has been reported that examines the existing user authentication practice adopted in the emergency communication systems and the challenges that users experience during the authentication process. Better understanding in this domain could lead to improved design that better accommodates the unique needs of the emergency responders and their supporting teams.

3 Methodology

We developed a survey and an interview to collect preliminary information about the current authentication practice adopted in the emergency communication systems. The targeted participants for the interview are directors and managers in the emergency communication centers across the United States. They were invited to participate in the study through email and phone calls. The targeted participants for the survey are managers and regular employees working in emergency communication centers in the

United States. They were contacted through their supervisors or professional groups on LinkedIn. The study was approved by the IRB of Towson University and is currently in progress. We are planning to conduct interviews with 12 to 16 communication center managers and collect information from approximately 100 survey respondents.

The survey and the interview questions were designed to collect information on user authentication from the following perspectives:

- demographic information such as age, responsibilities, and experience in emergency communication systems
- authentication methods in use at work and interaction experience with each method
- security problems of the authentication methods in use
- impact of user authentication on productivity
- preferred authentication methods.

4   Result

To date, we have collected data from five interview respondents and fifteen survey respondents. The five interview respondents are managers in emergency communication centers with more than twenty years of experience in the field. Four out of the five interview respondents are between the age of 40–50 years and the fifth person is above 50 years. The managers reported that the main system they are using is the Computer Aided Dispatch system and 9-1-1 phone system. They also use web-based applications such as Police records management and National Crime Information Center (NCIC).

The survey respondents include emergency communication center operators who respond to emergency calls from the public and dispatch appropriate emergency responders to handle the situation. Their ages range from 18 years to 50 years with varying years of experience in the field.

All the interview and questionnaire respondents are currently using username and password for authentication. Twenty-five percent of the respondents use a PIN in addition to username and password to gain access to their systems. This result suggests that the knowledge-based authentication method is still the dominant authentication mechanism in emergency communication centers. However, three of the five managers interviewed believed that knowledge-based authentication method could not provide an adequate level of security to their organization's system. They also complained about the usability of this authentication method. They mentioned that at times emergency center operators do forget their password, which may result in waste of time and reduction in productivity. Eighty percent of the survey respondents found it difficult to remember their passwords because of the complexity requirements.

Regarding preferred authentication methods, sixty-five of the interview and survey respondents prefer the biometric-based authentication method such as fingerprint because of the difficulty in remembering alphanumeric passwords or PIN. Thirty-five percent of the respondents prefer the possession-based authentication methods such as smart card or token.

5   Discussion and Conclusion

The responses received so far indicated that knowledge-based authentication methods are currently the dominant authentication method in emergency communication centers. There was no correlation between age or years of experience of the respondents and the reported usability of the authentication method. However, all survey respondents expressed their frustrations about the knowledge-based authentication method. From the employees' perspective, the respondents believed that the knowledge-based authentication method currently in use is affecting their productivity and suggested other user authentication methods should be implemented that are easier to use. Three out of the five managers interviewed confirmed that the user authentication method is affecting productivity. In addition, they emphasized that knowledge-based authentication method does not provide an adequate level of security for their systems and that there is a need to consider the implementation of other authentication methods such as fingerprint or smart card.

At the end of this study, there will be sufficient amount of data to help understand the current practice of user authentication in emergency communication centers. Based on the findings of the study, we will summarize the advantages and limitations of the current practice and make recommendations to stakeholders regarding possible solutions to improve the existing authentication methods in emergency communication centers. Our next study will focus on user authentication methods used by emergency responders who work at the scene of an emergency.

References

Acharya, S., Polawar, A., Pawar, P.: Two factor authentication using smartphone generated one time password. J. Comput. Eng. (IOSR-JCE) **11**, 85–90 (2013)

Braz, C., Seffah, A., M'Raihi, D.: Designing a trade-off between usability and security: a metrics based-model. In: Baranauskas, C., Palanque, P., Abascal, J., Barbosa, S.D.J. (eds.) INTERACT 2007. LNCS, vol. 4663, pp. 114–126. Springer, Heidelberg (2007). https://doi.org/10.1007/978-3-540-74800-7_9

de Bordea, D.: Selecting a two-factor authentication system. Netw. Secur. **2007**(7), 17–20 (2007)

Buttussi, B., Chittaro, L., Carchietti, E., Coppo, M.: Using mobile devices to support communication between emergency medical responders and deaf people. In: Proceedings of the 12th International Conference on Human Computer Interaction with Mobile Devices and Services, pp. 7–16 (2010)

Cohen, S., Ben-Asher, N., Meyer, J.: Towards information technology security for universal access. In: Stephanidis, C. (ed.) UAHCI 2011. LNCS, vol. 6765, pp. 443–451. Springer, Heidelberg (2011). https://doi.org/10.1007/978-3-642-21672-5_48

Fang, S-C., Chan, H.-L.: Human identification by quantifying similarity and dissimilarity in electrocardiogram phase space. Pattern Recogn. **42**, 1824–1831 (2009). https://doi.org/10.1016/j.patcog.2008.11.020

Hackers have taken down dozens of 911 centers. Why is it so hard to stop them? https://www.nbcnews.com/news/us-news/hackers-have-taken-down-dozens-911-centers-why-it-so-n862206

ISO 9241-11: Ergonomics of human-system interaction—Part 11: Usability: Definitions and concepts (2018)

Katsini, C., Belk, M., Fidas, C., Avouris, N., Samaras, G.: Security and usability in knowledge-based user authentication: a review (2016). https://doi.org/10.1145/3003733.3003764

Komanduri, S., et al.: Of passwords and people: measuring the effect of password-composition policies. In: Conference on Human Factors in Computing Systems – Proceedings, pp. 2595–2604 (2011). https://doi.org/10.1145/1978942.1979321

Portman, M., Pirzada, A.: Wireless mesh networks for public safety and crisis management applications. IEEE Internet Comput. 12(1), 18–25 (2008)

Riley, C., Buckner, K., Johnson, G., Benyon, D.: Culture & biometrics: regional differences in the perception of biometric authentication technologies. AI Soc. 24(3), 295–306 (2009)

Schneier, B.: Sensible authentication. ACM Queue - Game Dev. 74 (2004). http://queue.acm.org/detail.cfm?id=971595. Accessed Feb 2004

Yee, K.-P.: Aligning security and usability. IEEE Secur. Priv. 2, 48–55 (2004). https://doi.org/10.1109/MSP.2004.64

Helping Users Secure Their Data
by Supporting Mental Models of VeraCrypt

Eric Spero, Milica Stojmenović$^{(\boxtimes)}$, and Robert Biddle

Carleton University, Ottawa, Canada
{eric.spero,milica.stojmenovic,
robert.biddle}@carleton.ca

Abstract. VeraCrypt is a popular free and open source file encryption software that encrypts disks and partitions. It has known usability issues which limit its reach to a wider audience. One way of improving its usability is to better support user mental models by changing the functionality description. We did a Cognitive Walkthrough with usability experts to test VeraCrypt's interface and the effectiveness of an attempt to help ease use through a mental model builder (MMB) in the form of a short instructional text. They concluded that the MMB would be helpful for users. We also conducted a user study to verify VeraCrypt's usability and to test the MMB with users. Before the MMB, participants were asked to secure a file using VeraCrypt and none were successful. After our MMB, 4/5 participants were able to achieve at least one sub-task, with two successfully completing the entire task. However, the MMB was more successful with users with tech backgrounds, suggesting that a more detailed MMB would have been better for average users.

Keywords: Usable cybersecurity · Usable encryption · User and expert testing

1 Introduction

Journalists and researchers often collect highly sensitive data. One way for them to secure their data is to use encryption software. Encryption scrambles information so that only those with special knowledge can unscramble it. In the context of computing, it is often used to conceal sensitive data. Encrypting files on one's local machine ensures that those files cannot be read if an attacker gains access to one's computer.

One of the most popular [3] software encryption tools is VeraCrypt, shown in Fig. 1. It is free and open source software, which positions it well to reach a wide audience. It allows users to encrypt their entire file system, or to create a virtual encrypted disk inside a file. We focus on the second of these functionalities.

VeraCrypt retains the user interface (UI) of its predecessor, TrueCrypt, which has been the subject of usability criticism [2]. Gujrati and Vasserman [2] redesigned TrueCrypt's UI and showed that the new design improved system ease of use. However, none of the recommendations have been implemented.

Mental models (MMs) are internal representations of the external world [7]. People rely on MMs to use software [9]. Software usability, which is crucial in computer security [6], can be improved by supporting users' MMs. There are many ways

© Springer Nature Switzerland AG 2019
C. Stephanidis (Ed.): HCII 2019, CCIS 1032, pp. 211–218, 2019.
https://doi.org/10.1007/978-3-030-23522-2_27

of supporting users' MMs, and perhaps the simplest is changing the description of its functionality. To aid VeraCrypt users, and to test a minimal mental model change, we created a short textual mental model builder (MMB) to improve users' understanding of the software by likening its functionality to the creation of a virtual USB drive.

Fig. 1. VeraCrypt's UI

We designed a two-part study with a twofold purpose: (1) to test the ease of use of VeraCrypt, and (2) to see if a minimal textual MMB for VeraCrypt could increase its ease of use for users. Given that VeraCrypt's UI has not changed in the years since its usability issues were first discovered, it seemed to us that there must be some practical constraints preventing UI changes from happening, and that we should explore alternative methods of improving usability. Hence, we emphasize the secondary research purpose, which was to design and test the effectiveness of a short textual instruction that draws an analogy between the encrypted file container created by VeraCrypt and something we hoped would be more familiar to users: a USB drive.

2 VeraCrypt

With VeraCrypt, users create an encrypted disk by clicking the "Create Volume" button, and then following the "Volume Creation Wizard". In the wizard, users specify a filename/location for the encrypted volume. The volume can be mounted to the filesystem, whereupon it functions like a regular storage volume such as a USB drive: Users can add files to the volume, then read and delete files from the volume. Once unmounted, its contents are unreadable.

VeraCrypt is a fork of TrueCrypt, and retains its UI. This UI was the subject of criticism and a subsequent redesign, and a user study demonstrated the new UI's superior usability [2]. Much of the usability issues in TrueCrypt's UI stemmed from its use of technical language: terms such as "Mount", "Dismount", and "Volume". Changing these terms to more familiar terms such as "Open", "Close", and "File Container" had a positive effect on usability. However, as mentioned earlier, these changes were not implemented and the suggestions are now several years old.

Using technical terminology unfamiliar to most users fails to meet the challenge presented by the "Unmotivated User Property" of security [6], which states that users do not consider security to be a primary task, and therefore will not be motivated to read about how a security system functions. Designers should instead speak in terms that are familiar to users [4].

One unexamined alternative is to examine building user MMs to aid them in securing their files using VeraCrypt. Thus, we created a MM builder, described next.

2.1   VeraCrypt Mental Model Builder

Given that the usability of TrueCrypt [2] has been questioned, we created a mental model builder (MMB) for its successor. As previously mentioned, mental models are internal representations of the external world [7]. We created a text that served to instruct users on the nature of VeraCrypt, to see if it would help increase the usability of the software. The MMB text was:

VeraCrypt lets you create files that behave a bit like virtual USB drives. Like USB drives, they can be 'attached' and 'detached' from your computer's file system.

- *When 'attached', they behave exactly like normal usb drives: you can store and delete files in them, and read the stored files*
- *When 'detached', you cannot store nor delete files in them, and you cannot read the stored files*

  Hint: you will likely need to use File Explorer to add files to this 'virtual USB drive' after it has been 'attached'

This MMB may address some of its usability pitfalls, is easier to implement than UI changes, and it is less demanding of user than reading technical documentation.

3   Methodology

3.1   Participants

For the expert-based testing, two Human-Computer Interaction specialists (1 male, 1 female) worked together to evaluate the interface. Both had over ten years of experience in the area. For the user-based pilot testing, five participants (3 male, 2 female; aged 26–31) volunteered in our study. None of the users had prior experience with VeraCrypt and none were cyber-security experts. Each participant did the study separately, for approximately half an hour.

3.2   Materials

For the expert-based test, the specialists did two Cognitive Walkthroughs (CW) of the interface. In a CW, experts examine the design and note problems while working through specific tasks [8]. For the user-based test, we collected data through questionnaires issued through LimeSurvey, participant observation while executing the main tasks, and a semi-structured interview at the conclusion of the study. Questionnaires included the System Usability Scale [1], and a custom questionnaire targeting Nielsen's [4] 10 Usability Heuristics. We recorded success rates and time spent per sub-task. Both experts and users read the MMB between interactions with VeraCrypt.

3.3 Procedure

The study was split into two parts: before and after the VeraCrypt MMB. Experts did the Cognitive Walkthrough twice, before and after the textual MMB, both times trying to secure a file while mimicking the steps an average user would have to go through. Each step required to achieve the overall goal (i.e. to secure a file) and problems a user would encounter were noted.

After the demographics questionnaire, a description of the main task was delivered textually through LimeSurvey. Participants assumed the role of someone who had been given a file containing passwords to a Swiss bank account with a large amount of money. We asked them to use VeraCrypt to make it so that the contents of the file would be unreadable to an attacker who had gained access to their computer. We made it clear that the data in the file was too long to be memorized (30 20-character passwords), and the file could not be deleted without losing access to the money.

The main task (for experts and users) consisted of four sub-tasks: (1) Creating an encrypted volume, (2) Mounting the encrypted volume to the file system, (3) Copying the contents of Passwords.pdf to the mounted volume and deleting the original, and (4) Unmounting the encrypted volume. After the MMB, participants were asked if they found the extra information helpful, and then completed post-task questionnaires.

4 Results

We present the results of the Cognitive Walkthrough, before and after the MMB, and of the user-based testing results. For the user-based testing, to measure the overall usability of VeraCrypt, we looked at the success rates for completing the main task, the subjective usability measures, and our notes.

5 Cognitive Walkthrough Results

Before the MMB, the results are as follows. The first step in the walkthrough presents users with the UI in Fig. 1. The experts determined that users would not know what "Create Volume" meant and would go with the only option on the screen that made sense to them: "Select File" since their goal would be to secure the sensitive PDF *file*. Then, the user may attempt to "Mount" the file which prompts the user to enter a password, and the result is fruitless. This action does not lead the user towards their goal. Hence, the user would fail the task with the first step in the interface. However, to in order to catch other issues found later in the interface, the experts continued to examine the UI.

Assuming that the users clicked "Create Volume", then they would see the UI in Fig. 2. Given titles of the two options, a user may be persuaded to click "Hidden VeraCrypt Volume" since the word "Hidden" suggests that the file that they need to secure would be safer than the "Standard" default option, seen in Fig. 2. However, the Hidden path leads the user to create a hidden container within a hidden container, which is not what the user needs to do.

Fig. 2. What users are thinking as they use VeraCrypt.

Clicking "Next" provides the user with the UI in Fig. 3. This prompts the user to select a *file*. Therefore, the user would select none other than the file that they are trying to secure. However, this action leads to the file selected becoming the secure location – i.e. it overwrites the file one specifies. If the user selects the file they wish to save as the folder they wish to create in order to place the file in later, then they have destroyed their sensitive data. Indeed, once the file is selected, the system does prompt the user with a warning "file already exists, do you want to replace it, overwriting its contents?" However, the user would click "Replace" since this could, from their point of view, replace the sensitive file with a "hidden" copy. Following this, there are more UI screens that the user can easily click through and successfully destroy their sensitive data. Again, the user would fail the task and lose their data.

After having read the MMB, the experts went through the interface again. However, the Volume Location screen (Fig. 3) was still an obstacle that users may have a hard time overcoming, unless the label is renamed. Assuming that the correct container was selected here, then the MMB would be successful in prompting the user to mount the new volume and then use it as a storage container before dismounting it. The only potential pitfall in the interface after understanding the previous step is that VeraCrypt gives you no indication that it cannot place the file in the new container (this must be done outside of VeraCrypt—for example, with Windows Explorer). This is where the hint at the bottom of the MMB comes in handy, since it tells the users exactly that.

Overall, the experts identified major MM issues with VeraCrypt's UI, and found the MMB improved its coherence. They further suggest that some terms in the interface be changed. For example, "File" and "Volume" should he changed to "Vault" to differentiate it from a file that needs to be secured, and to imply that it is meant to be used as a secure container. However, the experts determined that building user MMs

Fig. 3. Users are tempted to select the file they are wishing to save as the secure location.

may be even more important since their objective with the software should be changed to create a secure location for the secret file, rather than to automatically save the file they need safeguarded, as the wording in the interface may suggest.

5.1   User Testing Results

User Main Task Success Rate. *None* of the participants were able to successfully complete the first sub-task in their first attempt, create an encrypted volume, *without also deleting the file they were supposed to protect*. Three participants created an encrypted volume but overwrote it in the process. One participant overwrote the file even in their second attempt, after the textual intervention.

Participants were overall more successful in their second attempt, after receiving the MMB. One participant was successful in completing the task without any extra prompting from the researchers. Another participant canceled the volume creation process at the very last step seemingly without realizing what they had done. We notified this participant that they had canceled the creation of the encrypted volume, which was enough information to enable them to complete the first sub-task, and they went on to complete the remaining sub-tasks with ease. Two participants successfully completed the first subtask but gave up during the second sub-task. Finally, one participant overwrote Passwords.pdf again. When asked if the extra information we provided to participants (i.e. drawing an analogy between the encrypted volume created by VeraCrypt and USB drives) was helpful, two responded "yes", two "no", and one "undecided". In a follow-up question asking why they answered the way they did, all participants who did not answer "yes," made reference to the fact that they failed to complete the main task.

User Subjective Usability Measures. Participants gave VeraCrypt a mean SUS score of 23.6, which is extremely low: the normative average SUS score is 68 [5]. The heuristics results were consistent: Only 4/50 questions were positively rated.

Participant Observation. All participants demonstrated signs of confusion at some point or another, through speech, body language, and the length of time it took to complete sub-tasks. In the follow up interview, participants expressed that referring to the encrypted container as a file, as VeraCrypt does, was *counter-intuitive* and *misleading*. All participants exhibited a strong tendency to try to mount the Passwords.pdf (i.e. the file with sensitive information), even after this action resulted in no observable consequences.

6 Discussion

Consistent with Gujrati and Vasserman's [2] (GV) findings, both the experts and the users found the usability of VeraCrypt to be extremely low. Yet, both experts and users found some promise in the MMB. None of the participants were able to complete a basic task without the MMB, most participants destroyed a sensitive file, and participants frequently expressed exasperation.

We echo the sentiments of GV and urge the developers of VeraCrypt to cease all references to the encrypted volume or container as a file, technically accurate though it may be, to help the average user. We also found that participants on average got closer to completing the task after receiving the MMB. We discuss this finding next.

6.1 Effect of the MMB

All but one participant performed better in the second attempt at completing the main task. However, the MMB appears to have helped some participants more than others. This pattern aligns with the respective technical computer knowledge of the five participants: the two who were most successful in their reattempts were the two most technically knowledgeable out of the group of five. We suspect that the success of the analogy is greater for users with greater technical knowledge. For the MMB to be helpful in the second sub-task, users must know that one step in making a USB drive available for use by the operating system is to mount the drive to the file system.

Both participants seemed to expect that the encrypted volume would become automatically available to them after creating it. This expectation may come from their experience in using USB drives: in the normal use case involving a USB drive, a user plugs it in to a USB input slot, and the drive is automatically mounted and made available for use. We suspect that the mounting step is not a part of these users' mental models for how a USB drive works, so the MMB did not sufficiently equip them to complete the task. This may also explain why only the two most technically knowledgeable participants answered "yes" to the question asking about the helpfulness of the MMB. That two participants were helped so much by the short instructional text, and that two more were helped a little, suggests that this is a promising method for improving the usability of VeraCrypt *without* modifying its interface. A future MMB should alter the text to better explain this.

If a short MMB is successful, it might provide a satisfactory alternative to altering the UI, while also not requiring users to technical manuals before using the software.

7 Conclusion

VeraCrypt is a popular file encryption tool with severe usability issues. We designed and tested effectiveness of a MMB to help users understand how the software works. The CW revealed that developing MM may help users successfully save their files using VeraCrypt. Participants' objective performance in using the software, as well as the results of subjective usability measures and semi-structured interviews, all point toward the extremely low usability of VeraCrypt, and the need for a MMB. After even our minimal MMB, 4/5 participants were able to achieve at least one sub-task, with two successfully completing the entire task. We suggest that the MMB was more effective for some participants because of differences in respective MMs for how USB drives work, and that a more detailed MMB may have been more successful.

References

1. Brooke, J., et al.: SUS: a quick and dirty usability scale. Usability Eval. Ind. **189**(194), 4–7 (1996)
2. Gujrati, S., Vasserman, E.Y.: The usability of TrueCrypt, or how I learned to stop whining and fix an interface. In: Proceedings of the Third ACM Conference on Data and Application Security and Privacy, pp. 83–94. ACM (2013)
3. Henry, A.: Most popular file encryption tool: VeraCrypt. https://lifehacker.com/five-best-file-encryption-tools-5677725/1685273934. Accessed 02 Oct 2018
4. Nielsen, J.: Enhancing the explanatory power of usability heuristics. In: Proceedings of the SIGCHI Conference on Human Factors in Computing Systems, CHI 1994, New York, NY, USA, pp. 152–158. ACM (1994)
5. Sauro, J.: A Practical Guide to the System Usability Scale: Background, Benchmarks & Best Practices. Measuring Usability LLC, Denver (2011)
6. Whitten, A., Tygar, J.D.: Why Johnny can't encrypt: a usability evaluation of PGP 5.0. In: USENIX Security Symposium, vol. 348 (1999)
7. Johnson-Laird, P.N.: Mental models and thought. In: Holyoak, K.J., Morrison, R.G. (eds.) The Cambridge Handbook of Thinking and Reasoning, pp. 185–208. Cambridge University Press, Cambridge (2005)
8. Petrie, H., Bevan, N.: The evaluation of accessibility, usability and user experience. In: Stepanidis, C. (ed.) The Universal Access Handbook, pp. 10–20. CRC Press, Boca Raton (2009)
9. Norman, D.A.: Some observations on mental models. In: Gentner, D., Stevens, A.L. (eds.) Mental Models, pp. 15–22. Psychology Press, London (2014)

A Framework for Enhancing Health Information Data Security: Application of the Consolidated Framework for Implementation Research to Breach Analysis

Niya Werts[1]([⊠]) and Subrata Acharya[2]

[1] Department of Health Sciences, Towson University, Baltimore, MD, USA
nwerts@towson.edu
[2] Department of Computer and Information Sciences, Towson University,
Baltimore, MD, USA
sacharya@towson.edu

Abstract. Health information security breaches continue to be a pervasive problem in a variety of health care environments. Security breaches compromise the integrity of sensitive health information and serve as a barrier to health care provider, stakeholder, and patient trust in the full integration of transformative health informatics tools (e.g. shareable electronic health records) into the US health care system. While the logistics of security breaches are technological in nature, security breach awareness and prevention require exploring the complex web of the health care environment and understanding how the environment itself paves a path for potential security problems. In an effort to better understand the nature of data security breaches in health care environments, the authors propose an innovative application of the Consolidated Framework for Implementation Research (CFIR) to security breach analysis. The authors build on their previous research on electronic health records engagement, breach analysis, and audit procedures in various health care settings. For the purpose of demonstration, the current paper analyzes the most relevant breach occurrences based on volume of patient records from the Health and Human Services (HHS. GOV) breach dataset. Breach types were mapped to relevant CFIR constructs. The authors present the results of the CFIR mapping and discuss the potential uses of the CFIR constructs to support health information security practitioners in their efforts to improve the health data security environment.

Keywords: Health data breaches ·
Consolidated framework for implementation research ·
Health information management · Audit · Compliance

© Springer Nature Switzerland AG 2019
C. Stephanidis (Ed.): HCII 2019, CCIS 1032, pp. 219–224, 2019.
https://doi.org/10.1007/978-3-030-23522-2_28

1 Background

Security and privacy concerns continue to be prominent issues in health informatics [1, 2]. Health information breaches can cause increased distrust in the use of health information technology and subsequently create harmful conditions for both health care providers and patients [3], damage industry reputations, and cause significant, negative financial repercussions for all stakeholders. While breach identification is an important first step in identifying security and privacy vulnerabilities, developing appropriate preventive strategies based on deeper analysis of the environment that created the breach is a necessary next step.

The Consolidated Framework for Implementation (CFIR) is a model from implementation Science [4, 5]. The CFIR explores an intervention's characteristics, the settings of the intervention's deployment, the characteristics of the individuals who will interact with the intervention, and the functional processes involved with implementing the intervention [4]. For the purposes of this research, the identified interventions are the implementation of security protocols and policies to prevent health data breaches. The CFIR can provide greater perspective on the nuanced interplay between the implementation environment, the human constituents functioning in the environment, and how the attributes of the intervention create conditions for implementation success or failure.

In this study, the authors build on their previous work utilizing the CFIR as a flexible framework for examining barriers to engagement with electronic health records (EHR) in critical care hospitals and outpatient care units [6]. As security breaches were one of the most oft cited and prominent barriers to engagement with EHR systems, the authors investigated whether the application of CFIR mapping specifically to the security breach domain could yield interesting and value-adding results to the health information data security field and its practitioners.

2 Materials and Methods

Section 13402(e)(4) of the HITECH Act [7] requires all nationally serving licensed healthcare entities to provide time bound and accurate breach notification to the Office of Civil Rights (OCR). The Office of Civil Rights maintains an investigative portal of various security and privacy breaches cases both currently under investigation and also from past archived cases. The breach portal is sorted based on various categories, namely type and name of healthcare covered entity; state of breach event; volume of patient records affected; breach submission date; type of breach; and location of breach. The highest impact category amongst these is the volume of patient records affected.

In this research, the authors conducted an evaluation of the active cases at the HHS breach portal and reviewed those with the highest impact (i.e. patient records affected) over the past 3 years. Both state and national level evaluations were conducted. A comprehensive security assessment of the healthcare breaches was conducted based on the HITRUST Common Security Framework [8], HIPAA/HITECH Act [7], and the NIST risk management framework [9]. The "Confidentiality, Integrity and Availability (CIA) principle" [10] was reviewed to identify the most critical security and/or privacy characteristic (s) violated for the breach event. Once identified, the construct table from the CFIR was utilized to map the applicable preemptive construct to address the breach. The identification and mapping of the construct was guided by the federal health information standards and the service provider input collected from the authors' previous research [6].

Table 1 illustrates a subset of CFIR construct domains, construct definitions, and construct examples most relevant to the current work (for a complete overview of all the CFIR construct domains and definitions, visit CFIR.org.).

Table 1. CFIR construct domains, definitions, and examples subset

CFIR construct domains	Definition	Construct examples
Intervention characteristics	Attributes and qualities of the intervention	Intervention source
Inner setting	Internal organizational forces shaping adoption and implementation	Implementation climate, tension for change (security changes)
Characteristics of the individual	Attributes of the stakeholders and end users	Self-efficacy
Process	Contextual specificities of the implementation process	External change agents, engaging

3   Results

Table 2 highlights the most relevant CFIR constructs based on the breach incident category and the number of patient records impacted. The "intervention source" construct was implicated via the mapping in 8 of 10 breach incident categories. The "engaging" construct was implicated in 7 of 10 breach incident categories. The "implementation climate" construct was implicated in 7 of the 10 breach incident categories. The "external change agents" and "tension for change" (security change in this context) constructs were implicated in 4 of the 10 and 5 of 10 breach incident categories respectively.

Table 2. Breach incident categories and CFIR construct mapping

Breach incident	Volume (patient records)	Location	Most relevant CFIR intervention constructs
Hacking/IT Incident	2.65 million	Network Billing Server	Intervention Source, Engaging, External Change Agents, Implementation Climate
Phishing/Spyware Incident	1.4 million	Business Email System	Intervention Source, Engaging, External Change Agents, Implementation Climate

(continued)

Table 2. (*continued*)

Breach incident	Volume (patient records)	Location	Most relevant CFIR intervention constructs
Unauthorized Access/Disclosure	1.25 million	Application Server	Intervention Source, Tension for Change (Security), Engaging
Misconfiguration/IT Incident	0.975 million	Database Server	Implementation Climate, Tension for Change (Security)
Theft	0.582 million	Data Storage (Paper/Films)	Intervention Source, Self-Efficacy, Tension for Change (Security)
Unauthorized Access/Credential Theft	0.566 million	Application Server	Intervention Source, Tension for Change (Security), Engaging, External Change Agents
Hacking/Ransomware Unauthorized Disclosure	0.502 million	Network & Application Server	Intervention Source, Engaging, External Change Agents, Implementation Climate
Malware/Server Misconfiguration	0.500 million	Database & Network Server	Implementation Climate, Tension for Change (Security)
Unauthorized Access/Disclosure	0.435 million	Portable Electronic Device	Intervention Source, Tension for Change (Security), Engaging
Unauthorized Access/Disclosure	0.417 million	Email Server	Intervention Source, Tension for Change (Security), Engaging

4   Conclusion

While the current work is a pilot implementation, the results highlight the flexibility of CFIR mapping for shaping a more detailed narrative about health security breaches. The construct mapping in Table 2 could inform the established best practice security audit cycle (Fig. 1 Appendix 1) for the preparation and implementation of a preemptive action plan to limit the scope and occurrence of a breach event in the future. CFIR constructs identified, such as intervention source, engaging, implementation climate, tension for change (security), and external change agents may be important elements to support secure healthcare posture and the maintenance of security and privacy compliance. Whether as a stand- alone tool [6] or integrated with established information security models, the CFIR construct domains and construct examples expand the vocabulary of health information security breach categorization and breach prevention strategic priorities.

Appendix 1

Best Practice Life cycle for Security and Privacy Aware IT Operation.

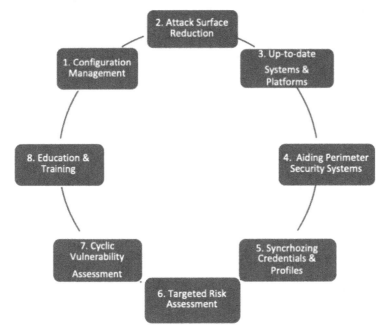

References

1. Liu, V., Musen, M.A., Chou, T.: Data breaches of protected health information in the United States. JAMA **313**(14), 1471–1473 (2015)
2. Wikina, S. B.: What caused the breach? An examination of use of information technology and health data breaches. Perspect. Health Inform. Manag. **11**(Fall) (2014)
3. Agaku, I.T., Adisa, A.O., Ayo-Yusuf, O.A., Connolly, G.N.: Concern about security and privacy, and perceived control over collection and use of health information are related to withholding of health information from healthcare providers. J. Am. Med. Inform. Assoc. **21**(2), 374–378 (2013)
4. Consolidated framework for implementation research guide. http://www.cfir.org. Accessed 3 Mar 2019
5. Damschroder, L.J., Aron, D.C., Keith, R.E., Kirsh, S.R., Alexander, J.A., Lowery, J.C.: Fostering implementation of health services research findings into practice: a consolidated framework for advancing implementation science. Implement. Sci. **4**(1), 50 (2009)
6. Acharya, S., Werts, N.: Toward the design of an engagement tool for effective electronic health record adoption. Perspect. Health Inform. Manag. **16**(Winter), 1g (2019)
7. HITECH Enforcement Act. https://www.hhs.gov/hipaa/for-professionals/special-topics/hitech-act-enforcement-interim-final-rule/index.html. Accessed 3 Mar 2019
8. HITRUST CSF. https://hitrustalliance.net/hitrust-csf/. Accessed 3 Mar 2019

9. NIST.   https://csrc.nist.gov/projects/risk-management/risk-management-framework-(RMF) Overview. Accessed 3 Mar 2019

10. Nieles, M., Dempsey, K., Pillitteri, V.: An Introduction to Information Security (No. NIST Special Publication (SP) 800-12 Rev. 1 (Draft), National Institute of Standards and Technology (2017)

Effects of Transparency of Service Design on User Attitude Toward 'Exchanging Information for Service'

Yu Zhang[⊠], Dandan Wang, Jianghua Mu, and Zengyao Yang

Department of Industrial Design, School of Mechanical Engineering,
Xi'an Jiaotong University, Xi'an 710049, China
{zhang.yu,xygfb,yangzengyao}@xjtu.edu.cn,
mjh279360984@stu.xjtu.edu.cn

Abstract. In the new wave of the 5G Era, greater use of innovative Internet and IOT services has created tremendous data values, as the same time, people fears are growing that personal information could be handled irresponsibly as a result. The study aims to improve the user experience for the e-mobility services in the future and establish a virtuous relationship between service providers and users in security and privacy aspects and think about how to design the user experience for trust and persuasion to build user confidence. The study explores Chinese's data-privacy-related perceptions and behaviors and places them in the context of various online services. The findings are based on a Chinese citizens questionnaire survey (N = 1003) and six focus groups (N = 48). The results show that users' attitude toward 'Exchanging Information for Service' is positively correlated with service demands, information sensitivity, cost-effectiveness and trust in service providers. Transparency of interactive interface such as understandable privacy policy visualized user interface, and control of the data produce positive effects on the willingness to share personal information.

Keywords: Exchanging information for service · Transparency ·
Service design · User experience · Interactive interface

1 Introduction

Nowadays, greater use of innovative Internet services has created tremendous data values. On the one hand, enterprises eager to get more valuable data from the users; on the other hand, people fears are growing that personal information could be handled irresponsibly as a result.

The user's awareness of privacy protection is related to their related knowledge, educational experience, related event experience, *etc*. It is constrained by the demand for services and the dependence on services, which determines the attitude and behavior toward personal information sharing. With the consequences of behavior, the individual's privacy security awareness is also awakened and enhanced [1]. Therefore, it is the primary prerequisite for building trust in service providers to make users enjoy

© Springer Nature Switzerland AG 2019
C. Stephanidis (Ed.): HCII 2019, CCIS 1032, pp. 225–232, 2019.
https://doi.org/10.1007/978-3-030-23522-2_29

a good user experience before users form a specific privacy awareness and attitude to service providers [2].

This study aims to improve the user experience for the e-mobility-related services and seek on the relationship between the online service design and the willingness to share personal information and how to design the user experience for trust and persuasion to build user confidence in the security and privacy aspect.

There are some theories used to explain the consumers' attitude and behavior about exchange information for service. Social exchange theory (SET) explain the behavior of a human in social exchange includes personal information [3]. The theory holds that people disclose personal information depends on the expectation of benefits in the future. Privacy calculus theory (PCT) proposes that an individual's intention to disclose personal information is based on the risk-benefit analysis. It is a balance between the amounts of personal information is willing to be shared, and the services are expected [4]. Therefore, it can be shown that sharing willingness, trust, reciprocity, and altruism will influence individuals' sharing behavior. Some researches about information sharing behavior depend on these social theories can be found in the literature. Taylor's research shows that trust can accelerate online information trading decisions and the behavior of experienced consumers intending to trade with the final electronic supplier they purchase depends on trust and perceived usefulness, perceived ease-of-use [5]. Chai found that there is a positive correlation between bloggers' trust and their knowledge-sharing behavior [6].

Forth more, many researchers think the willingness of consumers to disclose personal information depends on the sensitivity of different information. Sheehan argues that consumer concern and willingness to provide marketers with personal data vary dramatically by information type [7]. Bansal studied the impact of trust and sensitivity on users' online disclosure of personal information from the aspects of information sensitivity and trust. The results show that users perceive a greater risk to sensitive personal information. Individuals' intention to disclose healthcare related information depends on their trust, privacy concern, and information sensitivity, which are determined by personal dispositions—personality traits, information sensitivity, health status, prior privacy invasions, risk beliefs, and experience—acting as intrinsic antecedents of trust [8].

The topic involved exchange personal information for service is favorite in the Era of big data, but how to improve the user experience through service design is still under discussion. Transparency is critical to making more users willing for data sharing. A level of transparency about how data is collected and used is essential to build and maintain trust between businesses and consumers [9]. It is reasonable to believe that the willingness to share personal information and attitude toward "Exchanging Information for Service" will be more active under the premise of clear security measures and high transparency in use.

This study explores Chinese's data-privacy-related perceptions and behaviors and places them in the context of various online services. Interview, focus group and questionnaire survey involved attitude toward 'Exchanging Information for Service' across different user groups were implemented, and comparison among different groups was accomplished. Finally, Chinese netizens service design demands and privacy boundaries in typical online scenarios were summarized.

2 Methodology

2.1 Procedure

In order to design high-quality online service, an in-depth study on Chinese user attitudes toward sharing personal information and behavior with different service demands and scenarios was conducted. The main methods are as follows,

1st stage: Qualitative Research

(I) Interview/case studies: identify user's sensitivity to privacy in different online services scenarios.
(II) Focus group: identify the boundary of individual privacy and personas in 9 e-mobility related scenarios.

2nd stage: Quantitative Research

(I) Massive Questionnaire survey: measure user's attitudes on online privacy information sharing behavior via subjective scaling.
(II) Descriptive statistics and cluster analysis: generalize the levels of attitude toward 'exchanging privacy for service' attributed to different user groups.

2.2 Participants

In qualitative research, a total of 48 interviewees were divided into six groups, each with 7–8 people, who have some experience in using online services (as Table 1 shown). In quantitative research, 1003 questionnaires were received, who include 524 males and 479 females. Their average age is about 33 (ranges from 18–80). Participants were from 142 cities in China, and 67% (67) of them reached a bachelor's degree or above (as Table 2 shown).

Table 1. Demographics of the focus group interviewees

Age	Gender ratio	Education	Occupation
18–25	4:4	Bachelor or above	Student
26–35	5:4	Bachelor degree or above	Software engineer/staff/designer etc.
26–35	3:5	Bachelor degree below	Accounting/general staff etc.
36–45	4:4	Bachelor degree or above	Teacher/accounting/sales etc.
36–45	3:4	Bachelor degree below	Accounting/finance etc.
Over 45	4:4	Bachelor degree or below	Teacher/nurse/civil servant etc.

2.3 Personal Data and Scenario Categories

The classification of the personal data according to the 'personal data' definition of GDPR, which means any information relating to an identified or identifiable natural person [10] and some sociologic study practice about privacy and security [11].

Table 2. Demographics of the questionnaire participants

Age	18–25		26–35		36–45		46 or over	
	300		290		279		134	
Gender ratio	524(male): 479(female)							
Education	Middle school	High school		College	Bachelor		Master	Doctor
	31	137		163	506		144	22
Occupation	Student	Professional	Clerk	Manager	Freelancer	Civil servant	Self-employed	Worker	Others
	226	225	152	106	70	64	49	48	63
Income (rmb/Year)	None	<5,000	5,000–8,000	8,000–15,000	15,000–30,000	30,000–100,000	>100,000	Not shown
	201	168	178	201	90	29	2	134

We selected ten categories of personal data, that is, Network identity, demographic, biological, medical health, communication, social relationship, financial, location, behavior, and device information.

The online service scenarios were selected, which involved mobility, information transaction and new lifestyle of the netizens. The e-mobility related services include driving fatigue monitoring, environmental perception, travel planning, personalized driving, intelligent car lock, car payment, human-vehicle information interaction, voice control, and home-vehicle interconnection.

3   Results and Discussion

3.1   Chinese Citizens Attitude Toward 'Exchange Privacy for Service.'

More Chinese citizens hold a keen awareness of personal information protection. 83% of adults say they are often cautious about personal information. However, there is a general lack of privacy protection related education and common sense.

As Fig. 1 showed the five most sensitive personal information are: Financial Information (78% of adult think it is sensitive), Net Identification Information (74%), Personal Basic Information (68%), Bio-Information (63%), and Communication Information (61%).

There are nine items involved the attitude to exchange personal information for service, which four items are negative and five items are positive attitudes. As the Fig. 2 showed that few Chinese citizens are open and positive to 'exchange privacy for service,' 75% of adults tend to resist personal information be obtained without being informed, and accepted service with resignation. Around 1/3 tend to acceptable to "exchange privacy to service" and 16% incline to offer personal information in exchange for discounts.

The attitudes are different with age, gender, education level, etc. More youngers (18–35) view data as a tradeable asset that they can use to negotiate better prices and

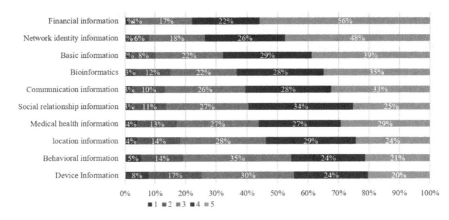

Fig. 1. Chinese citizens' sensitivity of personal information, which from 1 to 5 scores of Likert scales that means the most insensitive to the most sensitive.

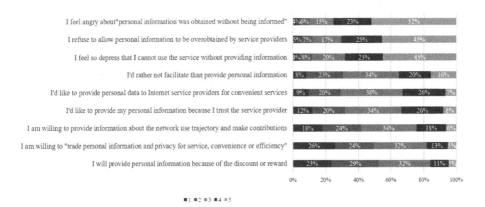

Fig. 2. Chinese citizens' attitude toward exchange personal information for service, which from 1 to 5 scores of Likert scales that means entirely disagree to agree.

offers; while older users (>35) are more public-spirited, and are willing to contribute to big data if it is helpful to public service. Females prefer to enjoy the convenience so relatively open despite their concern for safety (sensitive in financial and location information); while males tend to pragmatism, functionalism and are more cautious. Lower-educated (bachelor below) adults are more favorable to exchange privacy for convenience and efficiency and easy to follow the crowd.

3.2 Service Demands and Privacy Boundaries in Typical Online Scenarios

There are six online service scenarios involved in the survey: e-mobility, smart home, shopping online, financial service, healthcare, and others.

Service demands for various scenarios are correlated with age, gender, education level. The willingness to share information is affected by service demands, information sensitivity, cost-effectiveness and trust in service providers (see Fig. 3 shown).

Fig. 3. Service demands and willingness to share information, the demands and the sharing willingness are consistent in e-mobility, smart home, and healthcare; while the sharing willingness is lower than the demands in shopping online, financial and others services.

In the context of e-mobility, the highest demands for driving fatigue monitoring, environmental perception, human-car information interaction, intelligent voice control, the lowest demands for intelligent vehicle lock, home-vehicle interconnection (see Fig. 4 shown). The sharing willingness is basically similar to the service demands in the majority of cases, except driver fatigue monitoring and voice control, in which bio-information being required.

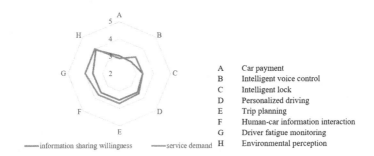

Fig. 4. Service demands and willingness to share information in the context of e-mobility services

Compare the attitudes toward exchange information for service in the focus group and the questionnaire. We found that the attitudes are more positive in the former because of more visualized service cases were showed. At the same time, more expectations and suggestions for service providers were proposed, such as more respectful for user's right to control personal data, strengthen data management, including grading, sensitive information transmission, and utilization to avoid data leakage. Especially the Transparency of user interface design such as understandable privacy policy visualized user interface, and control of the data would produce positive effects on the willingness to share personal information.

4   Conclusion

The study shows us Chinese citizen's general attitude toward exchange information for service, as well as the degree of sensitives on different information types. It discusses users' demands for service and their willingness to share information according to different service scenarios. Preliminary findings are that users' attitude toward 'Exchanging Information for Service' is positively correlated with service demands, information sensitivity, cost-effectiveness and trust in service providers. Transparency of service design such as understandable privacy policy visualized user interface, and control of the data is the key to continuing to build and maintain trust between businesses and consumers.

The paper is the inadequacy of the lack of analysis of the service design effects on the attitudes toward exchange information for service. We plan to go on with the next research is design exploration and verification as follows,

(I)   Detailed design in the context of e-mobility: design for the exchange information types that users expected and use flow.

(II) User evaluation: the sharing willingness was compared with the previous sharing willingness to verify the transparency of service interface design effect on user attitude. The factors affecting the user's willingness to share information in the interfaces will be further analyzed.

References

1. Milne, G.R., Rohm, A.J., Bahl, S.: Consumers' protection of online privacy and identity. J. Consum. Aff. **38**(2), 217–232 (2004)
2. Kim, D.J., Ferrin, D.L., Rao, H.R.: A trust-based consumer decision-making model in electronic commerce: The role of trust, perceived risk, and their antecedents. Des. Support Syst. **44**(2), 522–564 (2008)
3. Liu, Z., Min, Q., Zhai, Q., Smyth, R.: Self-disclosure in Chinese micro-blogging: A social exchange theory perspective. Inf. Manag. **53**(1), 53–63 (2016)
4. Majumdar, A., Bose, I.: Privacy calculus theory and its applicability for emerging technologies. In: Sugumaran, V., Yoon, V., Shaw, Michael J. (eds.) WEB 2015. LNBIP, vol. 258, pp. 191–195. Springer, Cham (2016). https://doi.org/10.1007/978-3-319-45408-5_20
5. Taylor, D.G., Davis, D.F., Jillapalli, R.: Privacy concern, and online personalization: The moderating effects of information control and compensation. Electron. Commer. Res. **9**(3), 203–223 (2009)
6. Chai, S., Kim, M.: What makes bloggers share knowledge? An investigation of the role of trust. Int. J. Inf. Manag. **30**(5), 408–415 (2010). https://doi.org/10.1016/j.ijinfomgt.2010.02.005
7. Kim, B.S., Mariea, G.H.: Dimensions of privacy concern among online consumers. J. Public Policy Mark. **19**, 62–73 (2000)

8. Bansal, G., Zahedi, F., Gefen, D.: The impact of personal dispositions on information sensitivity, privacy concern, and trust in disclosing health information online. Decis. Support Syst. **49**(2), 138–150 (2010)

9. GDPR Assessment. https://gdpr.report/news/2018/03/01/transparency-key-making-consumers-happy-data/

10. Olausson, M.: User control of personal data: a study of personal data management in a GDPR-compliant graphical user interface. Dissertation (2018)

11. Zhang, Y., Sun, X., Lu, J., Zhu, Q.: The empirical research on the willingness of information disclosure for mobile social platform users-taking Wechat as an example. Libr. Inf. **38**(03), 90–97 (2018)

Accessibility and Universal Access

Empathy Tool Design-Eye Disease Simulator Based on Mixed-Reality Technology

Jialiang Bai[✉], Zhefan Yu, Fengjie Zhang, and Yeshuai Cheng

Academy of Art and Design, Tsinghua University,
Shuangqing Road, Haidian District,
Beijing 100082, China
mubai_bjl@163.com, yuzhefanthu@163.com,
zhangfjl7@mails.tsinghua.edu.cn,
yangpeng_personal@163.com,

Abstract. People who are suffering from oculopathy have a tons of inconveniences in daily life due to cognitive difficulties. Our research results - eye disease simulator embrace inclusive design philosophy may make some changes. However, a kind of empathy tools aimed at helping designer experience eye disease has been lacking for a long time.

Our project brings out an eye disease simulator based on mixed reality technology (Microsoft Hololens) enable designers understand the eye disease patient better, and verify & optimize visual design through serious expert interviews, patient shadowing and other design methods.

Compared with the previously existed oculopathy simulator, our research result covers a variety of eye disease's traits, even more truly reveal the world of visually impaired groups can see. Getting the benefit from wearability and interactivity of Microsoft Hololens, visual designers can see world through transparent front glass simultaneously in an acceptable way, while recording issues on previous guide system through various interaction (including Leap-motion, eye tacking). Our research results can be widely used to guide system design in public space, web design and so on. In conclusion, our research project validates the effectiveness of eye disease simulator through actual design cases, and explores new approach that combines cutting-edge technologies with orthodox empathy design tools.

Keywords: Empathy toolkit · Mixed-reality · Vision guidance

1 Introduction

With the changes of social structure and the strength of the awareness of healthcare, all areas of society pay more and more attention to the vulnerable groups, design is no exception. By the change of the design paradigm, the research directions of 'Inclusive Design', 'Accessible Design' and 'Design for the special' have also been correspondingly developed. Although they have different titles, they are all vulnerable groups, including people with disabilities, left-behind children, empty nesters and visually impaired people involved in this article. As the number of visually impaired

C. Stephanidis (Ed.): HCII 2019, CCIS 1032, pp. 235–242, 2019.
https://doi.org/10.1007/978-3-030-23522-2_30

people grows, when designing the visual guidance system, the designers should not only serve the general public, but also special people. The visual guidance design tends to solve the cognitive problems that people may meet when they walk in unfamiliar spaces—they usually need the guidance system to locate space, direction and some functional areas.

This article takes patients with visual diseases and hospital space as examples. Visually impaired people are easily lost in the hospital, and they have serious judgment obstacles in the space with complicated functional areas. Our team design a toolkit, in the way of empathy, to help designers gain an intuitive impression of the visually impaired people on the space of the hospital. Our team adopt mixed reality technology to produce an empathy toolkit that combines a physical design tool with a virtual design tool, so the designers can verify the rationality of the solution with the patient's first-person perspective during the design process.

2 Preliminary Investigation

2.1 Empathy Tools

Empathy is the ability to think and recognize the emotions that others are experiencing while standing in the other's position. The so-called empathy tool is a technical approach–designers can experience the user's physical and psychological experiences–helping designers to understand user needs and user-centric product development.

2.2 Classification of Visually Impaired People

According to the relevant data, we divide the common vision diseases into four categories: sight discoloration, sight occlusion, sight blur and sight distortion. This classification helps us to visualize the design requirements.

Sight Discoloration. Color blindness is a common kind of the sight discoloration, including full color blindness, partial color blindness, and color weakness. Color blindness, also known as congenital color vision disorder, cannot distinguish a certain color or various colors in the natural spectrum, including red-green blindness; color weakness means that the color resolution ability is weak, although the color seen by normal people can be seen.

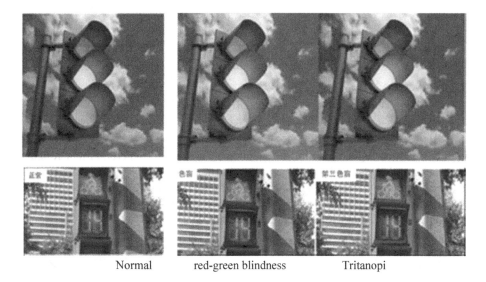

| Normal | red-green blindness | Tritanopi |

Sight Occlusion. Sight occlusion is common in diabetic retinopathy and glaucoma. Diabetic retinopathy is one of the serious complications caused by diabetes. Symptoms include blurred vision, shadows, spots, and pain. Glaucoma is caused by increased pathological intraocular pressure, visual field defects due to insufficient optic nerve supply, and decreased vision.

| diabetic retinopathy | glaucoma |

Blurred Vision. Eyesight blur is common in ocular diseases such as cataract, myopia, and hyperopia. Cataract patients are mostly elderly, the cause is opacity of lens protein denaturation, resulting in blurred vision and fog; myopia and hyperopia are due to lens hardening and can not adjust the relaxation, resulting in blurred vision in patients near or far.

Cataract   near-sighted or far-sighted

Sight Distortion. Sight distortion is common in macular degeneration and retinitis pigmentosa (flying mosquitoes). Macular degeneration is mostly the result of degeneration of the elderly, because the fluid leaking from the blood vessels will damage the macula, causing visual distortion and decreased vision; the mosquito is also a natural aging phenomenon, due to aging caused by aging.

macular degeneration   muscae volitante

3   Empathy Tool Design

3.1   Purpose

Taking patients with ocular diseases as an example, using mixed reality technology, a physical empathy tool combining physical design tools and virtual design tools helps designers to verify large public spaces (such as hospitals) in the design process with the patient's first-person perspective, stadiums, etc). The rationality of the design of the guidance system.

3.2   Methods

Hardware Support. Microsoft HoloLens is a pair of mixed reality smart-glasses developed and manufactured by Microsoft. Users can interact through eyes, voice and gestures. Our team choose this device as a hardware carrier for empathy tools, so the designers can move freely in the physical space.

Software Development. Our team use Unity and VisualStudio2017 as development tools, and use C# as the programming language. Our team adopt image processing technology and recode the video stream captured by the front camera of the Hololens, so the video stream is transformed to simulate different visual impairment pictures.

Interface Design. The top of the interface is the menu, user can select different visual impairment simulations by gestures. The left side is the adjustment of the degree of lesions, and users can move a sliding button up and down to simulate the severity of vision problems at different stages. At the same time, users can use gesture to mark the where they do not see clearly or the places they are confused in the scene (as red dots in the figure below). Then, they can click "Screenshot" button to save picture as evidence to improve the guide design.

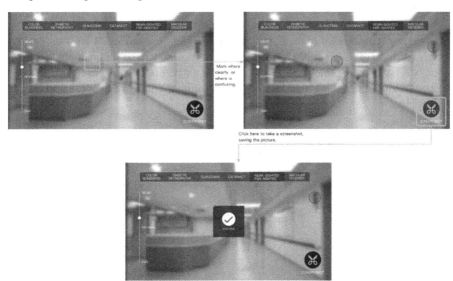

Interaction flow

Photograph for prototyping

4 Evaluation

Mockup is one of the most classic industrial design tools. At first, it appeared in the form of modified optical glasses. However, it did not meet expectations (for the reason that we cannot focus on the near scene and the distant one at the same time because of the physiological structure of human eyes). When Mockup simulates the visual effects of patients with eye diseases, most of them are blurred because the lens is too close to the eyeballs. In order to get better stimulation effects, we replaced the mockup with the more advanced device—Microsoft HoloLens.

For the purpose of verifying the rationality of the tool based on the first-person perspective in the actual hospital-guided design project, we contacted two senior visual designers, handing over the toolkit we produced to them. We selected three eye diseases: diabetic retinopathy, floaters, and color blindness. Through augmented reality technology, the designers could see the world in the eyes of patients with eye diseases from a first-person perspective.

By actual tests, we found that the information of the original guide design was too much and concentrated for diabetic retinopathy. In addition, too small information was partially occluded and centralized information was not easy to be found. With the aid of toolkit, we have found that the original design can be effectively improved by magnifying the area, enhancing the ductility (for example, changing to a long strip) and intensifying tone contrast (Fig. 1).

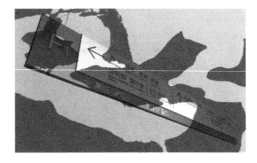

Fig. 1. Guide sign in the eyes of patients with diabetic retinopathy

For the floaters, we found that the information of the original guide design was too much, the font was too small and the information was blocked. With the help of toolkit, we have found that reducing and magnifying information while enhancing the tone contrast between graphics can effectively improve the original design (Fig. 2).

Fig. 2. Guide sign in the eyes of a floaters patient

For the yellow-gray blindness, we found that the color function and tone contrast of the original guide design were weak. In addition, the information was blurred and difficult to be identified (Fig. 3). With the assistance of toolkit, we have found that we can change the theme color while enhancing the color brightness contrast depending on various color blindness, which can effectively improve the original design.

Fig. 3. Guide sign and enhanced sign in the eyes of a yellow-gray blind patient. (Color figure online)

By means of our design tools, the two designers discovered the problems that different kinds of eye patients would encounter when looking at the guidance system. Combining the above three improvements, they produce a new guide design. The new one has a significant effect. If light is good enough, patients with three eye diseases mentioned above can observe the information on the guide signs more clearly (Fig. 4).

Fig. 4. Improved guide design

5   Conclusion

Our study of the visual guidance design toolkit is not totally equal to a research of standard design project. Although the design research results tend to be a kind of product which provide service for people, the aim of the early stage and the users are different.

First, our study fully reflects the philosophy of UCD (User-centered design). The toolkit can help the designers to learn the operating habit, physical condition, psychological thoughts and other information of users, and then these information can be transformed into different forms of data by technical means to help designers seek the breakthrough more explicitly during the design process.

Second, the service object of design toolkit is more complicated. A standard design project has an explicit service object, but design toolkit has two. The first one is the designers themselves sand the second one is the public.

Finally, empathy toolkits are presented differently. The toolkit maybe a simple mechanical structure, a device for digital information transmission, a space with deep interaction and so on. The process will help designers to have a new understanding of design, such as research, conception, drafting, prototype, design, display and so on.

The toolkit still has many parts to be improved in the future. The first one is the improvement of technology. We will continue to communicate with experts in relevant disciplines to make the toolkit more effective. Secondly, we should try to explore the possibilities of the project and make it applied to different fields in a suitable state.

References

1. Zhang, S.: Analysis of Epidemiological investigation data of cataract in China. Chin. J. Ophthalmol. (1999)
2. Zhou, H.: Prevalence of age-related macular degeneration in Caojiadu Street, Jing'an District, Shanghai. Chin. J. Ophthalmol. (2005)
3. Wang, N., Yu, S., Gou, B., Gong, X.: Research on computer aided color design technology for color blind people. Sci. Technol. Eng. (2007)
4. Bao, J., Wang, Y., Ma, Y., Gu, X.: Color blind correction method based on H component rotation. Prog. Biomed. Eng. (2008)
5. Abascal, J., Nicolle, C.: Moving towards inclusive design guidelines for socially and ethically aware HCI. Interact. Comput. **17**(5), 484–505 (2005)

Brain-Computer Interface for Motor Rehabilitation

Elizabeth Clark[1], Adrienne Czaplewski[1], Sean Dourney[1],
Ashley Gadelha[1], Khoa Nguyen[1], Patrick Pasciucco[1], Marimar Rios[1],
Ross Stuart[1], Eduardo Castillo[2], and Milena Korostenskaja[2,3(✉)]

[1] Department of Physical Therapy, AdventHealth University, Orlando, USA
[2] MEG Lab, AdventHealth for Children, Orlando, USA
milena.korostenskaja@adventhealth.com
[3] Functional Brain Mapping and Brain-Computer Interface Lab,
AdventHealth for Children, Orlando, USA

Abstract. Stroke is the fifth leading cause of death and disability in the United States with approximately 6.8 million people living with residual deficits and approximately \$34 billion spent on treatment annually [1, 2]. Simultaneously, dramatic healthcare shifts have limited extended care accessibility, with many individuals discharged from restorative therapy by three-months post-stroke. Decreased access and increased costs have led clinicians, and scientists to investigate more effective and efficient interventions to improve the function of the hemiparetic upper extremity of individuals post-stroke. One such modality is a brain-computer interface (BCI) technology that utilizes brain signals to drive rehabilitation of motor function. Emerging data suggests the use of BCI for motor rehabilitation post-stroke, facilitating an individual's return to function and improving quality of life [3–10]. Specifically, integration of virtual reality (VR) and functional electrical stimulation (FES) components is an innovative rehabilitation strategy with a strong potential to reinstitute central motor programs specific to hand function in patients' status post-stroke. By utilizing the Fugl-Meyer Assessment (FMA), researchers can monitor the motor function of the hemiparetic upper extremity pre/post-intervention, objectively quantifying the effectiveness of BCI for the restoration of upper extremity motor function [11]. Neurophysiological brain imaging techniques allow tracking changes in the neural substrates of motor function due to BCI intervention. Therefore, the purpose of our study is to demonstrate the utility of BCI-VR-FES intervention for motor rehabilitation of upper extremity, based upon the theory of neuroplasticity, in individuals' post-stroke by using functional (FMA) and neurophysiological outcome measures.

Keywords: Brain-computer interface · Virtual reality ·
Functional electrical stimulation · Stroke · Motor rehabilitation

© Springer Nature Switzerland AG 2019
C. Stephanidis (Ed.): HCII 2019, CCIS 1032, pp. 243–254, 2019.
https://doi.org/10.1007/978-3-030-23522-2_31

1 Introduction

Stroke and its Consequences. Stroke affects 795,000 Americans annually. It is the second leading cause of death worldwide, impacting approximately 6.5 million individuals globally in 2013 [1, 2]. The financial impact from stroke in the United States is an estimated $34 billion each year, including the cost of healthcare services, medications, and missed days of work [1, 2]. Individuals affected by stroke often experience serious long-term impairments to the motor, sensory, and language functions contributing to reduced mobility and reduced community reintegration. The post-stroke rehabilitation process is intricate and time-consuming, as the individual seeks to regain function lost due to damage to the brain. It is in the best interest of practitioners to investigate interventions that could provide an efficient means of rehabilitation and contribute to reducing the cost of health care. Therefore, due to the brain damage-related nature of functional impairments post-stroke, the development of brain activity-driven rehabilitation approaches is warranted. Recent advances in brain-computer interface (BCI) technology provide the means of integrating such technology into the rehabilitation process.

Sensory-Motor Impairments Post-Stroke and Rehabilitation Procedures. The nature of the impairments resulting from stroke varies widely and is determined by the location and severity of the stroke. Motor impairments can be extensive and can include hemiparesis of the upper or lower extremity contributing to asymmetric posture [12]. Patients also commonly present with reduced weight-bearing on the affected limb, severe balance dysfunctions, and increased risk of fall [13]. Sensory deficits may result in impaired detection and discrimination of sensory information [14, 15]. As a result, sensory impairments can further limit the motor output negatively impacting a person's quality of life. Therefore, rehabilitation that can simultaneously facilitate recovery of both motor and sensory functions becomes of particular significance.

Neuroplasticity and Motor Learning: Neuroplasticity is the brain's capacity to change and adapt as a result of interactions with the environment [16]. Cognitive and physical rehabilitation aim to facilitate neuroplasticity to improve functional outcomes. While the mechanisms regarding brain reorganization and its effects on functional outcomes need further attention, Kleim and Jones propose ten principles of experience-dependent neural plasticity that may exhibit a positive correlation to neuronal remapping within the brain and can be viewed in the Appendix 1 [16]. Some of the most common principles that appear to have a significant impact on the alteration of neuronal wiring include the following: specificity of the task, repetition of functional movements, and the incorporation of salient activities for each individual [7]. In an undamaged, healthy brain, neuroplasticity is evident, as the brain is continuously remodeled by experience-dependent exercises that are specific and intense in order to achieve a solution to a motor problem [16]. Research suggests that when an individual participates in problem-solving during frequent repetition of a salient task, neuroplasticity is enhanced [16].

Therefore, a critical component in the rehabilitation process after a stroke is facilitating neuroplasticity to promote motor learning. For example, when throwing a ball, a performer must gather sensory information such as what to look at or how the ball feels. Second, the performer needs to learn the concepts of the task. For example, when throwing the ball, knowing the mechanics of the ball, the angle at which to throw it, and any external forces affecting the direction of the ball. Third, when throwing the ball, the performer needs to have proper predictive/feedforward and reactive/feedback control mechanisms. The performer must know what to expect from each throw. In addition, if the performer throws too short or far, they would re-adjust the throw for the next one. Finally, the performer must incorporate higher level skills like spinning the ball [17]. Each of these components of task analysis is pertinent and closely related to the field of neurorehabilitation and motor learning theories, which are fundamental to maximize neuroplasticity and motor learning in individuals' post-stroke [18]. The integration of brain-computer interface together with virtual reality (VR) and functional electrical stimulation (FES) into neurorehabilitation of individuals post-stroke incorporates all these aspects of motor learning.

Brain-Computer Interfaces (BCIs) for Sensory-Motor Recovery After Stroke.
Brain-computer interface-virtual reality-functional electrical stimulation (BCI-VR-FES) is an innovative rehabilitation modality that has a strong potential to benefit patients suffering from both sensory and motor impairments, which may be particularly promising in restoring function in patients' status post-stroke [19–23]. Importantly, the principles of BCI-VR-FES rehabilitation are aligned with 10 principles of experience-dependent plasticity and promote neuroplasticity and neurorehabilitation outcomes, as highlighted in Appendix 1 [16, 18]. When reviewing each of the components separately, brain-computer interface (BCI) is a device that responds to neural processes occurring within the brain and translates detected neural signals into the desired action (e.g., wheelchair control; initiation of orthosis) [10]. It provides a direct communication pathway between the brain and an external device without the use of the typical neuromuscular pathways [10].

Electroencephalography (EEG). The computer-based system may use electroencephalography (EEG) to translate brain signals into commands for an output device to perform the desired action [24, 25]. In this way, even those patients with completely or severely impaired motor function can still potentially interact with the external environment by means of their brain activity, which can also be used for rehabilitation purposes.

Virtual Reality (VR) or Avatar Control. The BCI system can be combined with VR or Avatar, which utilizes a human-machine interface as a means of increasing patient engagement by providing a patient with visual feedback (for example, showing patient's moving hands on the screen). VR can be used for repetitive, task-specific training as the patient views the action. Calabro et al. has shown that the observation of an action recruits stored motor programs, which ultimately promotes recovery of movement execution and provides added value to the potential of using BCI systems for rehabilitation purposes [26].

Functional Electrical Stimulation (FES). Another addition, which can further strengthen the potential use of the BCI system in rehabilitation, is FES. It utilizes neuromuscular electrical stimulation to provoke the contraction of muscles local to skin electrode placement. Alon et al. has shown that it has beneficial effects on regaining upper-extremity function, including the ability to grasp, hold, move, and release objects [27]. Moreover, FES allows for sensory feedback, which makes it possible to combine rehabilitation of both motor and sensory function in a single procedure.

As a result, combining multiple modalities (BCI, VR, and FES) into one intervention (BCI-VR-FES) may improve efficiency of patient care and patient recovery of motor function after stroke [19–21].

2   Study Objectives

2.1   Outcome Measures

Our long-term goal is to improve motor recovery outcomes in stroke patients by expanding applicability and use of the BCI systems. The chosen primary outcome measures capture actual changes in motor recovery and functional mobility, as well as perceived changes in individuals post stroke after BCI-VR-FES. These measures include the Fugl-Meyer Assessment (FMA), Box and Block Test (BBT), Stroke Impact Scale (SIS), and Gait Speed (GS).

Fugl-Meyer Assessment (FMA). The Fugl-Meyer Assessment (FMA) is a comprehensive measurement tool of motor function of both the upper and lower extremity in individuals post stroke [8]. The FMA has previously been utilized when evaluating changes in subjects post stroke with BCI and FES interventions [8]. The FMA assesses motor function, sensory function, balance, joint range of motion, and joint pain across upper and lower extremity joints [8]. According to Gladstone et al., the FMA has exceptional reliability as well as construct validity [28]. A study performed by Kim et al. reported the FMA has a strong inter-rater reliability with intraclass correlation coefficients at 0.930 or higher among 50 patients with a history of stroke [28]. The same study showed good test-retest reliability within a two-week interval with intraclass correlation coefficients from 0.834 to 0.972 [11]. We intend to utilize the FMA to assess the upper extremity in this study. The minimally clinical important difference (MCID) for the FMA is 4.25 for grasping ability, 5.25 for releasing ability, 7.25 for the ability to move an arm, 4.25 for the ability to perform COPM, and 5.25 for overall UE function [29].

Generally, there is a correlation between lower FMA upper extremity scores and lower overall functional ability. It is ambiguous at times whether the score received from the FMA will depict the overall level of motor impairment. The analysis of previous research on the FMA stratification is presented in Appendix 2 [30–35] and highlights the inconsistencies in the use and stratification of the FMA to date. In order to minimize the ambiguity in the stratification and interpretation of FMA scores, considerations by researchers must also include type and chronicity of stroke, as well as the age of subjects. The literature findings shed some light, but still, lack clear and consistent stratification regarding the level of motor impairment. It is imperative for researchers and rehabilitation specialists to justify their stratification methods for effective selection and delivery of interventions to individuals.

Box and Block Test (BBT). Second, the Box and Block Test (BBT) is used to capture a change in a subject's dexterity. According to Chen et al., the BBT has a test-retest reliability with an intraclass correlation coefficient of 0.93 to 0.97 among 62 stroke patients tested 3 to 7 days apart [36]. The minimal detectable change (MDC) for the BBT is 5.5 blocks per minute [36]. Previous studies suggest that upper extremity rehabilitation may influence the lower extremities [37]. As such, the third outcome measure will be gait speed, captured using the GaitRite.

Gait Speed (GS). Gait speed is a reliable and valid means of assessing lower extremity function. It has a test-retest reliability range of 0.92 to 0.97 and has an intraclass correlation coefficient of 0.862, proving to be an effective means of determining functional mobility in the lower extremity [37, 38]. The MCID for GS is a change of 0.13 m/s or greater [39].

Stroke Impact Scale (SIS). Lastly, collecting patient reported outcomes on quality of life before and after the intervention is another important determinant efficacy. According to Duncan et al., the Stroke Impact Scale (SIS) questionnaire allows researchers to collect clinically meaningful change over time of the intervention [35]. Intraclass correlation coefficients for test-retest reliability of the SIS domains ranged from 0.70 to 0.92, excluding the emotion domain [35]. The MCID for the SIS is 9.2 for strength, 5.9 for ADL/IADL, 4.5 for mobility, and 17.8 for function [40].

Secondary Outcome Measures. Stroke causes both local (e.g., perilesional tissues) and global (e.g., networks) reorganizations within the brain [24–27]. The mechanism underlying the effect of rehabilitation therapy, that includes BCI-VR-FES or some of its components, on sensory-motor recovery might be closely linked to changes in cortical reorganization [28]. Indeed, changes in cortical brain activity after the BCI, VR, FES interventions (or different combinations of thereof) have been demonstrated in a number of neuroimaging studies. Importantly, these observed changes in brain activity significantly correlated with functional outcome measures observed over the course of the therapy [28]. In order to evaluate the effect of the BCI-VR-FES system intervention on brain activity, the following measures can be of particular significance [11, 29, 30]: BCI performance (e.g., classification accuracy); Magnetoencephalogram (MEG) and its averaged responses (also referred to as event-related fields - ERFs); Electroencephalogram (EEG) and its averaged responses (also referred to as event-related potentials - ERPs).

2.2 Objective/Aim/Goal/Hypothesis

Our *long-term goal* is to improve motor recovery outcomes in stroke patients by expanding applicability and use of the BCI systems. The primary objective of the current study is to evaluate the effect of the BCI-VR-FES system intervention on functional motor recovery after stroke. The following outcomes of BCI-VR-FES intervention will be explored: (1) changes in motor function (e.g., changes on the FMA, BBT, and GS); and (2) subject self-perception (e.g., SIS). The secondary objective of the current study is to evaluate neural changes associated with BCI-VR-FES intervention for motor recovery post-stroke. The third objective of the current study is to understand what contributes to the efficacy of the BCI-VR-FES system intervention, including: (1) epidemiologic/clinical (e.g., age, diagnosis, changes in motor function); (2) psychological (e.g., motor imagery characteristics); (3) neurophysiological (e.g., specific neural activation patterns or "signatures"); and (4) methodological (e.g., ipsilateral versus contralateral motor imagery; imagination approaches; imagined versus attempted movement; signal processing aspects).

3   Methods

3.1   Recruitment

Upon IRB approval from both AdventHealth and AdventHealth University, research investigators will provide detailed study information to outpatient rehabilitation therapists via email and in-person information sessions, to facilitate subject recruitment. Second, potential subjects, as identified by the outpatient rehabilitation therapists, will be provided with the primary investigators' contact information so that they can obtain additional study information, have questions answered, verify eligibility and provide informed consent. Potential subjects will be informed that recruitment from the outpatient clinic and subsequent eligibility verification by the researchers will in no way impact their current or future access to outpatient rehabilitation services. All HIPAA policies and procedures will be followed during the recruitment process, and throughout IRB approved study protocols procedures.

Inclusion Criteria. Inclusion criteria for this study include:

1. First-time stroke, resulting in hemiparesis of upper extremity
2. 18 years or older
3. Discharged from inpatient facility and currently attending outpatient rehabilitation
4. Demonstrate the ability to communicate with study personnel and execute tasks via verbal and written instruction

Exclusion Criteria. Exclusion criteria for this study include:

1. Inability to independently maintain the seated position
2. Pregnancy or indication of possibility of pregnancy
3. A history of any other neurologic disorder
4. Inability to participate in passive range of motion in the paretic limb or other UE diagnosis

3.2   Protocol

Initial and Subsequent Study Visits. During the first study visit, subject information will be collected and recorded in the Case Report Form. This will include demographic information and areas for data entry regarding the subject's performance on all outcome measures (FMA, GS, SIS, and BBT), and an area for results from EEG/MEG studies. Each subject in the *treatment group* will be required to attend 24 study-related intervention sessions in addition to their ongoing outpatient rehabilitation. Study interventions will be provided two to three times per week, for approximately one hour in duration, for 24 total visits.

Post-study Visits. Two visits will be required for *all subjects* in order to reassess outcome measures and determine if any study induced changes are maintained over time. The first post-study visit will occur: (1) immediately following the 24th intervention **session** (visit #25) for the treatment group, and (2) at 8–12 weeks post first visit for the control group - as closely time-matched to treatment group as possible. All subjects in the *imaging group* will be scheduled for MEG and MRI. The second/final post-study visit for all subjects will occur at three months follow up, to determine any retention.

3.3   Data Analysis

We intend to analyze each of the study outcome measures (BBT, FMA, GS, SIS), at pre, mid, post, and follow up timepoints to understand any relationship that may exist between the study subjects, the study interventions and final/retained subject functional outcomes over time. Additionally, we will seek to understand through statistical analysis if any relationship exists between our secondary measures, most importantly any changes in EEG/MEG signals and BCI responses as a result of this intervention, as well as comparison of this data in post-stroke subjects to other potential study populations.

4   Anticipated Results

4.1   Objective Outcomes

Primary Objectives. We are anticipating the BCI-VR-FES therapeutic intervention to induce clinically significant changes in the upper extremity sensory-motor function as assessed by the FMA and compare these changes to the those induced by standard rehabilitation. In addition, other outcome measures will be explored, such as change in the BBT and GS. GS is unique, **in** which we are looking to assess any restoration of overall posture and function of the LE through the use of BCI-VR-FES as an UE intervention for patients post-stroke. In addition to positive functional outcomes, we look to improve subject self-perception of motor function recovery as assessed by the SIS.

Secondary Objectives. We plan to evaluate neural changes associated with BCI-VR-FES intervention for motor recovery post-stroke. Evaluation of BCI performance over the course of the intervention will allow for correlation of changes in brain activity and functional outcomes for both the UE and LE. We will also evaluate data from MEG and EEG (including their averaged responses) changes in patients compared with healthy subjects.

Additional Objectives. Regarding the current protocol, we are looking to understand what contributes to the **efficacy** of the BCI-VR-FES system intervention, including: (1) epidemiologic/clinical; (2) psychological; (3) neurophysiological; and (4) methodological.

This study has been approved by AdventHealth IRB and is pending expedited review from AdventHealth University for IRB approval at the time of submission of this publication.

Acknowledgments. We would like to thank both the g.tech company, Austria for providing us with the RecoveriX device, as well as AdventHealth Sports Medicine & Rehabilitation for their collaboration on this study.

Appendix 1

Principle [16, 18]	Description [16, 18]	Anticipated Implementation: BCI-VR-FES
1. Use it or lose it	Failure to drive specific brain functions can lead to functional degradatio	Can be used on any stages after the traumatic brain event to facilitate motor learning and neuroplasticity
2. Use it and improve It	Training that drives a specific brain function can lead to an enhancement of that function	BCI-VR-FES utilizes a brain signal recorded from sensory-motor cortex to facilitate movement and provide sensory-motor-visual feedback
3. Specificity	The nature of the training experience dictates the nature of the plasticity	When training with BCI-VR-FES system, the patient is asked to visualize (imagine or even attempt) a skilled movement that he/she was able to perform before the stroke (e.g., hitting a tennis ball, playing a guitar, combing hair)
4. Repetition matters	Induction of plasticity requires sufficient repetition	BCI-VR-FES system provides hundreds of repetitions within relatively short period of time
5. Intensity matters	Induction of plasticity requires sufficient training intensity	The intensity of BCI-VR-FES training can be adjusted dependent on patient's capability and can vary within a broad range of intensity to promote neurorecovery
6. Time matters	Different forms of plasticity occur at different times during training	BCI-VR-FES approach has demonstrated its usefulness both for chronic and acute stroke patients. Moreover, it can be used on all stages of stroke recovery

(continued)

(*continued*)

Principle [16, 18]	Description [16, 18]	Anticipated Implementation: BCI-VR-FES
7. Salience matters	The training experience must be sufficiently salient to induce plasticity	BCI-VR-FES system provides constant feedback each time the patient is activating his/her sensory-motor cortex during motivational tasks, thus ensuring the salience of patient's experience during sensory-motor cortex activation versus other non-related activation
8. Age matters	Training-induced plasticity occurs more readily in younger brains	Although the plastic brain changes may be less profound in aging brain than in younger brain, the combination of approaches available within BCI-VR-FES allows for successful reorganization of brain tissue to produce desired outcomes
9. Transference	Plasticity in response to one training experience can enhance the acquisition of similar behaviors	It has been demonstrated that the BCI-VR-FES effect in restoring the function of upper extremity influences restoring the overall posture and the function of lower extremities through the promotion of concurrent/subsequent plasticity
10. Interference	Plasticity in response to one experience can interfere with the acquisition of other behaviors	BCI-VR-FES will occur outside of a subject's other therapies, potentiating neurorecovery to augment other therapeutic protocols, and not interfere with plasticity

Appendix 2

Publication	Type of stroke	Age of subjects (years)	Time since stroke (months)	Stratification
Woytowicz [30]	n/a	58.6 ± 11.8	>6	**With reflexes:** Severe (0–15), Severe-Moderate (16–34), Moderate-Mild (35–53), Mild (54–66); w/o reflexes: Severe

(*continued*)

(continued)

Publication	Type of stroke	Age of subjects (years)	Time since stroke (months)	Stratification
				(0–12), Severe-Moderate (13–30), Moderate-Mild (31–47), Mild (48–60)
Hoonhorst [31]	ischemic	64.8 ± 12.5	6	**With reflexes**: No UL motor capacity (0–22), Poor (23–31), Limited (32–47), Notable (48–52), Full UL motor capacity
Woodbury [32]	93% ischemic	69.8 ± 11	31 days ± 16.88 days	**Without reflexes:** Severe impairment (0–19 +/− 2), Moderate (19–47 +/− 2), Mild (47–60 +/− 2)
Michaelsen [33]	n/a	n/a	n/a	**With reflexes:** Moderate (20–64), Mild (65–66)
Pang [34]	n/a	n/a	n/a	**With reflexes:** 0–27, 28–57, 58–66
Duncan [35]	Ischemic	18–90	>3	**With reflexes:** 0–21, 21–50, 51–66

References

1. Center for Disease Control and Prevention. https://www.cdc.gov/stroke/
2. Benjamin, E., et al.: Heart disease and stroke statistics—2018 update: a report from the American Heart Association. **137**, e67–e492 (2018). https://doi.org/10.1161/cir.0000000 000000558
3. Cervera, M.A., et al.: Brain-computer interfaces for post-stroke motor rehabilitation: a meta-analysis. **5**, 651–663 (2018). https://doi.org/10.1002/acn3.544
4. Zhang, X., Elnady, A.M., Randhawa, B.K., Boyd, L.A., Menon, C.: Combining mental training and physical training with goal-oriented protocols in stroke rehabilitation: a feasibility case study. **12**, 125 (2018). https://doi.org/10.3389/fnhum.2018.00125
5. Mrachacz-Kersting, N., Aliakbaryhosseinabadi, S.: Comparison of the efficacy of a real-time and offline associative brain-computer-interface. **12**, 455 (2018). https://doi.org/10.3389/fnins.2018.00455
6. Frolov, A.A., et al.: Post-stroke rehabilitation training with a motor-imagery-based Brain-Computer Interface (BCI)-controlled hand exoskeleton: a randomized controlled multicenter trial. **11**, 400 (2017). https://doi.org/10.3389/fnins.2017.00400
7. Irimia, D.C., et al.: Brain-computer interfaces with multi-sensory feedback for stroke rehabilitation: a case study: BCI for stroke rehabilitation. **41**, E178–E184 (2017). https://doi.org/10.1111/aor.13054
8. Kim, T., Kim, S., Lee, B.: Effects of action observational training plus brain-computer interface-based functional electrical stimulation on paretic arm motor recovery in patient with stroke: a randomized controlled trial: effects of AOT Plus BCI-FES on arm motor recovery. **23**, 39–47 (2016). https://doi.org/10.1002/oti.1403

9. Pichiorri, F., et al.: Brain–computer interface boosts motor imagery practice during stroke recovery. **77**, 851–865 (2015). https://doi.org/10.1002/ana.24390

10. Ang, K.K., et al.: A large clinical study on the ability of stroke patients to use an EEG-based motor imagery brain-computer interface. **42**, 253–258 (2011). https://doi.org/10.1109/iembs.2009.5335381

11. Kim, H., et al.: Reliability, concurrent validity, and responsiveness of the Fugl-Meyer Assessment (FMA) for hemiplegic patients. **24**, 893–899 (2012). https://doi.org/10.1589/jpts.24.893

12. Hankey, G.J., Jamrozik, K., Broadhurst, R.J., Forbes, S., Anderson, C.S.: Long-term disability after first-ever stroke and related prognostic factors in the Perth Community Stroke Study, 1989–1990. **33**, 1034–1040 (2002). https://doi.org/10.1161/01.str.0000012515.66889.24

13. Calabrò, R.S., et al.: Robotic neurorehabilitation in patients with chronic stroke. Int. J. Rehabil. Res. **38**, 219–225 (2015). https://doi.org/10.1097/MRR.0000000000000114

14. Doyle, S.D., Bennett, S., Dudgeon, B.J.: Sensory impairment after stroke: exploring therapists' clinical decision making. Can. J. Occup. Ther. **81**, 215–225 (2014). https://doi.org/10.1177/0008417414540516

15. Doyle, S., Bennett, S., Fasoli, S.E., Mckenna, K.T.: Interventions for sensory impairment in the upper limb after stroke. Cochrane Database Syst. Rev. (2010). https://doi.org/10.1002/14651858.cd006331.pub2

16. Kiper, P., et al.: Computational models and motor learning paradigms: could they provide insights for neuroplasticity after stroke? An overview. J. Neurol. Sci. **369**, 141–148 (2016). https://doi.org/10.1016/j.jns.2016.08.019

17. Wolpert, D.M., Flanagan, J.R.: Motor learning. Curr. Biol. CB **20**, R467–R472 (2010). https://doi.org/10.1016/j.cub.2010.04.035

18. Kleim, J.A., Jones, T.A.: Principles of experience-dependent neural plasticity: implications for rehabilitation after brain damage. **51**, S225–S239 (2008). https://doi.org/10.1044/1092-4388(2008/018)

19. Cho, W., et al.: Hemiparetic stroke rehabilitation using avatar and electrical stimulation based on non-invasive brain computer interface. **5** (2017). https://doi.org/10.4172/2329-9096.1000411

20. Cho, W., et al.: Paired associative stimulation using brain-computer interfaces for stroke rehabilitation: a pilot study. **26** (2016). https://doi.org/10.4081/ejtm.2016.6132

21. Irimia, D., et al.: recoveriX: a new BCI-based technology for persons with stroke. **2016**, 1504 (2016). https://doi.org/10.1109/embc.2016.7590995

22. Monge-Pereira, E., et al.: Use of electroencephalography brain computer interface systems as a rehabilitative approach for upper limb function after a stroke. A systematic review. **9**, 918–932 (2017)

23. Venkatakrishnan, A., Francisco, G.E., Contreras-Vidal, J.L.: Applications of brain–machine interface systems in stroke recovery and rehabilitation. **2**, 93–105 (2014). https://doi.org/10.1007/s40141-014-0051-4

24. Ang, K.K., et al.: A randomized controlled trial of EEG-based motor imagery brain-computer interface robotic rehabilitation for stroke. **46**, 310–320 (2015). https://doi.org/10.1177/1550059414522229

25. Ang, K.K., Guan, C: EEG-based strategies to detect motor imagery for control and rehabilitation. **25**, 392–401 (2017). https://doi.org/10.1109/tnsre.2016.2646763

26. Calabrò, R.S., et al.: The role of virtual reality in improving motor performance as revealed by EEG: a randomized clinical trial. **14**, 1–16 (2017). https://doi.org/10.1186/s12984-017-0268-4

27. Alon, G., Levitt, A.F., McCarthy, P.A.: Functional electrical stimulation (FES) may modify the poor prognosis of stroke survivors with severe motor loss of the upper extremity: a preliminary study. **87**, 627–636 (2008). https://doi.org/10.1097/phm.0b013e31817fabc1

28. Gladstone, D.J., Danells, C.J., Black, S.E.: The Fugl-Meyer Assessment of motor recovery after stroke: a critical review of its measurement properties. Neurorehabilitation Neural Repair **16**, 232–240 (2002). https://doi.org/10.1177/154596802401105171

29. Page, S.J., Hade, E., Persch, A.: Psychometrics of the wrist stability and hand mobility subscales of the Fugl-Meyer Assessment in moderately impaired stroke. **95**, 103–108 (2015). https://doi.org/10.2522/ptj.20130235

30. Woytowicz, E.J., et al.: Determining levels of upper extremity movement impairment by applying a cluster analysis to the Fugl-Meyer Assessment of the upper extremity in chronic stroke. 98, 456–462 (2017). https://doi.org/10.1016/j.apmr.2016.06.023

31. Hoonhorst, M.H., et al.: How do Fugl-Meyer arm motor scores relate to dexterity according to the action research arm test at 6 months poststroke? **96**, 1845–1849 (2015). https://doi.org/10.1016/j.apmr.2015.06.009

32. Woodbury, M.L., Velozo, C.A., Richards, L.G., Duncan, P.W.: Rasch analysis staging methodology to classify upper extremity movement impairment after stroke. **94**, 1527–1533 (2013). https://doi.org/10.1016/j.apmr.2013.03.007

33. Michaelsen, S.M., Luta, A., Roby-Brami, A., Levin, M.F.: Effect of trunk restraint on the recovery of reaching movements in hemiparetic patients. **32**, 1875–1883 (2001). https://doi.org/10.1161/01.str.32.8.1875

34. Pang, M.Y., Harris, J.E., Eng, J.J.: A community-based upper-extremity group exercise program improves motor function and performance of functional activities in chronic stroke: a randomized controlled trial. **87**, 1–9 (2006). https://doi.org/10.1016/j.apmr.2005.08.113

35. Duncan, P.W., Wallace, D., Lai, S.M., Johnson, D., Embretson, S., Laster, L.J.: The stroke impact scale version 2.0: evaluation of reliability, validity, and sensitivity to change. **30**, 2131–2140 (1999). https://doi.org/10.1161/01.str.30.10.2131

36. Chen, H.M., Chen, C.C., Hsueh, I.P., Huang, S.L., Hsieh, C.L.: Test-retest reproducibility and smallest real difference of 5 hand function tests in patients with stroke. **23**, 435 (2009). https://doi.org/10.1177/1545968308331146

37. Fulk, G.D., Echternach, J.L.: Test-retest reliability and minimal detectable change of gait speed in individuals undergoing rehabilitation after stroke. **32**, 8–13 (2008). https://doi.org/10.1097/npt0b013e31816593c0

38. Webster, K.E., Wittwer, J.E., Feller, J.A.: Validity of the GAITRite walkway system for the measurement of averaged and individual step parameters of gait. **22**, 317–321 (2005). https://doi.org/10.1016/j.gaitpost.2004.10.005

39. Bohannon, R.W., Andrews, A.W., Glenney, S.S.: Minimal clinically important difference for comfortable speed as a measure of gait performance in patients undergoing inpatient rehabilitation after stroke. **25**, 1223–1225 (2013). https://doi.org/10.1589/jpts.25.1223

40. Lin, K., et al.: Minimal detectable change and clinically important difference of the Stroke Impact Scale in stroke patients. **24**, 486 (2010). https://doi.org/10.1177/1545968309356295

Requirements for a Framework of a Virtual Learning Environment for Deaf People Mediated by Avatar

Marta Angélica Montiel Ferreira[1]([⊠]), Laura Sánchez García[1], Juliana Bueno[1], and Tanya Amara Felipe[2]

[1] Informatics Department, Federal University of Paraná, Centro Politécnico, Jardim das Américas, Curitiba, PR, Brazil
zmontefer@gmail.com, sg.laura@gmail.com, oieusouaju@gmail.com
[2] Departamento de Ensino Superior – DESU2, Instituto Nacional de Educação de Surdos, Rua das Laranjeiras, 232-Laranjeiras, Rio de Janeiro, RJ, Brazil
tanyafelipe@gmail.com

Abstract. This work describes the process of Systematic Review of Literature, developed to collect requirements for the development of an avatar to be used in the Virtual Learning Environment applied to the literacy of deaf people. Two revisions were made. The first one with 23 articles on national and international bases from which it was possible to obtain a preliminary result of the necessary aspects for the Avatar as well as essential requirements for the Virtual Environment. The second one was carried out in the same databases, from which 34 articles were returned to collect the requirements of the Virtual Learning Environment. It can be verified that the deaf users accept the use of the Avatar. The review also served to verify the main technologies used. However, the research confirmed that a suitable avatar would not be sufficient for the proper functioning of a VLE with interface with interaction problems.

Keywords: Virtual learning environment · Avatar · Deaf · Literacy

1 Introduction

Although there are a variety of educational applications to support teaching and learning for the various areas of knowledge, it is perceived that for the deaf or student this environment still needs to be more accessible and more efficient [11, 37]. In addition, the principles of Human-Computer Interaction (HCI) were considered, in which it is emphasized that an ideal interface should be able to understand the intention of communication (pragmatic), that is, how people can understand their requests [7]. The environment is intended to use the Portuguese language written and signaled in Sign Language (Brazilian sign language) by an avatar. In this sense, a friendly and user-friendly interface should provide the user with the means to achieve what he wants according to his preferences, possibilities, intentions, obligations, among other aspects that require a broad understanding of interaction and communication.

© Springer Nature Switzerland AG 2019
C. Stephanidis (Ed.): HCII 2019, CCIS 1032, pp. 255–262, 2019.
https://doi.org/10.1007/978-3-030-23522-2_32

This research investigated the requirements for a virtual learning environment framework, as well as the avatar requirements for this environment, through literature review. This article describes the method of a Systematic Review of Literature - SRL, was conducted in two stages, the first selection contains 23 articles from national and international conferences and periodicals on the use of avatars in environments accessible to deaf users. The second step was selected 34 articles carried out on the same national and international bases. To perform the search, the string was created to perform searches on the selected bases. A protocol/method to be followed were chosen for the other phases of the research [18].

The present research is part of an ongoing thesis, which aims to develop a conceptual Framework of Virtual Learning Environment (VLE) for deaf people in the bilingual context (L1 the Brazilian sign language-Libras and L2, the Portuguese language, for the context of Brazil). According to Pivetta et al. (2014), the adoption of the avatar can make the environment more attractive, as well as being a more appropriate resource for deaf people [27]. According to some authors, there are several avatar characterizations and Meadows (2009) expressed that an avatar is an "active social representation of a user" [23]. For Theng and Aung (2012), an avatar is a humanoid created by computing [35].

Thus, the results of the authors' research pointed out that an avatar can arouse positive emotions in learning, but it is necessary to evaluate how to apply in a virtual environment, which includes several interaction options, considering the most appropriate way for the target audience of the research. In addition, you can list some requirements to be considered for the development of the avatar, as well as check which tools/software is most used for their design and recurring problems.

2   Theoretical Background and Related Work

In this section, we focus on the key concepts adopted in the article (Subsect. 2.1), and on the presentation of the theoretical reference, methods adopted, as well as previous work from researches (Subsect. 2.2).

2.1   Direct Way Methodology

The methodology selected for the proposed virtual environment of the direct way methodology was proposed by the French Association for Reading (AFL - *Association Française pour la Lecture*). Its objective is to train critical readers working on texts in a systematic way in order to go "from the message to the code" [1]. This methodology has been worked in French schools for more than 40 years and has proven results in the acquisition of a second language written by foreign students.

The research group that authors is part of, used these procedures, and found that they are adaptable and applicable to the teaching/learning of deaf people (Bueno 2014; Haiduski 2016). In Bueno (2014), the author proposed concepts for the construction of literacy to be applied in a bilingual virtual environment for deaf children [4]. In his research, the author performed an Action-Research based on the Direct Way Literacy, which was applied in the classroom of a bilingual deaf school, and brought positive results for deaf children [4].

For the present research, the results obtained in the Web Authoring Environment of Haiduski (2016), served as a basis for VLE issues, as well as the applicability of direct way methodology [14]. One can identify the need for a learning environment to support teachers from a literacy perspective [14]. However, it is not the objective of this research to develop the complete framework, but to provide support from the requirements for the construction of the same.

2.2 Related Work

There are available works on virtual learning environments for deaf people using avatar, who have performed an intermediate translation in Portuguese language glossaries for the translation of Libras, as well as capturing body, limb, head and face movements that allow a three-dimensional capture [6, 8, 26]. However, Do Amaral (2012) verified that the difficulty lies in the lack of knowledge of the grammatical structure of Libras [8].

Thus, this research proposal (in its macro view) aims to propose an environment of literacy that involves the grammar and lexicon of Libras. In Brazil, there are some applications that use avatar in accessible environments, among which we can mention Falibras [10], HandTalk [15], Rybena [16], and Vlibras [38], all these applications that propose to make a Portuguese translation for the Brazilian Sign Language. However, these translators' proposals work with a simplified grammar that does not account for several discursive morphsyntactic rules of Libras.

3 Systematic Review of Literature - SRL

A systematic review according to Kitchenham (2007) consists of a method that seeks to extract the most relevant publications on a subject or subjects, to quantitatively and qualitatively evaluate the studies already carried out in the area [18]. The environment has the purpose of using the Portuguese language written and signed in Libras by an avatar.

Following this method, research questions were defined for the two revisions that were answered through this process. In addition, the criteria for inclusion and exclusion of the articles found to carry out the searches were defined, so a keyword chain was developed.

3.1 Systematic Review of Literature - Avatar

To collect the data, the bases were defined and following the research method, two questions were elaborated. These questions were defined with the purpose of fulfilling the research objectives, they are:

- What are the requirements for an avatar of a virtual literacy environment?
- What are the requirements for a virtual environment?

Once the search was carried out, a protocol was selected to be followed for the other phases of the research. The first extraction in the international databases (ACM,

IEE, and Web of Science) and in the national databases (ACM-IHC, SBIE, and Google Scholar) selected 501.291 articles according to the search string.

After the search, the data file was exported to the Start-Ufscar-Lapes application, which returned 2.593 articles, according to the inclusion and exclusion criteria specified in the application. Then the 2.593 abstracts were read. From the reading of abstracts, 138 articles were selected, however, there was a need to make one more selection, since there were articles that addressed only virtual environments applied to other learning contexts (e.g., educational games, programming), this selection was done in the tool manually, and then the 79 articles were selected for full reading.

Following the complete reading of the articles, 23 articles were selected, which the present study used for the basement of the proposed study. Thus, it was possible to: (1) map the requirements: (2) the common problems, Fig. 1. Contains the requirements and common problems collected in the SRL:

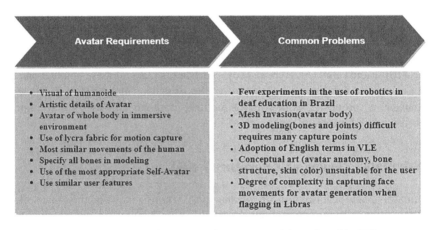

Fig. 1. Avatar requirements and common problems found in SRL

The requirements found in this SRL are the appearance of the avatar (i.e., size, weight, hair color, skin color and humanoid visual). In addition, the problems are the same that is difficulty in capturing face movements that requires many stitches, and the problem of mesh invasion.

Also mapped the Technologies used in the construction of the avatar. It is possible check the software Technologies for modeling, motion capture, text translation in sign language and 3D printing of the avatar (Kinect, Blender, 3DSMax, MakeHuman, Vision, MoCap, Simax, Unity, and Tinkercard). In addition, it is possible check where the searches were done. From this literature review, with the reading of the selected articles and complementary material, it is possible delineate the problematic of key issues for the initial understanding of the necessary requirements for the construction of a virtual environment of learning mediated by an avatar.

3.2   Systematic Review of Literature - Virtual Learning Environment

According to some authors, accessibility in environments is insufficient for deaf people [7, 39]. In addition, they stressed that it is important to consider the pedagogical aspects of VLE activities. They also emphasized that the tests could show the importance of the acquisition of sign language in the and for the acquisition of the second language [22]. The first extraction was carried out at the bases (ACM, IEE, Web of Science, Scopus and Manually (HCI-Brazil)).

Then, a second extraction was performed, of the 3.665 selected, 3.386 were rejected (reading the titles), and 276 were accepted for reading the abstracts. After reading, the abstracts 69 papers were selected for the complete reading that resulted in the selection of 34 articles to be used to collect the requirements for the environment. Allied to these data, the purpose of this research is to propose the learning environment that favors bilingualism. In addition, accessibility should also be considered for some authors, an environment for learning the second language might have resources such as a robot in which the child teaches theft to speak, so the child can practice the other language [20, 21, 34].

In addition to the requirements of the readings, the data will be used in the proposal of the environment, such as the use of a prototype translator for sign language, translating robots, and features that recognize hand gestures for the translation of sign language (e.g., mobile applications). As well as the uses of the Stanford CoreNLP system to process texts and apply writing rules and to retrieve language information, and the SECOND LIFE environment was used for language learning, another aspect to be considered social interactive tools, the use of storytelling for language learning [5, 32, 33, 36].

For some authors it is important to consider the phonological aspects for language learning, also the design of the activities should be aimed at bilingual literacy, and the use of signwriting can be applied from the web interface and with the help of avatar [3]. From the reading of the 34 articles selected, it was possible to classify the requirements into two groups that are (1) requirements for the environment and (2) pedagogical requirements, according to Fig. 2.

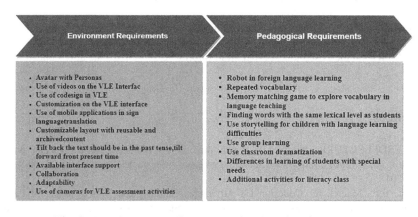

Fig. 2. Requirements environment and pedagogical found in SRL

From the readings performed, it was possible to identify the requirements mentioned above and others that are: simple interface, interface with good communicability, interface with good usability, interface that exploits the use of images and accessibility that can be facilitated by avatar for deaf people, use of videos is also important to be considered [2, 9, 13, 17, 19, 25, 28, 30, 31, 40, 41].

4   Results, Discussions and Limitations

The results obtained pointed out the importance of virtual (VLE) environments in the teaching-learning process. For the target audience of this research, it is important that the environment has the sign language, learning in its first L1 language and contains the writing of the second L2 language [4]. In addition, the accessible environment should provide computing resources that exploit visual aids, in this case the avatar [27]. Thus, it is possible that (VLE) environments become more accessible to deaf users [6, 12, 26, 27]. However, only those requirements will not be sufficient for the development of the conceptual framework, which needs further research.

5   Conclusion and Future Works

From the review, we obtained as a result a set of requirements of the conceptual Framework of the virtual learning environment (VLE) and requirements for the construction of the avatar. In addition, as a result, it is possible map the countries that have already conducted and published research on this subject. In addition, verify the critical issues for the development of the proposal of this research, in addition to the initial understanding of the problem.

From this research, it was understood the need of interaction of the environment followed the precepts of HCI. In this sense, a friendly and user-friendly interface should provide the users with the means to achieve what they want according to their preferences, possibilities, intentions, obligations, among other aspects that require a broad understanding of the interaction and communication [24, 29].

Acknowledgements. This study was financed in part by the Coordenação de Aperfeiçoamento de Pessoal de Nível Superior - Brasil (CAPES) - Finance Code 001. The Federal University of Paraná (UFPR) and the Postgraduate Program in Informatics (PPGINF) the development of this research.

References

1. ACTESDELECTURE: principes de la voie directe. N° 100. Association Française pour la Lecture, Paris (2007). http://www.lecture.org/revues_livres/actes_lecture.html. Accessed 05 Apr 2018
2. Alves, F.P., Maciel, C.: Codesign De Atividades Gamificadas: Uma Abordagem Participativa Do Design Instrucional Em Ambientes Virtuais De Aprendizagem. In: IHC 2014 Companion Proceedings - Master and Doctoral Consortium, Foz do Iguacu, Brazil (2014)

3. Boulares, M., Jemni, M.: A route planner interpretation service for hard of hearing people. In: Miesenberger, K., Karshmer, A., Penaz, P., Zagler, W. (eds.) ICCHP 2012. LNCS, vol. 7383, pp. 52–58. Springer, Heidelberg (2012). https://doi.org/10.1007/978-3-642-31534-3_9
4. Bueno, J.: Pesquisa-ação na construção de insumos conceituais para um ambiente computacional de apoio ao letramento bilíngue de crianças surdas. Tese de Doutorado, Curitiba (2014)
5. Chowdhuri, D., Narendra, P., Amrita, M.: Virtual classroom for Deaf people. In: IEEE International Conference on Engineering Education: Innovative Practices and Future Trends (AICERA), Kottayam, India, 19–21 July 2012 (2012)
6. De Martino, J.M., et al.: Signing avatars: making education more inclusive. Univers. Access Inf. Soc. Int. J. **16**, 793–808 (2017)
7. De Pinho, A.L.S., De Sales, F.M.J., Rosa, J.G.S., Ramos, M.A.S.: Technical and pedagogical usability in e-Learnig: Perceptions of students from the Federal Institute of Rio Grande do Norte (Brazil) in virtual learning environment. In: 10th Iberian Conference on Information Systems and Technologies (CISTI), Aveiro, Portugal, 17–20 June 2015 (2015)
8. Do Amaral, W.: Sistema de transcrição da língua brasileira de sinais voltado à produção de conteúdo sinalizado por avatares 3d. Tese de Doutorado, Unicamp-Campinas (2012)
9. Escudeiro, P., et al.: Virtual sign - a real time bidirectional translator of Portuguese sign language. In: 6th International Conference on Software Development and Technologies for Enhancing Accessibility and Fighting Infoexclusion (DSAI 2015), Sankt Augustin, Germany (2015)
10. Falibras. http://www.surdosol.com.br/tag/falibras/. Accessed 05 Apr 2018
11. Ferreira, M.A.M., Bueno, J., Bonacin, R., García, L.S.: The use of computational artifacts to support deaf learning: an approach based on the direct way methodology. In: Antona, M., Stephanidis, C. (eds.) UAHCI 2017. LNCS, vol. 10279, pp. 198–209. Springer, Cham (2017). https://doi.org/10.1007/978-3-319-58700-4_17
12. García, L.S., Guimarães, C., Antunes, D.R., Fernandes, S.: Architecture for deaf communities cultural inclusion and citizenship. In: Proceedings of the 15th International Conference on Enterprise Information Systems, Ange'rs, França, pp. 68–75 (2013)
13. Guimarães, C., Antunes, D. R., Garcia, L.S., Peres, L.M., Fernandes, S.: Pedagogical architecture - internet artifacts for bilingualism of the deaf (sign language/Portuguese). In: 46th Hawaii International Conference on System Sciences, Wailea, Hawaii, USA (2013)
14. Haiduski, A.S.d.L.: Ambiente de autoria web de apoio ao letramento infantil. Dissertação de Mestrado— UFPR, Curitiba (2016)
15. Hand Talk. http://www.handtalk.me/. Accessed 05 Apr 2018
16. Instituto ICTS. http://portal.rybena.com.br/site-rybena/sobre.html. Accessed 04 May 2018
17. Khenissi, M.A., Essalmi, F., Jemni, M., Kinshu: A learning version of memory match game. In: ICALT 2014: IEEE 14th International Conference on Advanced Learning Technologies, Athens, Greece, 7–10 July 2014 (2014)
18. Kitchenham, A.B.: Guidelines for performing systematic literature reviews in software engineering. EBSE Technical report (2007). https://userpages.uni-koblenz.de/laemmel/esecourse/slides/slr.pdf. Accessed 04 May 2018
19. Lima, P.S.R., De Brito, S.R., Silva, O.F., Favero, E.L.: Personalização De Interfaces Para Ambientes Virtuais De Aprendizagem Baseados Na Construção Dinâmica De Comunidades. In: CLIHC 2005, Cuernavaca, México, 23–26 October 2005 (2005)
20. Liu, C.-j., Wang, G.: Using second life in ESL/EFL teaching and teacher-training in the Web2.0 environment. In: IEEE Symposium on Electrical and Electronics Engineering (EEESYM), Kuala Lumpur, Malaysia, 24–27 June 2012 (2012)
21. Lu, Y., Chang, C., Chen, G.: Using a programmable storytelling robot to motivate learning second language. In: ICALT'- Seventh IEEE International Conference on Advanced Learning Technologies, Niigata, Japan (2007)

22. Luccas, M.R.Z, Chiari, B.M., de Goulart, B.N.G.: Reading comprehension of deaf students in regular education. Jornal da Sociedade Brasileira de Fonoaudiologia **4**(4), 342–347 (2012)
23. Meadows, M.S.: Avatar: the culture and consequences of having a second life. Br. J. Educ. Technol. **40**, 577–581 (2009). https://doi.org/10.1111/j.1467-8535.2009.00969_4.x
24. Nielsen, J.: Usability Engineering. Academic Press, Cambridge (1993)
25. Nunes, L.R.D.P., Braun, P., Walter, C.C.F.: Procedimentos e recursos de ensino para o aluno com deficiência: O que tem sido disseminado nos trabalhos do GT 15 da ANPED sobre estes temas? Rev. bras. Educ. espec. **17**(spe1), 23–40 (2011)
26. Paiva, F.A. dos S., De Martino, J.M., Barbosa, P.A., Benetti, A.B., Silva, I.R.: A transcription system for Brazilian sign language: the case of an avatar. Revista do Gel, São Paulo **13**(3), 12–48 (2016)
27. Pivetta, E.M., Saito, D.S., Ulbricht, V.R.: Surdos e Acessibilidade: Análise de um Ambiente Virtual de Ensino e Aprendizagem. Rev. Bras. Ed. Esp., Marília **20**(1), 147–162 (2014)
28. Pivetta, E.M., Ulbricht, V.R., Saito, D.S., Almeida, A.M.P.: Bilingual and accessible virtual learning environment. In: Proceedings of 2017 Twelfth Latin American Conference on Learning Technologies (LACLO), La Plata, Argentina (2017)
29. Rocha, H.V., Baranauskas, M.C.C.: Design e Avalição de Interfaces Humano-Computador, Campinas (2003). http://pan.nied.unicamp.br/publicacoes/livros.php
30. Rolim, A.L., Bezerra, E.P.: Um Sistema De Identificação Automática De Faces Para Um Ambiente Virtual De Ensino e Aprendizagem. In: WebMedia Companion Proceedings of the XIV Brazilian Symposium on Multimedia and the Web, Vila Velha, Espírito Santo, Brazil, 26–29 October 2008, pp. 129–132 (2008)
31. Schouten, D.G.M., Smets, N.J.J.M., Driessen, M., Fuhri, K., Neerincx, M.A., Cremers, A.H. M.: Requirements for a virtual environment to support the social participation education of low-literates. J. Univers. Access Inf. Soc. **16**(3), 681–698 (2017)
32. Setiawardhana, Hakkun, R.Y., Baharuddin, A:. Sign language learning based on Android for deaf and speech impaired people. In: International Electronics Symposium (IES), Surabaya, Indonesia, 29–30 September 2015 (2015)
33. Silva, L.C., Oliveira, F.C.M.B., Oliveira, A.C., Freitas, A.T.: Introducing the JLOAD: a Java learning object to assist the deaf. In: ICALT: IEEE 14th International Conference on Advanced Learning Technologies, Tunisia (2014)
34. Terashima, R.; Echizen-ya, H., Araki, K.: Learning method for extraction of partial correspondence from parallel corpus. In: International Conference on Asian Language Processing. Singapore (2009)
35. Theng, Y.-L., Aung, P.: Investigating effects of avatars on primary school children's affective responses to learning. J. Multimodal User Interfaces **5**, 45–52 (2012)
36. Thompson, R.H., Tanimoto, S.L., Berninger, V.W., Nagy, W.: Coding, reading, and writing: Integrated instruction in written language, Seattle, USA (2016)
37. Valente, J.A.: Informática na Educação: Instrucionismo X Construtivismo. 1997. Disponível em: http://www.futurarte.com.br/artigos/valente2. Accessed 12 Oct 2018
38. Vlibras. http://www.vlibras.gov.br/.Last. Accessed 04 May 2018
39. Waki, A.L.K., Dos Santos, G.F., Almeida, L.D.A.: Consolidação De Recomendações Sobre Jogos Acessíveis Aos Surdos In: IHC 2014 Proceedings - Short Paper, Foz do Iguaçú-Brazil (2014)
40. Zhang, R., Zhang, B., Zhu, J., Huang, H.: Development of multi-video based virtual classroom and its application in English as second language learning. In: International Symposium on Computer Science and Computer, Shanghai, China, 20–22 December 2008 (2008)
41. Zilio, L., Fairon, C.: Adaptive system for language learning. In: ICALT: IEEE 17th International Conference on Advanced Learning Technologies, Timisoara, Romania (2017)

Compensatory Visual Field Training Based on a Head-Mounted Display Eye Tracker

Katsuyoshi Hotta[✉], Oky Dicky Ardiansyah Prima,
Takashi Imabuchi, and Hisayoshi Ito

Graduate School of Software and Information Science,
Iwate Prefectural University, Takizawa, Japan
g231o027@s.iwate-pu.ac.jp

Abstract. The impact of visual field defects on conducting Activities of Daily Living (ADL) is significant. These defects include central and peripheral visual field loss. Many studies have revealed that patients of visual field defects need to increase visual scanning on performing visual tasks. Compensation training of eye movements has been shown to be effective to improve the visual exploration and extent the visual search fields. However, since it takes sufficiently long and intense period, the training needs to incorporate easy and fun tasks to promote an ongoing effort to patients. This study proposes a compensatory visual field training using game-like dynamic scenes presented by a head-mounted display eye tracker (HMD-ET). The head mounted display will eliminate the necessity of head movements during visual exploration. Each scene induces saccadic eye movements to complete given tasks. To simulate the patient of central scotoma, the participant's central visual field was masked while performing a training consists of obstacle course game. On the other hand, to simulate the patient with peripheral vision defects, the participant's peripheral visual field was partly masked. During training, eye movements were recorded at 240 Hz, which enable the detection of saccadic eye movements. Experiments using the proposed training conducted by 10 participants with normal visual acuity were able to reveal the differences in patterns of visual exploration between participants with simulated central scotoma and peripheral visual field defects. Questioners taken after the training shows that tasks and scenes used for the training are relatively easy and may encourage patients to continue the training.

Keywords: Visual field training · Preferred retina locus · Eye tracking

1 Introduction

Visual field defects (VFDs) are visual impairments where visual acuity is reduced compared to normal vision. VFDs cause various problems in conducting everyday activities. For many people, VFDs are often difficult to be recognized because of the filling-in mechanism in the human brain. VFDs can be broadly classified into peripheral vision defects and central scotoma (vision defects at the central vision). Peripheral vision defects, such as altitudinal field defects (vision defects above or below the horizontal), bitemporal hemianopia (vision defects at the sides), and homonymous hemianopia (vision defects at one side of the visual field for both eyes)

© Springer Nature Switzerland AG 2019
C. Stephanidis (Ed.): HCII 2019, CCIS 1032, pp. 263–268, 2019.
https://doi.org/10.1007/978-3-030-23522-2_33

create the sensation of seeing through a narrow tube, a condition commonly referred to as "tunnel vision." On the other hand, central scotoma, the most common defect observed on macular visual field testing covers the reading visual field causes reading inability.

VFDs are difficult to be completely recovered. Patients with central VFDs will suffer difficulties to estimate the distance to and the driving speed of lead cars. On the other hand, patients with peripheral VFDs will have more difficulties to detect stimuli in the periphery that will increase the risks of accidents with pedestrians approaching from the side [1]. There are approaches to treat the VFDs, such as field enhancement and rehabilitation techniques. The former is a field expansion by using optical systems incorporating prism to optimize the use of the remaining vision. The later includes saccadic training (compensatory visual field training).

The compensatory visual field training has been shown to be effective to improve the visual function [2]. This training uses a strategy to induce patients to deviate their gaze fixation point more of the visual scene towards their blind hemifield. However, since it takes sufficiently long and intense period, this training needs to incorporate easy and fun tasks to promote an ongoing effort to patients.

This study proposes a compensatory visual field training using game-like dynamic scenes. These scenes are presented by a head-mounted display eye tracker (HMD-ET). This type of eye tracker will decrease eye tracking errors affected by head movements during visual exploration. Each scene induces saccadic eye movements to complete given tasks.

2   Materials and Methods

2.1   Participants

Ten students from Iwate Prefectural University were recruited for our experiment. All participants had normal or corrected to normal vision (with contact lenses). Each participant voluntarily gave written informed consent in accordance with ethical guidelines.

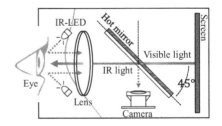

(a)   The HMD-ET   (b)   Mechanism of the HMD-ET

Fig. 1. HMD-ET used for this study

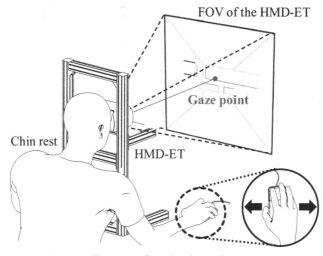

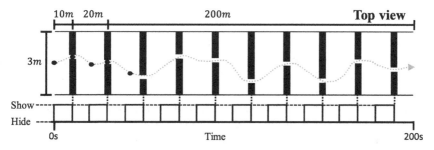

Fig. 2. Environmental equipment for the compensatory visual field training.

Fig. 3. A moving scene of obstacle course game used in the compensatory visual field training.

2.2 Apparatus

For this study, we have developed an HMD-ET. This device was employed to monitor eye fixations during a compensatory visual field training. Gaze points are sampled at 240 Hz. Figure 1 shows HMD-ET developed in this study. This device uses a 240 Hz infrared stereo camera to track the dark pupil reflected by two hot mirrors. The center of the pupil is estimated by fitting an ellipse to the boundary of the dark pupil that has been refined using the convex hull algorithm. Figure 2 shows environmental equipment for our compensatory visual field training. The HMD-ET is mounted on a chin-rest. Mouse is provided to change the horizontal self-position against the given stimuli for the training.

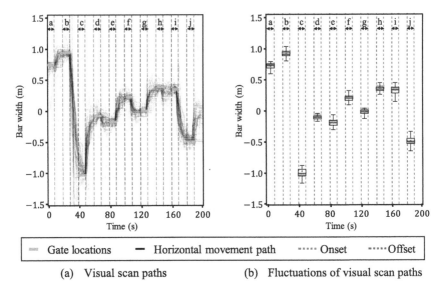

(a) Visual scan paths   (b) Fluctuations of visual scan paths

Fig. 4. Visual scan paths during the compensatory visual field training with a condition of peripheral vision defects.

2.3   Stimuli and Procedure

At the beginning of the experiment, eye calibration routine was performed using 9 points. Minimum requirement for the calibration accuracy was 1°. Each participant was required to meet this calibration accuracy before starting the experiment.

A moving scene of obstacle course game was shown on the monitor inside the HMD-ET. This monitor has a 100° Field of View (FOV) and consists of 960 × 1,080 pixels. A 3 m length bar with tiny gate was shown at around 10 m of the traveling direction. This bar would come close and arrive to the viewer location within 10 s. Participants were given a task to pass through the gate by using the mouse to move horizontally. 10 s break time was given before the next bar showing. Therefore, the training will complete in 200 s forgiven 10 bars. These tasks were repeated 5 times to complete the training. A fixed presentation order of the tasks was used for all participants. The stimuli were presented by using Unity game development platform [3]. Figure 3 shows scenes used in this study.

3   Results

All gaze fixation points were extracted, and the horizontal visual scan paths were visualized against the gates' appearance information. Figures 4 and 5 shows visual scan paths and horizontal movements during the compensatory visual field training with conditions of peripheral vision defects and central scotoma. Onset and offset of the appearance of each bar are shown in dotted lines. Visual scan paths of participants under a condition of peripheral vision defects shows large fluctuations than that of central scotoma. It is consistent to our expectation because under this condition, the narrowing of the visual field reduces the amount the participants can see when looking straight ahead. Hence, the participants intentionally increased their eye movements in order to pass the moving gates.

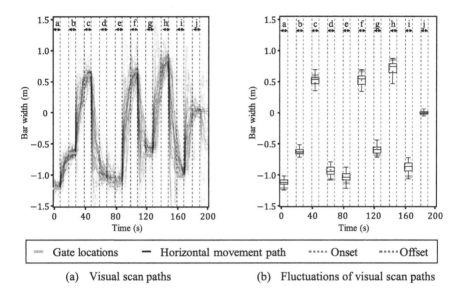

| (a) Visual scan paths | (b) Fluctuations of visual scan paths |

Fig. 5. Scan paths during the compensatory visual field training with a condition of central scotoma.

Table 1. ANOVA results

Effect	DF	Sum Sq.	F-value	p-value
VFDs	1	5.19E+02	0.28	0.59
Gate location	1	1.36E+04	7.43	0.006
VFDs × Gate location	1	1.89E+04	10.34	0.0001
Residuals	996	1.82E+06		

To analyze the fluctuations of visual scan paths quantitatively, the standard deviation of the coordinates of the visual scan paths for each gate's appearance time were calculated. Two-way ANOVA were performed with VFDs (peripheral vision defects and central scotoma) and gate locations from the center of the pathway (± 50 cm, ± 100 cm, ± 150 cm) for the standard deviations as dependent variables. Table 1 shows the ANOVA result. As expected, there was a statistically significant interaction between VFDs and gate locations from the center the pathway, $F(1, 996) = 10.34$, $p < 0.001$. The gate locations from the center the pathway also has a significant main effect.

4 Discussion

Our experiment results show that despite of the types of visual defects, all participants successfully completed tasks to pass through the gate of the training scenes. Participants put under a condition of peripheral vision defects tend to increase their eye movements to ensure the right path to complete the tasks than that of central scotoma. This eye movement behavior is important for people with VFDs to increase their Activities of Daily Living (ADL). This training may be useful to keep the driving license despite the visual field loss. Questioners taken after the training shows that tasks and scenes used for the training are relatively easy and may encourage patients to continue the training.

References

1. Donges, E.: A 2-level model of driver steering behavior. Hum. Fact. **20**(6), 691–707 (1978)
2. Pambakian, A.L.M., Mannan, S.K., Hodgson, T.L., Kennard, C.: Saccadic visual search training: a treatment for patients with homonymous hemianopia. J. Neurol. Neurosurg. Psychiatry **75**(10), 1443–1448 (2004)
3. Unity. https://unity.com/. Accessed 5 Apr 2019

Autoethnographic Approach to Studying the Affective Information Behavior of a Deaf Student

Kevin J. Mallary[✉]

University of Tennessee, Knoxville, USA
kmallary@vols.utk.edu

Abstract. Deaf and hard of hearing students in higher education—a growing population—may acquire substantially less information in the classroom than their hearing peers. Although assistive technologies (AT) are designed to help hearing-impaired students close that information gap, negative experiences using technologies can impede users' abilities to retrieve information and learn. The author of this study, who is a profoundly deaf Ph.D. student, has conducted an autoethnographic study of his affective experiences using AT in formal and informal educational settings. His experiences, which are documented in an *AT Use Diary*, have been analyzed using the framework of activity theory. Ultimately, the researcher plans to interview and survey fellow hearing-impaired students, hearing peers, and faculty and staff members, in order to recommend improvements to existing AT, and make higher education most inclusive for students with hearing loss.

Keywords: Deaf and hard of hearing students ·
Affective information behavior · Assistive technology ·
Autoethnography · Activity theory

1 Background

Deaf and hard of hearing students in higher education—a growing population [13]—may retain nearly 27% less information in the classroom than their hearing peers [10]. Assistive technologies (AT), including hearing aids, FM transmitters, speech recognition applications, and sign language interpreting services, may enable hearing-impaired students to close that information gap. However, a person's negative experience (e.g., frustration) using technology can impede his or her ability to accomplish essential tasks, such as information retrieval and learning [7].

As a profoundly deaf Ph.D. student, I have conducted an autoethnographic study of my affective experiences using AT to retrieve information in educational settings. Scholars contend that more studies of affective information behavior (IB) are needed [5, 12]. Although much empirical IB research embraces traditional methods (e.g., experiments, interviews, surveys) [5], scholars and practitioners have recommended innovative approaches, including autoethnography [4]. Autoethnography is ideal for exploring the author's experiences and critiquing the social structures in which the

© Springer Nature Switzerland AG 2019
C. Stephanidis (Ed.): HCII 2019, CCIS 1032, pp. 269–273, 2019.
https://doi.org/10.1007/978-3-030-23522-2_34

researcher functions [11]. To examine my affective experiences using AT, I have carefully documented my thoughts in an AT Use Diary. Diaries are useful for acquiring rich data in naturalistic settings, especially when users employ multiple technologies in various locations [8].

Since the majority of IB studies lack theory [5], my experiences using AT to retrieve information are examined through the lens of activity theory. This interpretive framework conceives technology use as contextual [1]. Activity theory is appropriate for understanding my experiences, because I employ AT in formal and informal educational settings (e.g., classrooms, online lectures, library), and in the presence of peers and faculty members.

2   The Study

Autoethnography is used to explore and critique social structures through the lens of the author's personal experiences [11]. Beginning in January 2019, I began documenting my experiences using AT to retrieve information in educational settings. I regularly use a combination of hardware and software tools, including my hearing aids and FM transmitter, which are both manufactured by Phonak [14]; and most recently, Android's [2] Live Transcribe mobile application. I have reflected on my experiences using these tools in a series of Word documents, which comprise my *AT Use Diary*. Diary studies, as I have learned conducting this study, are particularly valuable for collecting rich data from users in their environments [8].

3   My Experiences

Activity theory is an appropriate framework for interpreting my experiences using AT to retrieve information, because technology use is contextual [1]. This framework, per Engeström [3], is comprised of seven interrelated elements: subject, rules, community, division of labor, mediating artifacts, object, and outcome. These elements, which are depicted in *Fig. 1*, are defined as follows:

- The **subject** is the individual or group that is performing an action. As a student, I am the subject who is learning.
- **Rules** are norms or conventions that govern the activities of community members. Instructors' expectations, classroom activities (e.g., lectures, group activities), and time constraints, are some of the rules that shape the actions of individuals in the learning environment.
- The **community** is comprised of individual actors. Members of the academic community include faculty members and students, amongst others.
- **Division of labor** refers to the collective action of community members working toward a goal. Students who collaborate during group activities depend on each other to complete their required assignments.
- **Mediating artifacts** are either sources of information or tools used in the completion of intended goals. In my experience, AT (e.g., hearing aids and FM transmitter, speech recognition application) are tools that enable me to retrieve information.

- The **object** is the focus of an activity. Academic assignments, for instance, are the focal point of students in a learning community.
- The **outcome** is the product of an activity. In the context of higher education, enhancing student learning—and perhaps developing new tools or services—are outcomes. By understanding how I, and other students with hearing loss, deploy AT, new technologies could be developed.

Three moments from the past two months effectively illustrate my affective information behavior, and they also provide insight into the structure of higher education. During a recent graduate seminar in educational psychology, my Phonak hearing aids began producing static and made my experience listening to the instructor difficult. Suddenly, the batteries in my hearing aids died, which made me feel frustrated. To remedy the issue, I had to excuse myself from class so that I could first remove fluid from my aids. Then, I sprinted across campus to the nearest pharmacy to purchase new hearing aid batteries. This entire ordeal took me away from my obligation as a student for nearly 30 min. When I returned to the classroom, my instructor asked me if everything was okay. I responded that I was fine; however, I expressed concern that I missed some important concepts. Fortunately, my peers in the course offered to share their notes with me. I wondered if other students with hearing aids have shared similar experiences. In my *AT Use Diary*, I posed the question: Would their peers be willing to help them, too?

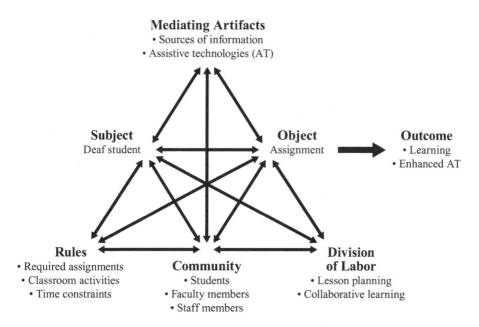

Fig. 1. Examining the author's affective information behavior via activity theory

Second, I recently began testing out Android's Live Transcribe mobile application. I first downloaded the application in its beta form, and I was excited about being able to use it. During a video conference with one of my peers, I felt disappointed when using the application, because at least half of the words being said were either misinterpreted or missing. These shortcomings prompted some confusion as I struggled to fully comprehend what was being said. I am fortunate, though, that my colleague is patient with me and does not hesitate to repeat statements or provide clarification. Thankfully, as the weeks have progressed, I have found that the application has gradually improved. The application is far from perfect; however, it is indeed performing better. As I remarked in my diary, I intend to continue using the Live Transcribe application, and I even plan to deploy it in group settings.

Finally, my Phonak FM transmitter has been an invaluable tool for helping me to retrieve information inside the classroom. Recently, my professor played a video on the classroom's projector. Although the video did not have captions, I was able to use my FM transmitter to listen to the presentation. The FM transmitter captures sounds and then sends them to the receivers embedded in my hearing aids. I managed to point the transmitter toward one of the speakers mounted on the wall. Doing so enabled me to understand more of the information than I would have if I did not have access to the technology. Fortunately, I am permitted to use my FM transmitter in the classroom because I have registered with my institution's disability support services. Had I not received permission from the institution to use AT, I would have been unable to comprehend the information presented in the video. Institutional support, as I articulated in my diary, is essential to my success.

Collectively, my affective experiences using AT demonstrate the value of social and institutional support in higher education. My peers and faculty members often help to fill in the gaps when I misinterpret or completely miss information that is presented. Although I have faced various technological setbacks (e.g., dead hearing aid batteries, inaccurate transcriptions), fellow members of the learning community have been unwavering in their support of my learning. I often ask myself: What if other deaf or hard of hearing students did not have adequate social support, or they did not receive appropriate AT? I believe that AT can be powerful tools for learning. However, students, faculty members, and staff members (e.g., disability support services), must be willing to offer their support if those technologies fail to meet users' needs. Technological failures may leave students feeling frustrated or ill-equipped to handle the rigors of higher education. I have experienced these emotions on numerous occasions when my AT have malfunctioned.

4   Conclusion

This autoethnographic study is a novel attempt at exploring the affective IB of a deaf student in higher education. Looking ahead, I will continue documenting my experiences using AT to enrich my findings. Additionally, I plan to interview other deaf and hard of hearing students enrolled in my institution. Ultimately, I aim to make theoretical contributions to the IB and activity theory literature. Practitioners may also benefit from my findings: disability support services, faculty members, and manufacturers of AT, could enhance their services and products to best meet the needs of students with hearing loss.

Although this study was limited for several reasons, these limitations present opportunities for improvement. First, although self-report methods (e.g., diaries, interviews) are "... efficient and easy techniques for obtaining emotion data" [9], triangulating self-report and physical data is ideal for measuring affect [6]. Going forward, I could collect physical or neurological data (e.g., eye tracking, facial recognition, galvanic skin response) to bolster the value of my findings. Second, I did not adequately capture all seven elements of activity theory. Since this study is autoethnographic, neither my peers nor faculty members were observed or interviewed. This restricted my understanding of community and division of labor. In a future study, I could administer surveys or conduct interviews with hearing students and faculty members to better understand their role in my learning experience. Finally, the amount of time spent collecting data was brief (i.e., approximately two months). Therefore, I should continue collecting data via a mixture of methods.

References

1. Allen, D., Karanasios, S., Slavova, M.: Working with activity theory: context, technology, and information behavior. J. Am. Soc. Inf. Sci. Technol. **62**(4), 776–788 (2011)
2. Android: Introducing Live Transcribe (2019). https://www.android.com/accessibility/live-transcribe/
3. Engeström, Y.: Activity theory and individual and social transformation. In: Engeström, Y., Miettinen, R., Punamäki-Gitai, R.-L. (eds.) Perspectives on Activity Theory, pp. 19–38. Cambridge University Press, Cambridge (1999)
4. Julien, H., Given, L.M., Opryshko, A.: Photovoice: a promising method for studies of individuals' information practices. Libr. Inf. Sci. Res. **35**(4), 257–263 (2013)
5. Julien, H., O'Brien, M.: Information behavior research: where have we been, where are we going? Can. J. Inf. Libr. Sci. **38**, 239–250 (2014). Paper presented at ACSI/CAIS 2014
6. Kahneman, D.: Experienced utility and objective happiness: a moment-based approach. In: Tversky, A., Kahneman, D. (eds.) Choices, Values, and Frames, pp. 673–692. Cambridge University Press, New York (2000)
7. Klein, J., Moon, Y., Picard, R.W.: This computer responds to user frustration: theory, design, and results. Interact. Comput. **14**(2), 119–140 (2002)
8. Lazar, J., Feng, J.H., Hochheiser, H.: Research Methods in Human-Computer Interaction. Morgan Kaufmann, Boston (2017)
9. Lopatovska, I., Arapakis, I.: Theories, methods and current research on emotions in library and information science, information retrieval and human–computer interaction. Inf. Process. Manag. **47**(4), 582 (2011)
10. Marschark, M., Sapere, P., Convertino, C., Seewagen, R., Maltzen, H.: Comprehension of sign language interpreting: deciphering a complex task situation. Sign Lang. Stud. **4**(4), 345–368 (2004)
11. Muncey, T.: Doing autoethnography. Int. J. Qual. Methods **4**(1), 69–86 (2005)
12. Nahl, D., Bilal, D. (eds.): Information and Emotion: The Emergent Affective Paradigm in Information Behavior Research and Theory. Information Today, Inc., Medford (2007)
13. Newman, L.A., Madaus, J.W., Javitz, H.S.: Effect of transition planning on postsecondary support receipt by students with disabilities. Except. Child. **82**(4), 497–514 (2016)
14. Phonak: Life is on (2019). https://www.phonak.com/us/en.html

Electromyography as a Suitable Input for Virtual Reality-Based Biofeedback in Stroke Rehabilitation

Octavio Marin-Pardo, Athanasios Vourvopoulos ,
Meghan Neureither, David Saldana, Esther Jahng,
and Sook-Lei Liew$^{(\boxtimes)}$

University of Southern California, Los Angeles, CA 90089, USA
marinpar@usc.edu, sliew@chan.usc.edu

Abstract. Virtual reality (VR)-based biofeedback of brain signals using electroencephalography (EEG) has been utilized to encourage the recovery of brain-to-muscle pathways following a stroke. Such models incorporate principles of action observation with neurofeedback of motor-related brain activity to increase sensorimotor activity on the lesioned hemisphere. However, for individuals with existing muscle activity in the hemiparetic arm, we hypothesize that providing biofeedback of muscle signals, to strengthen already established brain-to-muscle pathways, may be more effective. In this project, we aimed to understand whether and when feedback of muscle activity (measured using surface electromyography (EMG)) might more effective compared to EEG biofeedback. To do so, we used a virtual reality (VR) training paradigm we developed for stroke rehabilitation (REINVENT), which provides EEG biofeedback of ipsilesional sensorimotor brain activity and simultaneously records EMG signals. We acquired 640 trials over eight 1.5-h sessions in four stroke participants with varying levels of motor impairment. For each trial, participants attempted to move their affected arm. Successful trials, defined as when their EEG sensorimotor desynchronization (8–24 Hz) during a time-limited movement attempt exceeded their baseline activity, drove a virtual arm towards a target. Here, EMG signals were analyzed offline to see (1) whether EMG amplitude could be significantly differentiated between active trials compared to baseline, and (2) whether using EMG would have led to more successful VR biofeedback control than EEG. Our current results show a significant increase in EMG amplitude across all four participants for active versus baseline trials, suggesting that EMG biofeedback is feasible for stroke participants across a range of impairments. However, we observed significantly better performance with EMG than EEG for only the three individuals with higher motor abilities, suggesting that EMG biofeedback may be best suited for those with better motor abilities.

Keywords: Human-computer interfaces · Stroke rehabilitation · Electromyography · Biofeedback · Virtual reality

C. Stephanidis (Ed.): HCII 2019, CCIS 1032, pp. 274–281, 2019.
https://doi.org/10.1007/978-3-030-23522-2_35

1   Introduction

Repetitive task-specific practice is one of the main treatments for many individuals after stroke [1]. However, individuals with greater motor impairments and a limited range of motion are often unable to perform functional practice with their affected limb. Alternative treatments that do not require volitional movement are currently under study to help treat these individuals. Two such treatments are: (1) using biofeedback to give the patient direct control of their physiological signals, and (2) encouraging ipsilesional brain activity via the action observation network (AON).

First, biofeedback provides an individual with information about their own physiological signals and can be used to train individuals to directly control those signals. Previous studies have used neurofeedback of electrical signals from the brain, via electroencephalography (EEG), to encourage recovery of brain-to-muscle pathways following stroke [2, 3]. Similarly, biofeedback of electromyography (EMG) signals, which reflect electrical activity from contracting muscles, has also been used to strengthen the affected limb of patients with limited voluntary movement [4].

Second, the AON refers to the motor-related brain areas that are active both when a person performs and observes an action. Importantly, previous research has shown the feasibility of inducing activity in the AON [5] just via observation, in patients who do not have volitional motor ability, and that this results in enhanced motor recovery after stroke [6]. Moreover, virtual reality (VR) using an immersive head-mounted display (HMD) has been shown to enhance these AON-related activation patterns during motor observation and execution as well [7].

Therefore, a human-computer interface (HCI) that takes physiological signals as input and provides biologically relevant biofeedback of actions through HMD-VR could potentially take advantage of both HCIs and AON activity to enhance post-stroke motor recovery. We recently created a system capable of interchangeably use different types of biofeedback, called REINVENT, which can be easily tailored to meet each patient's needs [8]. We previously tested REINVENT using EEG-based biofeedback for individuals after stroke. Here, we further hypothesized that, for individuals with existing muscle activity in the hemiparetic arm, biofeedback of muscle signals, to strengthen existing brain-to-muscle pathways, may be more effective. Therefore, in this paper, we investigated (1) whether EMG amplitude could be significantly differentiated during active trials compared to baseline, allowing for its use as an effective biofeedback input, and (2) whether using an EMG signal would lead to more successful VR biofeedback control than an EEG signal.

2   Methods

2.1   Participants

In this experiment, 4 chronic stroke participants (1 female, 3 male) were recruited. They had an average age of 60 ± 5.8 years old and were all chronic stroke (time range of 6 to 16 years after stroke). They presented with varying levels of motor impairment (Fugl-Meyer Assessment, Upper Extremity scores: 13/66, 28/66, 37/66, 49/66), which were assessed by a trained occupational therapist. All participants gave written informed consent in accordance with the Declaration of Helsinki. This protocol was approved by the Institutional Review Board at the University of Southern California.

2.2   Study Design

We acquired simultaneous electrophysiological data (EMG and EEG) from the participants while they tried to move a virtual hand towards a virtual target within a set time frame (Fig. 1). The acquisition system was built on top of a previous VR-HCI training paradigm [8] and was updated to accommodate the needs of our current research question (see Materials).

Fig. 1. VR environment. For each trial, the following sequence applied: (1) No target (ball) on the table (baseline acquisition, 10 s); (2) Target appears on the paretic side of the participant, cueing movement (active acquisition, 12 s); (3) If sensorimotor desynchronization is present, the virtual hand moves towards the target; (4) If time runs out or hand reaches the target, a new trial begins.

For each participant, 640 movement attempt trials over eight 1.5-h sessions were recorded (4 blocks of 20 trials per session). Each trial consisted of a 10-s resting recording (baseline) and 12 s of motor execution, where participants were asked to actively contract the muscles that produce wrist extension. Successful trials, defined as when their EEG sensorimotor desynchronization (power of the 8–24 Hz band) during movement attempt exceeded the preceding baseline, drove the virtual arm towards the target (see Signal Processing).

Online EEG processing drove neurofeedback during the sessions, while offline EMG processing was used to identify active contractions for the current analyses. Additionally, each participant's performance, defined as the percent of trials per block in which there was a significant signal increase during active trials versus baseline, were assessed in both biofeedback modalities.

2.3   Materials

For EEG acquisition, a Starstim 8 (Neuroelectrics, Barcelona, Spain) system was used. Starstim is a wearable, wireless sensor system that allows recording and visualization of 8 channel 24-bit EEG data at 500 Hz. The spatial distribution of the electrodes followed the 10–20 system configuration [9] recording from somatosensory and motor areas: Frontal-Central (FC3, FC4), Central (C3, C4, C5, C6), and Central-Parietal (CP3, CP4).

Surface EMG was acquired from 4 muscles at 2000 Hz using a Delsys Trigno Wireless System (Delsys, MA, USA) with their proprietary software. Each sensor incorporated 4 differential Ag electrodes with amplification and filtering stages and a 16-bit A/D converter. Delsys Trigno EMG sensors were placed on Extensor Digitorum Communis (EDC), Flexor Carpi Ulnaris (FCU), Biceps Brachii (BB) and Triceps Brachii (TB) muscles of the paretic arm. Electrode positioning was determined by the experimenter by palpating the muscles while the participant performed elbow and wrist flexion and extension and was confirmed by visual inspection of the raw EMG signals. Skin preparation involved shaving the selected area and cleaning the area with iso-propyl alcohol and abrasive paste.

VR feedback was delivered via an Oculus Rift CV1 (Oculus VR, CA, USA). This HMD incorporates two OLED displays (1080 × 1200 resolution per eye, a 90 Hz refresh rate, and 110° field of view), 6 Degrees-Of-Freedom motion tracking (3-axis position and 3-axis rotation) and 2 3D-audio headphones.

All 3 devices (Fig. 2) were connected to a dedicated desktop computer (OS: Windows 10, CPU: Intel® Core™ i7-6700 at 4.00 GHz, RAM: 16 GB DDR3 1600 MHz, Graphics: NVIDIA GeForce GTX 1080) for data acquisition, signal processing, and VR task rendering. Since each device had different communication protocols and drivers, the Lab Streaming Layer (LSL) protocol[10] was used for data synchronization and recording (Fig. 2). Both EEG and EMG signal processing and statistical analyses were performed in Matlab (The Mathworks, MA, USA). The VR task was programmed in the Unity game engine (Unity Technologies, CA, USA) and rendered with the Oculus SDK.

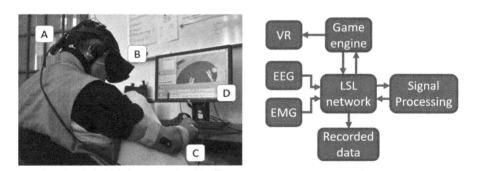

Fig. 2. Left: System devices: (A) EEG amplifier and electrodes, (B) HMD-VR, (C) EMG sensors, (D) VR task and signal processing computer. Right: System architecture: Devices stream data to the LSL network, signal processing reads raw data and sends processed data, game engine reads processed data and gives feedback through HMD, and all data is recorded from the network.

2.4 Signal Processing

EEG signals were processed in Matlab with the EEGLAB toolbox [11]. First, a bandpass filter was applied between 1–50 Hz, following bad channel removal. All EEG channels were re-referenced with an average reference and divided into epochs for every trial. Independent Component Analysis was used for removing all major artifacts related to power-line noise, eye blinking, ECG and muscular activity. Then, power spectrum and event-related Spectral Perturbation (ERSP) analyses were performed. ERSP values were converted to ERS/ERD percentages for the Mu (8–12 Hz) and Beta (12–30 Hz) bands over the C3 and C4 electrode locations to capture motor-related activation. Finally, hemispheric asymmetry was calculated as the power at the electrode contralateral to the movement (affected) side compared to the unaffected side.

EMG signals were processed in a custom Matlab script that, for each session, divided data in baseline and active contraction epochs, applied a DC-offset correction, filtered within 10–500 Hz, applied a full-wave rectification, and calculated the mean amplitude of the signal.

For both processing pipelines, a success rate was calculated as the number of successful trials (i.e., difference between computed values during baseline versus active trials) for each session block.

2.5 Statistical Analyses

First, a one-sample Kolmogorov-Smirnov test was applied to all distributions to assess normality. Given normality, next, paired-samples t-tests were used to detect a significant difference between baseline and active contraction trials of each participant, as well as between baseline and active contractions at the group level. Finally, a paired-samples t-test was used to investigate the difference between EEG and EMG performance across participants. All statistical analyses were performed in Matlab.

3 Results

3.1 Amplitude Differentiation

Although there was wide variation in signal amplitudes across participants (Fig. 3), there were significant differences in EMG signal amplitude between baseline and active states for each individual (paired-samples t-tests: Participant 1: $t(639) = -6.4$, $p < 0.0001$; Participant 2: $t(639) = -30.9$, $p < 0.0001$; Participant 3: $t(639) = -47.9$, $p < 0.0001$; Participant 4: $t(610) = -34.4$, $p < 0.0001$) and as a group (paired-samples t-test: $t(2530) = -41.6$, $p < 0.0001$), as shown in Fig. 4. This preliminarily suggests that we can use EMG to successfully distinguish between rest and movement attempt across severe, moderate, and mild stroke survivors.

3.2 Success Rate Comparison

We then asked if participants would have been more successful with EMG feedback versus EEG feedback. A paired-samples t-test between each modalities for each participant revealed a significant difference between the two medians (Participant 1: $t(31) = 5.4$, $p < 0.0001$, Participant 2: $t(31) = -14$, $p < 0.0001$, Participant 3: $t(31) = -19.5$, $p < 0.0001$, Participant 4: $t(30) = -7$, $p < 0.0001$). Specifically, the data showed that the participant with the worst motor impairments showed better performance with EEG

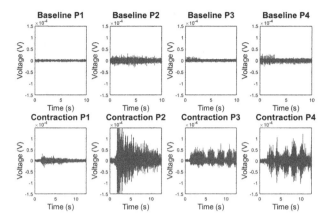

Fig. 3. Sample of EMG data recorded from Extensor Digitorum Communis of stroke participants. Top: EMG signal during baseline (no voluntary muscle activity). Bottom: EMG signal during active contraction.

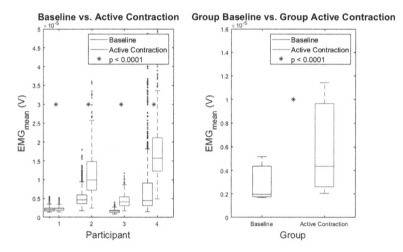

Fig. 4. Average EMG signal during baseline vs active contraction. Left: Distributions of the meanEMG values calculated from baseline (blue) andactive contraction (green) datasets for each participant. Purple * indicates a significant difference between the two states. Right: Distributions of the meanEMG values calculated from baseline (blue) andactive contraction (green) datasets across all participants. Purple * indicates a significant difference between the two states. Center line of the box-and-whisker plot represents the median value, the lower bound of the box represents the 25th percentile, and the upper bound of the box the 75th percentile. Whiskers extend to the most extreme data points not considered outliers, and outliers are indicated by dots. (Color figure online)

feedback compared to EMG feedback (Participant 1). However, the three participants with better motor ability showed greater success when using EMG biofeedback compared to EEG biofeedback (Participants 2–4; Fig. 5).

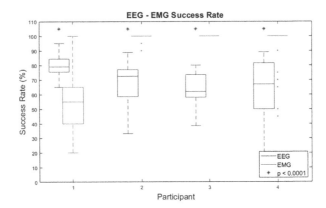

Fig. 5. Mediansuccess rates between EEG biofeedback (blue) and EMG biofeedback (green) for each participant. Purple * indicates a significant difference between the scores of the two modalities. Center line of the box-and-whisker plot represents the median value, the lower bound of the box represents the 25th percentile, and the upper bound of the box the 75th percentile. Whiskers extend to the most extreme data points not considered outliers, and outliers are indicated by dots. (Color figure online)

4   Conclusions

Our current results show that it is possible to identify between rest and active movement attempt in individuals with a wide range of motor impairments. In addition, this preliminary research suggests that participants with higher motor ability, and thus higher EMG signal amplitude differences, would have better control of EMG biofeedback compared to EEG neurofeedback. In contrast, for individuals with lower motor ability, EEG neurofeedback would be more successful. Overall, these findings provide preliminary data to support personalization of VR-based biofeedback based on motor impairment level. However, given the small sample size, further studies with larger samples are needed to confirm these findings. In addition, larger studies could examine whether there is a specific threshold of motor ability can predict which populations respond best to each type of feedback.

Acknowledgments. This research was supported by the American Heart Association through the REINVENT project (Grant #16IRG26960017) and a USC-CONACyT fellowship jointly given by the University of Southern California and the Mexican National Council of Science and Technology.

References

1. Langhorne, P., Bernhardt, J., Kwakkel, G.: Stroke rehabilitation. Lancet **377**, 1693–1702 (2011). https://doi.org/10.1016/S0140-6736(11)60325-5
2. Ramos-Murguialday, A., et al.: Brain-machine interface in chronic stroke rehabilitation: a controlled study. Ann. Neurol. (2013). https://doi.org/10.1002/ana.23879

3. Shindo, K.: Effects of neurofeedback training with an electroencephalogram-based brain-computer interface for hand paralysis in patients with chronic stroke: a preliminary case series study. J. Rehabil. Med. **43**, 951–957 (2016). https://doi.org/10.2340/16501977-0859
4. Armagan, O., Tascioglu, F., Oner, C.: Electromyographic biofeedback in the treatment of the hemiplegic hand: a placebo-controlled study. Am. J. Phys. Med. Rehabil. **82**, 856–861 (2003). https://doi.org/10.1097/01.PHM.0000091984.72486.E0
5. Garrison, K.A., Aziz-Zadeh, L., Wong, S.W., Liew, S.L., Winstein, C.J.: Modulating the motor system by action observation after stroke. Stroke **44**, 2247–2253 (2013). https://doi.org/10.1161/STROKEAHA.113.001105
6. Celnik, P., Webster, B., Glasser, D.M., Cohen, L.G.: Effects of action observation on physical training after stroke. Stroke. **39**, 1814–1820 (2008). https://doi.org/10.1161/STROKEAHA.107.508184
7. Vourvopoulos, A., Bermúdezi Badia, S.: Motor priming in virtual reality can augment motor-imagery training efficacy in restorative brain-computer interaction: a within-subject analysis. J. Neuroeng. Rehabil. **13**, 1–14 (2016). https://doi.org/10.1186/s12984-016-0173-2
8. Spicer, R., Anglin, J., Krum, D.M., Liew, S.L.: REINVENT: a low-cost, virtual reality brain-computer interface for severe stroke upper limb motor recovery. In: Proceedings of IEEE Virtual Reality, pp. 385–386 (2017). https://doi.org/10.1109/vr.2017.7892338
9. Klem, G.H., Lüders, H.O., Jasper, H.H., Elger, C.: The ten-twenty electrode system of the International Federation. Electroencephalogr. Clin. Neurophysiol. **10**, 371–375 (1999). https://doi.org/10.1016/0013-4694(58)90053-1
10. Kothe, C.: Lab Streaming Layer (LSL). https://github.com/sccn/labstreaminglayer
11. Delorme, A., Makeig, S.: EEGLAB: an open source toolbox for analysis of single-trial EEG dynamics including independent component analysis. J. Neurosci. Methods. **134**, 9–21 (2004). https://doi.org/10.1016/j.jneumeth.2003.10.009

HapTalker: E-book User Interface for Blind People

Ryoka Nakai[✉], Kiyohide Ito[✉], Hidekatsu Yanagi[✉], and Yoshiaki Mima[✉]

Future University Hakodate, Kamedanakano, 116-2,
Hakodate, Hokkaido 0418655, Japan
{g2118027,itokiyo,yanagi,mima}@fun.ac.jp
http://www.fun.ac.jp/

Abstract. This study proposes a novel user interface (UI) for electronic devices, such as e-book readers, for visually impaired people. Voice and touch interfaces such as the text-to-speech function and touch panel of e-book readers, respectively, have enabled such users to independently comprehend text and complete and individual sentences end-to-end. However, these users may find it inconvenient to skip certain sentences because the visual interface design of current e-book readers is primarily based on paper books. This study develops the "HapTalker" UI design prototype to overcome this inconvenience. A performance estimation model for this UI is also proposed.

Keywords: User interface · Text-to-speech function · Book reader · Visually impaired · Performance estimation

1 Introduction

This study aims to improve visually impaired people's ease of smartphone use for reading e-books. Currently, human "readers" convert a paper book (i.e., visual information) into audible media (i.e., audible information) to enable visually impaired people to read books. However, such conversions require time, and therefore, visually impaired people must wait before they can read books.

The invention and subsequent widespread use of e-books has changed this scenario because most e-books are equipped with functions to convert text to speech. These functions help visually impaired people read books without any conversion delays. E-books are becoming increasingly popular, and they are already recognized as a common medium for publishing textual information [1].

Unfortunately, e-books are not designed to be easy to use by visually impaired people. For example, such users face difficulties in pointing to a specific part on a display. Current product designs are based on the conventional graphical user interface (UI) model that is typically used by visually able people.

Before e-books emerged, visually impaired people used audiobooks. Digital Accessible Information SYstem (DAISY) is a technical standard that lists the

© Springer Nature Switzerland AG 2019
C. Stephanidis (Ed.): HCII 2019, CCIS 1032, pp. 282–288, 2019.
https://doi.org/10.1007/978-3-030-23522-2_36

specifications of digital audiobooks for visually impaired people. Various devices have DAISY-compliant hardware (Fig. 1) that is carefully designed for visually impaired people. Visually impaired people can operate such devices easily and quickly using only a few buttons to control all functions. These interfaces are therefore very helpful to such users.

Unfortunately, it is not easy to provide DAISY contents. In fact, several months are required for a person to convert text and additional information to voice for DAISY contents.

Fig. 1. Product example (using PLEXTALK [2])

This study proposes a human–machine interaction method for visually impaired people to easily use a smartphone. This method was implemented as a research prototype called HapTalker and an empirical evaluation was conducted. An operational model for performance estimation of visually impaired people's ease of reading was also provided.

2   Related Works

2.1   E-book Readers

E-book readers such as Kindle and iBooks are widely used. E-books store data as text and provide options to automatically convert text into voice. Thus, visually impaired people can use the voice function to read books.

Unfortunately, e-books have a conventional graphical UI. Specifically, the book text and UI components for various functions are placed at certain absolute positions on the screen. As a result, compared to visually able users, visually impaired users require more effort to specify target UI objects precisely [4]. Therefore, it is important to devise more convenient ways for visually impaired people to handle text on e-book readers.

2.2   User Interface for Visually Impaired People

Many previous studies have proposed UI designs for visually impaired people. For instance, Kane et al. introduced a touch-gesture-based interface [3] that enables control of touch panel devices without using vision. This method is applicable for

   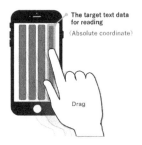

Fig. 2. Operation with an e-book reader   **Fig. 3.** Text placed at an absolute position

specifications on hierarchical data placed on the screen. Their study results showed that eight out of 10 users preferred using this method. As target objects are placed at absolute positions, users have to check which object is specified as the first target. If the system uses relative finger movements as the principal input information but not the absolute position, the meaning of interaction changes because users need not be concerned with what part of the display they have touched.

3   HapTalker

Visually impaired people can use the latest e-book readers with touch screens and voice feedback functions. However, the UI still inherits a perceptional model on a bit map screen. Typically, to enable human–computer interactions with a bit map screen, all UI components are specified with absolute coordinates. However, computer operations based on relative motions, such as gesture-based operations, are more useful for visually impaired people because they can then touch any part of the screen.

3.1   HapTalker Design Concept

In this study, we designed an e-book reader called HapTalker that provides audible and haptic reactions to users based on the following three principles.

1. Operate Using Relative Motion: Visually impaired people find it difficult to pinpoint an exact position on the touch panel. Thus, relative motion on the touch panel is used as the primary input parameter (Fig. 4). Relative operation detection using an acceleration sensor is also evaluated.
2. Use Text-to-Speech Interface: Voice is the primary output interface. Text content is read out using the text-to-speech function, and other information such as sentence numbers is provided using a sound interface.
3. Reaction with Vibration: The smartphone is equipped with a small vibrator to intuitively intimate any changes in the target text data.

In this paper, we do not discuss the reaction with vibrations owing to the lack of space.

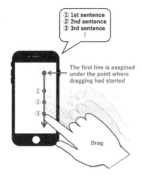

Fig. 4. First line assigned under the point where dragging motion starts

3.2 Data Model of HapTalker

HapTalker's text data model differs from that of a conventional e-book. In a conventional e-book, text is laid out as a rectangular frame to fit into a page, and it often breaks across lines because of the size limit of the page/frame. Further, all sentences must fit on the page. As our system does not lay out text/sentences visually, it does not need to break any line of text.

In our system, the document structure is defined as follows: a document consists of chapters, a chapter consists of sections, a section consists of paragraphs, and a paragraph is represented as an ordered list of sentences.

- When a user accesses the e-book, the system specifies one sentence.
- The specified sentence and sentence number are read out.
- The user can move from one chapter, section, paragraph, or sentence to another.

4 Three Proposed Models

Three different models were implemented and evaluated: straight line type, dial type, and doorknob type. HapTalker is implemented as an iOS application using the Swift4 programming language for iPhone8.

4.1 Straight Line-Type Model

Operations with a straight line-type model are based on "drag" and "tap." These actions are frequently used as touch gestures, thus affording ease of use. The basic operations for this model are as follows.

1. The height of one line (e.g., 17.5 mm) is specified.
2. An operation is started by dragging.
3. The system starts reading from the first sentence in the document. The first position is related to the current sentence.

4. When the finger is dragged downward by an amount equal to the height of one sentence, the current line number is increased by one.
5. The system maintains the current location (i.e., current sentence number).
6. When the finger is dragged upward by an amount equal to the height of one sentence, the current line number is decreased by one.
7. When the current line number indicates a change in the target line number, the corresponding target text is read using the text-to-speech function.
8. By moving two fingers together, users can move to the next or previous paragraph.
9. By moving three fingers together, users can move to the next or previous paragraph.

Users can mark a location in an e-book by sliding their finger to the left or right. If they drag their finger over a marked sentence, they feel a vibration.

4.2 Dial-Type Model

The dial-type UI responds to circular motions made using a finger (Fig. 5). This motion is similar to rotating a dial for increasing/decreasing an audio amplifier's volume or to that of an analog device controller used for winding or rewinding video tapes.

In this UI, dial rotation is perceived as the angle between two straight lines as specified by the starting position, center of the touch pad, and ending position.

The dial-type UI is somewhat restricted as it specifies only sequentially ordered sentences. Moreover, it is relatively difficult to extend its function compared to that of the straight line-type UI.

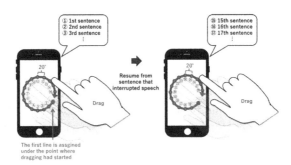

Fig. 5. Every 20° of rotation in the clockwise direction denotes moving forward by one sentence in the e-book

4.3 Doorknob-Type Model

The doorknob-type UI differs from the other two UIs in that it uses an acceleration sensor. Visually impaired people are familiar with the open-close operation of a door with a doorknob. In this model, rotating the smartphone (Fig. 6) by more than 30° in a specific direction takes the user to the next or previous sentence.

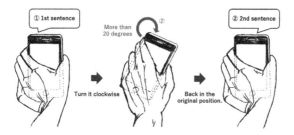

Fig. 6. Rotating smartphone by 30° in the clockwise direction allows the user to move forward by one sentence in the e-book

5   Performance Estimation

The time to access was estimated using the following formula.

$$T(n) = a * \log_2(1 + (n \bmod W)) + b * \lfloor n/W \rfloor. \tag{1}$$

where n is the distance from the current line to the target line, and W is the mean number of dragged sentences in one drag operation. a and b were obtained using empirical methods. In this study, the accuracy of the above equation was measured experimentally. Good accuracy was obtained for the second term, as shown in Fig. 7 below. We are also investigating the effect of the first term on T(n).

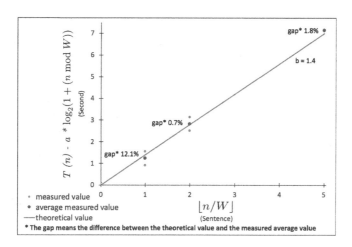

Fig. 7. Second term of equation

6   Concluding Remarks

This study proposed different input methods for a novel e-book UI called Hap-Talker for visually impaired people who want to read books/documents using smartphones. Three e-book reader prototypes were implemented and feedback was obtained from two postnatal visually impaired people.

The evaluators gave negative feedback for the data structure because it does not support the concept of a page, which they considered useful for sharing documents with other readers. Thus, the data model needs further improvement.

The evaluators gave their own preferences for the three types of operation.

- Line Type: One evaluator noted that the line-type model is straightforward to use and that it eases the data-handling operation. The evaluators had positive feedback about the use of vibrations for intimating users about sentences.
- Dial Type: The evaluators found the operation of the dial-type model to be more complex than that of the line-type one.
- Doorknob Type: The doorknob-type model required complex user motions, and therefore, the evaluators were hesitant to use this operation.

A formula for performance estimation was proposed. In the future, we will refine the performance estimation formula using the measured values.

References

1. Impress Research Institute: The Grid: Blueprint for a New Computing Infrastructure. Survey Report, Impress (2017)
2. PLEXTALK: http://www.plextalk.com/americas/top/products/ptn2/
3. Kane, S.K., Bigham, J.P., Wobbrock, J.O.: Slide rule: making mobile touch screens accessible to blind people using multi-touch interaction techniques. In: Assets 2008 Proceedings of the 10th International ACM SIGACCESS Conference on Computers and Accessibility, pp. 73–80 (2018)
4. Kane, S.K., Wobbrock, J.O., Ladner, R.E.: Usable gestures for blind people: understanding preference and performance. In: Proceedings of the 2011 Annual Conference on Human Factors in Computing Systems-CHI, pp. 413–422 (2011)
5. Aoki, R., et al.: Drag & Flick: character input method for the visually impaired using touch screen. In: Proceedings of Interaction, vol. 2013, pp. 72–79 (2013)
6. Ohashi, T., Miura, T., Sakajiri, S., Onishi, Y., Onotsuka, K.: An input/output interface using voice feedback for visually impaired users using touch screen terminals. In: Proceedings of the Information Technology Forum, pp. 565–566 (2015)

Can Exhibit-Explanations in Sign Language Contribute to the Accessibility of Aquariums?

Miki Namatame[✉], Masami Kitamula, Daisuke Wakatsuki,
Makoto Kobayashi, Manabi Miyagi, and Nobuko Kato

National University Corporation of Tsukuba University of Technology,
Tsukuba 3058520, Japan
{miki,m-kitamr,waka,nobuko}@a.tsukuba-tech.ac.jp,
koba@cs.k.tsukuba-tech.ac.jp,
mmiyagi@k.tsukuba-tech.ac.jp

Abstract. In this study, we aimed at improving the information accessibility of aquariums based on universal design and design for all. We designed the contents using sign language for the visitors who are Deaf and Hard-of-Hearing. We prepared QR codes in front of water tanks, so the visitors could access the content by using their mobile phone and/or tablet-PC easily.

We conducted a demonstration experiment at an aquarium with the university students who are Deaf and Hard-of-Hearing and gathered their opinions using a questionnaire. One opinion obtained was that the explanation was more impressive in sign language than in writing. As a result of our video analysis, when there was sign language content, the communication between visitors increased. It was highly appreciated to watch the fish while watching commentary in sign language. However, sign language content requires time to finish playing. In order to convey the comments in a short time, sign language as well as visual information, needs to be designed appropriately.

Keywords: Aquarium · Sign language · Accessible design

1 Introduction

People spend a lot of time outside of school in their lives. So, independent science learning outside of a school is important [1, 2]. In particular, places such as museums are important organizations of lifelong learning. Recently, access to buildings and information of the museums has been greatly improved with legal maintenance [3, 4]. The concept called "universal accessibility for the global citizen" is necessary at museums [5, 6]. In actuality, some museums prepare the barrier-free checklists [7] and the accessibility program for visitors and the universal guidelines for an exhibition. For example, the Smithsonian National Museum also prepare universal design manuals and specialized posts [8]. Some museums conduct tours for the impaired [9, 10], that has an inclusive design whereas others have displays and hands-on devices in sign language [11].

Unfortunately, there are few museums taking such actions in Japan. Most of the content for people with visual and/or hearing disabilities is insufficient from a viewpoint

© Springer Nature Switzerland AG 2019
C. Stephanidis (Ed.): HCII 2019, CCIS 1032, pp. 289–294, 2019.
https://doi.org/10.1007/978-3-030-23522-2_37

of universal design and accessible design. So we tried to improve information accessibility for the visitors who are Deaf and Hard-of-hearing at the aquarium as the first step to achieve this goal.

2   Research Question

What kind of disadvantages do deaf people face in an aquarium? By attempting to answer this, we suggest solutions to the problems and inspect the effect of their implementation through an experiment.

3   Method

3.1   Basic Research at the Aquarium

Ibaraki prefectural Oarai aquarium "Aqua World" tries to be barrier-free. However, barrier-free information does not consider the hearing-impaired.

Therefore, we researched what kind of disadvantages the hearing-impaired face in the aquarium through the simulated experience of the staff. We considered solutions to solve problems and implemented it in the aquarium (Fig. 1).

Fig. 1. Discovery from simulated experience: What is the disadvantage of hearing-impaired visitors in the aquarium? (Cut off external sound with white noise and ear muffs)

1. Experience Learning
   The experimental lesson is available in the Discovery room. Everyone can touch the creatures in the discovery room. However, the voice of the guide is often not noticed when visitors watch the tank during observation and concentrate on it. Therefore we prepared water-proof instruction cards in the aquarium and sank them underwater. This method was very effective for everyone.
2. Face-to-Face Commentary
   As for the commentary given by the aquarium, the hearing-impaired cannot get information mainly by sound. Even for the non-impaired person, it is hard to take information at the crowded place in particular. Therefore, I installed a directional speaker in this situation and improved the ease of information collection by sound (Fig. 2).

Fig. 2. Left: Attention card sunk in the water; Center: Face-to-face learning with directional speakers; Right: Text conversion by automatic speech recognition

3. Explanatory information using a microphone

   Speech to text conversion on devices converts a digital recording of a sound into written words. When a sound recorded beforehand is played on a speaker, this system is suitable. However, there are many ad libs at a live show. Therefore, we connect the microphone to the machine translation system and converted the sounds into written words.

4. Dolphins and California Sea Lion show

   The scenario of the Dolphins and California Sea Lion show changes according to the health condition of the dolphins and sea lions. Because there is so much reflection in the pool, we tried real-time, abstract note-taking. We will present the result of these practice experiments in ICOM.

3.2 Designing Multilingual Content

The aquarium contains a voice-guide system. The system can inform the visitor of the content of the displays at 47 places in the aquarium in Japanese, English, Chinese, and Korean. However, the voice guide is not useful to the hearing-impaired.

We assumed that the websites are a popular tool for many people to get information. Thus, we designed the web content by incorporating Japanese sign language. First, we noted the technical terms spoken in an aquarium audio tour. Then, we created the sign language video for each technical term and discussed them with the hearing-impaired. We thus designed the web content using sign language (Fig. 3).

Fig. 3. Screenshot of the sign language content

3.3   Field Experiment (27ᵗʰ Nov 2018)

We chose 20 exhibitions out of 47 places with audio guides and prepared water-proof cards in which the QR code in front of a fish tank and commentaries are printed.

We watched the sea creatures while reading the explanations in sign language gestures. We recorded it by using a video camera and investigated how sign language was used in the aquarium. We divided eight participants into two groups. Group A used the sign language content through an iPhone in the first half and used card commentaries in the latter half. Group B used card commentaries in the first half and the sign language contents through the phone in the latter half. Then, the questionary survey and the aquarium quiz were conducted (Fig. 4).

Fig. 4. Snapshot of the experiment (participants watching sign language animation)

4   Result and Analysis

4.1   Attributes of Participants and Their Communication Method

Eight experiment cooperators (average age: 21) were daily sign language users. Their communication methods with the hearing people are residual hearing ability and lipreading. All the members had the experience of visiting an aquarium, with either their school group, friends, or family. We asked about the likes or dislikes of the aquarium. Six of them answered "I like aquariums". Two of them answered "I'm not sure which side I am in". The number of visits ranged from 2 to 23 (the average was 8.1 times and the standard deviation was 7.9). The reasons to go to the aquarium were "the creature which I could not usually watch was seen (6 people)" and "New knowledge about a creature was provided (3 people)".

4.2 Post-questionnaire

We performed usability evaluations after the field experiment. Participants responded on a six-step Likert scale about Effectiveness, Efficiency, Learnability, and Satisfaction (1: Strong disagree, 2: disagree, 3: Weak disagree, 4: Weak agree, 5: Agree, and 6: Strong agree). "I enjoyed it" was 5.4 points. "I want to experience again" was 4.9 points. "Sign language commentary is good" was 4.4 points. Five people answered, "Mobile phone is better". The remaining three answered, "A commentary card is better".

We asked the participants about the effectiveness of sign language commentaries at an aquarium. They answered on the six-step Likert scale described above. "Sign language is necessary" is 4.1 points, "Sign language is useful" was 4.25 points, "I want to use sign language commentary" was 4.38 points, "I was able to gain new knowledge" was 5.0 points, "I could learn new sign Languages" was 3.25 points. About Satisfaction of the web content by incorporating Japanese sign language, "I was satisfied with the contents" was 4.13 points, "I want to introduce this website" was 4.75 points.

And next, we question the efficiency by using the same Likert scale, the participants answered the following. "Screen was easy to see" was 4.5 points, "Sign language was easy to see" was 4.5 points, "I got information easily" was 4.75 points, "I could use the QR code instantly" was 4.88 points, "I was able to operate the website without stress" was 5.38 points.

Finally, we asked about learnability, they answered that "Sign language was easy to understand" was 5.0 points, "Text is easy to understand" was 4.6 points, "Photos were effective" was 4.6 points, "Sign language promoted my understanding" was 4.5 points.

"I can gain new knowledge about creatures" being the reason for going to the aquarium with sign language commentary increased to 7 people; before the experiment, only 3 people gave this reason.

In their comments, five people answered that "it was fun because I could obtain information I did not know". There was also a comment saying, "I think that sign language commentary will be a tool to enjoy the aquarium". On the other hand, some commented that it took time to finish the explanation in sign language, so they worried that they might be causing trouble for other people.

In the quiz of a total of 20 points, group A scored an average of 16.25 (SD = 1.1), group B scored an average of 17.5 (SD = 0.5), and there was no significant difference between the groups, t (6) = 1.85, p = .12.

5 Discussion and Conclusion

Conducting a demonstration experiment at the aquarium for deaf and hard-of-hearing people, we gathered their opinions using a questionnaire. There was also an opinion that the explanation in sign language is more impressive than the written explanation. The video analysis showed that sign language content increased the communications between visitors. The people highly appreciated being able to see fish while watching the commentary in sign language. However, since sign language content takes time to finish playing, sign language as well as visual information should be designed appropriately to convey the content.

Cooperating with the aquarium staff, we clarified the disadvantages the hearing impaired faced in the aquarium and suggested solutions. In this study, we inspected the effect of sign language content with experimental proof.

Acknowledgements. This work was supported by JSPS KAKENHI Grant Number 18H01046 and Contract research of Ibaraki Prefecture (2017). This study has been approved by the research ethics committee of the Tsukuba University of Technology (H30-4). We thank Aqua World Ibaraki Prefectural Oarai Aquarium and the Tsukuba University of Technology students who helped with the research.

References

1. Falk, H.J., Donovan, E., Woods, R.: Free-Choice Science Education. Teachers College Press, New York (2001)
2. Abell, K.M., Lederman, G.M.: Handbook of Research on Science Education. Lawrence Erlbaum Associates, Hillsdale (2007)
3. Hamraie, A.: Building Access: Universal Design and the Politics of Disability, 3rd edn. University of Minnesota Press, Minneapolis (2017)
4. Paciello, M.: Web Accessibility for People with Disabilities, 1st edn. CRC Press, Boca Raton (2000)
5. Smith, M.J., Salvendy, G. (eds.): Human Interface 2007. LNCS, vol. 4558. Springer, Heidelberg (2007). https://doi.org/10.1007/978-3-540-73354-6
6. The inclusive museum. https://translate.google.com/translate?hl=de&sl=de&tl=en&u=https%3A%2F%2Fwww.museumsbund.de%2Finklusion%2F. Accessed 29 Mar 2019
7. https://www.lmb.museum/de/fach-und-arbeitsgruppen/ag-barrierefreiheit-ausstellungen/barrierefreiheit/. Accessed 29 Mar 2019
8. Smithsonian Guidelines for Accessible Exhibition Design. https://www.si.edu/Accessibility/SGAED. Accessed 29 Mar 2019
9. American Museum of Natural History. https://www.amnh.org/plan-your-visit/accessibility. Accessed 29 Mar 2019
10. Science Museum in London. https://www.sciencemuseum.org.uk/visit-us/accessibility. Accessed 29 Mar 2019
11. The National Palace Museum in Taipei. https://www.npm.gov.tw/en/Article.aspx?sNo=02007003. Accessed 29 Mar 2019

Consensus-Based Human-Agent Interaction Model for Emotion Regulation in ASD

Chung Hyuk Park[1]([✉]), Hifza Javed[1], and Myounghoon Jeon[2]

[1] The George Washington University, Washington D.C., USA
{chpark,hifzajaved}@gwu.edu
[2] Virginia Tech, Blacksburg, VA, USA
myounghoonjeon@vt.edu

Abstract. This paper presents a human-agent interaction framework for emotional regulation through emotional interaction with a virtual agent that uses a consensus-based algorithm. This model-based framework provides a parameterized and dynamic approach for emotional interaction with an agent that can be applied to social robot-based therapies and virtual agent-based socio-emotional interaction studies. The extended goal of this study is to develop a human-robot interaction framework that can implement emotion regulation (ER) for children with Autism spectrum disorder (ASD). This paper describes the algorithmic approach for the design of this framework, as well as a user study to evaluate its effectiveness as a tool to provide emotional interaction and emotion regulation to children with ASD.

Keywords: Human-agent interaction · Social robotics · Emotional interaction · Consensus model · Multi-agent emotion regulation

1 Introduction

Human-robot interaction is a fast-growing field of research, with applications in the fields of social interaction, assistive robotics, behavioral therapy, and educational robotics [3, 7, 8]. Research on regulating and expressing emotions through physical or animation-based facial expressions through robotic platforms has been conducted in several studies [2, 4]. However, an efficient framework for modeling and guiding emotional interactions between a human user and a robotic agent is yet to be achieved.

For interactions with a virtual or robotic agent to be effective, the agent must be equipped with its own control mechanism that can regulate its emotions, in order to conduct a meaningful interaction that can have a certain desired effect on the human. To this end, we use a consensus-based approach [5] to formulate an agent-based interaction framework. One specific aim of this study is to apply this framework to promote emotional interactions and implement emotion regulation among children with Autism Spectrum Disorder (ASD), who commonly experience difficulties in engaging in emotional interactions as well as in self-regulating the emotions they experience on an everyday basis.

© Springer Nature Switzerland AG 2019
C. Stephanidis (Ed.): HCII 2019, CCIS 1032, pp. 295–301, 2019.
https://doi.org/10.1007/978-3-030-23522-2_38

2 Consensus-Based Emotional Interaction Model

Previous research in the field focuses primarily on expressing artificial emotions through robotic systems, estimating emotional responses of humans, or assessing engagement in task-based settings, but not much emphasis has been laid on designing realistic models for naturalistic emotional interactions. In this work, we propose a novel consensus theory-based framework for emotional interaction that includes three emotional agents: a human user with an emotion state, a robotic agent with emotional expressions, and a target emotion goal for emotion regulation.

We use a 2-dimensional (2D) representation of emotions with arousal and valence values, as defined in Russell's circumplex model [6]. In this 2D plot (Fig. 1a), we represent the human's emotion state as xH and the robotic agent's emotion state as xR. By adding a goal state for emotion regulation, xG, we can then form a consensus equation as in (1), where aR is the approach rate:

$$\dot{x}_R = a_R \sum_{j \in \{H,G\}} (x_j - x_R) = a_R(x_H - x_R) + a_R(x_G - x_R) \tag{1}$$

The consensus approach guarantees the convergence of multi-agents. Although the human node, x_H, is not controllable, all the nodes exist in a bounded domain (bounded input, bounded output), thus enabling connected stability for emotional interaction and regulation. The equation above takes as input the emotion state of the human (x_H) and computes the next emotion state of the penguin (x'_R) with the aim of gradually guiding the human toward the goal emotion state (x_G).

3 Emotional Interaction Model for Socially Assistive Robotics

In applying the consensus algorithm, we design additional mechanisms for effective emotional interaction: *rapport formation* and *characteristic bias*.

Since the human agent is not directly controllable, the robotic agent is dynamically assigned a temporary target node such that it initially approaches the human's emotion state to form a rapport with the user and then gradually moves the temporary target state closer to the predetermined goal emotion in order to implement emotion regulation. Therefore, through continued interactions with a robotic agent that has a dynamically changing target state, the consensus algorithm gradually leads the human's emotion to a desired goal emotion state.

The second mechanism of characteristic bias is represented by $B()$, which is a character bias function, and a_R, which is an approach rate. The bias function enables different models of agent behavior to be designed. For example, in a *linear speed model*, the speed of emotional change on the 2D emotion domain is linear to the output of control algorithm (1). However, in a *spring-damper model*, the directional input of emotional change (spring term) and the resistance to abrupt emotional change (damping term) are taken into account to form unique emotional characteristics of the agent.

To assess the feasibility of our methodology, we created a graphical user interface (GUI)-based emotional game (shown in Fig. 1b) that uses emotional expressions previously designed for a robotic agent in [1], in which the agent and the human user both take turns to express their emotions. The protocol for a single iteration of the turn-based emotional interaction is as follows: (1) Robot expresses its initial emotion (displayed in the left panel), (2) Human responds with his/her current emotion state (displayed on the right panel), (3) Robot agent allocates a temporary target state and the final goal state (4) Robot computes its next emotion state based on the consensus equation and the current model of agent behavior, and (5) Robot displays its new emotional expression on the left panel.

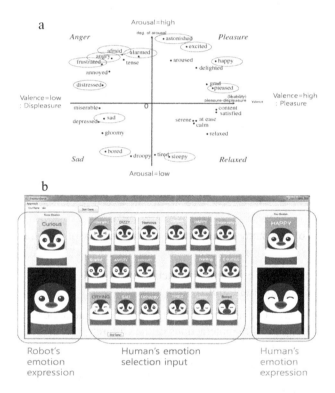

Fig. 1. Our emotion interaction framework: (a) the emotional mapping of our agent (robotic) system based on Russell's circumplex model [8] and (b) our GUI-based emotional interaction game with character-based agents.

4   User Study and Methods

We invited 5 typically developing (TD) children and 5 children with ASD to participate in our study, with the goal of verifying the potential of this framework. Table 1 presents the demographic details of the two participant groups. The mean age of both the TD and ASD groups was 8.4 years.

All participants were accompanied by their parents who remained with them through the length of their sessions. The children were familiarized with the purpose and procedure of the experiment and parental consent was obtained. The research protocol for the study was approved by the George Washington University (GWU) Office of Human Research and all requirements established by the GWU IRB #111540 were followed. The emotion game was run on a computer that was placed on a table in a room with the children seated in front of it. No instruction about how long the game could be played was given. Data from only a single interaction session per participant are included in this paper.

Table 1. Participant demographic information

ID	Gender	Age	Race	Group
1	M	10	Asian	TD
2	M	9	Caucasian	TD
3	M	9	Caucasian	TD
4	M	5	Caucasian	TD
5	M	9	South Asian	TD
6	M	7	Caucasian	ASD
7	M	8	Caucasian	ASD
8	M	10	Caucasian	ASD
9	M	8	Caucasian	ASD
10	M	9	Caucasian	ASD

The purpose of the study was to verify the usefulness of this framework in two ways:

(1) As a tool to promote emotional interactions, and
(2) As an emotion regulation tool.

To evaluate its effectiveness in promoting emotional interactions among children, we measured the lengths of the interactions of the children with the robotic agent as an indicator of the ability of this tool to engage the children. The length of an interaction was measured as the number of turns in the interaction sequence (the number of emotional states selected by the child while playing the emotional interaction game). To evaluate its usefulness as an emotion regulation tool, we evaluated the last 30% of the emotion selections of each child to measure the proximity of the emotion states to the goal state. A distance of less than 10% of the maximum possible distance in the 2-D emotion domain was considered to be a successful case of emotion regulation.

5   Outcomes

Figure 2a shows one case of interaction flow between the robotic agent and a participant, where the robotic agent utilizes the linear model to compute its emotion states. In this model, the robotic agent closely follows the participant's emotion states temporarily as if

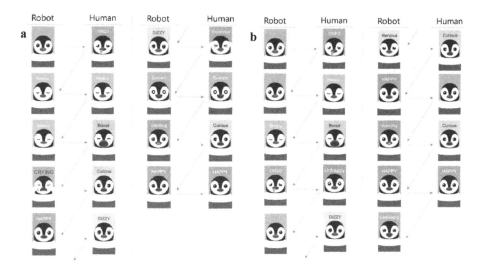

Fig. 2. Emotion game example with the robot's emotional change model (a) being linear and (b) including the damping component.

mimicking the user, but then gradually leads the user toward more positive emotional states. In Fig. 2b, the robotic agent utilizes the spring-damper model. The changes in emotion states in this case can be seen as "smoother" than the linear model, but sometimes give the impression of "indifference" to user's emotion state. These results show that this framework has the capacity to model different emotional characters.

Table 2 presents the results obtained for the two measures of interest described in Sect. 4. The lengths of interaction, the difference in emotion states of the participant and robotic agent towards the end of the interaction, as well as the success of emotion regulation are listed here for every participant.

We used this data to identify any differences in the interaction patterns of the participants from the two groups (ASD and TD). The average length of interaction for the TD group was 42.4 turns while that for the ASD group was 16.8 turns. The average emotional difference for the TD group was found to be 8.48 while that for the ASD group was 5.27. In addition, emotion regulation was found to be successful for 4 out of 5 participants in the TD group and 3 out of 5 participants in the ASD group.

One-way analysis of variance (ANOVA) was applied to these data in order to compare the performances of the two groups. Results from this analysis are shown in Tables 3 and 4. The emotion game was found to be more engaging to the participants in the TD group than those in the ASD group. A statistically significant difference in the length of interaction between TD and ASD groups was found, with a p value of 0.0034. However, in their emotional interaction with the robotic agent, both groups in general showed smooth guided progression towards the goal state, with an overall rate of success of emotion regulation being 70%. There was also no statistically significant difference in the success of the emotional regulation for the two groups (p-value of 0.5447), showing that the framework can be equally effective in regulation emotions for both the TD children and children with ASD.

Table 2. Key measures obtained from the collected data to evaluate the framework

ID	Length of interaction	Emotional difference	Success of ER	Group
1	47	4.06	Yes	TD
2	31	2.74	Yes	TD
3	44	7.57	No	TD
4	58	2.89	Yes	TD
5	32	0.89	Yes	TD
6	28	3.80	Yes	ASD
7	15	4.36	Yes	ASD
8	12	3.84	No	ASD
9	7	10.03	No	ASD
10	22	4.32	Yes	ASD

Table 3. One-way ANOVA to compare the lengths of interaction for both groups

Source	Sum. Sq	d.f.	Mean Sq.	F	Prob > F
X1	1638.4	1	1638.4	16.8	0.0034
Error	780	8	97.5		
Total	2418.4	9			

Table 4. One-way ANOVA to compare the success of ER for both groups

Source	Sum. Sq	d.f.	Mean Sq.	F	Prob > F
X1	0.1	1	0.1	0.4	0.5447
Error	2	8	0.25		
Total	2.1	9			

6   Discussion and Conclusion

In this work, we presented a novel, consensus-based, emotionally-expressive tool to engage children with ASD in emotional interactions, while simultaneously guiding the emotional exchange to perform the emotion regulation function.

Firstly, since this was only a pilot study meant to form an initial assessment of the effectiveness of this tool, a small participant size was considered to be sufficient. With a large-scale study in the future, we hope to collect more data to improve the validity and reliability of the results obtained from this pilot study.

From the current study, we found that the design of our emotion game was more engaging to the TD children than those with ASD. This may be attributed, in part, to the fact that the emotions in the display panel were labeled, and children with superior reading abilities could have an advantage over the other children. For children with weaker reading skills, the available choices could only be interpreted through the images used to depict each emotion. However, it must be pointed out that all children were familiarized with the game prior to the monitored interaction, where they were introduced to each emotion (with its label). We hope that continued interaction with this tool will bring improvements on this front, since further exposure to the game will help to increase familiarity and understanding of the game for the ASD children.

We also found that this tool offers similar benefits in terms of emotion regulation to children belonging to both groups. In the future, we hope to use this strategy to design emotional interactions with an embodied robot, which may be even more effective in expressing and regulating emotions in such a setting.

We also plan to incorporate reinforcement learning into this framework to allow the robotic agent to learn unique policies tailored to the individual preferences of every user with whom it interacts.

Acknowledgements. This research is partially supported by the National Institutes of Health (NIH) under grant # 5 R01 HD082914-04 through the National Robotics Initiative (NRI) program.

References

1. Bevill, R., et al.: Interactive robotic framework for multi-sensory therapy for children with autism spectrum disorder. In: The Eleventh ACM/IEEE International Conference on Human Robot Interaction, pp. 421–422. IEEE Press (2016)
2. Breazeal, C.: Emotion and sociable humanoid robots. Int. J. Hum.-Comput. Stud. **59**(1–2), 119–155 (2003)
3. Feil-Seifer, D., Skinner, K., Matarić, M.J.: Benchmarks for evaluating socially assistive robotics. Interact. Stud. **8**(3), 423–439 (2007)
4. Kim, H.-R., Lee, K., Kwon, D.-S.: Emotional interaction model for a service robot. In: 2005 Robot and Human Interactive Communication, ROMAN 2005. IEEE International Workshop on Robot and Human Interactive Communication, pp. 672–678. IEEE (2005)
5. Olfati-Saber, R., Fax, J.A., Murray, R.M.: Consensus and cooperation in networked multi-agent systems. Proc. IEEE **95**(1), 215–233 (2007)
6. Posner, J., Russell, J.A., Peterson, B.S.: The circumplex model of affect: an integrative approach to affective neuroscience, cognitive development, and psychopathology. Dev. Psychopathol. **17**(3), 715–734 (2005)
7. Robins, B., Dautenhahn, K., Te Boekhorst, R., Billard, A.: Robotic assistants in therapy and education of children with autism: can a small humanoid robot help encourage social interaction skills? Univers. Access Inf. Soc. **4**(2), 105–120 (2005)
8. Tapus, A., Mataric, M.J., Scassellati, B.: Socially assistive robotics [grand challenges of robotics]. IEEE Robot. Autom. Mag. **14**(1), 35–42 (2007)

Study on Contrast Sensitivity of Different Age Groups

Linghua Ran[1(✉)], Chaoyi Zhao[1], Xin Zhang[1], Xin Wu[2], Ling Luo[1], Hong Luo[1], Huimin Hu[1], and Wu Haimei[1]

[1] SAMR Key Laboratory of Human Factors and Ergonomics (CNIS), China National Institute of Standardization, No. 4 Zhi Chun Road, Haidian District, Beijing, China
{ranlh, zhaochy, zhangx, luoling, luohong, huhm}@cnis.gov.cn
[2] Beijing Huiyunyiting Technical Company, Beijing, China
89427978@qq.com

Abstract. In this experiment, the digital Mars contrast sensitivity check tables are used to test the contrast sensitivity value between two genders and three age groups. There was no statistically significant difference in contrast sensitivity between genders (P > 0.05) and between different eyes (P > 0.05). The contrast sensitivity of individuals of different groups was significantly different. The contrast sensitivity values of the left eye, right eye and both eyes increase with the increase of visual acuity.

Keywords: Contrast Sensitivity · Ages

1 Objective of Experiment

Evaluating binocular vision by binocular vision functions and other indicators have been quite common. In various examinations, visual acuity is the most common indicator of a person's visual acuity. In fact, visual acuity on the sight chart does not fully and accurately reflect the ability of human eye to distinguish in real life. The visual acuity chart is a visual target with a contrast of 100%. In daily life, there is hardly any object with such high contrast ratio. That is to say, the visual acuity chart only shows the ability of the human eye to distinguish the target with 100% contrast, which does not reflect the ability of human eye to distinguish different contrast objects. Contrast sensitivity is the ability of the visual system to recognize sinusoidal gratings of different spatial frequencies under bright contrast changes. It can reflect and predict visual function better than vision charts [1]. The advantage of Contrast Sensitivity (CS) examination is that it can not only evaluate the ability of a patient to distinguish objects of different sizes, but also reflect the ability of the human eye to distinguish different contrast images. CS, one of the important indicators of form and sense function, is the reciprocal of the threshold contrast that represents the perception of different spatial frequencies by the human eye, which means that, the contrast sensitivity equals 1/contrast threshold. Therefore, the CS examination can fully and accurately evaluate the subject's ability to respond to surrounding objects in different

© Springer Nature Switzerland AG 2019
C. Stephanidis (Ed.): HCII 2019, CCIS 1032, pp. 302–308, 2019.
https://doi.org/10.1007/978-3-030-23522-2_39

environments, and it can provide an important reference standard for clinical visual function tests.

Visual acuity is the focus of person's attention. Many people have taken regular visual examination as a basic health care activity. Contrast sensitivity is a key part of ophthalmic optics. The existing basic measurement methods of contrast sensitivity can be divided into four kinds [2]: the first is the positive metaphysics detection method, the second is the contrast detection of the vision meter, the third is the computer measurement algorithm, and the fourth is the contrast sensitivity measurement algorithm. The positive metaphysics detection method is the method of using the contrast of the dark and dark stripes. By analyzing the mutual transformation of the provisions of the dark, the mutual transformation of the contrast sensitivity is analyzed to reflect the high and low frequency. The visual acuity measurement refers to the use of the black and white stripes above the visual meter for the corresponding visual acuity test. The main tool in this process is an electronic or manual test chart. The computer measurement method is to use computers to carry out corresponding sensitive tests through a certain application control program. In the contrast sensitivity measurement algorithm, the contrast sensitivity is determined by the brightness of the black bar and the white interval, and the visual standard is designed strictly according to the contrast sensitivity threshold standard. Among the four methods, the first one is efficiency and time-saving. This experiment adopts the first method, that is, the positive metaphysics detection method. In order to explore the effect of gender and eyes to contrast sensitivity, 90 cases were studied in this study. The sensitivity of persons was measured and the data were statistically analyzed.

2 Experimental Equipment

This experiment uses the Mars contrast sensitivity test card as a test material. Mars contrast sensitivity test card, whose specification is 23 cm * 35.5 cm, includes 3 separate tables, and each table of measurements can represent the final result. Each table has a total of 48 Sloan letters. Each letter is 1.75 cm high and has a viewing angle of 2° at 0.5 m. It is divided into 8 lines with 6 letters per line. A letter of the alphabet corresponds to a contrast value. The contrast value gradually decreases from 91% (−0.04 log) to 1.2% (−1.92 log) in units of 0.04 LogCS per visual mark.

3 Experimental Subject

The participants in this experiment were recruited from the society. The subjects were aged between 18 and 75. A total of 90 people were divided into three age groups. The basic information of the subjects in each age group is shown in Table 1.

Table 1. Information of subjects

Age group	Number	Age range	Average age	Standard deviation
Youth group 18-35	67	19–35	25.5	5.3
Middle-aged group	65	45–55	49.4	4.8
Elderly group 60–75	59	58–72	63.2	3.8
Total	191	–	–	–

4 Experimental Environment

This experiment needs to be carried out in a bright laboratory, and the lighting conditions provided by the environment should be achieved. The brightness of the test table is 90–120 lx.

5 Experimental Procedure

The distance from the test to the Mars contrast sensitivity test card was 41–59 cm. The experimenter randomly selected a table from the three digital Mars contrast sensitivity check tables and performed left eye, right eye, and two eye tests on subjects respectively. During the test, the subjects were allowed to read from high contrast to low contrast, starting from top to bottom, allowing the head to move slightly to the left and right, reading each letter cannot exceed 30 s, until the continuous reading of the two marks was not possible or cannot be read, then the contrast sensitivity value was recorded.

The scoring system for the lettered Mars contrast sensitivity chart is from −0.04 Log CS to −1.96 Log CS at intervals of 0.04 Log CS; each letter represents 0.04 Log CS. The Log CS score obtained before termination is subtracted by the number of misreading letters multiplied by 0.04, and the resulting Log CS is the final contrast sensitivity value.

6 Data and Statistical Analysis

6.1 Data Result

The percentiles of mean value, standard deviation, and differential contrast sensitivity values for the comparison sensitivity data for different age groups are shown in the following table:

Table 2. Descriptive statistics of contrast sensitivity for each age group

Age group	Category	Mean value	Standard deviation	Least value	Median	Maximum value
Youth	Left eye	1.76	0.03	1.68	1.76	1.84
	Right eye	1.75	0.03	1.68	1.76	1.84
	Binoculus	1.80	0.05	1.76	1.80	1.92
Middle age	Left eye	1.74	0.06	1.44	1.76	1.76
	Right eye	1.73	0.06	1.44	1.76	1.76
	Binoculus	1.77	0.04	1.68	1.76	1.92
Elderly	Left eye	1.66	0.12	1.16	1.68	1.76
	Right eye	1.65	0.15	0.96	1.68	1.80
	Binoculus	1.72	0.08	1.40	1.76	1.84

6.2 Data Analysis

1. Differences in contrast sensitivity between different sexes

The values of males and females were analyzed after two groups of independent samples t-test analysis. There was no statistically significant difference in contrast sensitivity between genders ($P > 0.05$). See Table 3.

Table 3. Contrast sensitivity of different genders

Gender	Mean value	Standard deviation
Male	1.7642	.06179
Female	1.7681	.07027

2. Differences in contrast sensitivity between different eye types

The values of the right eye and the left eye were analyzed after t-test analysis of two groups of independent samples. There was no significant difference between the contrast sensitivity of different eyes ($P > 0.05$). See Table 4.

The contrast sensitivity of the binoculus of the 69 individuals was the same, accounting for 36% of the total number; the contrast sensitivity of the left and right eyes of the 124 individuals was different, but the contrast sensitivity of the left eye was basically smaller than that of the right eye.

Table 4. Contrast sensitivity of different eyes

CSF	Mean value	Standard deviation
CSF Left eye	1.7210	.08405
CSF Right eye	1.7143	.09990

3. Differences in contrast sensitivity between different age groups

The average contrast sensitivity of left eye, right eye and binoculus of different age groups is shown in the Fig. 1.

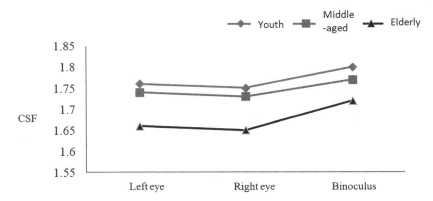

Fig. 1. Contrast sensitivity mean of left and right eyes and eyes of different age groups

It can be seen from Table 2 that, the contrast sensitivity of individuals of different groups was significantly different. For the comparison sensitivity of left eye, the contrast sensitivity of the elderly group was less than middle-aged group (t(58) = 4.25, p < 0.0001) and youth group (t(58) = 5.76, p < 0.0001), and the contrast sensitivity of middle age was less than that of the youth (t(64) = 2.54, p < 0.05); For the contrast sensitivity of the right eye, sensitivity of sensitivity in the elderly was less than middle-aged group (t(58) = 3.78, p < 0.0001) and youth group (t(58) = 5.27, p < 0.0001), and the contrast sensitivity of middle-aged group was less than that of youth group (t(64) = 2.90, p < 0.01); For the binocular contrast sensitivity, the same results were also found, with youth group contrast sensitivity greater than elderly group (t(58) = 6.55, p < 0.0001) and middle-aged group (t(64) = 4.47, p < 0.0001), and the sensitivity of middle-aged group was greater than that of elderly group (t(58) = 4.08, p < 0.0001).

As people grow old, the contrast sensitivity of human eyes to visual signals has decreased significantly. Under normal vision conditions, the main reason for the decrease in age-related contrast sensitivity is the decrease in the number of photore-ceptors caused by aging and changes in the neurological basis. At the same time, the analysis and extraction speed of visual signals in the elderly has decreased signifi-cantly, reflecting a significant increase in delay [2–4]. Their sensitivity to wavelengths has also been declining, which has led to a decrease in their ability to discriminate between color vision and spatial change. These can all lead to a decrease in visual quality.

4. The relationship between vision and contrast sensitivity

Subjects were divided into 3 groups according to their corrected visual acuity. The visual range of group A was [0.3, 0.8], 47 cases in total, accounting for 24%; The visual range of group B was [1.0, 1.2], 95 cases in total, accounting for 50%. The visual range of group C was [1.5, 2.0], a total of 51 cases, accounting for 26%. The contrast sensitivity statistics for the left eye, right eye and binoculus of these three groups are shown in Table 5:

Table 5. Contrast sensitivity statistics for the left eye, right eye and binoculus

		CSF left eye	CSF right eye	CSF binoculus
Group A	Mean value	1.6643	1.6435	1.7328
	Standard deviation	.13996	.17030	.10359
	P50	1.7200	1.7200	1.7600
Group B	Mean value	1.7343	1.7326	1.7731
	Standard deviation	.04808	.04821	.04265
	P50	1.7600	1.7600	1.7600
Group C	Mean value	1.7480	1.7448	1.7862
	Standard deviation	.02942	.03604	.05225
	P50	1.7600	1.7600	1.7600

As can be seen from the above table, the contrast sensitivity values of the left eye, right eye and both eyes increase with the increase of visual acuity, indicating that as the visual acuity increases, the contrast sensitivity of the human eye increases, and the human visual function improves in the meanwhile. It can be seen that people with good eyesight generally have better spatial resolution in high-contrast environments.

By One-way ANOVA, there was a significant difference in CSF values between group A and group B, between group A and group C ($p < 0.05$). There was no significant difference between group B and group C ($p < 0.05$). When the visual acuity standard is 1.0 or more, visual quality such as contrast sensitivity is not significant.

7 Discussion

Visual contrast sensitivity is a form-detection method that reflects the ability of the visual system to recognize sinusoidal gratings at different spatial frequencies under bright contrast. It can indirectly reflect the optical imaging quality of the external objects on the retina, represents the functional status of the retina, and to some extent reflects the visual quality of the human eye. In this experiment, a contrast sensitivity test card was used to test the contrast sensitivity of the three groups of people (youth, middle-aged, and elderly groups). It preliminarily explored the influencing factors of visual contrast sensitivity. The results showed that there was no significant difference between the contrast sensitivity of different genders and eyes. As people grow old, the contrast sensitivity of human eyes to visual signals decreases significantly; For people with better eyesight, contrast sensitivity is also better, that is, people with good eyesight have better spatial resolution. The relevant departments may use this detection method as the main detection method for the visual function of certain professional workers.

Acknowledgment. This research is supported by "Presidents Fund Project" (522017Y-5277), National Key R&D Program of China (2016YFF0201701), National Science and Technology Basic Research (2013FY110200).

References

1. Schade, O.H.: Optical and photographic analog of the eye. Opt. Soc. Am **65**, 721–739 (1956)
2. Li, J.: The application of contrast sensitivity in ophthalmic optics. Cardiovasc. Dis. J. Integr. Tradit. Chin. West. Med. 6(2) (2018)
3. Kline, D.W., Scialfa, C.T., Lyman, B.J., et al.: Age differences in the temporal continuity of gratings as a function of their spatial frequency. Exp. Aging Res. **16**(1–2), 61–65 (1990)
4. Diaz, F., Amenedo, E.: Ageing effects on flash visual evoked potentials (FVEP) recorded from parietal and occipital electrodes. Neurophysiol. Clin. **28**(5), 399–412 (1998)
5. Curran, T., Hills, A., Patterson, M.B., et al.: Effects of aging on visuospatial attention: an ERP study. Neuropsychologia **39**(3), 288–301 (2001)

Designing an Alternative Communication System for Dysarthria in Its Initial Stage in Amyotrophic Lateral Sclerosis (ALS)

Daniel Solano Cobos[(✉)] and Danilo Saravia Vargas[(✉)]

Universidad del Azuay, Cuenca, Ecuador
dsolanoc@es.uzuay.edu.ec, dsaravia@uazuay.edu.ec

Abstract. Dysarthria is one of the main speech impediments which cause verbal messages to be unintelligible as a consequence of a neurological injury of the speech motor system. An indicator of this is a poor articulation of phonemes. Dysarthria may be of different kinds: spastic, flaccid, hypokinetic, hyperkinetic, ataxic, mixed, etc. The aim of this research is focused on using user-centered design and emotional design as a methodology to contribute with a communication alternative for senior citizens suffering from dysarthria in its initial stage and having the need for a communication system. With the purpose of overcoming a deficiency occurring in our context and obtained in a field research by means of interviews to experts and visits to treatment centers, it was concluded that, as a consequence of having a technological gap, it is difficult that senior citizens learn and interact with the existing technological systems that surround us, so the validation of the need for designing a system that meets our users' specific needs was justified. By taking this into account, a portable, rechargeable, alternative communication board with an interface that is contemporary to users was designed. This considerably improves communication around them.

Keywords: User-Centered Design · Emotional design · Senior citizen · Usability · Motor function · Interface

1 Introduction

Dysarthrias are motor disorders characterized by poor articulation, without affecting mental function, comprehension, or verbal memory. It is caused by weakness, slowness, or lack of coordination of the muscles that control speaking production and, therefore, they are not language disorders in strict sense [1]. That is, people suffering from this illness have lost the capacity to articulate comprehensible verbal messages and have communication problems.

The aim of this research is focused on contributing with a communication alternative that uses user-centered design (UCD) methodologies and emotional design. They allow senior citizens suffering from this disorder to communicate again. For this purpose, a field research was conducted in order to collecting the necessary information to correctly deal with this problem and continuing with the appropriations of the previously mentioned design methodologies. It concluded with the construction of a functional prototype that links itself to senior citizens suffering from this communication problem.

© Springer Nature Switzerland AG 2019
C. Stephanidis (Ed.): HCII 2019, CCIS 1032, pp. 309–316, 2019.
https://doi.org/10.1007/978-3-030-23522-2_40

There are several tools that may be used to treat dysarthria as communication methods. These tools have been used as wireless warners in which the patient, by pressing a button, warns the caregiver that he/she needs help. They are also tablets that use a mobile application to transform them into an augmentative/alternative communication system. There also exist more complex tools like the head mouse or Irisbond that lets patients use a computer to browse their interfaces and transmit messages. Other tools are portable boards, such as Megabee and E-tran, which are assisted writing panels that use the user's movement and blinking of his/her eyes and that require a third person to code the message [2].

Nowadays, we can find some studies, devices, and alternative communication systems, like for example the case of Universidad Nacional de Córdova, that developed an integrating project called "Developing an Accessibility Service for Mobile Devices Controlled by a Portable Brain-Computer Interface". The aim was to design an accessibility service prototype by using a commercial brain-computer interface (BCI) as an assist device in the area of motor neurorehabilitation. The idea was that patients use this device in their daily lives. This device combines multimedia and electronic resources to develop an intangible item that interacts with users of the different commercial brain-computer interface [3]. This device controls a brain-computer interface which, in sum, is an electronic element that allows users to interact with their mobile phone and/or computer through a multimedia application, but, when tests were made, an inconvenience was found - users need to learn how to generate a stable and determined signal so they can deal with the different tasks that are going to let them interact with the application. In its turn, the training process for using this type of technology resulted to be frustrating for users.

Continuing with the research of these systems, we found the article titled "Non Verbal Communication Systems Enrich Augmentative and Alternative Languages with Accessibility and Usability Properties", developed jointly by the Unidad Académica Caleta Olivia (UACO) and Universidad Nacional de la Patagonia Austral (UNPA). This article focuses on "a contribution to reduce the existing gap between technology and disability". This contribution proposes an augmentative and alternative communication system which focuses on greatly reducing the barriers people with disabilities find when dealing with ITCs and the Internet. This system proposes a daily communication tool focused on cognitive disability and considering the degree of physical commitment. This project established the basis for the implementation of a web site where people with motor and/or cognitive disability are able to communicate through pictograms and interact and express themselves through an alternative and augmentative communication system. [4] It is worth mentioning that this way of using an alternative and augmentative communication system for designing web pages provides great benefits to end users who, in this case, are people with motor disability. This system is adjustable and/or personalizable, capable of converting itself into a daily effective communication tool that articulates spoken language and its equivalence to pictographic symbols.

Considering this background, this project focused on the development of a product that allows senior citizens communicate without having to go through complex learning curves or needing complex or little autonomous elements.

2 Proposal

By using the principles of User-Centered Design (UCD) and taking into account the idea of proposing a communication system that is in direct contact with an old-age user who is foreign to today's technological context, it was considered that this communication system had to be designed on a cognitive basis which is familiar to this kind of user. On this basis, Norman's hypotheses about UCD to simplify the structure of tasks were taken as the starting point at a direct interaction level with an interface where users are able to intuit the functioning of each part of the system configuration or, in certain cases, with a brief explanation, the user understands how to appropriately use this device [5].

With this user-interface-object relationship, it was concluded that, when correctly performing topography, which is the spatial compatibility between the location of commands and the system, the user would surely and immediately intuit that the product is useful and meets the specifications so that it may be adjusted to our user's characteristics. It was necessary to make a design considering an error margin as the last postulation of UCD. This characteristic is extremely important to design a communication system since, as it relates to a handicapped user who does not know about the technological context but still wants to get a feeling of independence, it is not an exaggeration to assume that users might incorrectly interact with the system either as a consequence of their limitation of mobility or for an external factor.

From the perspective of Emotional Design, it has been considered that the appearance (visceral characteristics) the communication system is going to have needs to take into account simple formal aspects which match a senior citizen's imaginaries; that is, it needs to look solid. This is the reason that basic geometric shapes have been used as the starting point [6].

Continuing with the levels proposed by Norman, let's consider that the second behavioral level; that is, usability, has to emphasize on our user's characteristics. For this reason, limitations of mobility, the possible interactions, ergonomic functions, and the distribution of the interface to be used, as well as the possible architecture of information, were considered. Regarding the limitations of mobility, it needs to be considered that, as it has been researched, patients suffering from ALS get to lose almost completely their fine motor skill while their gross motor skill is uncouth and very hindered. With these considerations, we may investigate the possible interactions and how ergonomics might minimize to the limit the errors regarding the system's usability. According to the National Institute for Safety and Hygiene at Work, 1989, "Commands represent the last link in this information circuit; badly designed commands may cause distortions in the system" [7]. Similarly, thinking of usability demands the investigation of the kind of action which is going to be taken, the type of command that corresponds to their position, which, according to NISHW, is necessary to leave a minimal separation among the buttons, 10 mm for occasional action and 12.5 mm for continuous action. This information is very useful considering our user has limitations of mobility in one or both his/her upper limbs [7].

Usability is also defined as a communication methodology, as observed in Fig. 1. Users directly interact with the device to transmit a message to the receiver, who may be a relative, his/her caregiver, or, in other words, his/her direct environment. The receiver uses this direct form of communication with the user to exchange information and turns the device into a communication channel which the user has to transmit his/her message again.

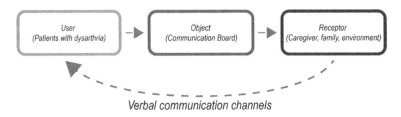

Verbal communication channels

Fig. 1. Communication process

3 Development

Beginning with the characteristics and considerations defined by the field research and information gathered, the user's profile was established. Similarly, it was considered that an advanced stage of dysarthria may be the beginning of the use of an alternative communication method or system. Another aspect considered was the use of this system to communicate. For this purpose, users need to have a good cognitive state (Fig. 2, Tables 1 and 2).

Table 1. User's characteristics

Category	Characteristic
Age	47–63 years old (M-W)
Level of dysarthria	Advanced
Functions patient keeps intact	Brain
Level of mobility	Able to use hands
Requirements	Needs a caregiver to perform daily tasks
Messages	Pain, lie down, sit down, use restroom, take a shower, change clothes, thirst, itching, needs food, among others
Additional needs	Interpreter

As an answer to the user's characteristics and in relation to the proposed conceptual model, both the characteristics and restrictions the communication system needs to meet and the information hierarchy used were defined. As follows, these characteristics are detailed:

1. Portable.
2. Contain modules or ways to communicate:
   a. Daily or routine actions.
   b. Method for transmitting more complex messages.
3. Alarm button to call caregiver.
4. Simple layout to allow easy and fast user's understanding.
5. Usability: Adjustable to left or right hand.
6. Communicate a person's most pressing needs.

Fig. 2. Usability outline

Table 2. Specifications of usability outline

Id.	Characteristic
1	First level of communication called warning call to caregiver through a text message sent from a mobile phone
2	First need actions (pain, restroom, sleep, or communicate with someone specific)
3	Second need actions or messages to start a simple conversation
4	Method for transmitting more complex messages through a screen and two interaction buttons (YES/NO)

Once the characteristics of the alternative communication system (ACS) have been defined, a study outline was made in order to validate how it functions with people outside the context of these kinds of disorders, with the purpose of seeing how they interact by simulating a situation of needing an alternative communication method, different from usual communication systems. In this way, a change in interface handling was evidenced, ending with the elimination and modification of some categories, with the purpose of letting users have more complex conversations or communication. This process caused the creation of a simple board at interface level, but with a good level of communication (Fig. 3).

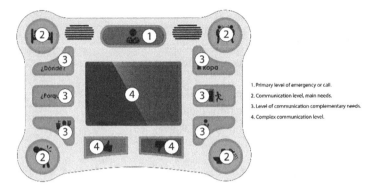

Fig. 3. Final interface of the communication board

The functional concretion of this device used an Atmega2560 microcontroller, which was utilized for handling the GLCD display that offers diverse options to have a more complex communication, as well as a series of buttons that include audio tracks that are reproduced when the buttons are pressed. There is also an audio amplifier to control the speakers and the RF 433 MHz Module, which was used to send warning signals to a receiver the caregiver brings along. Similarly, the corresponding PCBs that allow the different devices to interact were designed. This device is compact, repairable, and functions with a rechargeable battery (Fig. 4).

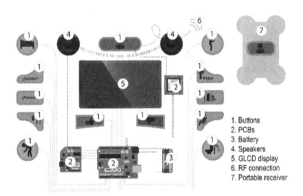

Fig. 4. Connection and operation diagram

The morphological concretion used 3D modeling programs to design the 3D-printed buttons, framework, fastening elements, PCB connectors, forms of assembly and distribution of the internal elements of the device.

4 Results, Validation, and Conclusions

Considering it is an alternative communication system (ACS) for senior citizens' dysarthria with ALS, big barriers to overcome were found, like for example the existing technological gap among generations, the lack of mobility caused by this disease, the usability of this device in relation to the hierarchy of information or the different options this language has and that the patient needs to transmit, the versatility and portability of this device, its weight, ergonomic characteristics, communication with relatives, and complexity of use. These were dealt with along the development of this research and are reflected in this prototype of alternative communication board which allows users to communicate in an easier way than with other devices offered in the market that are more complex to use. It also warns the caregiver by simply pressing a button that sends a signal that causes the receiver to vibrate and become an emergency warning mechanism or a need notice that tells the caregiver the patient needs help. Similarly, some predetermined messages or phrases have been programmed in each button and have been validated by different users. These messages or phrases allow a patient to communicate with his/her surroundings through sounds that emphasize his/her main needs and provide him/her with tools for a more complex communication on a screen that displays the patient's information, like for example emergency phones, doctors, among others. The outline of this prototype was made with pictograms, so that the board language may be interpreted by any main or indirect user (Fig. 5).

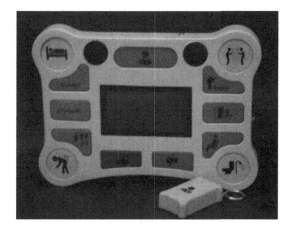

Fig. 5. Prototype of the alternative communication board

Having been able to use the user-centered design and emotional design method-ologies as a contribution to the development of this device, it was possible to take into account all the user's specific characteristics to construct a device that links the abovementioned methodologies. This opens a way for proposing new alternatives, like for example the possibility of changing the receiver for a mobile phone which will receive a message through a Telegram application that allows the patient to not only interact with the caregiver but also with more family members, and improve his/her performance in his/her surroundings. The aim is to provide the patient with future tools to strengthen the activities he/she has limitations with because of his disability, improve his/her quality of life, and give him/her back a certain level of independence and interaction with his/her surroundings.

References

1. Rhône-Poulenc Roder, S.A.: Esclerosis Lateral Amiotrófica una enfermedad tratable. In: Mascías Cadavid, J., Mora Pardina, J., Chaverri Rada, D. (eds.) Tratamiento de los problemas de comunicación, pp. 401–411. Prous Science, Barcelona (1999)
2. Asociación Española de Esclerosis Lateral Amiotrófica (adEla). Guía para la atención de la esclerosis lateral amiotrófica (ELA) en España. Ministerio De Sanidad Y Política Social, Madrid, España (2009)
3. Costa, H.A.: Repositorio digital UNC. Obtenido de Desarrollo de un servicio de accesibilidad para dispositivos móviles comandado mediante una interfaz cerebro-computadora portable (2017). https://rdu.unc.edu.ar/handle/11086/5172
4. Gonzáles, M., Sosa, H., Elba, A.: Revista de informes científicos técnicos UNPA. Obtenido de Non-Verbal Communication Systems. Enriching Augmentative and Alternative Languages with Accessibility and Usability Properties, 30 de Junio de 2014. http://ict.unpa.edu.ar/journal/index.php/ICTUNPA/article/view/ICT-UNPA-82-2014
5. Norman, D.: La psicología de los objetos cotidianos. Narea, Madrid (1990)
6. Norman, D.: Emotional Design; Why We Love (or Hate) Everyday Things. Member of the Perseus Books Group, New York (2004)
7. Instituto Nacional de Seguridad e Higiene en el Trabajo. NTP 226: Mandos: ergonomía de diseño y accesibilidad. España. Obtenido de, 15 de Junio de 1989. http://www.ladep.es/ficheros/documentos/ntp_226.pdf

Construction of a Japanese Sign Language Database with Various Data Types

Keiko Watanabe[1]([⊠]), Yuji Nagashima[1]([⊠]), Daisuke Hara[2],
Yasuo Horiuchi[3], Shinji Sako[4], and Akira Ichikawa[1]

[1] Kogakuin University,
1-24-2 Nishi-shinjuku, Shinjuku-ku, Tokyo 163-8677, Japan
ed13001@ns.kogakuin.ac.jp,
nagasima@cc.kogakuin.ac.jp
[2] Toyota Technological Institute,
2-12-1 Hisakata, Tempaku-ku, Nagoya 468-8511, Japan
[3] Chiba University,
1-33, Yayoicho, Inage-ku, Chiba-shi, Chiba 263-8522, Japan
[4] Nagoya Institute of Technology,
Gokiso-cho, Showa-ku, Nagoya, Aichi 466-8555, Japan

Abstract. We have constructed a sign language database which shows 3D animations. We are aiming at constructing an interdisciplinary database which can be used by researchers in various academic fields. This database helps the researchers analyze Japanese sign language. We have recorded nearly 2,000 Japanese signs to now, and we are planning to record on the database approximately 5,000 signs. Firstly, we decided to pick up frequently used Japanese words on the database. Each sign language expression corresponds to the Japanese words is examined. Secondly, we recorded 3D motion data of the determined sign language expressions. We used optical motion capture to record 3D motion data. The data format obtained through motion capture is C3D data, BVH data and FBX data, and frame rate is 120 fps. In addition, we also recorded a full HD video data at 60 fps, super-slow HD data at 30 fps, and depth data at 30 fps, for use in analysis of sign language.

These are recorded synchronously. In addition, we have developed a new annotation system which can reproduce different types of data synchronously to make the database the most effective. Because it is necessary for data analysis to reproduce synchronously all data, which have been recorded at different frame rates.

Keywords: Sign language · Motion capture · 3D animations

1 Introduction

Sign language is a form of language and a nonverbal means of communication used by people with a hearing impairment. Compared with spoken language, research on sign language is lacking in engineering and linguistics. One reason is the absence of a multipurpose database that can be commonly used by researchers from different areas, such as linguists and engineers. We created a Japanese sign language database to be used in many different areas of research.

© Springer Nature Switzerland AG 2019
C. Stephanidis (Ed.): HCII 2019, CCIS 1032, pp. 317–322, 2019.
https://doi.org/10.1007/978-3-030-23522-2_41

We decided to include sign language expressions in the database that are general and used more frequently. Although many sign language dictionaries are published in print form, sign language is inherently expressed by movement. Therefore, the database should be recorded as a set of video data and shows by movement. The database has more than one data format, such as motion capture data and depth data, for each video of a sign language expression. A system has also been developed to play the data for use in analyses of sign language. It is planned to make the sign language data in the database searchable by sign language expression, such as hand gestures, as well as by the meaning of an expression in Japanese spoken language. Ultimately, the database will include nearly 5,000 expressions.

This report explains how the sign language expressions were selected, how the sign language data was recorded, and the system we developed for playing sign language data.

2   Signs to Be Included in the Database

The database consists of sign language expressions that are general and used more frequently in daily life. Frequently-used Japanese words would be selected and a sign language expression would be recorded for each one.

2.1   Selecting Words to Be Included in the Sign Language Database

The selection of JSL expressions to be included in the database was based on data about the frequency of use of Japanese words. The terms of word familiarity are expressions with greater audio density, and those seen more frequently in Lexical Properties of Japanese [1] made by NTT, the Corpus of Spontaneous Japanese [2] and the sign language news [3] on NHK Educational TV were selected as candidates for inclusion in the database. From the list of candidates, Japanese sign language expressions to be included in the database were selected based on the expressions in the Japanese-JSL Dictionary [4]. The Japanese-JSL Dictionary, a publication by the Japanese Federation of the Deaf, includes more expressions than any other sign language dictionary published in print form. It contains nearly 6,000 expressions.

As a result, we chose 3,000 Japanese words, such as *Onaji* (same), gakko (school), at first. Furthermore, we plan to add other necessary words such as finger alphabet.

2.2   Discussion About Sign Language Expressions

We discussed how to sign language express each of the Japanese words selected in Sect. 2.1. The sign language expressions have been verified in cooperation with persons who use sign language as their primary language. Japanese words and their sign language counterparts do not correspond perfectly. If one sign language expression cannot be decided for one Japanese word, more than one sign language expressions are recorded.

For example, the word *namae* (name) can be expressed with different expressions. *Onaji* (same) may involve the same movement, but the position of the hands may differ among individuals. In some situations, it may be expressed using only one hand. *Hiraku* (open) can also involve differences—in sign language, it depends on what will be opened. In this situation, two or more sign language expressions were recorded for a single Japanese word.

We also placed importance on consistency in the sign language expressions included in the database. For this reason, the sign language expressions for *hiraku* (open) and *tojiru* (close) correspond in an antonymous manner in the database.

2.3 Recording Data of Signs

To ensure accuracy in the analyses of sign language behavior, all of the selected sign language expressions were shot in video form. The shooting was recorded in three data formats. Recording the 3D behavioral data involved the use of optical motion capture. The 3D behavioral data included in the database are C3D data at 120 fps, BVH data and FBX data at 119.88 fps. Recording depth data involved the use of Kinect 2. Depth and infrared images were recorded at a maximum of 29.97 fps. Furthermore, high-resolution camcorders were used to record video data at a frame rate of 60 fps. It has been also decided that video data will be recorded by three HD camcorders at 59.94 fps and by a super-slow HD camcorder at 119.88 fps (29.97 fps for playing). The data at different frame rates was synchronized before being recorded.

Fig. 1. Appearance of the recording studio

Figure 1 shows how an image was shot and recorded. 42 motion capture cameras were installed and used for recording in detail, including the delicate movements of a hand during an exchange using sign language. A Kinect 2 unit was set in front of the person doing the sign language. Three high-resolution camcorders were placed in front, to the left, and to the right of each person. In addition, full-HD videos at 119.88 fps (29.97 fps for playing) were also recorded as a reference. Until now, 1,400 signs have been recorded using these data formats.

Two people, one man and one woman, worked as sign language models during the shooting. Both are native signers of Japanese sign language. They are the deaf, and were born in a Deaf family. They were also chosen based on a criterion to use a type of Japanese sign language which is ease to read.

3 Development of a System for Playing Videos

The data synchronously filmed as written in Sect. 2 differs in terms of frame rate. For analysis, however, the video data must be synchronized and played. To this end, we developed a system for synchronizing and playing the video data.

3.1 Function of the System for Playing Videos

The annotation system that is being developed will consist of a viewer part and an analysis support part. The viewer part has two subparts: a viewer for 3D motion data developed by Unity and another viewer for video data developed by .NET Framework. Major functions of the viewer include the following.

- Divide the screen into a maximum of four portions to synchronize and play arbitrary data recorded in the database;
- Data in the BVH file format to draw 3D computer graphics;
- Use of C3D data to draw marker points;
- Drawing motion capture data from arbitrary perspectives and view angles;
- Background drawing of motion capture data is possible with arbitrary data;
- Drawing in the BVH file format involves the selection from two male models and three female models; and
- Recording replay screens.

The screen of the viewer can be divided into a maximum of four portions, each of which can display data. Allowing data to be synchronized and played at different frame rates makes it possible to check and analyze multiple data in accordance with a time axis.

The animation of sign language involves female and male models that can be altered arbitrarily. Figure 2 shows a screen divided into four portions to display data: BVH data (a female model, a male model and a skeletal animation) and C3D data. Figure 3 shows a screen playing video data using .NET Framework. This two-screen show same scene.

Details of the system will be reported later.

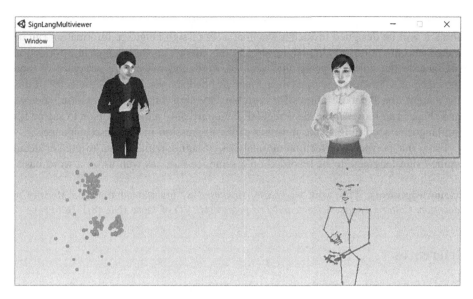

Fig. 2. A screen divided into four portions to display data using UNITY

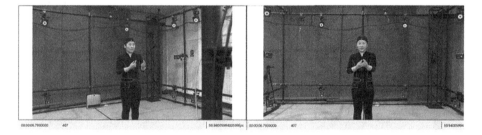

Fig. 3. Video data playing unit using .NET Framework

4   Conclusion

This paper is about the Japanese sign language database that is currently being created.

We considered the Japanese words to be included in the database. With the cooperation of native sign language speakers, we selected the sign language expressions corresponding to the Japanese words. Each sign selected was recorded in video form. Three types of data, including 3D behavioral data, depth data, and high-resolution data were synchronously recorded. To date, nearly 2,000 signs corresponding to 1,400 Japanese words have been recorded. We have planned to record nearly 5,000 signs. In the future, the remaining data will be recorded with an aim to complete the database.

A system has also been developed for synchronizing and playing the data. The system will be able to simultaneously play data at different frame rates.

The system for playing videos currently involves selecting data names. In the future, it will be designed in such a way that a set of sign language information can be entered into the corresponding signs already recorded. The sign language information will include the part of speech and type of word, the morpheme structure of sign language and sign language movement, such as hand shapes. Through the entry of this information, the database allows for searching by sign language expression, such as hand shapes and moves, whereas a regular dictionary only allows a person to search for sign language according to the meaning of the expression in Japanese language.

From our perspective, facilitating analyses of sign language data in greater detail requires sign language to be recorded on a sentence basis as well as on a word basis.

Acknowledgements. This work was *partly supported* by grant-in-aid from the *Ministry of Education, Culture, Sports, Science and Technology (MEXT)* of Japan (No. (S)17H06114).

References

1. Amano, S., Kasahara, K., Kondo, T. (eds.): NTT Database Series [Lexical Properties of Japanese], vol. 9, Word Familiarity Database (Addition), Sanseido, Tokyo (2008)
2. Corpus of Spontaneous Japanese. http://pj.ninjal.ac.jp/corpus_center/csj/. Accessed 29 Nov 2018
3. Katou, N.: Japanese Sign Language Corpus on NHK News. In: 2010 NLP (the Association for Natural Language Processing) Annual Meeting, pp. 494–497 (2010)
4. Japan Institute for Sign Language Studies (ed.): Japanese/Japanese Sign Language Dictionary. Japanese Federation of the Deaf, Tokyo (1997)

Design and User Experience Case Studies

Icon Design for a Tourism Mobile App

Claudia Regina Batista(✉) ⓘ, Adhemar Maria do Valle Filhoⓘ,
Amanda Mafioletti, and Maria Helena Novakoskiⓘ

Federal University of Santa Catarina, Florianópolis, Brazil
claudia.batista@ufsc.br

Abstract. This article shows the icon design process for the *FloripaTour App* - a tourism mobile app created to help tourists visiting Florianópolis Island. Five icons were developed to represent these categories of tourist attractions: natural landscapes, architectural and urbanistic elements, singular cultural elements, gastronomy and festive symbols. The icon design process was performed according to these steps: research, analysis, image refinement process, standardization through the same graphic style and evaluate the comprehensibility of icons.

Keywords: Icon · Design process · Mobile APP

1 Background

The *FloripaTour App* is a tourism mobile app created to help tourists visiting Florianópolis[1]. This app shows the city's main tourist attractions, such as: beaches, restaurants and regional cuisine, local culture, route mapping, and more.

The main tourist attractions were grouped into five categories: natural landscapes, architectural and urbanistic elements, singular cultural elements, gastronomy and festive symbols. These categories gave rise to the app's navigation structure (see Fig. 1):

These five categories will be shown on the screen in the navigation menu. In this case, describing the categories through textual information is not a good option because it takes up a lot of space on the screen. Visual communication and the use of icons in navigation menu is an effective alternative to overcome the lack of screen space on mobile devices. These small pictorial symbols on mobile app interface improve the effectiveness of sending and receiving information.

The design process of five icons representing Florianópolis tourist attraction categories are presented below.

2 Methods

The icon design process was performed in these five steps:

---

[1] Florianopolis is the capital city of the state of Santa Catarina, situated on an island located at the Brazil's Southern Coast. This charming landscape full of natural beauty attracts many tourists.

C. Stephanidis (Ed.): HCII 2019, CCIS 1032, pp. 325–330, 2019.
https://doi.org/10.1007/978-3-030-23522-2_42

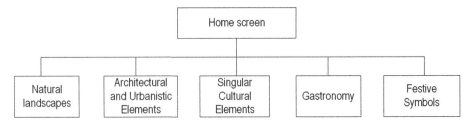

Fig. 1. *FloripaTour App* navigation structure

– Step 1: Identify elements that represent the five tourist attraction categories.
– Step 2: Choose the elements that best represent each category and draw illustrations about these themes.
– Step 3: Image refinement process: eliminate superfluous lines and adornments, starting from the illustration until obtaining the synthesis of the image. The purpose of this step is to obtain the best graphic representation capable of transmitting the meaning of the information.
– Step 4: Standardization of five icons through the same graphic style, framing, chromatic treatment and border application (which delimits the button area).
– Step 5: Evaluate the comprehensibility of icons.

3   Results

Initially, a field survey was conducted to identify the elements that best represent these categories: natural landscapes, architectural and urbanistic elements, singular cultural elements, gastronomy and festive symbols (see Fig. 1).

In step 2, some illustrations were created to represent each category. Easily identifiable images were desired. Then in step 3, the superfluous details of the drawings were eliminated to make them simple and clear.

In step 4, the application of the visual graphic style, chromatic treatment and circular border finalized the process.

The visual graphic style adopted is simple and it uses two-dimensional elements with application of vibrant and contrasting colors.

"I am Floripa" sign is a city landmark where tourists like to photograph. The vibrant colors of the letters express: hot climate, tropical country, island, sea, sun, nature, casual people and cheerful place. This atmosphere inspired the color palette of the icons for the *FloripaTour App* (see Fig. 2).

The Table 1 shows the elements that best represent the tourist attractions categories and icons created for each category.

In step 5 an evaluation of the comprehensibility of icons was performed in order to verify if the icon meaning is communicated with effectiveness. Forty people with similar profiles to app users participated in this evaluation.

In the test based on the recognition method, each icon was shown in isolation, in the absence of a text label or of other interface elements. The person participating in the

Fig. 2. Color palette of the icons for the *FloripaTour App*

test must guess what that icon symbolizes. When the answers unrelated to the information you want to communicate, then this icon must be redone.

The evaluation results are shown in Table 2.

Observing the evaluation results, it can be said that in general the five icons communicate or express the desired meaning. But in some interpretations there was ambiguity. When the icons represent very abstract concepts, it will be difficult for the user to make a correct analogy, so this image must be accompanied by a text label.

Table 1. The icons created to represent the tourist attractions categories

Categories	Elements that best represent the tourist attractions	Icons for FloripaTour App
Natural landscapes	Sunset at the beach.	
Architectural and urbanistic elements	Hercílio Luz bridge: *a famous city landmark.*	
Singular cultural elements	Bernunça: a regional folk character.	
Gastronomy	Shrimp, among other seafood.	
Festive symbols	Regional festivities.	

Table 2. Evaluation results

Icons	Results
Natural landscapes	100% of the answers were related to the "natural landscape" theme. People's answers: beach, sun, Floripa, island, natural place, nature, sea.
Architectural and urbanistic elements	No answer was exactly related to the "architectural and urbanistic elements" theme. But, 100% of people responded Hercílio Luz Bridge. As the bridge is a famous *city landmark*, then the association was made immediately.
Singular cultural elements	No answer was exactly related to the "singular cultural elements" theme. 75% of the answers are similar to the theme meaning, because they indicated Bernúnça (a regional folk character), Boi de mamão (other regional folk character) and folklore. 25% of the answers were wrong. People cannot understand the icon meaning. Tourists do not know the local culture elements, so they cannot make the association with the icon meaning.
Gastronomy	100% of the answers were related to the "gastronomy" theme. People's answers: shrimp, seafood, restaurants.
Festive symbols	100% of the answers were related to the "festive symbols" theme. People's answers: party, June's party, regional festivities.

Icons are, by definition, a visual representation of an object, action, or idea. If that object, action, or idea is not immediately clear to users, the icon is confusing and frustrating.

The authors of this study emphasize that the evaluation provides valuable feedback to the icon designers. In this step, it is possible to perform a redesign to improve the designs that did not perform well during an evaluation.

References

1. Harley, A.: Icon Usability. In: Visual Design Navigation. Nielsen Norman Group, 27 July 2014. https://www.nngroup.com/articles/icon-usability/. Accessed 20 Aug 2018
2. Horton, W.: The Icon Book: Visual Symbols for Computer Systems and Documentation. Wiley, New York (1994)
3. ISO/IEC. The International Organization for Standardization and the International Electrotechnical Commission – ISO/IEC 11581 – part 1–6. Information technology – User system interfaces and symbols—Icon symbols and functions (2000)
4. ISO. The International Organization for Standardization – ISO 9186-1:2014 Graphical symbols – Test methods – Part 1: Methods for testing comprehensibility (2014)

Measuring Critical Reception in Kids Through Consumption of Risky Challenges Videos in YouTube

Jeniffer Cruz Vera, Alejandro Reyes García, Gadi Reyna Miranda,
Alejandro Rosales Martínez$^{(\boxtimes)}$, Margarita Espinosa Meneses,
Gabriela Ramírez-de-la-Rosa, and Dina Rochman Beer

Universidad Autónoma Metropolitana (UAM) Unidad Cuajimalpa,
05348 Mexico City, Mexico
{2173800123,2173806036,2173800114,2173800025}@alumnos.cua.uam.mx
{mespinoza,gramirez,drochman}@correo.cua.uam.mx

Abstract. This project researches if critical reception facing YouTube content can be promoted in children between nine and eleven years old, focusing in analysis, evaluation and taking a stand facing the videos of risky challenges. This is an interdisciplinary project that used a mixed methodology, mostly quantitative which consists in four phases, two of them will be exposed in this paper. One phase let us know what the kids like and consume. The other phase allow us to measure the level of three abilities of critical thinking. We found that even if the kids do not consume a lot of channels with risky challenges, it is important to enhance the ability to take a stand in order to avoid that children hurt themselves.

Keywords: Critical thinking · YouTube · Risky challenge ·
Consumption habits · Critical reception · Risky contents

1 Introduction

Tide Pod and Bird Box are examples of videos showing dangerous challenges that became viral on internet. The emulation of those activities caused injuries in some people who did them. What needs to be done to prevent kids watching this videos from harming themselves? One possibility is prohibition, as YouTube's recent policy update [1] is doing; another more effective way is by promoting critical thinking in the user. In this era of immerse technology, we believe that we need to focus on the user's instead of the technology itself.

According to Scriven and Paul "Critical Thinking is the intellectually disciplined process of actively and skillfully conceptualizing, applying, analyzing, synthesizing, and or evaluating information gathered from, or generated by, observation, experience, reflection, reasoning, or communication, as a guide to belief and action" [2].

© Springer Nature Switzerland AG 2019
C. Stephanidis (Ed.): HCII 2019, CCIS 1032, pp. 331–338, 2019.
https://doi.org/10.1007/978-3-030-23522-2_43

Our main project researches if critical reception facing any kind of content in YouTube can be promoted in children between nine and eleven years old through an Educational Communication Strategy (ECS). To this end, we used a mixed methodology: quantitative but mostly qualitative, which consists in four phases, two of them will be exposed in this paper. We center this study around *risky challenges* that we formally defined as: "Challenging or provoking an individual to participate in or engage in an activity in which there is a possibility of harm to the physical integrity of a person."

The rest of this paper is organized as follows. Section 2 shows the description of the first two phases in the methodology used. In Sect. 3 a complete report of our finding will be given. After that, in Sect. 4 we expose the conclusions reached and the future work for this project.

2   Methodology

The general methodology used for the entire project is formed by four phases where were included qualitative and quantitative techniques. First, the exploration phase involves researching the consumption habits in YouTube of children between nine and eleven years old. The second phase aims to evaluate the level of critical thinking of our target population by using a rubric that measures three features: analysis, evaluation and taking a stand. The third phase involves the development design of a interdisciplinary proposal which promotes the critical reception in kids from nine to eleven years old. The last one, it is about the evaluation of the final technological proposal to measure the critical reception in kids using our communication strategy. In this paper we will focus solely on the two first phases.

2.1   Participants

According to Piaget, *the concrete period of cognitive development* in the human beings start in the childhood, particularly between 9 and 11 years old. In this cognitive stage children begin to use logic and reasoning as part of higher cognitive functions, in order to solve complex problems. Also, they start to relate previous and empiric knowledge with new one in order to acquire a different meaning of their environment [3]. That is why in this project we focused on this key stage in order to promote a cognitive development and the critical reception for the media information.

Therefore, in this study we considered the participation of children from nine to eleven years old attending 4th, 5th and 6th grade at Primary School from two private schools and two public ones. These schools are located near to Cuajimalpa community within Mexico City (influence area of our University). The total number of children participating in the study is 370 (184 girls and 186 boys). We considered three ages such as we have 128 participants of age 9, 103 participants of age 10 and 139 children were 11 years old.

2.2   Phase I: Exploration to Investigate Kids Consumption Habits on YouTube

The main goal of the Exploration phase is to investigate YouTube consumption habits in our participants in order to detect possible risky content available to our subjects in that platform. Therefore we designed an evaluation tool called "Your likes on YouTube" the aim was to define the analytical categories: thematic areas, type of audience, interactions and consumption habits.

The key concepts that we considered were *Media Literacy* and *Digital Culture*. This classification allowed us to design the elements of the survey to obtain information, such as the early diagnosis of possible warnings about risky content in YouTube.

To investigate the thematic areas of interest in this platform, we asked for how much each child likes or not the twelve predefined type of content; this classification is given by YouTube[1]. To know the type of audience we included a section where general information about each participant was asked: gender, age and school grade.

To identify the consumption habits of the children according to the frequency of usage on YouTube there was the question: How often do you watch YouTube per week?, the possible answers were: Everyday, 5 or 6 days a week, 3 or 4 days a week, 1 or 2 days a week and Never.

For evaluating the category of risky challenges or the possible warnings in the content provided by the digital platform the question was: Write which are your three favorite channels on YouTube. Moreover, there were questions to assess about risky content consumption, like dangerous challenges, fights and blows, sexual content or other. The request was to mark anything that they had watched or heard on YouTube and specify in which channel or video they had seen that. Besides, four options were given: Swearwords, Blows and fights, Risky challenges, Sexual content and Other.

2.3   Phase II: Measure of the Critical Thinking in Kids

The main goal of this phase is to evaluate the children skills of *analysis*, *evaluation* and *taking a stand* when they watch a video of a risky challenge. A secondary goal is to identify how children conceptualize the term "challenge". To achieve this goals, two activities were developed by using a focus group technique.

First, the children were asked to form mixed teams in order to create their own challenge using a variety of materials provided by us. After that, the children acted the challenge for the rest of their fellow participants as if they were on a YouTube video. Meanwhile, the other teams evaluated the "video" with like or dislike props[2].

---

[1] The complete list of this categories are in https://creatoracademy.youtube.com/page/lesson/overview-categories?cid=platform&hl=es#strategies-zippy-link-1.

[2] Word used in Marketing to describe an object that attracts the attention of people used in any audiovisual production.

On the second activity, the children watched a YouTube video belonging to a channel that they see the most (according to the results of the first phase of exploration). In this video[3], the youtuber Kimberly Loaiza gives instructions to make a challenge in which she ignites and burns her hand fingers with antibacterial gel and doesn't feel any pain, explaining the warnings to consider. For instance, she suggests twice being very careful to perform the challenge.

After watching the video, a series of questions were asked to the children in order to measure their level of critical thinking. We use the rubric shown in Fig. 1 taken as a base one published by University of Northeastern Illinois, published in 2006[4]. Hence, a judge would had to measure where the answers of a kid are in the rubric to evaluate him. Later on this paper we describe the children's status according to this approach.

Name: XXXX	Grade of assessment			
		4	3	2	1
	Concept indicator	Outstanding	Satisfactory	In progress	Beginner
Analysis	Identifies	Identify in a clear and detailed manner the risks, dangers or possible physical damages	Identify the risks, dangers or possible physical damages	Partially identify the risks, dangers or possible physical damages	Do not identify the risks, dangers or possible physical damages
	Interprets	Make precise, comprehensive and convincing interpretations of the intentions of the youtuber	Make precise, comprehensive and convincing interpretations of the intentions of the youtuber	Make one interpretation of some of the intentions of the youtuber	Do not make interpretations of the intentions of the youtuber
Evaluation	Evaluates	Give a detailed judgment or conclusion based on the rirsky challenge	Give a judgment or conclusion based on the dangerous challenge	Give an imprecise judgment based on the dangerous challenge	Do not give a judgment or conclusion based on the dangerous challenge
Taking a stand	Takes a stance	Decide not to perform the challenge and present detailed arguments about the risks and possible consequences of doing it.	Decide not to perform the challenge and present one argument about the risks and possible consequences of doing it.	Undecided about performing the challenge and anticipates some possible consequences of doing it	Decide to perform the challenge and do not present arguments about the risks and possible consequences of doing it.

Fig. 1. Rubric to evaluate the skills of critical thinking in children who participate

3   Results

3.1   Phase I

Consumer Habits. The results of this phase about the user habits exploration on YouTube, allows to show the frequency of children in their usage of YouTube. After our exploration, we get that more than a half of the children referred to watch YouTube daily, followed by a frequency of 3 to 4 days a week with more than 19%; only 1.4% of the children reported not watching YouTube at all.

---

[3] https://www.youtube.com/watch?v=qnfxYE28gh8.
[4] http://homepages.neiu.edu/~ctl/bulletins/Bulletin11.pdf.

We found a clear preference for entertainment content. For instance, *Los Polinesios*[5] is the channel with unanimous preference in the four schools evaluated without distinction of age or gender. The Polinesios upload a wide range of topics: personal videos, travel videos, pranks and daily experiences with a comic and funny style, challenges, tutorials and video games. Furthermore, the Video Games and Gameplays channels were the most popular for boys, with channels such as *Fernanfloo*[6] and *Ninja*[7] standing out. In the case of the girls, they prefer channels like *Gibby*[8] or *Kimberly Loaiza*[9] where they find diverse contents such as sketches, challenges, adventures and trips, among others.

Risky Contents. As part of this first phase of exploration, it was important to detect the possible risky contents to which the children were exposed within the platform. Figure 2 shows the percentage of consumption in boys and girls participants who have been exposed to certain risky contents according to their own report.

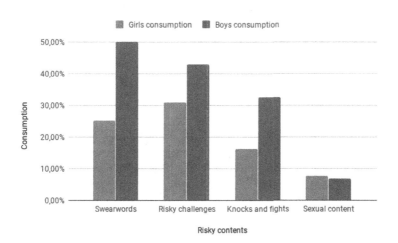

Fig. 2. Consumption (auto-reported) of risky content

Even though swearwords was the highest reported category, we decided to focus on videos containing risky challenges (second most reported). We put swearwords aside due to the highly subjective definition, interpretations and versatility of contexts on which swearwords are used. Additionally, risky challenges are considered a latent danger for children who try to perform them as a trendy topic.

Based on this, we decided to carry out a manual review of 100 videos of risky challenges, starting from channels that children indicated as their favorites, with the goal of detecting the level of risk in this challenges. Also, we elaborated a taxonomy according to the type of damage or injury that could be caused, such as asphyxiation, physical injuries, gastrointestinal or respiratory damage and burns. After watching all these videos we found that gastrointestinal and respiratory damage categories constitute more than 30 videos, followed by asphyxia videos with 16. Finally, burns and respiratory harm categories just have 2 videos per each one.

3.2 Phase II

A Challenge Structure. One goal of this phase was to identify how children conceptualize the term challenge. In order to know that, the kid's representations of a video were diagrammed with flowcharts. Without the details, the basic structures allowed to compare and to analyze their ideas. Diagrams in Fig. 3 show how children used cards to loop were an action must be done. What to do and how they do it is what make them different but in general terms they follow a basic structure, as we can see in Fig. 4.

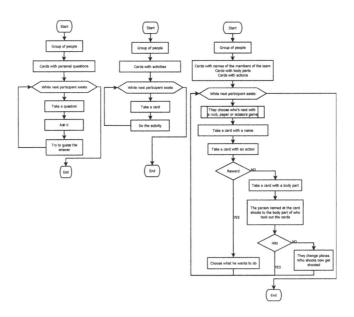

Fig. 3. Flowcharts of the challenge performed by teams of children. Cards initiates some activity and all members have to do it

There are two more structures that do not have a set of cards with established actions to begin, they have the loop where every participant have to develop some motor coordination activity. As a result of these diagrams, we could say that the participants have a common understanding of challenge and this is: within a group of people, propose an activity to be carried out by everybody.

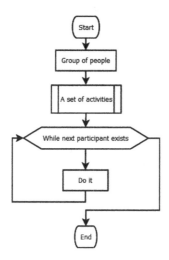

Fig. 4. Basic structure of challenge

The Level of Analysis, Evaluation and Take a Stand in Children Who Participated. The other goal of this phase was to evaluate children skills of *analysis, evaluation* and *taking a stand* about a video of a risky challenge for instance Kimberly Loaiza video which shows ignition and burns using antibacterial gel.

For the *analysis* skill, seventeen kids in a sample of twenty seven showed an "In progress" status, see Fig. 5. Which means that they can extract and overview

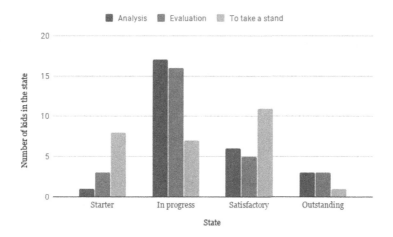

Fig. 5. Number of children in each state (grade of assessment) of the skill evaluated

a problem, getting the main argument of it, but no further more. About the *evaluation* skill, a similar overall assessment is shown: sixteen children have a "In progress" status, this means that they gave an imprecise judgment about the played video. Finally, the *take a stand* ability has a balanced sample, but also more "Starters" than in progress. Which could end with children doing what they saw on the video.

4   Conclusion and Future Work

In conclusion, even children favorite channels are not the ones which produce risky challenge, the kids are consuming them. So, if they watch risky challenges on YouTube they should be capable to decide not to do them. With the current evaluations, there are a lot of possibilities that kids simulate what they saw. This is because to *take a stand* ability it has more "Starter" kids than other status. Finally, there is an opportunity to improve their skills for getting the "In progress" population into a "Satisfactory" status.

On the basis of the results obtained, the viability of the different technological prototype proposals collected in phase 2 of our methodology will be evaluated, with the aim of choosing the most suitable one for the fulfilment of the objective in this research project: to promote critical reception skills in children. After the design of the prototype, it is planned to go to the evaluated schools and test it with them. Finally, we will have to evaluate the repercussion of our intervention.

Acknowledgments. This work was partially funded by CONACYT under scholarships numbers 869762, 870435, 869682 and 836519. We also thank to UAM Cuajimalpa for the provided academic support.

References

1. Camilla: Announcement: Strengthening enforcement of our Community Guidelines (2019). https://support.google.com/youtube/thread/1063296?hl=en
2. Scriven, M., Paul, R.: A statement presented at the 8th Annual International Conference on Critical Thinking and Education Reform (1987). http://www.criticalthinking.org/pages/defining-critical-thinking/766
3. Piaget, J., Inhelder, B.: Psicología del niño, 8th edn. Morata Publisher, Madrid (1920)

The Research on the Characteristics of Furniture Hardware Design Through 3D Printing

Cynthia Chun Yu Hsieh[(⊠)] and Shao Wei Ku

Chung Yuan Christian University, 200 Chung Pei Road, Chung Li District,
Taoyuan City 32023, Taiwan, R.O.C.
ch0315@arch.nctu.edu.tw

Abstract. With the improvement of living standards and self-conscious, design begins to transform from simplification to diversification including furniture hardware. From the literature review, we had found the type and specifications of today's hardware components are mostly more fixed and limited. With its manufacturing advantage of small amount of customization and diversification, 3D printing has become a perfect solution for this need of change. Therefore, this study hopes to solve the bottleneck caused by mass production in the hardware process through 3D printing technology, and to provide diverse and form-free hardware components.

Keywords: 3D printer · System furniture · Hardware

1 Introduction

Furniture design has always been a very important part of residential design. The traditional furniture is mainly made by hand during the production process. After World War I, the main demand of design strives towards the standardization, systematization and low cost. Lu (2014) believes that the standard modular and systematic furniture is one of the successful examples in the modern furniture industry. The modular system of standardized furniture not only focuses on the environmental protection standards in the production process, but also has a quick and easy assembly mode which has produced a huge demand in the market. However, with the improvement of living standards and self-conscious, personalization issues are gradually being emphasized (Lu 2009). Design begins to transform from simplification to diversification. For the interior space, changes in furniture scale and the way people use them influence each other. The systematic furniture, with its original existing portfolio and building-block style, is gradually unable to meet the expectations of consumers and interior designers for their needs in function and style; therefore it is facing the pressure from the need of a change. From the literature review, we had found out that most systematic furniture is assembled and designed from different sizes of the plate, which is closely related to hardware components, in line with the principle of the standardization of mass production, the type and specifications of today's hardware components are mostly more fixed, which can't really allow users to have great experiences.

© Springer Nature Switzerland AG 2019
C. Stephanidis (Ed.): HCII 2019, CCIS 1032, pp. 339–347, 2019.
https://doi.org/10.1007/978-3-030-23522-2_44

With its manufacturing advantage of small amount of customization and diversification, 3D printing has become a perfect solution for this need of change. This model of production, developed from rapid prototyping (Bateman and Cheng 2006), is unlike traditional processing techniques that removes material. It can produce complex shapes and can be used to directly engage in activities and thus eliminates cumbersome assembly procedure. Its applications evolved from early model-assisted design and the small-scale validation of product functionality to today's components which can even directly manufacture functional products. Therefore, this study hopes to solve the bottleneck caused by mass production in the hardware process through 3D printing technology, and to provide diverse and form-free hardware components. The study is divided into two major steps: 1. 3D print hardware elements operational factors and case analysis. 2. 3D printing hardware implementation and prototype testing, in order to view 3D print materials in the structural constraints to execute the construction of a new hardware production process.

2 Factor Analysis on Furniture Hardware Characteristics

We must first understand the characteristics of furniture hardware nowadays if we want to adopt 3D printing for them. Wang (2003) and Wang (2007) stated that modern metal essential components should have the following features—functionality, decorativeness, practicality, economy and safety. As for traditional and modern metal hardware comparison, Mu (2010) pointed out functionality, decorativeness, durability and safety. Moberg and Forsman (2016) believed the fundamental concept of design is that the metal decoration on furniture pieces should be pleasing to the eye. Besides the systematicness and functionalities seen on various kinds of furniture pieces, whether the chosen material is durable should be thoroughly evaluated. If furniture metal pieces are mostly used to accommodate mass production, Klímová (2009) stated that the primary goal is to be practical and economical. Ho (2009) categorized the form of furniture metal pieces into 8 features: systematicness, precision, functionality, decoration, practicality, economy, durability and safety.

Comparing with traditional metal hardware, Liao (2013) put forward a new feature-freeness for the 3D-printed metal design so far. He believed that free formation should be the core value of 3D printing and this characteristic is far more important than the others. Ridding the procedures of traditional manufacturing models and the limitation, free-form physical models with complexity can be created fast and precisely. Šebková (2013) thought that the most influential change 3D printing brings to us is effectiveness. With digital creation and design, it enhances the decorativeness, functionalities, practicality and durability of the product in a highly efficient manner. 3D printing can even integrate cross-disciplinary data and demonstrates its systematicness, precision and functionalities (Tavsan 2015). Chou (2016) further illustrated that when 3D printing is incorporated in furniture component design, one should emphasize on exploring humanity, customization and free form. This study will go through the above literary works and have the relevant factors consolidated in the following table (Table 1).

Table 1. Metal essential component feature/factor literature analysis and summary

Hardware characteristics	Literary works
Systematicness	Ho (2009), Moberg and Forsman (2016), Tavsan (2015)
Precision	Ho (2009), Tavsan (2015)
Functionality	Ho (2009), Klímová (2009), Šebková (2013), Tavsan (2015), Moberg and Forsman (2016), Mu (2010), Wang (2007), Wang (2003)
Decoration	WeiHsin Ho (2009), Moberg and Forsman (2016), Šebková (2013), Mu (2010), Wang (2007), Wang (2003)
Practicality	Ho (2009), Wang (2003), Wang (2007), Šebková (2013),
Economy	Ho (2009), Wang (2003), Wang (2007), Klímová (2009)
Durability	Ho (2009), Mu (2010), Moberg and Forsman (2016), Šebková (2013)
Safety	Ho (2009), Wang (2003), Wang (2007), Mu (2010)
Freeness	Liao (2013), Chou (2016)

Considering that it is not specific enough about how the chosen material can determine the durability and the cost of how 3D printing is incorporated in different industries is also not explicit yet, durability and economy will be excluded from this study. This paper will only put emphasis on 7 factors: systematicness, precision, functionality, decoration, practicality, safety and freeness.

3   Case Studies

Numerous real practices on 3D-printed hardware can be found online. They are primarily works about assembling or combining objects. This study will classify the combined objects as boards (surfaces) and tubes (lines). In this study, 6 pieces of work that have been tested and sold online were selected for analysis.

Case 1, tubes (line) vs. tubes (line): Ti-Join's 3D-printed hardware design uses metal material. From Fig. 1 below, we can see that it's a structure of connected ending points. The overall planning focuses on the freeness and decorativeness of the appearance and hardware design.

Fig. 1. Case 1 Ti-Join's (left), case 2 Cross Tenon Coat Rack (right)

Case 2, tubes (line) vs.tubes (line): Cross Tenon Coat Rack is tubular metal connection; the detailed parts harness the feature of mortice and tenon joints to enhance safety when the piece is being used. To examine this piece in a holistic manner, the simple joining approach and fixed tenons fit the systematicness of this study, but it lacks variety in terms of usage and appears to score low in functionality.

Case 3, board (surfaces) vs. board (surfaces): Link Furniture's 3D-printed metal design mainly uses triangular boards, leveraging standardized boards for highly changeful and flexible composition. The customized setting of the angles creates fairly high precision. Systematicness can also create a different touch to the work by accommodating the process techniques of traditional boards.

Case 4, board (surfaces) vs. board: Print to build is hardware used to connect quadrilateral boards. These objects are comparatively smaller units, fastening the connection of different boards. The safety performance needs to be tested repeatedly. The diversity of this combination enhances the precision of 3D-printed hardware (Fig. 2).

Fig. 2. Case 3 Link Furniture's (left), case 4 Print to build (right)

Case 5, board (surfaces) vs. tubes (line): SACK's design is more inclined to traditional hardware components. Because of its simple, minimal look, these objects can go to mass production easily. But the slice shape and changeless forms prevent the maker from leveraging the freeness of 3D printing. In the design, holes are reserved so that other essential components can be connected to the work. This feature enhances the systematicness that this study wants to examine (Fig. 3).

Fig. 3. Case 5 SACK's (left), case 6 The Design 3.0 series (right).

Case 6, board (surfaces) vs. tubes (line): The Design 3.0 series starts from simple fashion. It shows the attempt to use only one 3D-printed component as the key supporting point of the furniture in order to achieve the minimum in quantity of the objects and the maximum in efficiency and safety. Metal components of the same style can be arranged in different ways so as to create furniture pieces for various purposes even though the objects' sizes and angles have to be adjusted.

Based on the above 6 cases, this study conducted a 5-point scale analysis on the following 7 characteristics—systematicness, precision, functionality, decorativeness, practicality, safety and freeness— via questionnaires. In total, 50 valid questionnaires were collected and the respondents are all personnel involved in interior design. According to the statistics, the advantage and the weakness of the 6 cases in terms of each characteristic are shown in Fig. 4 below. Based on a comprehensive comparison on the result, the objects generally score either 3 or 4 points for the 7 factors in the questionnaire. Among them, SACK outperforms the others as the most systematic. Its minimalist structure style makes it easier to systematize and combine various systems furniture. Link Furniture & Print To Build are found to be the best in precision and functionality. Link Furniture uses metal screws for combination, so the accuracy of the installation is efficiently improved. In addition, correction on the angles makes the piece fitter for numerous user behaviors. As for the simple connection board seen in Print To Build, it can be used as diversified systematic cabinets since cabinets have the highest demand in the furniture market. Ti-join scores exceptionally in decorativeness and freeness. The metal hardware itself fully plays to the strength of digital software, constructing streamlined and organic shapes, and yet each joint is configured differently. For metal hardware, this is unprecedented achievement. In terms of practicality, The Design 3.0 Series and SACK are both optimal design. The assembly types and the enabled functions have covered almost all of the current commonly-used connection approaches of systems furniture. Lastly on safety, Ti-Join is structured and formed by parameter settings before being 3D-printed with metal material. Ti-Join and The Design 3.0 Series are both designed for one single purpose, giving up risky and highly changeable factors to ensure safety. On the contrary, Print To Build can be disassembled and assembled in numerous ways. During the transformation process, a lot of safety variables could surface, and hence it scored the lowest in safety. If traditional metal components can be used as fasteners in this piece of work, its safety can be significantly improved.

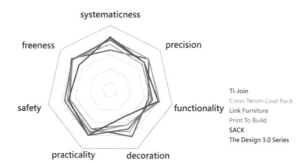

Fig. 4. The statistics of the 6 cases in terms of each characteristic.

To summarize from examining the above cases of 3D-printed hardware components, it is found that most of the designs are quite incomprehensive in planning. The issues are stated as follows: 1. Ignoring the freeness in style and decorative presentation in order to present the focus of functionality. 2. To display freeness in style and decorative features without considering the function development and extended usage. 3. Focusing on creating new structural combination system but ignoring how systems furniture and metal components were integrated in the past. 4. Adopting special formation approach or structure without experimenting on the possibilities of alternative operation methods. 5. Integral shaping has been considered for the design, but few attempts have been made to combine with different materials.

Table 2 illustrates 4 solutions to address the 5 issues derived from case analysis. Issue 5 indicates that different materials should be combined for metal printing, but due to the limitations on cost and machinery of this preliminary study, all the materials used

Table 2. Experimental phase.

Steps	Issues	Description	Concept
Approach 1	Issue 1	To enhance the decorativeness and freeness of traditional metal furniture component with 3D printing. To supplement the shortcomings in style by using 3D-printed objects as an extended component for combination	Softening
Approach 2	Issue 2	Continue to use functional items of traditional metal components, change the way they work with 3D-printed manufacturing, and then add more functionalities and decorations	Incremental change
Approach 3	Issue 3	Follow how traditional metal components are used. Use 3D printing technology to facilitate integration with traditional metal components	Spiral
Approach 4	Issue 4	Special 3D printing formation does not only improve the monotony from the appearance, but also establish a new way of operation, presenting new opportunities of how metal can work as a part of the furniture	Mutation

will be the ordinary 3D filament (ABS/PLA). This study will not consider using other materials for now. This is a limitation and yet it can be explored in the future for further research.

4   Conceptual Prototype

This chapter continues on the discussion on 4 recommended solutions mentioned in Table 2 and hence this study proposes 4 conceptual prototype development approaches. With digital drawing and 3D printing techniques, the threshold is lowered and many free-form styles and objects can be designed directly. The research results are described as follows:

The main idea of concept 1 is softening the work by defining it as a preliminary decoration on the outside of the model instead of the stereotypical vertical/horizontal structure. This is an attempt to soften the rigid frame of the object with flexible curve. In Fig. 5, objects underwent twisting and stretching in the design process. The existing

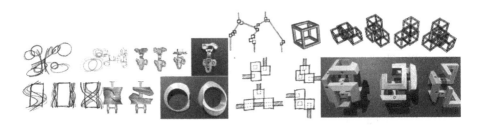

Fig. 5. (Left) concept 1,softening. (Right) concept 2, incremental change.

block was modified and beautified. When the objects were twisted and pulled to different directions, adjustment was made so the mass can adapt to different angles and height. Finally the mass is softened and decomposed into 2 objects that can be combined as a whole, making it easier to be fixated on existing metals.

The main idea of concept 2 is incremental change, which is to add more functionalities and purposes of the object. Therefore, the cubical structure is hollowed out and dragged out. By adding changes in angle and combination rather than joining on the fixed direction like how it was done before, the objects that used to always look the same are now given with new possible functions and outward appearance. Considering that the existing 3D-printing furniture types are mostly joints with tubes and panels, this study takes rectangular surrounding shape as the basic design pattern. All the tubes used to form the rectangle are altered slightly with size coordination and proportion adjustment. The surfaces on the outside are finished with a bevel angle so as to enrich the decorativeness and to get rid of the rigid, vertical angle.

The principal idea of concept 3 is spiral. The process started with twisting a single piece of object, and then it was adjusted through different lengths and thicknesses, which not only increases the decorativeness, but also improves and ensures the safety required when it's being used. The spiral torsion was then carried out with plural pieces. During this stage, for the thickened part, the layer of different sizes has been taken into consideration so as to amplify the artistic look and ensure the safety at the same time. Finally, the central axis of the spiral was added to the main frame, and then tested and adjusted at different lengths (Fig. 6).

Fig. 6. (Left) concept3, spiral. (Right) concept 4, mutation.

The main idea of concept 4 is mutation, which is the driving force of biological evolution. When it comes to how people perceive furniture metal is manufactured, the sequential improvement approach is taken as the basis of design and production, either for selected fittings or assembly patterns. Yet, with mutation, it means to leverage different thoughts and thus this study came up with an object that is designed unconventionally. The conceptual object's core functionality is based on the principle of magnetic force, mainly the rejection force. By pressing the whole object, different components will pop out.

5   Conclusion

This study conducted literature analysis and summarized 9 properties/factors of existing metal hardware. 7 of them have been selected (systematicness, precision, functionality, decoration, practicality, safety and freeness) to analyze 6 3D-printed metal cases. From the analytical result, it is difficult for all the current 3D-printed metal to be equipped with aesthetics and functionality at the same time. The ones with safety and functionality are usually lack of freeness and decorativeness. Furthermore, there's no integration of 3D-printed metal hardware with traditional metal that is widely used in the market and manufactured in big volume. Therefore, 3D-printed metal is only suitable for some furniture in particular shapes. 3D printing technology cannot be used to upgrade the old traditional metal hardware. Finally, in terms of application, 3D-printed metal still faces the limitation imposed by traditional metal and there's no further development for 3D printing material, either. That is the reason why this study proposes 4 conceptual prototypes in order to address the aforementioned issues: (1) softening, (2) incremental change, (3) spiral, (4) mutation. These 4 conceptual prototypes address the issue that 3D-printed metal nowadays has to compromise and give up freeness in exchange of functionality. It also takes us to think further on how 3D printing can be applied to create new styles or to combine with traditional metal It is expected to establish a new system where traditional metal and 3D-printed metal can intermingle or be used in the same structure. However, this study is still in the early phase of prototype development. It will require further testing for actual use and installation on real furniture pieces. Moreover, the implementation also needs to be evaluated by vendors in the industry. This is a limitation of this study but it can also be taken as a direction for subsequent studies and development.

References

Bateman, R.J., Cheng, K.: Extending the product portfolio with 'devolved manufacturing': methodology and case studies. Int. J. Prod. Res. **44**(16), 3325–3343 (2006)

Chou, P.P.: Research on innovation design of furniture model under the influence of 3D printing technology. MING (Attitude) **10**, 69–70 (2016)

Forsman, M.: Development of adjustable furniture legs, Master's thesis, Jönköping University (2016)

Ho, W.S.: The system furniture material and the essential hardware component of the housing space to explore, Master's thesis, Shu-Te University (2009)

Klímová, B.J.: Manufactre of driving rollers, Master's thesis, Brno University of Technology (2009)

Liao, Y.S.: New trends in manufacturing 3D printing technology. NTU Alumni Bimonthly **88**, 16–23 (2013)

Lu, T.H.: Collaborative agent based mass customization manufacture information system research, Ph.D. thesis, National Tsing Hua University (2009)

Lu, C.H.: Modular research of system cabinets style, Master's thesis, Taipei Tech EMBA (2014)

Mu, C.Y.: Comparative research between traditional and modern hardware of furniture. Furniture Inter. Des. **9**, 80–81 (2010)

Tavsan, F.: Biomimicry in furniture design. J. Proc. Soc. Behav. Sci. **197**, 2285–2292 (2015)

Wang, T.Q.: Application and developing tendency of modern furniture hardware. Furniture Inter. Des. **12**, 18–19 (2003)

Wang, D.J.: Development and evolution of foreign modern furniture hardware. Furniture Inter. Des. **1**, 79–81 (2007)

Šebková, B.M.: Progressive technologies in furniture design, Master's thesis, Mendel University in Brno (2013)

Can Chatbots Help Reduce the Workload of Administrative Officers? - Implementing and Deploying FAQ Chatbot Service in a University

Keeheon Lee[1,2], Jeongwon Jo[1], Jinyoung Kim[3],
and Younah Kang[1,3(✉)]

[1] Underwood International College, Yonsei University, Seoul,
Republic of Korea
{keeheon,jjw48,yakang}@yonsei.ac.kr
[2] Graduate School of Information, Yonsei University, Seoul, Republic of Korea
[3] Graduate School of Communication, Yonsei University, Seoul,
Republic of Korea
{marykim1013,yakang}@yonsei.ac.kr

Abstract. Recently, it is often considered that chatbots can reduce customer service costs and handle a number of customers at the same time and thus, they have been widely used for administrative work. In this study, we developed a chatbot for Frequently Asked Questions (FAQs) in a college and deployed it to students and department offices. We then conducted an experiment with two offices, with and without chatbot, to analyze whether the introduction of chatbot affects the administrative workload. Office workers' workloads were measured using the National Aeronautics and Space Administration Task Load Index (NASA-TLX) questionnaire in addition to observations and the log data of chatbot usage. This report contains our findings and analysis of how the introduction of chatbot influenced the administrative work patterns and the workers' perceived workload.

Keywords: Chatbot · Workload · NASA-TLX · Administrative work · College

1 Introduction

Development of information technology has brought in computer systems into working environments and allowed office automation. Office automation is to leverage on computer software or hardware to process repetitive tasks, minimizing human engagement. Office automation was positively proven to make it easier for employees to finish tedious and repetitive tasks including typing, filing, document management, and telephoning and to lower the number of needed workers [1, 2]. Previous research done to measure the impact of office automation on librarian's productivity demonstrates that it augmented workers' productivity. With office automation, skill levels of workers augmented as they completed tasks rapidly and controlled tasks at hand [3].

© Springer Nature Switzerland AG 2019
C. Stephanidis (Ed.): HCII 2019, CCIS 1032, pp. 348–354, 2019.
https://doi.org/10.1007/978-3-030-23522-2_45

The representative office automation has been an automatic response system (ARS) on phone which sends a pre-designated replies for incoming inquiries. However, it turned out that the satisfaction index is higher for the screen-based ARS (41.1% answered 'satisfied') than that for the voice-based ARS (26% answered 'satisfied') although the screen-based ARS is less prevalent [4]. 51.2% of respondents that were satisfied with the screen-based ARS said they prefer to confirm information visually. Due to development in natural language processing, the application of the screen-based ARS can be extensively expanded with the introduction of chatbot.

Chatbot is an automated response system that provides an intuitive, conversation-like approach to answering inquiries [5]. By providing an effective natural language interface, chatbots support users to perform their tasks without having to directly interact with human agents through calling or emailing [6]. Chatbots are used in a wide range of fields for alternatives to traditional customer service such as e-commerce, education, and counselling [7] as they typically use simple questions and commands, tailored for specific scenarios and tasks [8]. The present study provides insights into how chatbots for administration at college can be adapted to answer students' FAQ and analyzes if chatbots can save labor costs of administrative offices.

2   Use of Chatbot for University's Administration Service

Administration service at university embraces simple, repetitive question and answer, and formulaic information request and response. Recently, several universities have begun to adopt chatbots that can respond to certain formulaic questions from students in order to raise the efficiency of administrative officers' work and to enhance the experience of students [9]. For instance, the University of Canberra has developed two chatbots called Lucy, the chatbot for students, and Bruce, the chatbot for support staff [10]. They currently offer support via email, phone calls and FAQ's, and are aimed at quickly performing repetitive tasks and answering commonly asked questions. The University of Manchester's Timetabling Office has introduced a messaging app-based chatbot that delivers basic timetable information to students [11]. The apps available for such chatbot services include Facebook Messenger, Telegram, LINE, Kik, and Viber, and it is planned to be released through Twitter and Google Assistant. Since it is provided through existing messenger platforms, it establishes a service environment that raises accessibility and lessens users' unfamiliarity. Students are able to ask for information such as the location of school buildings and timetable for lectures. The effects of such chatbots at universities, however, have not been fully examined. It is still unanswered whether chatbots can actually resolve students' specific inquiries without human intervention, alleviating the workload of office staffs. In this study, we seek to examine whether incorporating chatbots into university administrative services is beneficial, specifically with regards to office staffs' workload.

3   Methodology

3.1   Development of Chatbot for FAQs in a College

For the study, we have developed an interactive chatbot for Frequently Asked Questions (FAQs) in an international college in Korea. We focused on the fact that university administrative offices are receiving a large amount of inquiries, most of which are rather simple questions that can be answered by simply browsing the college website. Furthermore, an FAQ has the advantage over other corpus training sets in that there are clear equivalents of "user" (Question) and "chatbot" (Answer) which simplifies modelling of turn-taking [12]. The chatbot is based on KakaoTalk which is the most popular chat application in the country [13]. It uses KakaoTalk API to deploy the bot in Python to KakaoTalk. Anyone can search the chatbot in the messenger and ask inquiries either by typing their questions as they would chat with a human or by traversing items in the menu to access necessary information. In short, the chatbot incorporated both contextual and menu-based chabot type. Google's DialogFlow was used to understand the context of user's input when one freely typed their question, not using items in the menu. Items in the menu contained academic notices or announcements, employment notices, faculty directories, and academic regulations including graduation requirements. Ultimately, this chatbot service aims at providing information such as majors, graduation requirements, notices, and events inside a campus without interacting with human.

3.2   Measures

In order to figure out if chatbot actually does alleviate workloads of office staffs, we decided to compare the objective amounts of tasks and how they subjectively feel before and after the introduction of the chatbot. We conducted two stages of experiments, pre-chatbot introduction experiment and post-chatbot introduction experiment, on two administrative offices, office A and B, with two staffs from each office. Having office A as an experimental group and office B as a control group, the pre-chatbot experiment was conducted before introducing the chatbot for seven work days. In order to analyze the precise effects of the chatbot, we promoted the chatbot service to students of department A with the support of department president, but not to those of department B. We then implemented the post-chatbot experiment for six days on the same two administrative offices with respect to comparing differences between a group in which chatbot was introduced to students, office A, and a group in which it was not, office B. The objective was to analyze whether the workload of the employees has been reduced after the introduction of the chatbot.

With an aim to compare the difference in objective amounts of tasks, we measured the number of inquiries staffs receive via email per day. Also, in order to track any variations in the contents of inquiries, we asked the staff members in office A and B to fill in an observation sheet where they entered the number of inquiries they received per day through each predefined category including faculty directory, academic regulations, academic schedule, department exclusive programs, graduation requirement, academic affairs, student services, and etc.

Office workers' perceived workload was also collected quantitatively through the National Aeronautics and Space Administration Task Load Index (NASA-TLX). NASA-TLX is a subjective workload assessment technique that relies on a multidimensional construct to derive an overall workload score based on a weighted average of ratings on six subscales: mental demand, physical demand, temporal demand, performance, effort, and frustration level [14]. The analysis method is that the higher the score, the higher the subjective workload but regarding performance, the lower the score, the higher their work performance. We asked them to answer the NASA-TLX questionnaire every day after work during the experiment.

Additionally, to scrutinize the usage pattern of chatbot, we analyzed the usage statistics including the number of users and the usage frequency of each feature.

4   Results

To measure and compare the amounts of workload of office A and office B, we initially analyzed the amount of email inquiries they received from students. First of all, with regard to the observation sheets specified in Table 1, office A has received an average of 16.3 inquiries per day, 114 in total when chatbot was not yet introduced to students. For office B, on the other hand, the average number of inquiries they received was 12.14, 56 in total, which was fewer than that of office A. However, once the chatbot was introduced, the situation reversed. The number of email inquiries office A received decreased by 27.19%, recording 83 emails in total and 13.8 emails on average. On the other hand, the number of email inquiries office B received augmented by 71.43% with 96 emails in total and 16 emails on average. The numbers imply that the actual amount of workload for office A, who took advantage of office automation by chatbot, did decline.

Table 1. Amount of inquiries each office A, B, and chatbot received

	Before Chatbot				After Chatbot				Overall			
	Total	Avg.	Max	Min	Total	Avg.	Max	Min	Total	Avg.	Max	Min
A	114	16.3	26	9	83 (−27.19%)	13.8 (−15.34%)	23 (−11.54%)	8 (+11.11%)	197	15.15	26	8
B	56	12.14	29	6	96 (+71.43%)	16 (+31.8%)	20 (−31%)	13 (+116.67%)	152	11.7	29	6
Chat-bot	With overlap				20							
	Without overlap				8							

Figure 1 shows the contents of the inquiries office A and B received from students via email and it also demonstrates a difference between the contents of the inquiries. Many of the emails office A received were concerned with academic schedule and graduation requirement before the chatbot was introduced. With the introduction of chatbot, inquiries about graduation requirement decreased and most inquiries were relevant to other personal inquiries. In terms of office B, when chatbot was not introduced, most inquiries were about academic schedule and graduation requirement, as office A. However, during the experiment period when chatbot was introduced to students, most of the inquiries for office B were concerned with faculties directory which can be simply resolved with the chatbot.

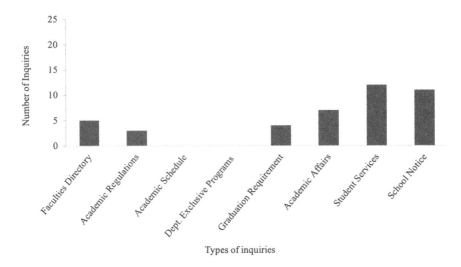

Fig. 1. Types of inquiries chatbot received after introduction of chatbot

The frequency of chatbot usage during the experiment period was 20 without overlapping users. The types of inquiries were analyzed to comprehend the usage patterns and objectives behind using chatbot. The usage frequency of each feature is indicated in Fig. 1. Students frequently used chatbot to overview recently updated notices and events, which are provided in the menus of 'School Notice', 'Student Services', and 'Academic Affairs.' Users can select a title of each notice and be directed to the website for specific information. They also often visited 'Graduation Requirement' menu where they can directly download the pdf document that specifies required courses and credits according to their majors (Table 2).

Table 2. Results of NASA-TLX compared by average score of total sum

Office	Average of total sum of 6 categories	
	Pre-chatbot	Post-chatbot
A	67.8	63.5
B	72.3	70.4

In terms of NASA-TLX, for the pre-chatbot experiment, the average score of office A was 67.8 whereas the one of office B was 72.3. Thus, the subjective workload of office A's staff member turned out to be about 5 points lower than the one of office B, which represents the degree in which the staff member at office B felt her workload was higher than that of office A. For the post-chatbot experiment, the average score of office

A turned out to be 63.5, which was about 4 points less than its score of the pre-chatbot experiment. In terms of office B, the average result was 70.4, about 2 points less than the one of the pre-chatbot experiment. Thus, analyzing the difference between the scores of the pre-chatbot and post-chatbot experiment of each of the offices respectively, there was a greater reduction in workload for office A, which implies that the introduction of chatbot exerted a positive influence.

5   Discussion

The present study has been conducted with an aim to examine the effects of chatbot for administrative office. The results indicate the tendency that the chatbot has reduced the amount of workload at an administrative office. First, there was striking decrease in the number of inquiries received by email once the chatbot was introduced. Secondly, the subjective evaluation of the difference in workload before and after the introduction of chatbot was analyzed through NASA-TLX. The average score of office A from NASA-TLX showed a greater reduction than the one of office B did, implying that the subjective workload of office A was improved after the introduction of chatbot.

The study has several limitations. First of all, there was a lack of promotion in chatbot service to students in department A, as it was promoted only via KakaoTalk chat room by department president. In addition, the experiment was conducted over a short period as it demands and is dependent to the support of office A and B, because they need to manually categorize each email inquiry. Lastly, there was no means to figure out whether students have actually thought of using the chatbot before asking to the office right away.

Our study presented new evidence that the introduction of chatbot can reduce workers' workload in the context of a college administrative office. Future studies need to be conducted with more measures, variables, and users to further explore this theory.

Acknowledgment. This work has been conducted with the support of the "Design Engineering Postgraduate Schools (N0001436)" program, a R&D project initiated by the Ministry of Trade, Industry and Energy of the Republic of Korea.

References

1. Vary, T.: Coates: office automation: productivity, employment and social impacts. Inf. Technol. People **4**(3), 315–326 (1988)
2. Lee, S.Y., Brand, J.L.: Effects of control over office workspace on perceptions of the work environment and work outcomes. J. Environ. Psychol. **25**(3), 323–333 (2005)
3. Yaghi, K., Barakat, S.: The impact of office automation on worker's productivity at all organizational levels at King Abdul-Aziz University Library: a case study. Kärntner Botanikzentrum **21**, 26–34 (2014)
4. Jung, H.K., Kim, C.S., Yoon, Y.J.: A study on the improvement of ARS (automatic response system) service. Korea Inf. Soc. Dev. (2011). 11-Jin Heung-Da-11
5. Sofy Carayannopoulos.: Using chatbots to aid transition. Int. J. Inf. Learn. Technol. **35**(2), 118–129 (2018)

6. Dale, R.: The return of the chatbots. Nat. Lang. Eng. **22**, 811–817 (2016)
7. Serban, I., et al.: A Deep Reinforcement Learning Chatbot. ArXiv e-prints (2017)
8. Abu Shawar, B.A., Atwell, E.S.: Chatbots: are they really useful? J. Lang. Technol. Comput. Linguist. **22**(1), 29–49 (2007)
9. Park, D.: A study on conversational public administration service of the chatbot based on artificial intelligence. J. Korea Multimed. Soc. **20**(8), 1347–1356 (2017)
10. Use cases for a campus chatbot. http://www.aftabhussain.com/chatbot_uses.html. Accessed 24 Mar 2019
11. University Uses Messaging Apps as Chatbot. https://www.insidehighered.com/blogs/student-affairs-and-technology/university-uses-messaging-apps-chatbot. Accessed 25 Mar 2019
12. AbuShawar, B., Atwell, E.: ALICE chatbot: trials and outputs. Computación y Sistemas **19**(4), 625–632 (2015)
13. Jung, H.-S.: The evolution of Korean social network service focusing on the case of Kakao talk. J. Dig. Convergence **10**(10), 147–154 (2012)
14. Cao, A., Chintamani, K.K., Pandya, A.K., Ellis, R.D.: NASA TLX: software for assessing subjective mental workload. Behav. Res. Methods **41**(1), 113–117 (2009)

User Experience Design Methodology for Optimizing Kids' Toy Customization Platform Architecture: A Case Study

Xiang Li$^{(\boxtimes)}$ and Xuelian Song

Faculty of Art and Design, Wuhan University of Technology, Wuhan, China
lixiang8100@whut.edu.cn

Abstract. There is a study concerning the optimization of kids' toy customization platform architecture with user experience design methodology. In this paper, we aimed at the kids' toy internet customization platform, analyzed the basic characteristics of children who are the main target users of service and described dual user mode. This paper presented a case study on the Kids Creation Station toy customization platform. There are the characteristics of complex service process, many stakeholders and many users with special feature on kids' toy internet customization platform, therefore, this paper synthesized and implemented some methods and tools in interaction design and service design, and used behavior logic to organize processes, contact points and interfaces to build a better user experience. Basing on the case analysis and following with the dual user mental model, we applied the methods of service blueprint analysis to evaluate, insight and optimize existing platforms, proposed the architecture of the kids' toy internet customization platform with 3D printing technology. We explored the compared and comprehensive approach in service design and interaction design. This research conceived the future overall services format based on the principle of customization-design-manufacture-logistics-social, and provided reference for the development and promotion of personalized customization and intelligent manufacturing.

Keywords: User experience design methodology · Kid's toys · Individual customization

1 Introduction

Research shows that in recent years most consumers want their own clothing and supplies to be different from others, and like to have their own characteristics in China [1]. Consumers are not satisfied with the same product of mass and standardization, and begin to pursue their own individuality and unique lifestyle. With the rapid development of modern technology, personalized service has become the hotspot in many fields. As a new intelligent information service mode, personalized service is more targeted than traditional service mode. Nowadays, there are customization in various material and non-material fields. It is one of the key factors of commercial success that customization platform provides users with personalized products and exclusive

© Springer Nature Switzerland AG 2019
C. Stephanidis (Ed.): HCII 2019, CCIS 1032, pp. 355–362, 2019.
https://doi.org/10.1007/978-3-030-23522-2_46

services from the user's point of view, and help consumers have a better personalized experience, which has become a development trend.

The increasing number of personalized services for kids' toys is due to the fact that toy products play an important role in children's physical and mental health development, brain development and creativity. For designer of kids' toys and provider of commercial services, the children's characteristics in the process of cognitive development should be taken into account as an important basis for the design and service of toy products to meet children's needs for personalized products. [2].

In this paper, we aimed at the kids' toy internet customization platform, firstly analyzed the two basic characteristics of children who are the main target users of service:

(1) Kids are in the stage of fast development. According to the cognitive-developmental theory proposed by the psychologist Jean Piaget, the growth process of children can be divided into the following four stages, and the types of toys used by children at each stage are listed (see Table 1).

Table 1. Analysis of children's characteristics in the ages based on cognitive-development theory.

Age range	Description of stage	Developmental phenomena	Toys
Birth–2	Sensorimotor	• Objective • Stranger anxiety	Bell, tumbler, rattle-drum, Trojan horses
2–6 years	Preoperational	• Pretend play • Egocentrism • Language development	Jigsaw, balance beam, music box, ping pong
7–11 years	Concrete operational	• Conservation • Mathematical transformation	Board game. Ball game, bicycle, Lego, books
12– adulthood	Formal operational	• Abstract logic • Potential for mature moral reasoning	Sports equipment, mobile phone, computer

(2) Dual user mode. The choice of children's toy products, to a large extent, is the reflection of parents' subjective volition to cultivate children [3]. Children are the users of customized toys when parents are the main users and decision makers of personalized customization services. The whole service interaction is shared by two users-children and parents. The user experience of two users should be taken into account in the process of the kids' toy internet customization platform architecture.

In 1990 s, Professor Richard Buchanan clearly defined the object of interaction design as behavior. "creating and supporting human activities through the mediating influence of products" [4]. The service design that has been focused in recent years follows the development of the economic model, it's changed from the simple attention of single product design to the integrated attention to the comprehensive service system design [5]. In general, it is from the design of "objects" to the design of "relation", from the design of single "element" in system to the overall design of "relation" in system [6]. Service design focuses on the interactions between people and individuals or systems, and creates services for them. Therefore, interaction design and service design are both comprehensively design approach to improve the user experience by focusing on the elements which are behavior, integrated system and relations.

2   A Case Study

There are the characteristics of complex service process, many stakeholders and many users with special features on kids' toy internet customization platform, therefore, this paper synthesized and implemented some methods and tools in interaction design and service design, and used behavior logic to organize processes, contact points and interfaces to build a better user experience.

2.1   Mental Model Analysis

In 1984, Donald Norman first introduced the concept of mental model into the field of design [7]. Mental model refers to the cognition of things formed by people through external sensory stimulation, learning and experience, which is the thinking activity of people to complete various tasks [8]. Mental models can help designers and business service providers build empathy.

In this paper, we used three methods – Surveys and Questionnaires, Focus Group and Interview and Participatory Design to qualitatively capture the user's mental model which is applicable to kids' toy internet customization platform. We presented the basic mental space of two users for this task (behavior) by using the behavioral affinity graph in the macro mental model, which help the designer macroscopically construct the entire interaction process (see Fig. 1 and Fig. 2). We find that children focus on the experience of using customized toys after customization, while parents are more focused on whether the experience is good in the process of customization.

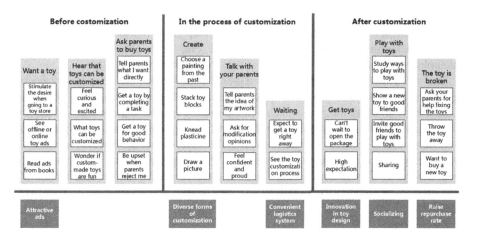

Fig. 1. The mental space of children's behavior.

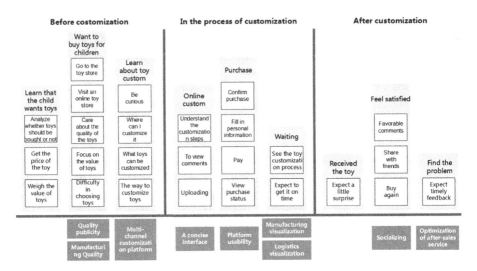

Fig. 2. The mental space of parental behavior.

2.2 Kid's Creation Station

Kids Creation Station established by a start-up company is that a personalized toy customization service platform that can help children turn their ideas into 3D models and provide 3D printing services. We conducted a case study on the Kids Creation Station toy customization platform and extracted the page flow and navigation architecture of the platform (see Fig. 3). We found that the platform simplified the problems such as the time-consuming process of 3D model printing and the difficulty in processing model data into three steps: hand-painted graffiti (user)-photo uploading (user)-physical printing (platform) during the experience. In this process, users only upload their hand-painted artworks to the platform, which greatly facilitates users and improves the interoperability between users and the platform [9].

In this paper, the tools of stakeholder analysis, user persona, and user journey were implemented to qualitatively and quantitatively analyze for exploring the design flaws in user experience. First, we built the stakeholder map of the platform service system to target to determine the response strategy (see Fig. 4). It concludes that its core stakeholders are parents and children and that they influence each other.

The user role models of parents and children which is two main types of users on the customized platform are built (see Fig. 5), which reconstructed the scenes of characters when using the platform and summarized the core characteristics of parents and children. The main characteristics of parents: young parents who have children and are willing to accept new things, therefore, the corresponding demands are mainly about the quality of toys, the convenience of shopping, the quality of service and a good experience. The main characteristics of children are a group of 5–16 years old who have clear requirements on toys and innovation and interesting of toys were considered.

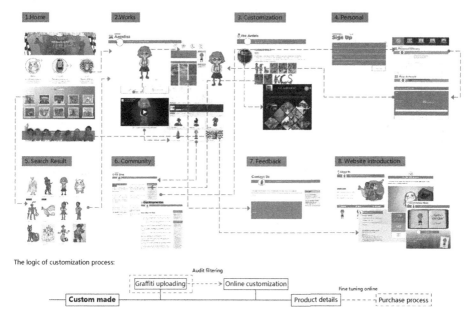

Fig. 3. The platform page flow of Kids Creation Station

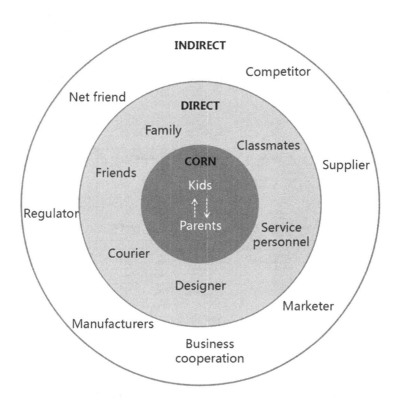

Fig. 4. Stakeholder map on Kids Creation Station

Fig. 5. User role model on Kids Creation Station

The customer journey map is summarized and drawn by integrating the experience emotional data of user roles, merging similar conclusion and distinguishing the different conclusion (see Fig. 6). The user experience journey map is used to describe the platform service process from six dimensions: service stage, service touch point, behavior path, experience emotion, user demand and opportunity point. It can be clearly seen that in the stage of ordering the user's emotion is expressed as the lowest value, which are the products obtained by the customization have a large deviation from the scheme provided by the user, the communication between the user and the designer is not smooth, the customization mode is single which can't meet the needs of different users.

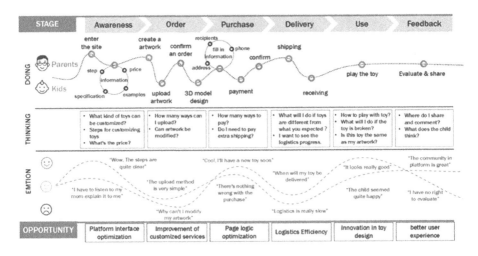

Fig. 6. Customer journey map on Kids Creation Station

3   Discussion

Basing on the case analysis and following with the dual user mental model, we applied the methods of service blueprint analysis (Fig. 7), proposed the architecture of the kids' toy internet customization platform with 3D printing technology (Fig. 8). The interaction logic of the architecture is: (1) Analyze and determine the users' personalized needs by using a variety of interactions and techniques, including: video, graphics, texts and 3D scanning. (2) Distinguish the needs of personalized customization of toy products, which can be divided into three categories according to the children's degree

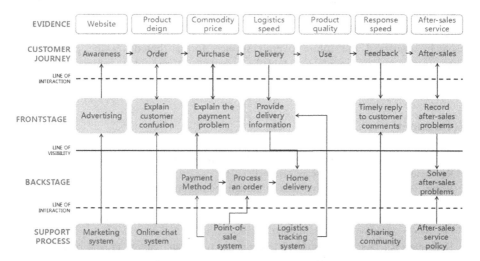

Fig. 7. Service blueprint of kids' toy internet customization platform

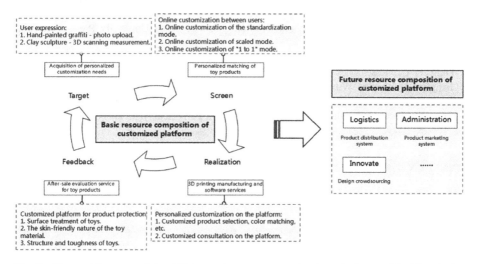

Fig. 8. The architecture of the kids' toy internet customization platform with 3D printing technology

of practicability in customizing ideas. (3) Designers and users create toy products together and customize them based on 3D printing technology. (4) In order to make the customized toy products have good quality and the users can obtain continuous service after purchase, the platform provides the function and interaction of quality inspection and after-sales service tracking for customized toys.

4   Conclusion

In this paper, we analyzed the interactive characteristics of the kids' toy internet customization platform and presented a case study in which multiple research methods and tools were used to evaluate, insight and optimize existing platforms. We explored the compared and comprehensive approach in service design and interaction design. This research conceived the future overall service format based on the principle of customization-design-manufacture-logistics-social, and provided reference for the development and promotion of personalized customization and intelligent manufacturing.

References

1. Fashion magazine, Zero research consulting group. 2016 China High-Income Urban Residents Fashion Index Research Report (2016)
2. Wang, X.: Study on children's toys design based on growth of cognition. Qingdao Technological University, Qingdao (2016)
3. Tang, J.: A study on the design of infant thermostatic milk bottles based on dual-user experience. Shandong University (2017)
4. Buchanan, R.: Design as inquiry: the common, future and current ground of design. In: Redmond, J., et al. (eds.) Future Ground: Proceedings of the International Conference of the Design Research Society, Monash University, Melbourne, Australia, November 2004 (2005)
5. Moritz, S.: Service Design: Practical Access to an Evolving Field, 3rd edn. Köln International School of Design, Cologne (2005)
6. Liu, G.: The Theory of Object and Relations. Central South University Press, Changsha (2006)
7. Norman, D.A.: The Design of Everyday Things. Basic Books, New York (1984)
8. Ding-lv, C.: Researches on Significations Based on Mental Models in Product Design. Jiangnan University, Wuxi (2009)
9. Jesse, J.G.: The Elements of User Experience: User Centered Design for the Web and Beyond. Mechanical Industry Press, Beijing (2011). FAN Xiao-yan, Translate

Research of Interactive Device Based on Intelligent Toy Receiving Box Design

Yi Lu[1(✉)] and Guoqi Lu[2]

[1] Beijing University of Technology, Beijing, China
7679067@qq.com
[2] Beijing Institute of Graphic Communication, Beijing, China
593044843@qq.com

Abstract. The purpose of our research is to design intelligent toy receiving box based on the interactive behavior and toy receiving habits of preschool children, so as to guide children to develop good receiving habits. We use qualitative and quantitative research methods such as questionnaire, competitive analysis, user interviews and user portrait, etc. The children's physiological characteristics, receiving behavior and problems in the receiving process were refined. At the same time, it refers to the tangible interaction design method [1] to carry out innovative design practice. Through the research on the intelligent toy receiving box, the interactive, funning and intelligence innovation mode of the children's toy receiving box is realized. Finally, this study is used to help children develop good receiving habits and classification management skills, and promote emotional communication between parents and children.

Keywords: Tangible interaction · Toy receiving box · Intelligent product · Preschool children

1 Introduction

The problem of children's toy receiving is a common problem faced by current children's families. At present, the receiving box on the market has a single function, it is simple and lack of interest, and does not systematically guide children to develop the habit of active receiving [4]. This study intends to design intelligent toy receiving box that meets children's cognition through discussion the way of interesting interactive receiving, guide children to manage their toys in a neat and orderly manner, cultivate children's sense of responsibility and classification, so as to help children develop good living habits.

2 Requirements on Intelligent Toy Receiving Box

2.1 User Research

Qualitative Analysis

We interviewed 35 preschool children aged 3–5 years in Beijing 21st Century International Kindergarten, and understood how children play toys and after games. The preliminary research data are summarized as follows:

© Springer Nature Switzerland AG 2019
C. Stephanidis (Ed.): HCII 2019, CCIS 1032, pp. 363–370, 2019.
https://doi.org/10.1007/978-3-030-23522-2_47

- Preschool children look for their favorite toys every day.
- Preschool children rarely have the habit of organizing toys by themselves.
- Preschool children often fail to find and lose toys in their homes.
- Most preschool children have been criticized and educated by their parents for littering toys.

Quantitative Analysis

Based on qualitative analysis, we still analyzed the quantitative data collection of questionnaires, and observed the preschool children receiving habits in the home. At the same time, the quantitative survey data are summarized as follows:

- Preschool children have the problem of placing toys randomly, which make toys easily lost;
- Preschool children need parents' help to organize their toys, increasing parents' burden;
- Preschool children have not formed the habit of organizing toys and looking for toys by themselves;
- Parents usually adopt reward mechanism and reasoning methods to help children develop good habits;
- Toy receiving boxes tend to be three-dimensional and closed;
- Parents will think about the characteristics of children's personal preferences when buying toy receiving products.

User Portrait

Based on preliminary research of preschool children's toy receiving, we analyzed children's behavior by journey map (Fig. 1). Then we further summarized the opportunity points of the design requirements as: (a). rational planning of toy receiving space; (b). children developing the habit of receiving toys by themselves; (c). the need for a toy receiving box that combines interesting and practical features; (d). enhancing interaction between children and parents.

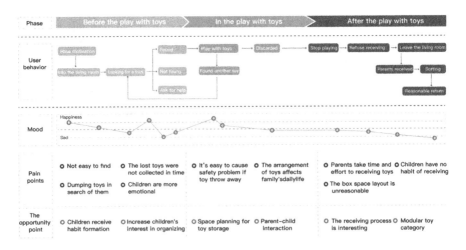

Fig. 1. Analysis of children's toys receiving process

The user portrait finally constructed as shown in Fig. 2. It is specifically described as a 5-year-old girl Lucy, who is lively and cheerful, she likes to imitate the behavior and sound of various anime characters in cartoons; there are many toys in her home, and a receiving box which cannot only receiving toys interestingly, but also classify and manage different types of toys. She likes the combination of all kinds of small objects and toys. She hopes that there are many kinds of toys, but she doesn't want to pack toys. She often loses them.

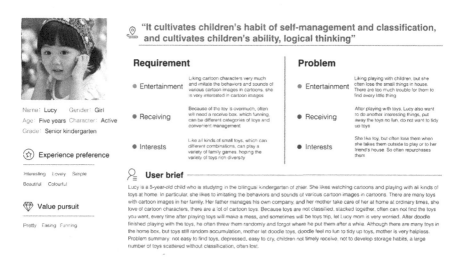

Fig. 2. Typical user portrait

3 Pilot Design

3.1 Hardware Design

The hardware design of the intelligent toy receiving box mainly shows the aspects of function design, modeling design, interaction technology, prototype production, etc. Based on the user portrait, we summarized the functions of toy receiving box as follows. Use scenario of the product is shown in Fig. 3.

- The complete set of toy receiving box includes a plurality of independent intelligent boxes which are convenient and fast to assemble;
- Each toy box body has diversified shapes and colors, built-in sound and light sensors, and provides visual interactive feedback when storing toys;
- The mobile app can be provided with toys to be placed in each box. When the toys are misplaced in the box, there will be voice and light reminders. When it comes to receiving time, the toys will have corresponding voice and light prompts when they forget to put them back;
- The mobile app can set game time and record reminding content, and intelligently control game time through voice changing reminding;

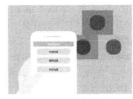
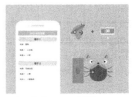

Step 1: Children alway leave toy everywhere.Only mother tidied up the toys.

Step 2: Connect the box to the mobile app. Different materials or types of toys can be set sep-arately.

Step 3: Parents and children attach FRID labels to toys to in-crease their communication and interaction

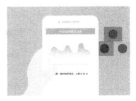

Step 4: When the toy is put into the storage box, there will be correct judgment and voice and light prompt.

Step 5: Parents can set time, voice and mode in the app.

Step 6: The parents check the data analysis and score of the doodle receiving situation in the app.

Fig. 3. Scenario of intelligent toy receiving box

- The mobile app can view the data analysis of children's daily accommodation and the data analysis of one week or one month's accommodation, so as to understand and encourage children to develop the accommodation habit through visual feedback.

Modeling Design

As shown in Fig. 4, the intelligent toy receiving box is designed with a three-dimensional effect diagram and a combined color scheme. The whole set of combined box is composed of box body with embedded multiple sensors. The combination mode is flexible and the ears are stacked and plugged with multiple boxes. In detail design, the box has round and lovely edges and corners, and the side handshaking slot can be moved, making it easy for simple interactive operation. The tag design of accessory parts is integrated into the abstract cartoon shape of animals, and the blank part in the middle of the tag allows children to write a mark in the tag.

Fig. 4. 3D mode & label design of toy receiving box

Hardware Technology

The main hardware components of the intelligent toy receiving box include a speaker, a pressure sensor, a lamp band, a sound sensor, an M 2100 module, an antenna, an RFID tag, a HC05 Bluetooth module, etc. When children put toys in and out of the toy box, they will drive the data of the pressure sensor to change. At the same time, the RFID detector will identify and match the tag information. When the tag information matches successfully, it will send the correct sound prompt to the MP3 module, and if there is no corresponding tag information in the match, it will play the wrong sound prompt. Every change in weight will make the RFID detector recognize the tag once. If the tag information does not match, an error message will be generated. In addition, the Bluetooth module can connect the hardware with the mobile phone,

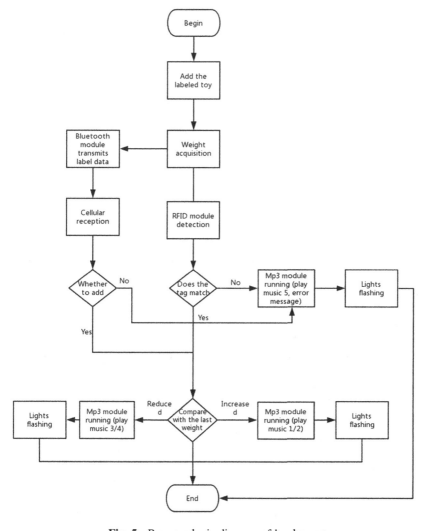

Fig. 5. Program logic diagram of hardware

open the app and connect Bluetooth, and then put the toy with the tag into the box. If you click add, the tag will be automatically entered into the system. The specific interactive hardware module and program logic are shown in Fig. 5.

Prototype Production

We prints out the various parts of the toy (the eyes are transparent) through 3D printing technology, assembles them together, and finally sprays the model effect with spray paint. The final prototype model is shown in Fig. 6.

Fig. 6. Prototype of intelligent toy receiving box

3.2   Software Design

The software design mainly focuses on the parent mobile App "Yummy". The homepage of the interface "Yummy" displays visual charts such as play time distribution, tag distribution and favorite toy ranking of the receiving box. In the process of using the toy receiving box, the system will collect and count the tag data, upload receipts to the mobile through the Bluetooth communication module, and display them on the mobile in the form of charts. The data will be analyzed and collected in three dimensions of week, month and summary. On the device page, click 'Setting of receiving box', parents can organize the labels of each toy box by themselves, such as add, delete and rename. After connect Bluetooth and then put the toys with labels into the box. The Bluetooth module will transmit the label information to the mobile phone, and the user can check the label information code at the mobile phone. Click 'Add' to send the label information to the program, and the label addition is completed. On the setting page, the intelligent toy receiving box can be flexibly set for intelligent game time control, toy box name classification setting, voice volume adjustment, personal basic information and so on, so that parents can pay attention to the receiving situation of their children. While children are using the physical toy receiving box, app will synchronize the children's receiving records to the data detection, and parents can understand the changes of children's receiving habits according to the data feedback. The main interface is shown in Fig. 7.

Fig. 7. App UI design of intelligent toy receiving box

4 Pilot Evaluation

During the product evaluation, we invited two children aged 3–5 in using "Yummy" toy receiving box and analyzed the problems in the use process (Fig. 8). Children were very satisfied with the creative design of the prototype [3], but also found some problems in the design. Such as young children have a biased understanding of the box shape and think cats should have beards; young children easily ignored the false prompts; the way toys are labeled and classified is relatively complicated for young children; parents are in the leading position and like to help children solve problems; label entry procedures are cumbersome and audio selectivity is limited. In the future iterative design, we will modify the design based on feedback questions: (a) the box shape can be slightly figurative in combination with children's cognitive preferences; (b) the number of prompt interaction modes of the receiving box increases, such as different changes of lights; (c) the mode of receipt information transmission has changed, and the label entry procedure has been optimized. The testing process is shown in Fig. 8.

Fig. 8. Prototype testing for children

5 Conclusion

Based on the characteristics of children's cognitive behavior and receiving habits [6], this study adopts a systematic tangible interaction design method, extracts the elements of interaction design from four levels of senses, behavior, emotion and space, and carries out innovative design through design practice [2]. The innovative features of "Yummy" are summarized as follows: (a). intelligence. According to their own needs, they can freely set up functions, receive toys in multiple functions, and intelligently control game time; (b). Multi - channel interaction. Toy receiving box provides visual feedback, voice reminding and other multi-sensory interaction ways to guide children to interact with it in an interesting way; (c). Emotionalization. The toy receiving box can help parents enhance parent-child interaction education [5], help children develop good receiving habits, and has the characteristic of entertainment and learning.

References

1. Yi, L.: Research on toy design for preschool children based on entity interaction. Doctoral thesis, Tsinghua University (2018)
2. Katriina H.: Digital natives and cardboard cubes: co-creating a physical play(ful) ideation tool with preschool children. In: Proceeding of Interaction Design and Children Conference, Stanford, CA, pp. 541–547. ACM Press (2017)
3. Iversen, O.S., Smith, R.C., Dindler, C.: Child as protagonist: expanding the role of children in participatory design. In: Proceeding of Interaction Design and Children Conference, Stanford, CA, pp. 27–37. ACM Press (2017)
4. Zhang, Junli: Design of children's toy storage device. Light. Ind. Technol. **24**(10), 121 (2008)
5. Lu, Y., Tang, H.: Research on emotional design of educational toys for preschool children. Packag. Eng. **39**(10) (2018)
6. Liu, J.: Research on bionic design of infant puzzle box. Master thesis, Changchun University of technology (2016)
7. Guha, M.L., Druin, A., Fails, J.A.: Cooperative Inquiry revisited: reflections of the past and guidelines for the future of intergenerational co-design. Int. J. Child Comput. Interact. **1**(1), 14–23 (2013)
8. Santer, J., Griffiths, C., Goodall, D.: Free Play in Early Childhood: A Literature Review, pp. 1–114. National Children's Bureau, London (2007)
9. Druin, A.: Cooperative inquiry: developing new technologies for children with children. In: Proceedings of the SIGCHI Conference on Human Factors in Computing Systems, pp. 592–599. ACM (1999)
10. Hains, S.M.J., Muir, D.W.: Effects of stimulus contingency in infant-adult interactions. Infant Behav. Dev. **19**(1), 49–61 (1996)

Development and Evaluation of Gamified Multimodal System to Improve Experience Value of Floor Wiping

Ryota Makabe[1,2(✉)], Kodai Ito[2], Tsubasa Maruyama[2],
Natsuki Miyata[2], Mitsunori Tada[2], and Michiko Ohkura[1]

[1] Shibaura Institute of Technology, 3-7-5, Koto, Toyosu, Tokyo
135-8548, Japan
al15088@shibaura-it.ac.jp
[2] National Institute of Advanced Industrial Science and Technology, 2-3-26,
Koto, Aomi, Tokyo 135-0064, Japan

Abstract. It is difficult to keep motivation for daily house cleaning as people must repeat the same task monotonically. Floor wiping is a task to wipe the entire floor, but it is usually difficult to complete the task due to such obstacles as furniture. Therefore, the purpose of this study is to provide a system that supports a complete and enjoyable floor wiping by multimodal feedbacks including tactile and auditory feedbacks. We developed a system composed of floor wiper, optical motion capture system for reconstruction of the location of the wiper, tactile feedback device, Bluetooth surround sound headphone, and PC. In addition, we implemented "rhythm game" to increase enjoyment, and 3D surround sound and vibration to present unwiped area. As a result of the evaluation experiment of our developed system, cleaning became fun with our system. However, the improvement of feedbacks as well as the accuracy of the wiper's location restoration remain as future work.

Keywords: Floor wiping · Gamification · Multimodal feedback

1 Introduction

It is difficult to keep motivation for daily house cleaning, as people must repeat the same task monotonically. Previous studies proposed a system to enhance an enjoyment in cleaning by applying a gamification technique [1–3]. Gamification is an attempt to apply the elements of the game to other fields [4], for example, rehabilitation [5, 6] and education [7, 8], which effectively increased motivation. Moreover, a common house-cleaning problem is that a complete cleaning such as wiping the entire floor evenly, cannot be done due to such obstacles as furniture. A previous study proposed a system to support a complete cleaning by showing on a PC display such visual feedback as an unwiped area [9]. However, it was considered too difficult to clean and check the visual feedback on a PC display simultaneously. Therefore, this research proposed a gamified system with multimodal (tactile and auditory) feedbacks for floor wiping. The purpose of this study are as follows:

C. Stephanidis (Ed.): HCII 2019, CCIS 1032, pp. 371–377, 2019.
https://doi.org/10.1007/978-3-030-23522-2_48

- To provide gamified system that increases fun in floor wiping
- To provide system that supports a complete floor wiping

2   Methods

2.1   Developed System

The configuration of our developed system is shown in Fig. 1. This system consists of floor wiper, optical motion capture system (OptiTrack), tactile feedback device (ADTEDS), Bluetooth surround sound headphone (SONY WH-L600), and PC. We used the motion capture system to simulate the wiper's location in a room in real time. In addition, we used the vibration from the tactile feedback device and the surround sound from the headphone.

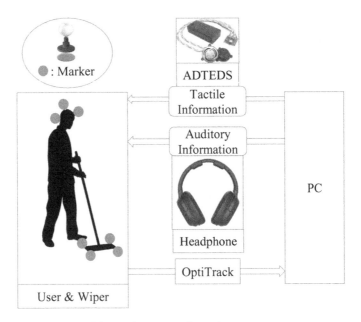

Fig. 1. System configuration

2.2   Feedbacks

We implemented the following tactile and auditory feedbacks. The details are described as follows:

- Tactile feedback: The device vibrated according to number of times that each area was wiped: the vibration was strong in unwiped area, and then stopped after wiping it for three times.

- Two auditory feedbacks:
  - 3D surround sound: It was used to direct users to unwiped area and notify them when the floor was completely cleaned (i.e. the floor was wiped for three times).
  - A "rhythm game": It was used to enable users to synchronize their wiping movement according to the tempo. If user's movement matched the tempo, the system played the successful sound and added points. In this system, we set the tempo to 150 beats per minute (BPM).

2.3 Evaluation Experiment

To evaluate the effectiveness of the feedback, we set the following four feedback conditions:

- No feedback
- Only tactile feedback
- One auditory feedback (only 3D surround sound)
- Both auditory feedbacks (3D surround sound and rhythm game)

Before performing the experiment, we attached retro-reflective markers of the motion capture system to the wiper and the headphone (Fig. 2), attached the tactile feedback device to the dorsal side of participant's right hand, and put the headphone to participant's head. We set up a living room with such furniture as chairs and a table as obstacles, and marked the yellow line as wiping area (Fig. 3). We instructed participants to wipe the floor for three times including the areas under the furniture. Moreover, we did not specify the place to start wiping, the order of the place to wipe, and the wiping speed.

Fig. 2. Wiper and headphone with markers

We performed the experiment with 10 Japanese participants: five males and five females who were in their 20's to 30's. They performed the same floor wiping tasks for all four feedback conditions (two minutes each), and answered the following questionnaire about their opinions of using our system under each condition using 5-point Likert scale (1: Strongly disagree, 5: Strongly agree) and free description.

- Question 1: "Did floor wiping become fun by using the system?"
- Question 2: "Was feedback information appropriate?"

Fig. 3. Experiment room

In addition, our system recorded log data during their wiping task to measure percentages of the number of wiped times.

3   Results and Discussion

3.1   The Effectiveness of Rhythm Game to Increase Fun

The results of Question 1 were used to confirm the effectiveness of the rhythm game to increase fun in floor wiping. We compared the results between two feedback conditions: no feedback and both auditory feedbacks in which the rhythm game was included. The results indicate that participants felt more fun with rhythm game than no feedback (Fig. 4).

3.2   The Effectiveness of Feedbacks to Support Complete Cleaning

Figure 5 shows the result of the questionnaire whether the feedback information was appropriate or not (Question 2). We compared the results among three feedback conditions: only tactile feedback, one auditory feedback (only 3D surround sound), and both auditory feedbacks (3D surround sound and rhythm game). The results indicate that the feedbacks were not appropriate because of the following reasons.

- The strength of vibration sometimes did not match the number of wiped times. The reason was that the markers attached to the wiper were hidden from the camera by furniture and the body of participants.
- It was hard to understand the direction of surround sound. The reason was that the change of position of the sound source was too fast.
- The tempo of rhythm game was too fast. The reason was that 150 BPM was set in all conditions.

In addition, we calculated the percentages of the number of wiped times (once, twice, and three times) over two minutes from the log data (Fig. 6). The results indicate that the participants wiped wider area with no feedback than with tactile or auditory feedbacks because they were distracted by the feedbacks.

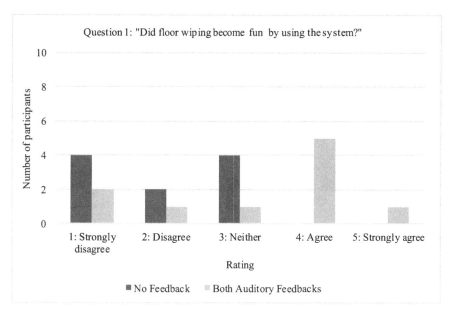

Fig. 4. Result of the questionnaire whether floor wiping becomes fun or not (Question 1)

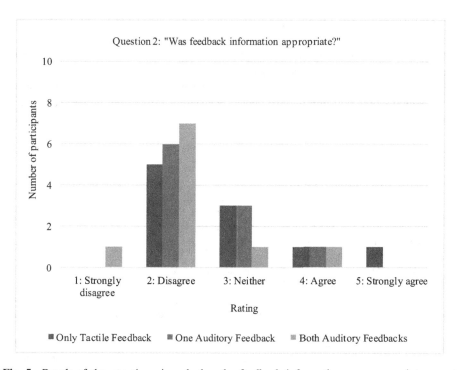

Fig. 5. Result of the questionnaire whether the feedback information was appropriate or not (Question 2)

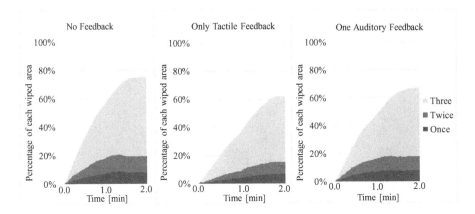

Fig. 6. Log data showing the percentages of the number of wiped times

4 Conclusion

In this research, we developed and evaluated a system to improve the experience value of floor wiping. The purpose of this research is to provide a system that supports a complete and enjoyable floor wiping with multimodal (tactile and auditory) feedbacks. The 3D surround sound and the vibration were used to present the unwiped area, and the rhythm game was used to enhance enjoyment in the floor wiping. From the experimental results, we confirmed that our developed system increase fun in floor wiping. On the other hand, the feedbacks for complete cleaning were still not appropriate due to the difficulty to understand the direction of sound, the mismatch between the strength of vibration and the number of wiped times, and the fast tempo of rhythm game. Future works will improve the detection accuracy of the floor wiper and perform further experiment to evaluate various feedback conditions.

References

1. Ichimura, S., Yazawa, T., Tomaru, S., Watanabe, H.: Attempt to make household chores gamification: application to cleaning. In: Multimedia, Distributed, Cooperative, and Mobile Symposium 2014, pp. 1285–1290 (2014). (Japanese)
2. Kosaka, T.: Monster Cleaners: a serious game using vacuum cleaners. Entertain. Comput. **2016**, 148–151 (2016). (Japanese)
3. Yamaki, T., Ogasawara, R., Siio, I.: Information presentation with interactive cleaner. In: The 78th National Convention of IPSJ (Interface), pp. 129–130 (2008). (Japanese)
4. Deterding, S., Sicart, M., Nacke, L., O'Hara, K., Dixon, D.: Gamification: using game-design elements in non-gaming contexts. In: Proceedings of CHI Extended Abstracts, pp. 2425–2428 (2011)
5. Alimanova, M., et al.: Gamification of hand rehabilitation process using virtual reality tools: using leap motion for hand rehabilitation. In: Proceedings of the 1st IEEE International Conference on Robotic Computing, Taichung, Taiwan, pp. 10–12 (2017)

6. Cikajlo, I., et al.: Telerehabilitation of upper extremities with target based games for persons with Parkinson's disease. In: 2017 International Conference on Virtual Rehabilitation (ICVR), pp. 1–2. (2017)
7. Robledo-Rella, V., García-Castelán, R.M.G., Medina, L., de Arellano, J.M.R., Guerrero, I.: CocoGame: a funny app to learn physics and math. In: 2017 IEEE Frontiers in Education Conference (FIE), pp. 1–4 (2017)
8. Fathoni, A.C.A., Delima, D.: Gamification of learning kanji with "Musou Roman" game. In: 2016 1st International Conference on Game, Game Art, and Gamification (ICGGAG), pp. 1–3 (2016)
9. Tanaka, H., Igaki, H. Inoue, H.: Vacuum sweep history visualization system. In: The 74th National Convention of IPSJ 2012(1), pp. 335–336 (2012). (Japanese)

Neural Generative Model for Minimal Biological Motion Patterns Evoking Emotional Impressions

Asuka Minami[✉], Hideyuki Takahashi, Midori Ban, Yutaka Nakamura,
and Hiroshi Ishiguro

Graduate School of Engineering Science, Osaka University, 1-3, Machikaneyama,
Toyonaka, Osaka 560-8531, Japan
{minami.asuka,takahashi,ban,nakamura,ishiguro}@irl.sys.es.osaka-u.ac.jp

Abstract. Humans can infer the body shapes, actions, and emotions of
an animal by observing a pattern of moving white dots. This phenomenon
is called "biological motion." However, at times, humans feel perceive
animacy even via motion patterns comprising more simple geometric
shapes, for example, a circle and a triangle. In this study, we attempted
to create generative models of biological motion patterns of up-down
circular motion with emotional expressions. We collected motion patterns created by naïve participants and attempted to devise generative
models that could generate biological motion with emotional expressions
based on the gathered data. Our result implied that generative models
of biological motion with emotional expressions may be acquired from
the collective creations of many individuals.

Keywords: Biological motion · Minimal design ·
Perception of animacy

1 Introduction

It is known that humans are capable of imagining the actions and emotions of
animals by simply observing moving patterns of geometric shapes. The movement patterns of multiple point lights were sometimes perceived as biological
motions of specific animal [1,2]. Furthermore, Heider and Simmel demonstrated
that movements of geometric shapes can be inferred to possess anthropomorphic
intentions and emotions [3].

The physical parameters of the moving patterns directly affect the strength
and content of imagined biological or anthropomorphic impressions. Tremoulet
et al. investigated how the strength of animacy perception was modulated by various parameters in the movements of geometric objects, for example, the shape,
velocity, and trajectory [4]. Takahashi et al. suggested that the low frequency
band (up to 2 Hz) tends to evoke animacy perception, and this frequency characteristic of animacy perception commonly exists among different perceptual
modalities (visual, tactile, and auditory) [5].

© Springer Nature Switzerland AG 2019
C. Stephanidis (Ed.): HCII 2019, CCIS 1032, pp. 378–384, 2019.
https://doi.org/10.1007/978-3-030-23522-2_49

We believe that these scientific findings contribute to the development of human-friendly anthropomorphic interfaces. However, quieter stimuli are required for the design of computer interfaces for daily use. We define quiet stimuli as one which will be familiar with daily life and will not make human feel annoying. With this motivation, in this study, we created a neural generative model for motion pattern with emotional expressions using only the up-down movements of one dot.

2 Participants for Training Data Collection

In the first stage, we collected motion patterns created by naïve participants for training the generative models.

2.1 Subjects

Fifty-three university students participated in this experiment. We recruited participants regardless of their expertise in art and/or creative performance. The experiment was planned in accordance with the requirements of the ethics committees of the Graduate School of Engineering, Osaka University. The intent and procedure of the experiment were explained to the participants before the experiment commenced, and they agreed to participate voluntarily after signing a consent form.

2.2 Software

We used a graphical motion builder to let the participants create motion patterns (Fig. 1). The white circle on the right of the screen moves up and down according to the time sequence indicated by the black line on the left of the screen. This software enabled the participants to create up-down motion patterns freely and intuitively. The motion pattern information was stored in a CSV file as a set of cycles and position coordinates of 226 pixels, which make up the black line.

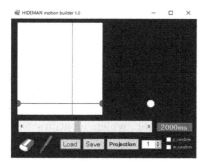 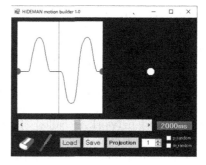

Fig. 1. Motion builder

2.3   Procedure

The participants were instructed to create the following types of motion patterns.

– Biological-Happy
– Biological-Sad
– Biological-Relaxed
– Biological-Nervous
– Non-Biological

In this paper, we refer to these themes as "Happy," "Sad," "Relaxed," "Nervous," and "Non-Biological" respectively. Each participant was asked to create a total of six patterns, two for "Non-Biological" and one each for the other themes. A total of about 15 min was provided to the participants to complete their respective patterns.

2.4   Results

A total of 318 patterns were collected. Three additional subjects observed and evaluated these motion patterns. In order to improve the performance of the generative model, we considered some of these samples as training data. This selection depended upon how well the movement matched the stated theme (Table 1).

Table 1. Samples used as training data

Theme	Quantity
Happy	48
Sad	45
Relaxed	51
Nervous	48
Non-biological	102

3   Generation Method

We trained the generative models using the collected data and evaluated new motion patterns obtained from the model. We used Wasserstein generative adversarial networks (WGAN-GP) [6], one of the derivative forms of GANs [7]. This method enables simultaneous learning. It involves two networks. The first network is called the generator, which generates data similar to the training data, and the second network is called the discriminator, which identifies the real training data from fake data by referring to the training data (Tables 2, 3).

We prepared as many GANs as the studied themes, namely 5 WGANs. The waveform of the sample data was resampled at 30 Hz to obtain a 120-dimensional waveform. Furthermore, the range of values in each dimension of this waveform

Table 2. Structure of the generator

Layer	Details
Input	Input: (10,1)
Dense	Output: (128, 1)
Batch normalize	-
Activate	ReLU
Dense	Output: (617,1)
Batch normalize	-
Activate	ReLU
Zero padding	
Convolution	Filters: 5 Filter length: 5 Stride: 1
Batch normalize	-
Activate	ReLU
Zero padding	-
Convolution	Filters: 1 Filter length: 20 Stride: 5 Outputs: (120, 1)

Table 3. Structure of the discriminator

Layer	Details
Input	Input: (120, 1)
Zero padding	-
Convolution	Filters: 50 Filter length: 5 Stride: 1
Activate	ReLU
Drop out	-
Dense	Output: (1, 1)

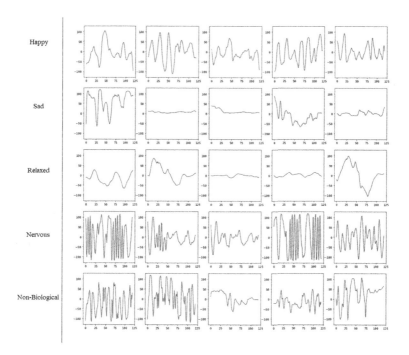

Fig. 2. Samples generated during the experiment

was normalized to $[-1, 1]$. The waveform obtained in this manner was used as training data. The generator considered 10-dimensional Gaussian noise as an input and outputted a 120-dimensional waveform as a motion pattern. Examples of the motion pattern generated by each generator after training are shown below (Fig. 2).

4   Evaluation Method

We conducted an evaluation experiment to assess whether the generative model obtained was appropriate.

4.1   Participants

Twenty-five university students participated in the evaluation experiment. We recruited participants regardless of their expertise in art and/or creative performance. The experimental procedure was planned in accordance with the requirements of the ethics committees of the Graduate School of Engineering, Osaka University. The intent and procedure of the experiment were explained to the participants before the experiment commenced, and they agreed to participate voluntarily after signing a consent form.

4.2   Stimuli

When the user presses the start button, a white circle moves up and down on the screen for 4 s according to the generated 120-dimensional waveform. The motion movie could be repeated if a participant so desired it.

4.3   Procedure

The participants were instructed to sit facing the wall on which the stimuli were presented. After watching the movements of one dot projected on the wall, they provided their respective impressions of the movement by choosing one of the following five options: "Happy", "Sad," "Relaxed," "Nervous," and "Non-Biological." This trial was repeated 50 times per person. Each motion pattern was evaluated by five participants.

4.4   Results

A confusion matrix was created using the answers obtained from the above experiment (Fig. 3). The result shows that samples other than "Sad" tend to elicit the intended impression most accurately. However, when all the answers of the participants were checked, it was found that "Non-Biological" accounted for 29.9% of all the answers. Thus, the result may be attributed to this biased choice towards the "Non-Biological" option rather than the performance of the generative model.

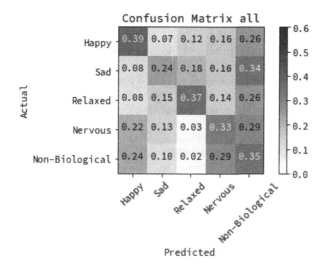

Fig. 3. Results of the evaluation experiment

5   Discussion

The results of the tests verified that the motion patterns generated by the generative model could be interpreted as intended to a certain extent. However, the accuracy of the estimation varied depending on the theme.

Referring to Russell's Ring [8], which is a two-dimensional model of emotion expressed by the indexes of arousal and pleasure, "Happy" and "Sad," and "Relaxed" and "Nervous" are diametrically opposite emotions. The results of the evaluation experiment show that at least these emotion pairs are less likely to be confused. This result implies that the neural generative model might be capable of acquiring the minimal essence of the studied emotional impressions from the motion patterns. However, additional research is required to confirm this.

We used five themes, "Happy," "Sad," "Relaxed," "Nervous," and "Non-Biological," but it is unclear whether the number and titles of these themes are appropriate for the experiments. Because the amount of information contained in one-dimensional motion is limited, the number of emotion types that can be estimated is also restricted. In this study, we adopted the choice-type answering format, but it is also necessary to devise or include another answering format, such as free descriptions requesting participants about their impressions on "what is being expressed?" or "what emotion do you feel?" We hope to expand the experiments accordingly in the near future.

References

1. Johansson, G.: Visual perception of biological motion and a model for its analysis. Percept. Psycho. **14**(2), 201–211 (1973)
2. Troje, N.F.: Decomposing biological motion: a framework for analysis and synthesis of human gait patterns. J. Vis. **2**(5), 2 (2002)
3. Heider, F., Simmel, M.: An experimental study of apparent behavior. Am. J. Psychol. **57**(2), 243–259 (1944)
4. Tremoulet, P.D., Feldman, J.: Perception of animacy from the motion of a single object. Perception **29**(8), 943–951 (2000)
5. Takahashi, K., Mitsuhashi, H., Murata, K., Norieda, S., Watanabe, K.: Frequency-dependence in haptic, visual, and auditory animacy perception. IEICE Trans. (Jpn. Ed.) **95**(4), 1048–1055 (2012)
6. Gulrajani, I., Ahmed, F., Arjovsky, M., Dumoulin, V., Courville, A.C.: Improved training of Wasserstein GANs. In: Advances in Neural Information Processing Systems, pp. 5767–5777 (2017)
7. Goodfellow, I., Pouget-Abadie, J., Mirza, M., Xu, B., Warde-Farley, D., Ozair, S., Courville, A., Bengio, Y.: Generative adversarial nets. In: Advances in Neural Information Processing Systems, pp. 2672–2680 (2014)
8. Russell, J.A.: A circumplex model of affect. J. Pers. Soc. Psychol. **39**(6), 1161 (1980)

Hierarchical Structuring of the Impressions of 3D Shapes Targeting for Art and Non-art University Students

Saki Miyai[1(✉)], Kenji Katahira[1], Masashi Sugimoto[1],
Noriko Nagata[1], Kunio Nikata[1,2], and Keigo Kawasaki[2]

[1] Kwansei Gakuin University, 2-1, Gakuen, Sanda, Hyogo, Japan
`saki-M@kwansei.ac.jp`
[2] Kanazawa College of Art, 5-11-1, Kodatsuno, Kanazawa, Ishikawa, Japan

Abstract. The spread of digital fabrication technologies such as 3D printers has increased opportunities to utilize 3D data. A support system for users without specialized knowledge must model the relationships between impressions received from shapes and the shapes' physical elements. Regarding the structure of impressions, previous works have hypothesized that a hierarchical structure with a lower layer closely related to physical parameters and an upper layer representing more abstract impressions. To extract the hierarchical structure of impressions for 3D shapes in this work, we conducted the Evaluation Grid Method to visualize an impression's hierarchical structure. Ten art university students and 10 non-art university students participated in the experiment and provided impressions they had formed from the 3D shapes presented as photographs. We extracted the hierarchical structure, including the impressions used in previous works in the upper side. The impressions representing the state and the features of shapes were extracted in the lower side. By classifying the language expressions representing the state and features from aspects of the shape's local features, the language expressions were classified into some similar viewpoints between participants' groups. While the language expressions representing abstract impressions varied between groups, and the language expressions related to "activity" were extracted only from art students. These findings revealed that there is not only a generality in the viewpoint strongly related to physical quantity but also differences based on knowledge and experience among individuals with regard to the more abstract impression.

Keywords: Kansei · Hierarchical structure · Evaluation grid method

1 Introduction

In recent years, the spread of digital fabrication technologies representing 3D printers has increased opportunities for personal fabrication. In addition, the development of information and communication technology (ICT) has made it possible to freely share the 3D data and knowledge required to create 3D models. Thus, the opportunities to utilize 3D data are increasing even for general users. However, utilizing 3D data requires specialized knowledge and skills, so it may be difficult for general users to

C. Stephanidis (Ed.): HCII 2019, CCIS 1032, pp. 385–393, 2019.
https://doi.org/10.1007/978-3-030-23522-2_50

create 3D models. On the other hand, even such general users express their feelings (Kansei) such as 'pretty' or 'soft' when they look at objects. Therefore, support for creating based on Kansei is considered effective. One example of support for creating based on Kansei is a proposal system for shapes that is close to the user's desired impression. Thanks to this system, general users can utilize 3D data more intuitively. This support system necessitates structuring the impressions (Kansei) that people receive from the shapes and grasping the relationships between Kansei and the physical elements of 3D shapes.

Regarding the structuring of Kansei, various previous works have hypothesized a hierarchical structure that shows the relationship between a person's psychological quantity and the physical elements of objects [1–4]. Although the hierarchical structure of Kansei hypothesized in these research has various names, a common point is that impressions and images are caused by physical elements and attitude, behavior and emotions that include such as 'favorite' are evoked. In this research, we define the hierarchical structure of Kansei consisting of three layers based on this common point: physical element, impression, and emotion as shown in Fig. 1. This hierarchical structure assumes a causal relationship between factors and results. The lower side shows the factor, and the upper side shows results evoked by the factor. We show the definition of each layer in order from the lower side. The physical element shows the physical parameter of stimuli. The impression layer shows the evaluation of the stimuli based on knowledge and experience. The emotion layer shows comprehensive evaluations of the stimuli, emotions, and attitudes based on comprehensive evaluations.

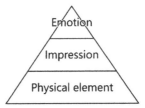

Fig. 1. The hierarchical structure of Kansei

2   Previous Work

Regarding evaluations based on Kansei, many works [3, 6–9] target various objects using Osgood's SD (Semantic Differential) method [5]. The SD method determines an impression of objects by evaluating the objects with adjectives (pairs of adjectives).

In the work considering the hierarchical structure of Kansei, Katahira et al. [3] conducted a experiment using the SD method for 3D shapes. As a result, the "Uniformity (Evaluation) Factor", the "Potency Factor" and the "Activity Factor" were derived as the main factors that related to the impression layer as shown in Table 3. They also extracted the main factor related to the attitude of preference in our emotion layer, and they modeled the relationship between the impression layer and the emotion layer.

The previous work revealed the relationship between the impression layer and the emotion layer but not the relationship between the impression layer and the physical element. It is difficult to expose the relationship between the impression layer and the physical element because the impression layer mixes concrete impressions strongly associated with physical element and abstract impressions strongly associated with the emotion layer. Understanding the relationship between the concrete impression and the abstract impression could reveal more details about the correspondence between the impression layer and the physical element.

3 Purpose

This work aims to clarify the impression's hierarchical structure. To extract the impression's hierarchical structure, we conduct an experiment with the evaluation grid method [10], which is a semi-structured interview. The evaluation grid method approach extracts the causal relationship between evaluations of what people perceive from object and what they evaluate from the percept. First, we focus on the participant's evaluation (language expression) of the object. By performing ladder-up to get an impression evoked from the language expression, we extract a comprehensive and abstract language expression. Alternatively, by performing ladder-down to get the factor of the language expression, we extracted an objective and concrete language expression. By performing ladder-up and ladder-down, we collect the causal relationship data between evaluations of objects. From the obtained data, we clarify the impression's hierarchical structure. We also investigate whether there is a difference in the impression layer's hierarchical structure depending on the presence or absence of production knowledge, for university students who have knowledge of art and university students who do not have knowledge of art.

4 Evaluation Grid Method Experiment for Extracting Causal Relationship of Language Expressions

4.1 Stimuli

The stimuli are 90 screenshots from 3D shapes' animations used in the previous work [3]. The screenshots were located where the shapes' features were considered most representative. We show the stimuli in Fig. 2. We presented 18 pictures per participant. In selecting 18 stimuli, to avoid variability in the similarity of stimulus set, we conducted a cluster analysis using the score for each stimulus obtained in previous work [3]. We selected almost the same number of picture at random from three obtained clusters and produced five sets with 18 pictures each.

Fig. 2. Example of screenshot

4.2   Participant

The participants are 10 university students majoring in art (art students) and 10 university students majoring in other (non-art students). Two participants from each student group evaluated for one stimulus set.

4.3   Procedure

Participants classified the stimuli into 3 to 7 groups in terms of "similar impressions". Next, they mentioned the "different impressions" between and within stimuli groups as far as they could think. By conducting ladder-up and ladder-down on the obtained language expressions, we extracted the causal relationships of the impressions of 3D shapes.

5   Extracting the Hierarchical Structure of Impression Layer

5.1   Analysis

Using E-Grid (a visual analytics system for evaluation grid method) [11], we conducted an analysis to categorize language expressions with the same meaning among the language expressions obtained from the participant groups. E-Grid can extract an evaluation structure diagram that is easy to interpret by setting a threshold to exclude language expressions whose contribution to the evaluation structure is small due to few

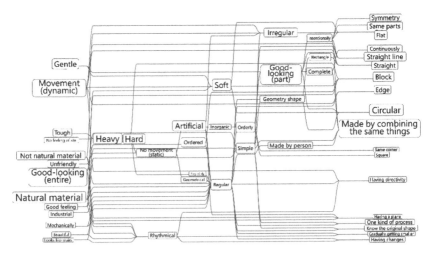

Fig. 3. Relationship diagram of impressions for non-art students

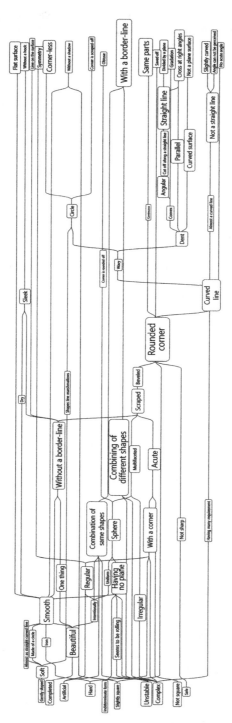

Fig. 4. Relationship diagram of impressions for non-art students

appearances and little connection with other language expressions. In this work, we set the threshold to 0.06, which includes less language expressions mentioned by only one person and more occurrences of categorized language expressions.

5.2 Result

We show the hierarchical structure of impressions for 3D shapes obtained by analyzing each participant group (Figs. 3 and 4). The left side of each figure shows the more abstract upper concept. The right side of each figure shows the more concrete lower concept. An item's size increases as its language expression is used more often. In the non-art university students' result, language expressions like 'symmetry', 'same parts' and 'squared' are obtained in the lower concept. Language expressions like 'unstable', 'soft' and 'hard' are obtained in the upper concept. In the art university students' result, language expressions like 'straight', 'square' and 'symmetry' are obtained in the lower concept. Language expressions like 'beautiful', 'heavy' and 'active' are obtained in the upper concept. These results showed that many impressions used in the previous SD method experiments [3, 6–9] appear as abstract impressions in the upper concept and that the states and features of shapes appear as concrete impressions in the lower concept.

6 Comparison of Language Expressions of Non-art University Students and Art University Students

6.1 Analysis

From the results of the hierarchical structure of impression layer for each participant group, we extracted the concrete impression that represented the state and feature of shapes and the abstract impressions such as adjectives used in the previous SD method experiment. To investigate which part of the 3D shapes participants viewed and evaluated, we classified the concrete impressions into 3D shape viewpoints.

6.2 Result

Table 1 shows the results of classifying the concrete impressions into the 3D shapes' viewpoints. The concrete impressions extracted from the non-art students' result were classified into eight viewpoints: Feature of shapes, Processing of corner, Outline of shape, Split into elements, Feature of element, Arrangement, Plane and Surface. The concrete impressions extracted from the art students' result were classified into six viewpoints: Feature of shapes, Processing of corner, Outline of shape, Feature of element, Arrangement and Plane. Because concrete impressions were classified into almost the same viewpoints among the participant groups, it is clear that there is no difference in the viewpoints when a person evaluates 3D shapes, regardless of their knowledge about creating.

The results of extracting the abstract impressions are shown in Table 2. The results show that the language expressions of competence used in the previous work [3], such

Table 1. The concrete impression and its viewpoint for each participants' group.

Art university students		
View point	**Impression representing state & features**	
Feature of shapes	Rectangle	Square
	Circular	Block
	Geometry shape	
Processing of corner	Edge	
Outline of shape	Straight	Straight line
Feature of element	Same parts	Same corner
	Made by combining	One kind of processing
	Same things	
Arrangement	Symmetry	
Plane	Flat	Having plane

Non-art university students			
View point	**Impression representing state & features**		
Feature of shapes	Sphere	Circle	Triangle
	Circle base	Similar to sphere	Not rectangle
	Rectangle	Cube	Not sphere
	Angular	Acute	Rounded corner
Processing of corner	Meet and form right angle	With corner	Scraped
	Acute angle	Corner less	Beveled
Outline of shape	Single line	Curved line	Not straight line
	Arc of circle	Billowing	
Split into elements	Single thing	Not single line	Without border line
	With border line		
Feature of element	Combination of different things	Combination of same things	Different shaped (parts)
	Same size	Same parts	
Arrangement	Symmetry	Overlapped	
Plane	Flat surface	Having plane	Multifaceted
	Divided by plane	Curved surface	Having no plane
Surface	Sleek	Thorny	Not dented
	Harsh	Gradation	Dented

Table 2. The abstract impressions of each participants' group.

Art university students			
Abstract impression			
Gentle	No movement (static)	Having changes	Soft
Unfriendly	Movement (Dynamic)	Intentionally	Inorganic
Tough	Not feeling of stir	Mot natural material	Orderly
Good feeling	Heavy	Natural material	Simple
Good-looking (whole)	Rhythmical	Hard	Having directivity
Beautiful	Irregular	Industrial	Know original shape
Ordered	Good-looking (part)	Mechanically	Geometrical
Regular	Made by person	Artificial	Exquisitely

Non-art university students			
Abstract impression			
Soft	Iron	Regular	Intentionally
Completed	Beautiful	Uniform	Irregular
Hard	Seems to be rolling	Unstable	Not sharp
Complex	Smooth	Safe	Artificial

as 'hard' and 'soft,' and the language expressions of evaluation, such as 'unstable' and 'irregular' are obtained from non-art and art university students. On the other hand, the art student results show language expressions of activities, such as 'with movement' and 'heavy' and language expressions of impressions they had of people, such as 'friendly' and 'cold'. Because the language expressions representing the abstract impressions differed depending on the participant groups, it turned out that there is a difference based on knowledge and experience regarding more abstract impressions.

7   Conclusion

The purpose of this work is to clarify the hierarchical structure of the impression layer and investigate the difference of impression depending on the presence or absence of knowledge and experience with creating. For these purposes, we employed the evaluation grid method to extract the detailed hierarchical structure of impressions for 3D shapes. Moreover, we compared the results between two participants' groups varied in that levels of knowledge and experience for creating, that is, non-art university students and art university students. As a result of analyzing the causal relationship of evaluation using E-Grid, the impressions used in previous SD method works were extracted as abstract impression in the upper side. The impressions represent the state and features of shapes were extracted as concrete impressions in the lower side.

While there was no difference between participants' groups in the concrete impressions, some differences between participants' groups were found for the abstract impressions. These results suggest the generality in the concrete impressions that are considered to be strongly related to the physical quantity, and the differences based on the knowledge and experiences in the abstract impressions. This work aid the development of a support system for users with less specialized knowledge and experience.

Appendix

See Table 3.

Table 3. The main factor of 3D shapes & adjective pairs in each factor in previous work [5].

Factor name	Adjective pairs			
Potency	soft – hard	weak – strong	smooth – rough	intense – mild
	relaxed – tense	distinct – vague	blunt – sharp	
Activity	active – passive	gay – sober	excitable – calm	delicate – rugged
	cheerful – cheerless	dynamic – static	heavy – light	
Evaluation	healthy – unhealthy	ordered – unordered	stable – unstable	connected – disconnected

References

1. Okamoto, S., Nagano, H., Kidoma, K., Yamada, Y.: Specification of individuality in causal relationships among texture-related attributes, emotions, and preferences. Int. J. Affect. Eng. 15(1), 11–19 (2015). https://doi.org/10.5057/ijae.ijae-d-15-00018
2. Chen, X., Barnes, C.J., Childs, T.H.C., Henson, B., Shao, F.: Materials' tactile testing and characterisation for consumer products' affective packaging design. Mater. Des. 30(10), 4299–4310 (2009)
3. Katahira, K., Muto, K., Hashimoto, S., Tobitani, K., Nangata, N.: The hierarchical approach to the semantic differential method. Trans. Jpn. Soc. Kansei Eng. 17(4), 453–463 (2018). https://doi.org/10.5057/jjske.tjske-d-17-00075
4. Yamada, A., Hashimoto, S., Nagata, N.: Automatic Impression Indexing based on Evaluative Expression Dictionary from Review Data. Trans. Jpn. Soc. Kansei Eng. 17(5), 567–576 (2018). https://doi.org/10.5057/jjske.tjske-d-18-00065
5. Osgood, C.E., Suci, G.J., Tanenbaum, P.H.: The nature and measurement of meaning. Psychol. Bull. 49(3), 197–237 (1952)
6. Takahashi, S.: Aesthetic properties of pictorial perception. Psychol. Rev. 102(4), 671–683 (1995)
7. Inaba, Y., Ishi, H., Kochi, J., Gyoba, J., Akamatsu, S.: Manipulating higher-order impressions of a class of 3D objects using the morphable 3D model: measurement of impressions by the SD method and psychological evaluation of the transformation. Inst. Electron. Inf. Commun. Eng. 109(28), 13–18 (2009)

8. Tanaka, Y., Oyama, T., Osgood, C.E.: A cross-culture and cross-concept study of the generality of semantic spaces. J. Verbal Learn. Verbal Behav. **2**(5–6), 392–405 (1963)
9. Kawachi, Y., Kawabata, H., Kitamura, M.S., Shibata, M., Imaizumi, O., Gyoba, J.: Topographic distribution of brain activities corresponding to psychological structures underlying affective meanings. Jpn. Psychol. Res. **53**(4), 361–371 (2011)
10. Sanui, J.: Visualization of users' requirements: Introduction of the Evaluation Grid Method. In: Proceedings of the 3rd Design and Decision Support Systems in Architecture and Urban Planning Conference, Japan, vol. 1, pp. 365–374 (1996)
11. Onoue, Y., Kukimoto, N., Sakamoto, N., Koyamada, K.: E-Grid: a visual analytics system for evaluation structures. J. Vis. **19**(4), 753–768 (2016). https://doi.org/10.1007/s12650-015-0342-6

Proposal of a Bin to Change Human Behavior with Positive Emotion

Masayuki Takahashi$^{(\boxtimes)}$ and Namgyu Kang

Future University Hakodate, 116-2 Kamedanakano, Hakodate, Hokkaido, Japan
{g2119023,kang}@fun.ac.jp

Abstract. In general, people need to remove plastic bottle caps when they throw away PET bottles. A preliminary survey found that 79% of plastic bottles were thrown away with the cap. This paper introduces an experiment which tried to encourage people to remove the cap before discarding the bottle. In the experiment, a separate bin for bottle caps was designed using "Fun Theory", which encouraged people to remove the caps without feeling bothered. It utilized a voting system. A prototype of this bin was created and placed in a public space within a university. Using this prototype, it was observed that 27% of plastic bottles were thrown away with the cap. Furthermore, a second improved prototype was developed which added sound effects. The second experiment was conducted to evaluate the users' experience when throwing away PET bottles. Results showed that participants enjoyed using the prototype and wanted to use it again. From the above, it was clarified that the proposed product was able to change human behavior through positive emotion.

Keywords: Kansei engineering · Fun Theory · Bin

1 Introduction

1.1 Background

Garbage separation can be troublesome for people. Although systems for garbage separation vary from town to town, it is generally necessary to sort waste into various types, such as burnable trash and non-burnable trash, plastic and PET bottles. PET bottles are, in Japan where this research took place, the common name for the plastic bottles containing drinks sold at stores, vending machines, etc.

According to a survey by Fumoto and Sakakibara (2002), university students have some knowledge of the environment. However, the percentage of people who can sort waste correctly is low [1]. Furthermore, according to a survey by Shinogi, Abe and Komatsu (2011), only about 20% of people answered that garbage separation is fun [2]. In other words, people need to separate garbage, but almost all people feel bothered by it.

© Springer Nature Switzerland AG 2019
C. Stephanidis (Ed.): HCII 2019, CCIS 1032, pp. 394–401, 2019.
https://doi.org/10.1007/978-3-030-23522-2_51

Ishihara and Nagamachi (2013) said: "Kansei is a collection of methodologies that support manufacturing from the perspective of human sensibility." (p. 1) [3]. There have been various successful attempts at changing human behavior with positive emotion.

The Fun Theory is an idea that the pleasure of positive sensitivity can change human behavior. There are many product productions using the Fun Theory. Piano Stairs is an example. Its steps are colored black and white like a piano keyboard and a sound is played when people walk on the steps. The number of people choosing the stairs over the adjacent escalator increased by more than 66% [4].

1.2   Research Purpose

The focus of this research is garbage separation; in particular the separation of bottle caps. The hypothesis is that a recycle bin using a voting action metaphor can encourage people to remove PET bottle caps with positive emotion. The purpose of this research is to verify the hypothesis and determine the usefulness of a recycle bin that promotes the removal of caps from PET bottles.

2   A Survey About Garbage Separation

2.1   A Survey About How Many People Know the Rule of Garbage Separation

According to an online questionnaire regarding waste separation that was answered by 3,442 Japanese people [5], 91.4% separated PET bottles from their trash, however only 41.1% removed the caps beforehand. However, it was possible that many people did not know the rules of garbage separation. Therefore, a survey was conducted in order to find out the percentage of people who know the rules of garbage separation.

This survey was conducted from November 5 to 6, 2018, targeting 32 university students living in Hakodate City in Japan. The questionnaires, created with Google Forms, were sent to respondents by e-mail. From the result of the questionnaire, about 53% of respondents answered that they knew the rules of garbage separation regarding plastic bottles.

2.2   A Survey About the Reality of PET Bottle Cap Separation

In this research, I propose a product to encourage people to remove caps from PET bottles when discarding them. It is necessary to obtain normal data as an evaluation criterion in order to evaluate whether the product can promote garbage separation. Therefore, a survey was conducted to get the data about the condition of PET bottles garbage separation.

This survey was conducted on 30 Future University trash bins in public areas from May 14 to 18, 2018. Twice a day at a fixed time, the discarded

PET bottles were retrieved and the number of bottles with removed caps was counted. As a result of this survey, it was found that of the 1079 PET bottles that were discarded in 5 days, 227 (approximately 21%) were without a cap (Fig. 1). Analysis of variance using the number of PET bottles with cap and without a cap was conducted (F (1,8) = 46.81, p <0.01).

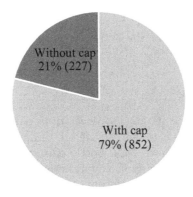

Fig. 1. The data about the condition of PET bottles garbage separation

2.3   Discussion

From the above results, the separation of plastic bottle caps is not done even if the rules of separation are known. It is assumed that this is because removing the cap is considered troublesome. Therefore, it was necessary to create a trash bin that encourages people to remove the cap, regardless of whether people knew the sorting rules, in order to increase the garbage separation rate.

3   Creating Prototype and Evaluation Experiment

3.1   Prototype1

Concept. In this research, based on the above mentioned Fun Theory, the author proposes a product which promotes the removal and recycling of caps from PET bottles, and compares it with the action of voting while discarding PET bottle caps. This product allows individuals to use the action of recycling their bottle cap to make a single vote on a simple question. Individuals make their vote by placing their bottle cap in one of two holes, each of which is connected to a separate half of the bin. The bin is transparent so everyone can see the results of the vote by looking at the number of bottle caps in the two halves of the bin.

Also, if there are too many voting items, it is considered that the voters feel stress when throwing away the plastic bottle cap. Therefore, this product is displayed two voting items.

In addition, this product is manufactured in approximately the same size to give a cohesive impression, as it is assumed that it will be installed with the trash cans used at Future University.

Structure. The material used was a transparent acrylic plate. Since the current recycle bins placed at the university where this research was conducted are at 22 cm wide, 32 cm deep, and 60 cm high, the prototyped recycle bin were manufactured to be almost the same size.

I used a 32 × 32 LED panel to display voting items which was easy to read even in the dark. The LED display program displays "Vote Me!" for 4 s, then "Which Do You Like?" for 4 s, and finally displays two voting items from right side to left side (Fig. 2). Instead of the static display using a board, I used dynamic display using LED panel because it is able to attract more attention to the user.

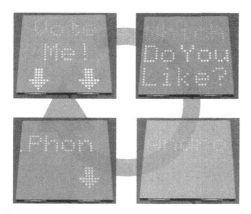

Fig. 2. The flow of LED panel

3.2 Evaluation Experiment 1

The product proposed in this study is based on the hypothesis that the trash bin using the metaphor of voting action can encourage people to remove PET bottle caps. Therefore, Evaluation experiment 1 was conducted to clarify how much the separation rate of PET bottle caps is increased compared to normal situation by using Prototype 1.

In this evaluation experiment, Prototype 1 was placed next to a recycle bin in the university on weekdays for 5 days (Fig. 3). The discarded PET bottles were retrieved and the average number of PET bottles with removed caps on one day was calculated. This evaluation experiment was conducted between June 26 and July 2, 2018. In addition, the data before this Prototype 1 was placed was 5 days on weekdays from May 14 to May 18 in the same place.

Fig. 3. Prototype 1 placed next to a recycle bin in the university

Result *Quantitative Evaluation.* The total number of PET bottles discarded in the standard recycle bin at the same location Prototype 1 was place before being placed this prototype was 56, and the number of PET bottles without cap was 3. That is, only about 5% of the caps were separated. After Prototype 1 was place, 82 PET bottles were thrown away at the same location, and 60 were uncapped. In other words, about 73% of the caps were separated (Fig. 4).

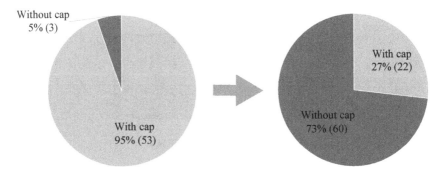

Fig. 4. Comparison between before placing Prototype 1 and after

Analysis of Variance. Analysis of variance was performed to clarify the effectiveness of Prototype 1 as a product that encourages people to separate PET bottle caps. From a result of the analysis, it became clear that there is a very significant difference in average $(F\ (1, 8) = 217.\ 90,\ p < 0.01)$.

Discussion. From the result of Evaluation experiment 1, the separation rate of the caps became much higher than before by placing Prototype 1. Furthermore, there is a very big difference in average before and after placing Prototype 1. In other words, it is judged that Prototype 1 was able to encourage people to remove PET bottles cap.

3.3 Prototype 2

Ideas to Improve Prototype 1. It is confirmed that Prototype 1 was able to encourage people to remove PET bottle caps by using the metaphor of voting action. However, Prototype 1 didn't have active interaction with users. Almost all attempts based on Fun Theory have active interaction with users and have good action acceleratory. Therefore, it is assumed that having an interaction is important to make Prototype 1 better.

I chose to use sound as the interaction between the user and the Prototype 2. It has been recognized that sounds and emotion have a deep relationship and it is said that listening to music may make people enjoyed [6]. Therefore, it is possible to give people positive emotion by making a reaction with some kind of sound when a plastic bottle cap is thrown away in Prototype 2. Thus, a sound is played when the plastic bottle is thrown away as an improvement plan.

In Prototype 2, a BlueTooth speaker was used in order to make a sound when the PET bottle cap was discarded. In addition, Prototype 1 had a transparent lid. There was a problem that the wiring used to control the LED panel could be seen by the user. Therefore, a low gloss black sheet was added to the lid for Prototype 2.

3.4 Evaluation Experiment 2

Evaluation experiment 2 was conducted to clarify whether users enjoyed using Prototype 2, wanted to use it again, and if it motivated them to recycle.

Evaluation experiment 2 was conducted for 2 days in 2019, targeting 30 university students. The participant was given a PET bottle and instructed to "discard the PET bottle". The participant discarded a PET bottle under two conditions: one without Prototype 2 (condition A) and one with it (condition B). "Dog" and "Cat" were selected as voting items. Each animal's sound was played using the mobile speakers connected to Bluetooth manually by experimenter when the participant voted. After the experiment, the participants answered a questionnaire regarding their feelings under the two conditions. Participants gave rankings on a five grade evaluation for 5 questionnaire items. Those were "pleasant", "easy to throw away", "troublesome", "wanted to use it again", and "wanted to separate". Finally, the participants wrote down the reason why they thought "pleasant" or "not pleasant" in free-form.

Result. Figure 5 shows the questionnaire results of all participants. As a result of the Evaluation experiment 2, it is clarified that condition B was evaluated higher than condition A in all items. In particular, the evaluation of condition B was very high in the items "pleasant", "wanted to use it again", and "wanted to separate".

From the answer of free-form of "pleasant" or "not pleasant", some participants were a little surprised by the sound. However, almost all participants using Prototype 2 answered that they enjoyed the sound effects.

Discussion. From the result of Evaluation experiment 2, it is judged that users enjoyed using Prototype 2. In addition, it is assumed that users had positive feedback for using Prototype 2 and separating garbage because the two items "want to use it again" and "want to separate" were highly evaluation. Furthermore, It is judged that there were few people who had a negative reaction even if they use Prototype 2 on a daily basis because the two items of "easy to throw away" and "troublesome" were positively evaluated.

In free-form answers, there are many descriptions related to sound. Therefore, it is judged that using sound as interaction with the user is useful. In addition, a participant wrote "it was fun to recycle in a natural way without being forced or reprimanded". From this statement, it is judged that the purpose of this research to change human behavior without feeling bothered was achieved.

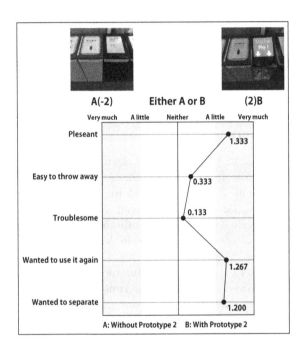

Fig. 5. The result of evaluation experiment 2

4   Conclusion and Future Perspective

4.1   Conclusion

This research has created a system which attempts to encourage people to remove the cap from PET bottles when discarding them.

From the evaluation results, it was revealed that Prototype 1 could greatly increase the separation rate of PET bottle caps. Furthermore, Prototype 2 included the addition of sound increased interaction between the user and the bin. From the Evaluation experiment 2, it became clear that the user enjoyed using this product. In other words, this product was able to encourage people to recycle PET bottle caps with a positive emotion.

From the above results, it is judged that the hypothesis recycle bins using a voting action metaphor can encourage people to remove PET bottle caps with positive emotion was proven true, and the effectiveness of this research is revealed.

4.2 Future Perspective

In this research, it was confirmed that a recycle bin that casts a vote based on Fun Theory promotes the removal of bottle caps, so it is planned to apply it to different situations and develop it further.

References

1. Fumoto, S., Sakakibara, N.: On Students' Consciousness for Segregating Home Trash (in Japanese). Kyoto University of Education Environmental Education Research Annual report No. 10, pp. 19–28 (2002)
2. Shinogi, M., Abe, K., Komatsu, Y.: The dilemma of social rationality between local governments and residents (in Japanese). Environ. Sociol. Res. **17**, 19–34 (2011)
3. Ishihara, S., Nagamachi, M.: Evolution of manufacturing and kansei engineering. Chugoku Reg. Res. Cent. **17**(2), 1–19 (2013). Special Issue: Kansei and Manufacturing) (in Japanese)
4. Unprofessional Development. https://unprofessionaldevelopment.org/portfolio/the-fun-theory/
5. DIMSDRIVE: http://www.dims.ne.jp/timelyresearch/2017/170314/
6. Ohgushi, K.: Music and emotion (in Japanese). J. Soc. Biomech. **30**(1), 3–7 (2006)

Expressing Segmentation in d-Comics

Xinwei Wang[1(✉)], Jun Hu[2], Bart Hengeveld[2],
and Matthias Rauterberg[2]

[1] Xi'an Jiaotong-Liverpool University, Suzhou, China
xinwei.wang@xjtlu.edu.cn
[2] Eindhoven University of Technology, Eindhoven, The Netherlands
{j.hu,b.j.hengeveld,g.w.m.rauterberg}@tue.nl

Abstract. Comics as a storytelling medium is constructed by panel sequences. The comics author defines how the panel sequences are segmented with specific storytelling intentions to enhance aspects such as: curiosity, suspense, surprise, emphasis, storytelling pace, etc. In printed comics, the intended segmentations are embodied because they are physically printed on the pages. However, different electronic devices that have different screen sizes and support different ways of interaction can all gain access to the same panel sequence of d-Comics (digital comics). Therefore, the question emerges how to express author intended segmentations in d-Comics. This article collects several design prototypes that explore the relationship between narrative structure, visual space, and interaction in d-Comics. Prototype 1 discusses how the background layer can express the segmentation. Prototype 2 explores how differences in movement speed of visual layers can express segmentation. Prototype 3 visualizes different shape changes when a reader interacts with the panel sequence to express segmentations. Prototype 4 explores different layouts of panels with interactivity linked to zooming in and out. And finally, prototype 5 uses spatial distance to show segmentations.

Keywords: Interactivity · Digital comics · Layout

1 Introduction

Comics as a storytelling medium is constructed by panel sequences [1, 2]. The comics author defines how the panel sequences are segmented with specific storytelling intentions to enhance aspects such as: curiosity, suspense, surprise, emphasis, storytelling pace, etc. In printed comics, the intended segmentations are embodied because they are physically printed on the pages. However, different electronic devices that have different screen sizes and support different ways of interaction can all gain access to the same panel sequence of d-Comics. Therefore, the question emerges how to express author intended segmentations in d-Comics.

Based on previous experiments [3, 4], we proposed a new vocabulary to describe how panels are segmented in d-Comics – Phasel:

A *phasel* (created by combining "phase" and "sequel") in d-Comics is represented by one panel or multiple panels that belong to each other. The author cannot

© Springer Nature Switzerland AG 2019
C. Stephanidis (Ed.): HCII 2019, CCIS 1032, pp. 402–409, 2019.
https://doi.org/10.1007/978-3-030-23522-2_52

decompose these further into smaller phasels. A phasel describes a strong relation among a certain number of panels and a significant difference with other phasels, determined by the author's interpretation.

2 Designed Prototypes

With the understanding of the vocabulary, we explored the design space of d-Comics with several prototypes. We created a twenty-four panels comics – Hedgehog Day – and identified eight phasels (Fig. 1).

Fig. 1. The twenty-four-panel-comics with 8 phasels.

2.1 Prototype 1: Background

The spatial arrangement as a panel segmentation strategy has several aspects such as the spatial distance between panels and different visual elements. To express a phasel gap, the common practice would be to increase the spatial distance of the phasel gap (Fig. 2).

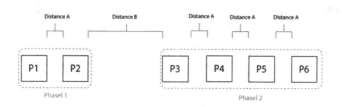

Fig. 2. Example of different distances between phasels.

Prototype 1 explores the "environment" aspect in the visual elements to express panel sequence segmentation. But instead of altering drawings inside panels, this prototype uses the space outside the panel. Each panel can be considered as one visual element, and the rest of the visual space displayed on the canvas would be the environment—since in the digital environment there can be different digital layers. Figure 3 illustrates the appearance of prototype 1. A panel sequence is placed horizontally on a virtual canvas. The background (environment) of Phasel 1 is wood grain, while the background of Phasel 2 is sand. When the reader scrolls through the panel sequence, the background changes based on the current phasel to which the current panel (the panel in the centre of the display) belongs to.

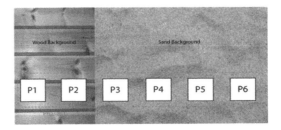

Fig. 3. An example of using differences in background to express segmentation.

The environment difference could be varied with other patterns. Different colours could also be applied for expressing the segmentation.

2.2 Prototype 2: Moving Speed of the Background

In the digital environment, images can be placed on top of each other in virtual layers. This is different from print comics where there is only one static layer, including the background. Moreover, in d-Comics interactions can be used to move between different layers. For example, the user could drag the background, while the foreground remains at the same place. One existing example of separating panel layer from the background layer is *The Boat* from Huynh [5]. The foreground layer contains the static panels, while the background layer is one animated sea image. Another example of using layers can be found in Stu's [6] *These Memories Won't Last*.

Fig. 4. A screenshot of Prototype 2

Figure 4 is a screenshot of Prototype 2, which has two layers: the foreground layer for placing the panels, and the background layer for the cloud image. The panels are the twenty-four panels created by the author of this article. The cloud image has been designed and programmed (using HTML, CSS and JavaScript) to occur constantly so that it appears as an infinite cloud background. The two layers all react to the same vertical scrolling input. When the reader scrolls the panels, the moving speed of the front layer remains the same. However, the background layer moves faster when it is a phasel gap, and slower when it is a normal panel gap. The reader can observe the differences only when interacting with the d-Comics. Once the interaction is stopped, both the foreground and background become static.

2.3   Prototype 3: Shape Change

The idea of this prototype is to consider the panel gap as a visible object. Figure 5 illustrates the mechanism of the prototype. Each panel gap has the same appearance when there is no input from the reader. The reader can scroll horizontally to move the panel sequence. In reaction to the reader's input, the visual gaps within a phasel change shape less dramatically than when there is a phasel gap. The visual effect is to mimic an elastic effect.

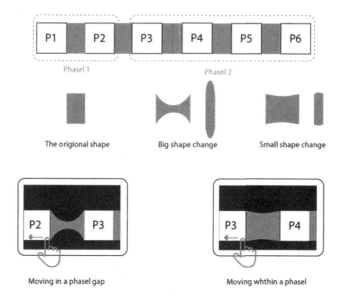

Fig. 5. A prototype in which different shape changes are used as the output to express segmentation.

2.4   Prototype 4: Zoom

Two existing examples of applying a zooming effect in d-Comics are McCloud's [7]. *The Right Number* and the zoom version of xkcd's *Click and Drag* adapted by Wesch [8]. Prototype 4 contains two sub-prototypes with different panel layouts: 4A and 4B (Fig. 5). The twenty-four-panel comics were applied with two different layouts. The prototypes were programmed with HTML, CSS and JavaScript. The zooming inter-action relies on the two "zoom in" and "zoom out" buttons located on the bottom right of the screen. Layout 1 starts with Panel 1 as the first stage. When zooming out, the presentation zooms to four, nine, sixteen and twenty-five panels in four steps. Layout 2 applies a zoom out starting from Panel 1 in the centre of the panel sequence, zooming to nine and twenty-five panels in only two steps. In both Layout 1 and 2, a guiding line has to be applied to indicate the reading order to the reader. The reason that the two layouts with the same zoom interaction require a different number of steps is that we have defined that each zoom in input should make at least one more panel visible. Then because of the different layout, the required steps to view a certain number of panels are different (Fig. 6).

Zoom layout 1

Zoom layout 2

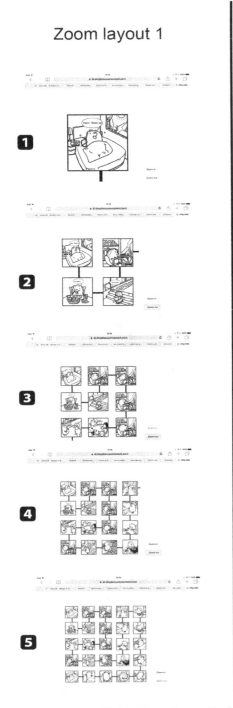

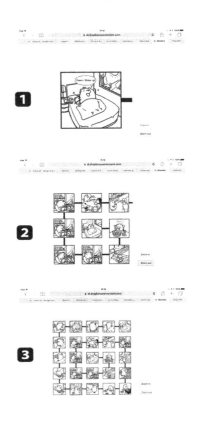

Fig. 6. Zoom layout 4A (layout 1) and 4B (layout 2).

2.5   Prototype 5: 3D Virtual Space

Prototype 5 aims to explore the three-dimensional virtual space. The author made 24 panels and identified eight phasels. The phasels were adopted and placed in three-dimensional virtual space in Unity. As Fig. 7 shows, panels that belong to the same phasel were placed horizontally on the x-axis, while different phasels were located vertically on the y-axis. By converting this setting with ARToolKit, we were able to experience reading d-Comics in Augmented Reality from a tablet. Figure 8 is a screenshot of the tablet used to read this prototype. The starting position was standing straight and holding the tablet perpendicular to the floor. By moving the tablet horizontally, we can see panels in the same phasel. By moving the tablet forward or backward, we can switch between phasels.

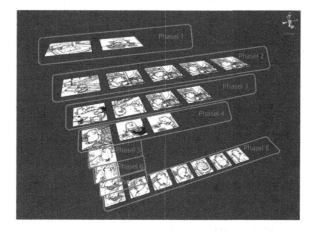

Fig. 7. An example of using the x-, y-, and z-axis to express segmentation.

Fig. 8. Screenshot of the augmented reality prototype made using unity and ARToolKit.

The problem of this prototype is that when a small phasel is on top of a large phasel (for example, Phasel 1 and Phasel 2), the large phasel won't be visually covered. Therefore, when reading Phasel 1, the reader can already see some panels in Phasel 2. One solution could be to use an angle between the phasels to separate them on different axes. For example, Fig. 8 shows a rebuilt 3D virtual space where the phasels are rotated 90°. The spatial arrangement will bring many interesting challenges, such as how to create a good 3D digital panel segmentation in virtual space (Fig. 9).

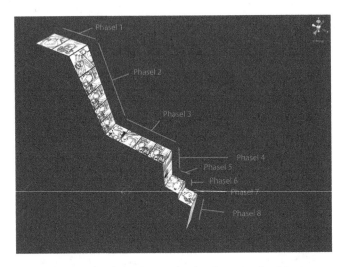

Fig. 9. Improved 3D scene where the rotation has been used to express segmentation

3 Conclusion and Future Work

To summarize, the prototypes described in this article explored the combination of visual space (the distance between panels, the background layer change of all panels, zoom in/out, virtual 3D space) and interaction (scrolling, dragging, moving the tablet in real space), with the purpose of expressing the panel sequence segmentations in d-Comics. The relation of segmentation with narrative structure, visual space and interaction can be described as tight and complex. This brings also the design space for exploring the storytelling possibilities. The future work will further explore how to bridge the author's storytelling intention with narrative structure, visual space and interaction.

Acknowledgements. The authors would like to thank the Chinese Scholarship Council and Eindhoven University of Technology for the support.

References

1. Eisner, W.: Comics & Sequential Art. W.W. Norton & Company Inc, New York (2008)
2. McCloud, S.: Understanding Comics. William Morrow Paperbacks, New York (1993)
3. Wang, X., Hu, J., Hengeveld, B., Rauterberg, M.: Segmentation of panels in d-Comics. In: Brooks, Anthony L., Brooks, E., Sylla, C. (eds.) ArtsIT/DLI - 2018. LNICST, vol. 265, pp. 28–37. Springer, Cham (2019). https://doi.org/10.1007/978-3-030-06134-0_4
4. Wang, X.: Segmentation of panels in d-Comics (doctoral dissertation). Eindhoven University of Technology, Eindhoven (2019)
5. Huynh, M.: The Boat. http://www.sbs.com.au/theboat/. Accessed 1 Mar 2019
6. Campbell, S.: These Memories Won't Last. http://www.sutueatsflies.com/portfolio/these-memories-wont-last/. Accessed 1 July 2017
7. McCloud, S.: The Right Number. http://scottmccloud.com/1-webcomics/trn-intro/index.html. Accessed 1 Aug 2016
8. Wesch, F.: A zoomable visualization of XKCD - Click and Drag. https://xkcd-map.rent-a-geek.de/#8/1.100/0.200. Accessed 1 July 2017

User Experience Evaluation of Intelligent Tunnel Digital Monitoring Interface Based on Cognitive Psychology

Lei Wu[1]([⊠]) [iD], Yao Su[1], Juan Li[2], Lijun Mou[1], Yue Sun[1],
Yekai Wei[1], Huai Cao[1,3], and Chong Feng[3]

[1] School of Mechanical Science and Engineering, Huazhong University
of Science and Technology, Wuhan, China
lei.wu@hust.edu.cn
[2] Department of Art and Design, Wuhan Huaxia University of Technology,
Wuhan, China
[3] Guangdong HUST Industrial Technology Research Institute, Dongguan, China

Abstract. This paper report on two experimental studies on digital monitoring interface to measure the user experience in intelligent tunnel monitoring system. Based on cognitive psychology theory, we conducted two experimental evaluation studies. The study 1 was using questionnaire method to explore and survey the end users. The study 2 was a comparative research study which were undergoing 7-point Likert user experience questionnaire. The prototypes of the study 2 were designed based on the study 1. Through the study 1 and study 2, we found that the target user needs of the digital monitoring interface were: (1) the interaction mode guided by logic of behaviors is more suitable for the design of tunnel data monitoring system; (2) professional background differences have lower significance on system availability; (3) data visualization should be different in different application scenarios. The research results can help us to deeper understand the design of digital monitoring interface in the related working scenarios.

Keywords: Digital monitoring interface · Cognitive psychology ·
User experience · Experimental evaluation · Interaction logic

1 Introduction

At present, the complex digital management system with the core of "internet of everything", "digitalization" and "user experience" has set off a new round of production revolution [1–3]. The "cyber-physical system" is an important carrier of this revolution. The cyber-physical systems have changed the way that humans manage the physical environment [4]. It is an intelligent control and management system that integrates computers and physical devices. In the era of traditional industrial development, computer-based digital interactive systems exist as analog control tools [5]. However, in the era of Industry 4.0, the digital physics system which is composed of computers, communication and control technologies can work together more reliably and efficiently [6]. The tunnel data monitoring system is a typical complex information

© Springer Nature Switzerland AG 2019
C. Stephanidis (Ed.): HCII 2019, CCIS 1032, pp. 410–417, 2019.
https://doi.org/10.1007/978-3-030-23522-2_53

physics system. As a system in the exploration and discovery stage, it is necessary to exquisitely design the demand characteristics, interaction characteristics and interface visualization direction.

2   Study1 - User Survey

2.1   Introduction

The tunnel data monitoring system is managed by the municipal operation and maintenance supervision department. The system mainly includes an operating system and a display system. Most of the operators are highly educated computer professionals and the age is generally younger. At the same time, the target group of the large-screen display function of the tunnel monitoring system is the inspectors.

2.2   Questionnaire Survey

Before designing the questionnaire, the author conducted interviews and investigations on the operation mode of the Guanggu Intelligent Tunnel Monitoring Platform of the Wuhan-Guangzhou Urban Construction Investment Development Group and the basic information and working conditions of the platform operators. The author learned the following points in the interview:

1. This system has been functioning as an iterative power;
2. The user's need for consistency in processing tasks is urgent;
3. The monitoring system has extremely high requirements for emergency handling;
4. The various visual expressions of the system are unreasonable.

Based on the above understanding, the staff of the data engineer and software engineer positions were selected as the experimental subjects for questionnaire survey. The subjects' selection requirements were: having a bachelor's degree or above, being engaged in or about to engage in data or background system related work. Finally, 37 valid questionnaires were received.

There are mainly four modules in the questionnaire design of tunnel data monitoring system: 1. basic information 2. suggestions about the product 3. the visual preference 4. operating habits. The specific content of the questionnaire is shown in the Fig. 1.

2.3   Date Analysis

Among the 37 valid questionnaires, there were 26 men, accounting for 70.27% of the total number of participants. In terms of educational level, there are 22 undergraduates, accounting for 59.46% of the total number of students. The rest are all bachelor's degree or above, generally high level of knowledge practitioners, the practitioners are generally high levels practitioners, and the subject is still undergraduates. 27 out of 37 people who participated in the survey were exposed to the data monitoring background

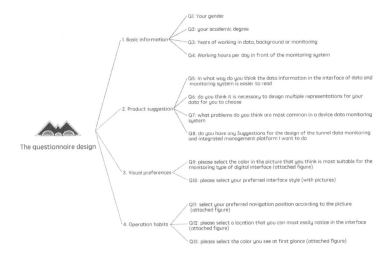

Fig. 1. The questionnaire design of tunnel data monitoring system

system for more than 5 h every day, accounting for 72.97% of the total number, and practitioners face computer work time at work is generally longer.

As shown in Fig. 2 and Table 1 that the problem points due to the difference in the working years are also different. The requirements of the interaction logic decrease with the increase of the working years; the requirements for the data presentation mode increase with the increase of the working years; the working years Longer people pay less attention to the loading time of data; in the problem of data classification, there is a "high-low-high" U-shaped curve; obviously, the problem of finding the desired data is more handy with the increase of working years; the requirements of information level problems have not changed much, but the trend is that the longer the working years, the smaller the problem; The inconsistency of task operation is the most prominent problem. the change is V-shaped, which is reduced from the initial 100% to 57% and then to 86% at the beginning of the year. Finally, at work for 3 years and above, up to 92% of the human eye. The design in this area is problematic.

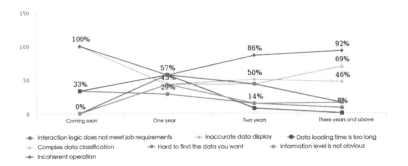

Fig. 2. Cross-sectional analysis of working years and outstanding problems

Table 1. Cross-analysis data sheet for years of work and outstanding problems

Working years	Interaction logic does not meet job requirements	Inaccurate data display	Data loading time is too long	Complex data classification	Hard to find the date you want	Information level is not obvious	Incoherent operation
Coming soon	1 (33.33%)	0 (0.00%)	1 (33.33%)	3 (100.00%)	0 (0.00%)	0 (0.00%)	3 (100.00%)
One year	2 (28.57%)	3 (42.86%)	4 (57.14%)	3 (42.86%)	4 (57.14%)	3 (42.86%)	4 (57.14%)
Two year	2 (14.29%)	7 (50.00%)	1 (7.14%)	6 (42.86%)	2 (14.29%)	2 (14.29%)	12 (85.71%)
3 years and above	1 (7.69%)	6 (46.15%)	0(0.00%)	9 (69.23%)	2 (15.38%)	2 (15.38%)	12 (92.31%)

From the above data cross-analysis results, we have found that some of the problems are caused by the short working years, so we filter and screen the problems. In design, we should focus on the most prominent issues, such as "inconsistent task operations", and we will seriously consider the problem of "inaccurate data presentation" and "complex data classification".

3 Study2 – Experimental Evaluation

3.1 The Service Blueprint Analysis

The advantages of the service blueprint are intuitive, easy to communicate, and easy to understand [7]. The system is divided into five levels, namely data acquisition layer, data conversion layer, data storage layer, data application layer and data access layer; users are divided into IT personnel, internal users (operators) and external users (inspectors). The chart reveals different information that can be accessed and the physical evidence in the operation for analysis. Through the service blueprint, the differences of responsibility between different users are clarified, which facilitates the information boundary of the system for different users and also provides the information they need for different users to avoid data confusion. As shown in Fig. 3.

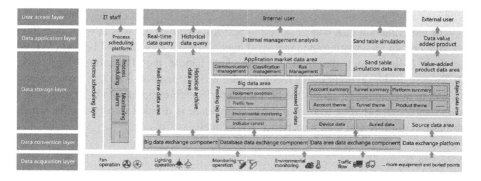

Fig. 3. The service blueprint of tunnel monitoring management system

3.2 Experimental Design

The subjects of this study were 10 undergraduate or postgraduate students in the department of industrial design and 10 graduate students in the department of computer science from Huazhong university of science and technology.

The experimental independent variables are: experimental materials and user background. Among them, the experimental materials independent variable is the System design based on logic of things and logic of behaviors (If "reasonable organizational behavior is used as the basis for decision making" as "logic of behaviors", then "the basis for decision-making that emphasizes the rational allocation of the property's own attributes" can be called "logic of things" [8]), as show in Figs. 4 and 5. The background of the user is divided into two directions, namely the computer background and the design background. The experimental dependent variable is the user experience score, and the five user experience evaluation indicators specified in ISO9241-11 are used.

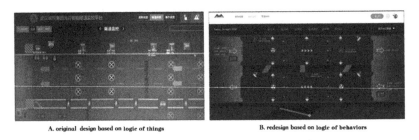

A. original design based on logic of things   B. redesign based on logic of behaviors

Fig. 4. Experimental materials of A&B interface

① Cursor searching   ② Browsing abbreviated information   ③ Entering the live details   ④ Checking a specific data

Fig. 5. Interactive prototype based on logic of behaviors

The experimental task was designed to perform two typical tasks at work: handling hazard alerts and navigating the inner workings of a tunnel, as detailed below: (1) Find the fault light, output the fault problem, and handle the dangerous alarm task. (2) Browse inside a tunnel and record problem information. And the experimental evaluation questionnaire adopts the 5E user experience questionnaire (1–7 rating and 7 is very satisfied) [4]. The design of the questionnaire is divided into two parts, which are basic questions and user experience respectively.

3.3 Data Analysis

The results of the questionnaire were analyzed by SPSS statistical analysis using descriptive analysis and correlation analysis, the specific experimental results were obtained as follows (Fig. 6):

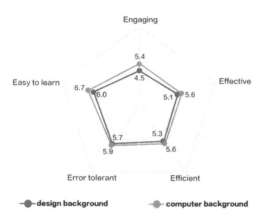

Fig. 6. Comparison of the average scores of experiences of different background users on improved system

From the scores of various experience indicators as show in Fig. 5, it can be seen that the user experience of different professional backgrounds is very close, but the design background of the subject is more strict on the user experience. The improved system was highly evaluated on "easy to learn" and "error tolerant" that is proved that in this survey, different information channels are given for different user types, and the behavioral line of the operation task is used as interactive logic to suit the background of system design.

Table 2. The correlation analysis

Engaging	Correlation coefficient	−0.388
	Pearson correlation	0.091
Effective	Correlation coefficient	−0.344
	Pearson correlation	0.137
Efficient	Correlation coefficient	−0.224
	Pearson correlation	0.342
Error tolerant	Correlation coefficient	−0.134
	Pearson correlation	0.574
Easy to learn	Correlation coefficient	−0.482
	Pearson correlation	0.031

As show in Table 2 that correlation analysis is used to study the correlation between the fault-tolerant ability of attraction efficiency and the lack of professional differentiation, pearson correlation coefficient is used to indicate the strength and weakness of the correlation. The specific analysis shows that: the correlation values between the effectiveness and efficiency of attractiveness were -0.388, -0.344, -0.224, -0.134, both close to 0, and the P value was >0.05, It shows that there is a significant negative correlation between majors and ease of learning. According to the statistical data, the computer background is easier to learn the system.

3.4   Conclusion

Through quantitative evaluation of user experience and through correlation analysis using SPSS, the conclusion is drawn as follows:

(1) The independent background of the subject's background has little influence on the user experience. Therefore, designers should pay attention to the commonality of people's cognition to guide the design of information physics system.
(2) According to the survey, the user experience of the tunnel monitoring management system designed with interaction base on logic of behaviors is better than interaction base on logic of things. The results of this survey provide a reference for the similar cyber-physical systems design.

4   Results and Discussion

Due to the rapid development of the Internet of Things and smart cities, our demand for information management systems has also changed dramatically. The first change is reflected in "visual usability", and the proper expression and information guidance of a large amount of data is particularly important. Secondly, the interactive characteristics of data information should be more concerned. The choice about logic of things and logic of behaviors has different effects on the use of the system. The ease of use of the digital interactive interface and the efficiency of processing each task can also greatly enhance the user experience of the system. The design of an excellent physical information system urgently requires an interactive experience, cognitive psychology, and visual visualization to be put on the agenda.

In summary, through the design survey, it is found that the overall design of the data monitoring and management system of the cyber-physical system should be based on the effective communication of information and the high consistency of the main operational tasks. From the perspective of researching a mental model that meets user expectations, we can develop products with clear logical relationships and satisfying users.

At the end, some content of this article can be extended. First of all, the subjects were only in the high-knowledge group throughout the survey, it has not been explored for a wider population. Secondly, the collection of experimental materials and experimental data is not obtained in the real use of the scene, and the user behavior is greatly affected by the scene, emotion, etc., which may have an impact on the experimental results. Finally, with the development of big data, the exploration of data application products must be forward, it is hoped that through sufficient practice exploration and induction and can obtain design rules that can be widely used.

Acknowledgments. The research financial supports from the Natural Science Youth Foundation of Hubei Province (Project No: 2017CFB276), Hubei Provincial Teaching Research Project (Project No: 2017055), Hubei Provincial Department of Education Humanities and Social Sciences Project (Project No: 18G002), Program of Introduction of Entrepreneurial Talents in Dongguan.

References

1. Blažević, N.: Internet of everything. Mob. Inf. Syst. **2017**, 1–3 (2017)
2. Yuan-Zhuo, W.: Network big data: present and future. Chin. J. Comput. **36**(6), 1125–1138 (2013)
3. Hassenzahl, M., Tractinsky, N.: User experience - a research agenda. Behav. Inf. Technol. **25**(2), 91–97 (2006)
4. Wen, J., Wu, M., Su, J.: Cyber-physical system. Acta Autom. Sin. **38**(4), 507–517 (2012)
5. Liu, C., Xu, X.: Cyber-physical machine tool-the era of machine tool 4.0. Procedia CIRP **63**, 70–75 (2017)
6. Khan, M., Wu, X., Xu, X., Dou, W.: Big data challenges and opportunities in the hype of industry 4.0. In: IEEE ICC 2017. IEEE (2017)
7. Bitner, M.J., Ostrom, A.L., Morgan, F.N.: Service blueprinting: a practical technique for service innovation. Calif. Manag. Rev. **50**(3), 66–94 (2008)
8. Xin, X.: Interaction design: from logic of things to logic of behaviors. Art Des. **261**(1), 58–62 (2015)

Using Ergonomics in Adjustable Switch Panel Design

Chii-Zen Yu[1,2(✉)], Fong-Gong Wu[1], and Huan-Ting Chang[3]

[1] Department of Industrial Design, National Cheng Kung University,
Tainan, Taiwan
ycz@mail.toko.edu.tw
[2] Department of Animation and Game Design, TOKO University,
Chiayi, Taiwan
[3] DaWan High School, Tainan, Taiwan

Abstract. In the field of ergonomics, compatibility is defined as the level of consistency between human expectations and the reality of the relationship between a controller and the controlled component. Therefore, compatibility enhancement is a critical factor that must be considered when designing a system. Researchers have confirmed that when the controller and controlled component are physically similar, their performance (i.e., response time, error rate, and information leakage) is optimal. The objective of this study is to enhance compatibility by applying an adjustable switch panel for decreasing the error rate during operations. An adjustable switch panel combines the switch buttons of the electric light, fan, and other commonly used electric appliances in the same switch panel. The switch buttons are fixed on the switch panel, which is assembled according to the position of the appliances, and a blank button indicates that there is no corresponding appliance. The switch panel can be freely matched and assembled. It can also be arranged according to the available space; moreover, illustrations of the electric light, fan, and appliances atop the switch button enable users to instantly identify the switch buttons. This design also enables several users to use the pane list down the advantages and disadvantages, which can serve as a reference for further design revisions.

Keywords: Ergonomics · Compatibility · Adjustable switch panel

1 Introduction

Compatibility is defined as the level of consistency between human expectations and the reality of the relationship between a controller and the controlled component. Thus, compatibility enhancement is a critical factor that must be considered when designing a system. Compatibility can be categorized into concept compatibility, mobile compatibility, spatial compatibility, and pattern compatibility. Current research on compatibility can be summarized as follows. Fitts and Seeger confirmed that when the display unit and controller are physically similar, their performance (i.e., response time, error rate, and information leakage) is optimal [1]. Researchers have investigated the error rates incurred by operating various combinations of control switches and stoves [2, 3]. Others have compared approaches that are based on Warrick's principle, scaled ipsilateral

© Springer Nature Switzerland AG 2019
C. Stephanidis (Ed.): HCII 2019, CCIS 1032, pp. 418–421, 2019.
https://doi.org/10.1007/978-3-030-23522-2_54

principle, and right-handed increase principle [4, 5]. Studies have demonstrated that when the aforementioned principles are consistent, the stereotype response of the subject is stronger. Osborne and Ellingstad added a sense line connection between the control knob and the hob to reduce the error rate of control [6].

The objective of the invention described in the present paper is to enhance compatibility by implementing an adjustable switch panel for decreasing the error rate during operations. The aims of this study were to improve spatial compatibility by sensing the design of the cue, reduce the error rate of manipulation, and assess the degree of spatial compatibility improvement.

2 Adjustable Switch Panel Design

Most controllers and controlled components in public places do not follow the principle of spatial compatibility. Because the control panel is designed in a fixed form, users can only operate the controlled components by adopting the trial-and-error method.

The designed adjustable switch panel with wall attachment follows the spatial compatibility principle. Specifically, each button on the control panel corresponds to a controlled component (e.g., ceiling lights and fans). The research team analyzed user experience of the designed panel to evaluate the improvement in spatial compatibility provided by this panel.

Adjustable switch panels can be classified into two according to the spatial relationship between the controller and controlled components. In the first type, the controller and controlled components are designed on the same plane. A common example is the broadcast system used in a computer classroom, in which the broadcast system is the controller and computers are the controlled components. The spatial compatibility is designed to equivalently arrange the controller and controlled components. In the second type of panel, the controller and controlled components are designed on a vertical plane. Common applications of this design are ceiling lights and fans in a classroom, where the switch panel on the wall is the controller and the lights and fans on the ceiling are the controlled components. Generally, in this type of spatial compatibility, the controller and controlled components are arranged in mirror symmetry.

On the basis of feedback from 10 users, the research team enhanced the controller–components compatibility of the adjustable switch panel designed in this study (Fig. 1). The design process was as follows: an adjustable switch panel was developed to create spatial compatibility between the controller and controlled components. The design was then applied to commonly used ceiling lights and fans. Each button on the panel corresponds to the relative position of the actual fan or light that it controls. The buttons have simple icons that inform users of their corresponding controlled components (Fig. 2).

According to the results of a cognitive analysis of spatial compatibility among 10 users, two types of cognition were identified: reflection (90%) and translation (10%). Two methods were adopted to enhance the spatial compatibility of the designed panel: 1. the control button and its corresponding controlled component were labeled with the same color; 2. the included angle between the plane of the controller and the plane of the controlled component was reduced. After these methods were implemented, the cognition results of the 10 users were all reflection (100%).

Fig. 1. Adjustable switch panel

Fig. 2. Adjustable switch panel and controlled component

3   Conclusions

We designed an adjustable switch panel in which each button on the control panel corresponds to a ceiling light or fan (controlled component) according to the principle of spatial compatibility. This panel has the following advantages:

1. According to feedback provided by users, the spatial compatibility between the controller and controlled components was improved.
2. Users were provided with a signal (label color or included-angle reduction), which improved their cognitive consistency toward spatial compatibility.
3. The designed panel can be connected to a touch screen or smartphone, thereby increasing the operational flexibility of the system.

References

1. Fitts, P.M., Seeger, C.M.: S-R compatibility: spatial characteristics of stimulus and response codes. J. Exp. Psychol. **46**(3), 199–210 (1953)
2. Chapanis, A., Lindenbaum, L.: A reaction time study of four control-display linkages. Hum. Factors **1**(1), 1–7 (1959)
3. Ray, R.D., Ray, W.D.: An analysis of domestic cooker control design. Ergonomics **22**(4), 1243–1248 (1979)
4. Brebner, J., Sandow, B.: The effect of scale side on population stereotype. Ergonomics **19**(5), 571–580 (1976)
5. Petropoulos, H., Brebner, J.: Stereotypes for direction-of-movement of rotary controls associated with linear displays: The effects of scale presence and position, of pointer direction, and distances between the control and the display. Ergonomics **24**(2), 143–151 (1981)
6. Osborne, D.W., Ellingstad, V.S.: Using sensor lines to show control-display linkages on a four burner stove. In: Proceedings of the Human Factors Society, 31st Annual Meeting, pp. 581–584. Human Factors and Ergonomics Society, Santa Monica (1987)

Novel Design of the Music Operation Interface

Chii-Zen Yu[1,2(✉)] and Fong-Gong Wu[1]

[1] Department of Industrial Design, National Cheng Kung University,
Tainan, Taiwan
ycz@mail.toko.edu.tw
[2] Department of Animation and Game Design, TOKO University,
Chiayi, Taiwan

Abstract. Smartphones have become popular in recent years. With the development of various smartphone applications (apps), smartphone functions are becoming increasingly advanced. However, functions are limited by the area of the smartphone screen, meaning that some apps are less convenient to operate. App designers can change the interface of an app to enhance operational convenience. This study presents a new music operating interface design concept and designed a smartphone app. This concept is an electronic instrument or music operating interface (such as for application in smartphones, flat panel computers, or other electronic products). The right hand plays the melody, and the left hand adjusts the octave. The app may also simply play all of the notes of a given song to facilitate user learning. This study recruited several participants to use the designed app and note its advantages and disadvantages, which can serve as a reference for revised designs.

Keywords: App · Smartphone · Music operation interface

1 Introduction

Technology can have life-changing influences. An increasing number of people use mobile electronic devices such as smartphones. The user of a smartphone can download applications (apps) with various functions. Among them, virtual keyboard apps are often downloaded to simulate the activity of playing an actual keyboard. The operations of the keyboard can affect users' intention to use the app.

The piano is a type of keyboard instrument used in Western classical music. It was formerly an ancient piano. It is commonly used for solo, ensemble, accompaniment, and other performances and is highly convenient for music composition and rehearsal. When pressing the keys on the keyboard, the player touches the muslin in the piano, which then taps the wire string to produce a sound. The piano has a wide range of sounds (88-degree range), and its tones are loud, crisp, rich, and varied.

The keyboard has a rich library of sounds that simulate various instruments. Players can select the appropriate sound, rhythm, and chords according to the needs of the music to produce a variety of performances. Part of the performance of the keyboard is fulfilled by automatic chord accompaniment. The pronunciation principle of a keyboard app is similar to that of the keyboard, but it is limited by the area of the smartphone screen, thus rendering the operation of existing keyboard apps less

C. Stephanidis (Ed.): HCII 2019, CCIS 1032, pp. 422–425, 2019.
https://doi.org/10.1007/978-3-030-23522-2_55

convenient. App designers can change the operating interfaces of the apps to increase operational convenience. The purpose of this study was to create a new keyboard app (in chord input mode) and propose a new keyboard app operating interface. In the chord input method, two or more buttons can be pressed simultaneously to achieve an output; this can reduce the number of required buttons. Ten participants were recruited in this study to compare the advantages and disadvantages of the existing input mode and chord input mode.

Each input device has unique characteristics and may not be suitable for all products. Inappropriate input tools can lead to inefficiency [1]. Therefore, for the input requirements of mobile products, it is necessary to provide a suitable new mobile input method and investigate its performance [2–5]. This study used a keyboard app to study mobile products and compare existing input methods with a new chord input method. The goal was to identify the optimal input method for improving input efficiency and accuracy.

2   Novel Design of the Music Operating Interface

Keyboard apps are available on the App Store and Google Play for users to write or play a song similar to how they would when playing an actual keyboard. As simulator apps, virtual keyboard apps generally have two types of interfaces. The first design (Interface A) presents a fixed keyboard with a range of 11 notes (Fig. 1). The other design (Interface B) exhibits a movable keyboard with a range of 52 notes in which users can slide the screen to switch between octaves. Although the use of Interface A is simple with high input accuracy, the player cannot play an entire song in most cases because of the limited range. By contrast, the range of Interface B allows the user to play a complete song, but the player must slide the keyboard to play in different octaves, resulting in lower input accuracy. To identify a solution for the aforementioned drawbacks, this study designed a novel keyboard app (Fig. 2).

Fig. 1. Keyboard app Interface A

Fig. 2. Keyboard app Interface B

The novel design can be applied to develop both actual instruments and keyboard apps. When using the designed app, users can play melodies with their right hands (the screen presents notes of a C major scale) and switch between octaves with their left hands (each button denotes a different octave). By simultaneously pressing a button and key, users can play notes in any octave. The operations are thus simple (Fig. 3). A total of 10 participants used the designed app and recorded the advantages and disadvantages they experienced while using the app, which can serve as a reference for future improvements. The designed app has a range of 49 notes and a fixed keyboard interface (Fig. 4). This range can be expanded by adding more octave buttons on the left.

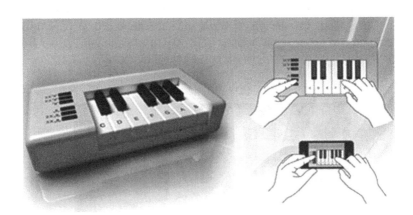

Fig. 3. Design concept of the novel app interface

Fig. 4. Keyboard interface of the designed app

3   Conclusions

The feedback provided by 10 participants after using the novel keyboard app and two existing keyboard apps is summarized as follows:

1. The app with Interface A demonstrates simple use with high input accuracy. However, the range is narrow. Consequently, most songs cannot be played in their entirety, resulting in limited usability. Conversely, the range of the app with Interface B is sufficiently wide and enables the user to play a complete song; however, the app has a lower input accuracy because the user must slide the screen to switch between octaves.
2. The novel keyboard app has a fixed keyboard with 49 white keys (a C major scale on the screen), and the user can switch between octaves using buttons provided on the left. The range can be expanded by adding more buttons for other octaves. Nevertheless, the current range is sufficiently wide for the user to play most songs.
3. For the novel keyboard app, users reported higher efficiency and accuracy when using numbered musical notation compared with Western musical notation.

References

1. Nishinaka, Y., Tsujino, Y., Tokura, N.: A pointing method for graphics. Syst. Comput. Jpn. **21**, 13–22 (1990)
2. Wu, F.G., Luo, S.: Design and evaluation approach for increasing stability and performance of touch pens in screen handwriting tasks. Appl. Ergon. **37**(3), 319–327 (2006)
3. Applied Ergonomics **37**(5), 629–639 (2006)
4. Wu, F.G., Huang, H.Y., Chen, C.H.: Chord input arrangement for the mobile computer. In: 11th International Conference on Human-Computer Interaction. Las Vegas, USA, file 87 (2005)
5. Wu, F.-G., Chen, Chun-Yu., Chen, C.-H.: Improvements of chord input devices for mobile computer users. In: Stephanidis, C. (ed.) UAHCI 2007. LNCS, vol. 4555, pp. 1026–1035. Springer, Heidelberg (2007). https://doi.org/10.1007/978-3-540-73281-5_112

Reasons and Measures of Low Work Quality of Airlines Safety Manager Based on SHELL Model

Yuan Zhang[✉], Yanqiu Chen, Yijie Sun, and Rong Zhao

Aviation Safety Research Division China Academy of Civil Aviation Science and Technology, Engineering and Technical Research Center of Civil Aviation Safety Analysis and Prevention of Beijing, Beijing, China
zhangyuan@mail.castc.org.cn

Abstract. The low work quality of safety manager seriously affects the safe operation of airlines, and there are few studies on this issue at present. Through the investigation and SMS audit of airlines, the types of low work quality of safety managers are summarized, and some examples are given. Based on SHELL model, the specific reasons for the low work quality of safety manager are analyzed in detail from five aspects, which are software, hardware, environment, collaboration and safety manager themselves. For these reasons, specific measures to improve the work quality of safety manager are put forward from five aspects, which are cultural construction, clear responsibilities, personnel recruitment, supervision and incentive mechanism, and safety management tools.

Keywords: Work quality · Safety management · Airlines · SHELL

1 Introduction

Safety is an important foundation and guarantee for the smooth and healthy development of air transport industry. With the rapid development of air transport industry, airlines pay more and more attention to safety management. In terms of safety management, resources have been invested, including personnel, equipment, funds and so on.

At present, airlines are equipped with safety manager. However, although safety managers carry out daily safety management, the quality of their work is low, and they fail to give full play to the role of safety protection.

Through literature collection and analysis, the following are found:

Firstly, in the field of air transportation, academia mainly studies the human factors in the aviation operation, including flight operation, aircraft maintenance, dispatch and release, aircraft design, air traffic management, airport operation, and carries out an analysis of the human factors in aircraft accidents. Ref. [1] mainly carries out human factor training and pilot psychology evaluation in hainan airlines. The psychological quality of pilots and the training of human factors are studied. Ref. [2] mainly carries out human factors analysis of aviation maintenance errors based on structural bayesian equation model. Ref. [3] mainly carried out human factor analyses on dispatch based

© Springer Nature Switzerland AG 2019
C. Stephanidis (Ed.): HCII 2019, CCIS 1032, pp. 426–432, 2019.
https://doi.org/10.1007/978-3-030-23522-2_56

on AHP. Ref. [4] mainly carried out preliminary human factor evaluation model on display color set in civil aircraft flight deck. Ref. [5] mainly carried out design of physical sign data collection system for human factors. Ref. [6] mainly carried out analysis and suggestion of midair collision accident based on HFACS. Ref. [7] mainly carried out a simulation study of human risk infection behavior in airport flight area. Ref. [8] mainly carried out study on ECAR model for human error analysis of aviation accident/incident.

Secondly, there is less research and analysis on the work quality of civil aviation safety manager. Refs. [9, 10] mainly study on competency model of safety manager in civil aviation operation organizations.

Through literature collection and analysis, there were in-depth study on the operational safety problems in airlines, but there was not a comprehensive and in-depth analysis and research on the reasons for the low work quality of safety manager in airlines. It is of great significance to carry out in-depth analysis the reasons for the low work quality of airlines safety manager and put forward targeted improvement measures for improving airlines safety management.

2   Specific Manifestations of Low Work Quality of Safety Manager

Through SMS auditing the safety management of several airlines, the main manifestation of the low work quality of safety manager is following.

1. The output of safety management is not in conformity with the actual safety situation, and fails to find out the safety problems in operation comprehensively and pertinently. For example,

- Safety inspection. Safety manager carry out safety inspection in accordance with the regulations. However, through safety inspection, no actual safety problems in operation have been found, or only some safety problems have been found. The results of safety inspection are inconsistent with the actual situation.

2. The safety management is not deep enough. It only pays attention to the appearance, but fails to find and deal with the safety problems at the organizational and system levels. For example,

- Incident investigation. After the occurrence of unsafe incidents, the results of the investigation failed to find out the real cause of the incidents. Or fail to find out the problems at the organizational level.

3. The effectiveness of safety management is not high, and the actual safety problems can not be thoroughly solved. For example,

- Risk control. Despite the implementation of some risk control measures, after the implementation of the measures, the risk has not really been reduced to an acceptable level.

- Safety training. Although safety training has been carried out for employees, the technical level and management ability of employees have not been effectively improved.

4. There is some meaningless safety management, which consumes safety management resources. For example,

- Safety information collection without clear purpose. Because there is no clear purpose of collection and specific information analysis method in advance, there is no further information analysis in the follow-up. Ultimately, safety information collection becomes meaningless.
- Safety meetings without clear conclusions. Although some safety conferences were held, it was useless, because there is no conclusion or output.

5. The automation level of safety management is low, and the work efficiency is relatively low. For example,

- Safety information collection. Collecting safety information through forms and personnel transmission not only consumes a lot of manpower and time, but also is inefficient.
- Safety information analysis. Information analysis by manual or EXCEL table is time-consuming, laborious and difficult to analyze in depth.

6. The mechanism and method of safety management are lack of innovation. For example,

- Be accustomed to afterwards management. Failure to try new safety management concepts and methods, adhere to the old management tools. Ultimately, the management efficiency is low and the management effect is not good.

3   Cause Analysis

Through investigating and interviewing the safety manager of several airlines, the reasons why the work quality of safety manager is low is analyzed deeply based on SHELL mode. It mainly includes the following aspects.

3.1   Software

- Lack of clear safety management manual, procedures, standards, methods, forms, etc. For example, lack of safety information collection and analysis procedures, safety checklist, safety information reporting standards, etc.
- Improper or unclear assignment of safety management responsibilities. For example, the safety responsibilities of safety management department and operation department are not clearly distinguished, and the responsibilities of investigation are not clear.

- Lack of necessary safety management IT systems, software, tools, etc. For example, there is a lack of safety information reporting system, safety information analysis software, safety monitoring system and so on.

3.2 Hardware

- Lack of necessary safety management equipment and facilities. For example, there is a lack of necessary office rooms, conference rooms, vehicles, computers, printers and so on.

3.3 Environment

- There is not a good safety culture and policies in airlines, which lead to employee not to pay enough attention to safety. For example, the airlines takes operation as its primary task. In the absence of serious unsafe incidents, employee does not attach importance to safety management.
- Airlines acquiesce in the existence of some major safety problems and lack the determination to solve them. For example, the top managers know that there are some serious safety problems in operation, but solving these safety problems requires a lot of resources, and there has not been a serious unsafe incident. In this case, top managers are unwilling to invest a lot of resources to solve safety problems.
- Airlines do not invest enough resources in safety management, such as human resources, education and training, safety incentives, equipment and facilities.
- There are not detailed process checks on safety management, and lack of final quality inspection. For example, for the safety management at all levels, it is only concerned about whether or not it is done, and the quality in each link is less concerned. Little attention has been paid to whether the safety management has produced actual results.
- The recruitment criterion for safety manager is low. For example, recruited safety managers lack professional knowledge or safety management knowledge. Safety manager have low salaries, and it difficult to recruit suitable personnel.
- Lack of comprehensive training for safety manager. For example, there is a lack of initial and regular safety management training for safety managers. The quality of safety management training is relatively low and fails to improve the working ability of safety manager.
- Lack of positive and fair incentive mechanism for safety manager. For example, there is no specific incentive or punishment mechanism for good or bad safety management. As a result, employees are not motivated to provide quality of work.

3.4 Collaboration

- Failure to reach an agreement with top management on safety management concepts and methods. For example, safety managers believe that safety management should be based on the results of information analysis. Departmental managers believe that safety management should be based on subjective perception.

- Failed to reach an agreement with the operation department on the concept and method of safety management. For example, safety managers believe that standard operating procedures should be strictly followed. Operating departments believe that as long as no unsafe incidents occur, it is safe, and it is not important to comply with the standard operating procedures.
- Operating departments do not cooperate with safety management, and there is concealment or fraud in safety issues, safety information, etc.
- The implementation quality of risk control measures in operation department is not high. For example, although a lot of risk control measures are carried out daily, the risks still exist and the safety problems have not been solved.

3.5 Safety Manager

- Lack of basic knowledge and ability in communication, coordination and so on. For example, safety manager have low educational background and lack of practical work experience.
- Lack of correct understanding of safety management. For example, the importance of safety and the purpose of safety information analysis are not well understood.
- Lack of knowledge and skills in safety management. For example, unknown the technology and method of safety management.
- Lack of understanding of the specific operation content and knowledge.
- The ability of learning and innovation is poor. For example, the acceptance of new ideas and affairs is relatively difficult.
- Satisfied with the present job. The enthusiasm for improving the quality of work is not high.
- The working attitude is not correct and the sense of responsibility is not strong.

4 Countermeasures

In view of the above problems, the following improvement measures are put forward.

1. Build a good safety culture from top to bottom. On the one hand, senior managers should establish correct safety concept and safety management concept, really attach importance to safety, pay attention to safety, invest sufficient resources in safety, and take effective measures to control safety risks in operation. Through the leading role of senior managers, influence and guide the safety management of safety managers, so that they really attach importance to safety and carry out safety management with high quality. On the other hand, the operation departments should enhance their awareness of the importance of safety, clarify their own safety responsibilities, and actively cooperate with safety manager to implement safety management.

2. Clarify the safety responsibilities and powers of safety manager at all levels. On this basis, clear and applicable safety management processes and methods are established to guide safety manager to carry out daily safety management.
3. Establish clear and reasonable recruitment and salary standards for safety manager, and regularly conduct safety management training to ensure that safety manager have sufficient knowledge and ability to carry out safety management.
4. Establish supervision and incentive mechanism of safety manager's work quality. Regularly evaluate the quality, attitude, enthusiasm and innovation of safety manager. Take necessary measures, including incentive measures and punitive measures, according to the evaluation results.
5. Establish and improve safety management tools and IT systems, improve the automation level of safety management, improve the efficiency and depth of safety management.

5 Conclusion

1. Through the investigation and SMS audit of airlines, this paper summarizes the types of low work quality of airlines safety managers, and lists some examples.
2. Based on SHELL model, the specific reasons for the low work quality of safety manager are analyzed in detail from five aspects, which are software, hardware, environment, collaboration and safety manager themselves.
3. In view of the specific reasons for the low work quality of safety manager, specific measures to improve the work quality of safety manager are put forward from five aspects, which are cultural construction, clear responsibilities, personnel recruitment, supervision and incentive mechanism, and safety management tools.

References

1. Hainan Airlines Carries Out Human Factor Training and Pilot Psychology Evaluation. Int. Aviat. (5), 44–46 (2004)
2. Che, Ch.Ch., Wang, H.W., Ni, X.M.: Human factors analysis of aviation maintenance errors based on structural bayesian equation model. Chin. J. Ergon. **24**(5), 11–16 (2018)
3. Tan, Zh.Y.: Human factor analyses on dispatch based on AHP. J. Civ. Aviat. Univ. China **35**(4), 54–57 (2017)
4. Chu, J.P.: Preliminary human factor evaluation model on display color set in civil aircraft flight deck. Aeronaut. Comput. Tech. **47**(6), 93–95 (2017)
5. Xia, Y.X., Fu, Sh.: Design of physical sign data collection system for human factors in civil airplane cockpit. Embed. Technol. **37**(5), 35–38 (2011)
6. Gan, X.Sh., Cui, H.L., Gao, W.M., Dai, Zh.: Analysis and suggestion of midair collision accident based on HFACS. J. Saf. Sci. Technol. **11**(10), 96–102 (2015)
7. Tang, X.X., Luo, F.: A simulation study of human risk infection behavior in airport flight area. Ind. Eng. J. **20**(4), 108–115 (2017)
8. Sun, R.Sh., Zhao, Q.: Study on ECAR model for human error analysis of aviation accident/incident. Chin. Saf. Sci. J. **22**(2), 17–21 (2012)

9. Wang, X.: Study on competency model of safety managers in airlines. J. Nanjing Univ. Aeronaut. Astronaut. (Soc. Sci.) **16**(3), 63–68 (2014)

10. Chen, F., Guo, N., Han, Sh.Sh.: Empirical study on competency model of safety management personnel in civil aviation operation organizations. J. Saf. Sci. Technol. **14**(6), 165–170 (2018)

Research on the Influence of New Technology on Radiotelephony Communication in the Cockpit

Youxue Zhang[✉], Sha Liu, Jiaying Liu, and Qian Wang

Flight Technology College of CAUC, Tianjin, People's Republic of China
434304820@qq.com

Abstract. In the paper, the concept of technology and technology update will be expounded first. Technologies that have profound impact on radiotelephony will be mainly classified as communication technology, navigation technology and monitoring technology. Meanwhile, it will expound the role that air-ground radiotelephony plays, the language features of radiotelephony and radiotelephony phraseology. Secondly, this paper will briefly analyze what impact new technologies (including new communication technology, new navigation technology and new monitoring technology) will cause on phraseology used in cockpit radiotelephony using the method of contrast. Then, put forward some strategies for the teaching of pilots' radiotelephony according to our own teaching needs and experiences combining with the study of this paper. And finally draw some conclusions about the influence of technology update on pilot air-ground communication.

Keywords: Communication · Navigation · Monitoring · Phraseology

1 Introduction

1.1 Significance of the Research

This paper will take airports, terminal areas and air routes as examples to briefly analyze how technology innovation impacts on air-ground radiotelephony terminology that is extremely systemic and theoretical, through analyzing the innovation of communication, navigation and monitoring technologies and the features of pilot air-ground radiotelephony.

1.2 Ideas and Methods of the Research

This paper is divided into five parts. Firstly, the definition of technology update and air-ground radiotelephony is expounded and the history of air-ground communication in aviation industry is described. Secondly, from the aspects of communication, navigation and monitoring, the basic concept of them and the classification and characteristics of air-ground radiotelephony is briefly introduced. In the third part, the paper analyzes the influence of technology update on pilot air-ground communication from the aspects of communication, navigation and monitoring through contrast and case analysis.

© Springer Nature Switzerland AG 2019
C. Stephanidis (Ed.): HCII 2019, CCIS 1032, pp. 433–441, 2019.
https://doi.org/10.1007/978-3-030-23522-2_57

Then, some teaching strategies are put forward for those students who are still in the education process to acknowledge technology update's impact on pilot air-ground radiotelephony. Finally, the summary of the main embodiment of the technical update and its implementation on the pilot air-ground radiotelephony terminology.

2 New Technology and Radiotelephony Communication

2.1 New Technology Classification

There are three kind of new technology, communication, navigation and surveillance. The continuous development of communication technology, making it possible for pilots to communicate with controller in the height of 10,000 m without barriers, also provides us a good guarantee of flight safety. Updating technology timely will have a great impact on communications techniques, we will use the Controller-Pilot Data Link communication (CPDLC).

Civil aviation navigation technology is mainly composed of three navigation systems: inertial navigation system, ground-based radio navigation system, satellite-based radio navigation system.

This article will introduce the detail of the RNP and RNAV navigation systems, and their impact on radio communication.

"Civil aviation surveillance system" is mainly used to know the real-time position of the aircraft, the interval between aircraft, ATC instructions, and to show the real flight track of the aircraft. The precise monitoring can provide a good aircraft take-off and landing instructions, greatly improved the flight safety coefficient. The following chapter will focus on ADS-B surveillance system, analyze its impact on pilot air-ground radiotelephony.

2.2 Radiotelephony Communication

What is the Air-Ground Radiotelephony? It is the transportation of the instructions between controllers and pilots. However, it is not the normal conversation, it includes a series of designated special expressions. In 2003, English has been designated as universal language in Air-Ground Radiotelephony.

With the deepening of economic globalization, English has been designated as universal language in Air-Ground Radiotelephony in 2003. The language level evaluation system has put into effect for the aviation personnel (including flight crew, controllers) from 2008. The implementation of all international flights, pilots and work at the international airport or district tune controllers, must obtain ICAO4 English level endorsement. It has the features of sound standardization, meaning simplification no rules of grammar with three categories of clearance, instruction and information.

3 Influence of New Communication Technology on Radiotelephony Communication

3.1 New Communication Technology

Ground-to-Air data link communication in civil aviation contains mainly four areas, which are VHF data link, HF data link, Secondary Surveillance Radar Mode S and Satellite data link communication.

Applications of data link system in civil aviation of China are as follows:

a. Pre-Departure Clearance (PDC)
b. D-ATIS
c. CPDLC: Controller Pilot Data Link Communication
d. Automatic Dependent Surveillance (ADS)

ACARS, currently in used air-ground data link communication, mainly employed by data service company for providing corresponding service to airlines. It has been widely used in fields of ATM and services (PDC, D-ATIS, ADS, CPDLC). ACARS as a term refers to the complete air and ground system, consisting of equipment on board, equipment on the ground, and a service provider.

3.2 Influence of New Communication Technology on Radiotelephony Communication

With the development of technology, CPDLC is invented. CPDLC uses date link system while traditional method of communication uses VHF bands for line-of-sight communication, SATCOM (INMARSAT), and HF bands for long-distance communication (such as remote and oceanic area). CPDLC, based on more reliable air-ground communication, offers a possible strategy to reduce pilot's workload and cancel semantic misunderstandings created by voice radio communication.

In-Flight Communication. CPDLC data link communication impacts pilots and controllers mainly in routine radio communications. In emergency radio communications, voice radio communication is used.

a: CPDLC data link communication can replace voice radio communication under routine conditions.

Because of CPDLC data link, many routine conversations can be omitted. For example, conversation showing below can be omitted so that minimize the probability of phonetical ambiguities.

More examples:

PIL: Leaving FL200, climbing to FL280
PIL: Heading120, correction, 140

Receiving instructions in the format of text, pilots can avoid problems like "to" and "two".

The below is a brief introduction to the application of CPDLC during departure phase, based on the example of pilots' radio comminutions during a departure phase of

Tianjin Binhai International Airport (ZTSN). The figure is departure chart of Runway 16L/R of ZTSN.

Normally, if the pilot uses VYK-01D for departure, the conversation between controllers and pilots would be like this (assuming CCA 1331 is the call sign):

PIT: Tianjin Ground, CCA1331. Airborne.
CTL: CCA1331, Tianjin Ground. Maintain runway heading. Climb to 300 m.
PIT: Maintaining runway heading. Climbing to 300 m, CCA1331.
(Approaching 300 m)
CTL: CCA1331, turn right heading340. Climb to 3000 m.
PIT: Right turn heading340. Climbing to 3000 m, CCA1331.
(Approaching m)
CTL: CCA1331, turn left heading280.
PIT: Left turn heading280, CCA1331.

In routine condition, above conversation can be completed omitted. Text versions of permissions, instructions and messages prevent phonetical ambiguities.

b: In emergency situation, CPDLC data link communication can replace voice radio communications.

In emergencies or CPDLC failure, crews can still establish radio communications to ensure flight safety.

PIL: CPDLC unserviceable, request to revert to voice communication
PIL: Disregard my last CPDLC request for climb. We have a system problem and will maintain present level for now
PIL: CPDLC terminated due to failure, reverting to voice communication.

These terms have been included in English Test for Chinese Civil Aviation Pilot-900 sentences. These are terminologies for student pilots as well as for frontline airline pilots to study and use.

Updated communication technologies have had a significant impact on pilots' air-to-ground communications.

Voice radio communications and data communications are compatible.

D-ATIS: Digital Auto-Terminal Information Service. Automatic Terminal Information Service, or ATIS, is a continuous broadcast of aeronautical information in high activity airports. ATIS transmissions on a discrete VHF radio frequency provide essential flying information such as weather, runway in use, air pressure and altimeter setting, etc.

4 Influence of New Navigation Technology on Radiotelephony Communication

4.1 New Navigation Technology

Navigation technology is the main technology of civil aviation transportation system. With the rapid development of China civil aviation, new aviation technology also constantly promote the industry's rapid progress. In recent years, part of the airports in China announced the RNAV program and RNP program based on PBN (performance-based navigation)

4.2 Influence of New Navigation Technology on Radiotelephony Communication

The development of traditional navigation technology has a great effect on the radiotelephony. Mainly from the following two aspects to elaborate.

Departure Phase. The development of traditional navigation technology has a great effect on the radiotelephony. For instance,

ATC: "CNN400, Orlando Departure, radar contact"
ATC: "CNN400, Turn left heading 310"
ATC: "CNN400, Do not exceed 1600 until further advised"
ATC: "CNN400, Turn left heading 280"
ATC: "CNN400, Turn left heading 260"
ATC: "CNN400, Climb and maintain 2000, give me a good rate through 12"
ATC: "CNN400, Out of 2000 turn left heading 230"
ATC: "CNN400, Heading is 230 contact departure 119.4"

This controller needs to issue eight instructions, while with regional navigation, controllers just send out three simple instructions.

ATC: "CNN400, Orlando departure radar contact"
ATC: "CNN400, Climb maintain 2000"
ATC: "CNN400, contact departure 119.4 good day"

This is a communication between pilots and air traffic controllers during departure. When we use the navigation, we have to make a series of two-way calls. The controller needs to keep sending heading instructions to the pilot to make sure that the aircraft arrived at the designated navigation station. Comparing to the second example of satellite based navigation uses, when radar contact, the controllers can see the aircraft on the radar screen, so they don't have to vector the plane to the fixed station. Therefore it reduces a lot of two-way communications, instructions reduced from eight to three with time saved, which greatly enhanced the work efficiency of pilots and controllers.

Arrival Phrase. Let' see another example of the approach.

PIL: "Winton Approach, SF150"
CTL: "SF150, Winton Approach"
PIL: "SF150, FL50, estimating RED 32, information M"
CTL: "Reduce speed 250 knots, cleared RED"
PIL: "Cleared RED, reducing 250 knots"
CTL: "SF150, expect straight in ILS approach, runway 07 QNH1005 report established"

Here, what pilot needs to do is ILS approach based on Ground-based navigation, that from the beginning of the approach, pilot needs to report to controller their position and the distance from the next station, and after known by the controller's leadership, the pilot can report establish eventually, and then contact tower. If they used satellite-based navigation approach (GPS) RNAV, it would be a easer way with relative ease.

PIL: "Winton Approach, SF150, request RNAV approach for runway 07"
CTL: "SF150, squawk 4236, heading 100, maintain 2000 until establish, cleared RNAV approach runway 07"

The using of satellite-based navigation makes all instructions easily within several words, which makes the life of controller and pilot much easier.

5   The Influence on New Surveillance Technology on Radiotelephony Communication

Airspace surveillance system includes all the equipment for surveillance of flight movements of aircraft in the airspace. It is an important method to protect safety of flight and improve the efficiency.

5.1   New Surveillance Technology

The widely use of air traffic control in china is the traditional radar monitoring. It guaranteed safety of flight In a certain period of time. But it still has limitation because of the method difference.

Primary surveillance radar is used to monitor uncoordinate targets and weather. The limitation is that the range will be short influenced by electromagnetic wave. Secondary Surveillance Radar is more cheap.it can identify target and keep the data base. Automatic dependent surveillance is a monitoring method which divide position and monitoring. the position process will be done by target. Since the Automatic dependent surveillance can rely on many kinds of data base, we can divided it to ground base monitoring and satellite-based surveillance system, which Completely overcome the affected by topography

5.2   Influence of New Surveillance Technology on Radiotelephony Communication

We will describe the influence to pilot about this new monitoring technology in two different aspects.

First, there are three aspects of influence to radio telephonic by using the ADS-B in controlled air space.

Position Report. During flight we will make self-report as required, such as:

PIL: "SF150, good morning"
CTL: "Go ahead, SF150"
PIL: "SF150 R at 35. flight level 310 estimating Y at 45"
CTL: "Roger SF150 next report at Z"

R, Y, Z are the points we usually report position. If we don't use ADS-B, we will have to report the distance and estimate arrival time to controller. But if we have ADS-B, they will know that from system so that we can just directly skip that.

Activity Report. When controller realize any unknown activity in that space, they will have to notify the pilot concern activity.

C: "SF150,unknown traffic, 10 o'clock.5miles crossing left to right"
P: "SF150, negative contact, request vectors"
C: "Turn left, heading 050"
P: "Turn left, heading 050 SF150".
C: "SF150 clear of traffic, resume own navigation"

This conversation is about the traffic information. Normally we will need to be noticed and guided from ATC to avoid traffic. Because we have no idea about other aircraft position. But if we have ADS-B system, the aircraft have the same system will see each other during the flight. Then they could avoid traffic without any noticed or guidance.

Other New Phraseologies. The most important influence to routine radio telephonic by using ADS-B system is some new terms, for example:
Our ADS-B transmitter appears to be malfunctioning. terminating further ADS-B transmissions.
ADS-B equipment degradation, will advise when able to resume operations.
GPS unreliable, terminating ADS-B transmissions.
Our ADS-B has malfunctioned. Is there any weather advisory at our destination?
We made an overshoot because our ADS-B indication a possible runway incursion.
Secondly, in uncontrolled air space. ADS-B enhance the coordination from air to air, it also improved capability of aircraft monitoring each other.
There is no uncontrolled airport in china. So people always misunderstand the meaning of uncontrolled airport. It doesn't mean we don't need to make radio call, it turned out just the opposite, it become to the most important way to make flight safe because of no ATC monitoring.
Here we got a exactly example to make a further explain for last phase. We are in an uncontrolled airport Orlando Apopka (X04), Multicom frequency is 123.05 MHz, and we are in C172 doing a VFR flight. Call sign: CONNECTION 222(CONN222), runway in use: 33.
We will make first self-advise at about 10 to 15 nautical mile to the filed. It include your position, altitude and remark information.
PLT: Apopka Traffic; Cessna CONN 222 is ten northeast at one two thousand five hundred; request airport advisory; Apopka Traffic.
We make this radio call 5 miles each time. If pilot doesn't get any information like runway in use or weather, we will maintain at least 500 feet above the TPA so we could check the wind sock to decide which runway we are going to use, the radio call will be:
PLT: Apopka Traffic; Cessna CONN 222 is 5 northeast at two thousand; will cross mid-field at one thousand and five hundred for wind indicator check; Apopka Traffic

When pilot over the Apopka field and decide to land runway 33, he will maneuvering to make a 45° enter the downwind leg. Radiocall is:

PLT: Apopka Traffic; Cessna CONN 222 is 45° maneuvering to join left downwind runway 33 at one thousand; Apopka Traffic.

Now we are on downwind:

PLT: Apopka Traffic; Cessna CONN 222; left downwind runway 33; Apopka Traffic

PLT: Apopka Traffic; Cessna CONN 222; turning base runway 33; Apopka Traffic

Then final:

PLT: Apopka Traffic; Cessna CONN 222; final runway 33; full stop; Apopka Traffic

If pilot want take off right away after touch down:

PLT: Apopka Traffic; Cessna CONN 222; final runway 33; followed by a touch-and-go; Apopka Traffic

ADS-B cost less, more accurate, strong signal. All these advantage is making it better to be used in busy traffic. We can easily tell that it overcome a lot of disadvantage from traditional surveillance. It will become a master way in surveillance. However, this technology is in beginning stage in china. We just have it on some route for west of china. Civil aviation in china is developing. Airspace, fleet and type of airplane are all growing up. Air traffic control equipment is going to be improved and better.

6 Conclusion

In view of the rapid development of aviation industry and the importance of pilot air-ground radiotelephony, this paper has drawn the following conclusions.

First of all, the influence of new communication technology on pilot air-ground radiotelephony is mainly in three aspects. Which is,

(1) The Communication During the Entire Flight

a: Under normal circumstances, voice communication can be replaced by CPDLC digital communication.

b: Under unconventional circumstances, voice communication can be replaced by CPDLC digital communication.

In the event of an emergency or CPDLC failure, the crew can still establish voice communications to ensure aviation safety.

(2) Pre-Departure Clearance (PDC).

(3) Digital Auto Terminal Information Service(D-ATIS).

Under normal circumstances, Voice and Data shall co-exist, CPDLC only used in non-critical communications, Decision to use CPDLC shall be at the discretion of controller and/or pilot, ICAO Annex 11, Chap. 3, para 3.5.1: « A controlled flight shall be under the control of only one air traffic control unit at any given time ».

Secondly, the impact of new navigation technology on pilot air-ground radiotelephony is mainly manifested in two aspects. Which is,

(1) Departure phrase.
(2) Arrival phrase.

Finally, the impact of new monitoring technologies on pilot air-ground radiotelephony is mainly manifested in three aspects. Which is,

(1) Position report.
(2) Traffic information report.
(3) Other new phrases used in air-ground communication and air-air communication

The impact of communication, navigation and monitoring technologies on pilot air-ground radiotelephony is mainly in the aspect of vocabulary, phrases and related expressions. Specific can be seen in the appendix. As pilots, controllers and related staff, the development trend of new technologies must be learned on time in order to acknowledge air-ground communication English in an active way. Thus can we learn, understand and apply new technologies timely.

Finally, due to the limited level of academic capacity and practical experience of the author, the shortcomings of the paper could be seen. Experts and teachers are welcome to criticize and correct, thank you!

References

1. Personnel Licensing, ICAO. Annex 1
2. Manual on the Implementation of ICAO Language Proficiency Requirements
3. ICAO. Document 9835
4. Manual of Radiotelephony
5. ICAO. Document 9432
6. ICAO. Annex 11, Chapter III
7. Roberson, F.A.: AIRSPEAK-Radiotelephony Communication for Pilots. Cambridge University, Cambridge (2011)
8. Radiotelephony Communications for Pilots and Controllers, CAUC (2005)
9. Information System Management (2003)
10. Study on the Speech Style of Radiotelephony Communication in Civil Aviation
11. The Characteristics and Translation of Radiotelephony Communication English
12. Airspeak—Radiotelephony Communication for Pilots
13. On the Stylistic Features of Radiotelephony communication in English between Pilots and Air Traffic Controllers
14. The characteristics of civil aviation air speak English and translation
15. An Analysis of Ambiguity in Air-ground Communication
16. https://en.wikipedia.org

Author Index

Printed in the United States
By Bookmasters